SPYMASTER

HELEN FRY

SPYMASTER

The Man Who Saved MI6

YALE UNIVERSITY PRESS
NEW HAVEN AND LONDON

For information about this and other Yale University Press publications, please contact:
U.S. Office: sales.press@yale.edu   yalebooks.com
Europe Office: sales@yaleup.co.uk   yalebooks.co.uk

Set in Adobe Garamond Pro by IDSUK (DataConnection) Ltd
Printed in Great Britain by TJ Books, Padstow, Cornwall

Library of Congress Control Number: 2021941542

ISBN 978-0-300-25595-9

A catalogue record for this book is available from the British Library.

10 9 8 7 6 5 4 3 2 1

Sir David Jason, OBE
in admiration of one of Britain's finest actors,
who is inspired by Kendrick's story

The spies in history who can say from their graves,
the information I supplied to my masters,
for better or worse, altered the history of our planet,
can be counted on the fingers of one hand.

Frederick Forsyth, CBE

CONTENTS

CONTENTS

PLATES

1. Thomas Joseph Kendrick in Vienna, 1930s. Courtesy of Barbara Lloyd.
2. Kendrick with army colleagues, South Africa, 1901. Courtesy of Barbara Lloyd.
3. Norah Kendrick (née Wecke). Courtesy of Barbara Lloyd.
4. Gladys Kendrick on her wedding day to Geoffrey Walsh, Vienna, 29 March 1931. Courtesy of Barbara Lloyd.
5. Kendrick with granddaughter Barbara Walsh, Vienna, c. 1937. Courtesy of Barbara Lloyd.
6. Clara Holmes with daughter Prudence at an Austrian ski resort, 1930s. Courtesy of Prudence Hopkinson.
7. Adolf Hitler salutes as he enters the Hofburg in Vienna, 14 March 1938. Sueddeutsche Zeitung Photo / Alamy Stock Photo.
8. Dr Erwin Pulay, Vienna. Courtesy of Jessica Pulay / the late Roger Lloyd-Pack.
9. Sigmund Freud, London, 1938. Courtesy of the Freud family.
10. Kendrick saying goodbye to his daughter and grandchildren at Vienna train station, 19 July 1938. Courtesy of Barbara Lloyd.
11. Gladys Walsh and children Barbara and Ken leaving Vienna, 19 July 1938. Courtesy of Barbara Lloyd.
12 & 13. Willi Bondi's passport, Czechoslovakia. Courtesy of Peter Barber.
14. The wedding of Countess Marianne Szápáry and Günther von Reibnitz, December 1941.
15. Rex Pearson, Kendrick's brother-in-law. Courtesy of Barbara Lloyd.

PLATES

33. Non-commissioned officers, Latimer House, *c.* 1944. Courtesy of the late Fritz Lustig.

34. Kendrick with friends at his house in Oxshott, Surrey, *c.* 1960s. Courtesy of Barbara Lloyd.

35. Kendrick with Hans and Mary Schick, *c.* 1960s. Courtesy of Barbara Lloyd.

36. Kendrick with sister Mary Rowlands and his wife Norah at Briarholme, Oxshott, Surrey, 1960s. Courtesy of Barbara Lloyd.

ACKNOWLEDGEMENTS

My first thanks are to Heather McCallum, the managing director at Yale University Press and my commissioning editor, for her enthusiasm and support for this book. She is an inspiration and, with her staff, an incredible support to authors during the writing and publication process. My sincere thanks to my brilliant editor, Marika Lysandrou, for the meticulous edits, patience and care over this book, in which she pushes for the best writing from me. I am equally grateful to my agent, Andrew Lownie, for his continued support throughout.

This book could not have been written without the help and close friendship for over 15 years of the grandchildren of Colonel Thomas Joseph Kendrick OBE: my love and thanks to his granddaughter Barbara Lloyd and her brother, the late Ken Walsh. Much appreciation, too, to Kendrick's great-granddaughters Anne Marie Thorpe and Christina Sutch, veteran Eric Sanders, and to others who have played a part in interviews and material for this book: Prudence Hopkinson, John Vignoles, Anne Walton, the late Roger Lloyd-Pack, Lord George Weidenfeld, Wolf Suschitzky and Derek Nudd.

Heartfelt thanks go to the special veterans who are no longer with us, but who were part of the journey of discovery and who worked at Kendrick's wartime sites: the late Eric Mark, Fritz Lustig and Susan Lustig, Paul Douglas, Peter Hart, Cynthia Turner (née Crew), Evelyn Barron and Elisabeth Bruegger (née Rees-Mogg). Thanks must go also to Robin Lustig, Stephen Lustig, Nigel Morgan, Helen Lederer, Loftus Jestin, Jennifer Jestin and Caroline Jestin, Miriam Mark, Sandra Robinson, Anne Mark, Richard Benson, Andrew Benson, Ernest Newhouse, Arthur Fleiss, Peter Oppenheimer, Jessica Pulay, Trixy Tilsiter, Diane

ACKNOWLEDGEMENTS

O'Shea, John Francken, Adam Ganz, Peter Barber, Sam Beer, Dudley Lambert Bennett, Otto Bennett, Michael Bottenheim, Lesley Allocca, Michael Allocca, Carol Curties, Andrea Evers, Mimia Umney-Gray, Professor Hugo de Burgh, Richard Deveson, Tom Deveson, Dr Anthony Eisinger, Susan Gompels, Stella MacKinnon, Melanie McFadyean, Dr Jonathan Simon, Edgar Samuel, Andrew Samuel, Jeremy Samuel, Mark Austen, David Wilson, Lesley Wyle, Cameron Woodrow, Robin Gedye, Sam Lambert, Dr David Cassidy, Peter Quinn, Robert Fabre, the late Patrick Filsell, Barbara Horwitz, Roger Marshall, Paul McNamara, Fiona McNamara, Hamish Cassels, Veronica Pettifer, Sir Michael Tugendhat, Tom Tugendhat, Andrew Leach, David Birnbaum, Peter Leslie, Robert Chester, Liz Driscoll, John Ross, Alasdair Macleod and Joanna Weatherby.

I am indebted to historians and researchers Phil Tomaselli, Lee Richards, Michael Smith, John Howes, Dr Claire Hubbard-Hall, the late Professor Keith Jeffery, Dr Jim Beach, Trudy Gold, Steven Kippax, Dr Brian Parritt, Dr Nick van der Bijl, Sarah Paterson, Mark Scoble, Colonel John Starling, Norman Brown, Neil Fearn, Mark Lubienski, Dr David King, Steve Mallinson, Mark Birdsall and Deborah McDonald. Huge thanks to Jacques Mostert in Cape Town who enthusiastically researched material for me in the archives in South Africa on military material on the Boer War and First World War in South Africa. I have been lucky to enjoy the support of Fred Judge (official Intelligence Corps historian), Joyce Hutton (senior archivist) and Major Bill Steadman (senior curator) at the Military Intelligence Museum, Chicksands; Dr Jim Beach; Iain Standen (CEO of Bletchley Park); René Bienert, archivist of the Vienna Wiesenthal Institute for Holocaust Studies; Frode Weierud; and Peter Helps. In addition, it has been a pleasure to receive active support from the Trustees of the Museum of Military Intelligence and the trustees of the Friends of the Intelligence Corps Museum. Last, but by no means least, to staff at Latimer House, who have been incredibly tolerant of the historian who turns up on the doorstep. They have taken an active interest in Kendrick as the wartime commander of Latimer House.

To my family, for their loyal support and encouragement over all the years – thank you. Finally, my heartfelt appreciation to those who helped with the book but who have asked not to be named.

ABBREVIATIONS AND GLOSSARY

Abwehr	German military intelligence
ADI(K)	air intelligence section attached to CSDIC
ATS	Auxiliary Territorial Service, the women's branch of the army during the Second World War
BSC	British Security Co-ordination, an MI6 organization in the US
Comintern	Communist International organization
CSDIC	Combined Services Detailed Interrogation Centre
DDMI	deputy director of Military Intelligence
DMI	director of Military Intelligence
FBI	US Federal Bureau of Investigation
Gestapo	Geheime Staatspolizei, German Secret State Police
GHQ	general headquarters
HUMINT	intelligence gained from humans
JIC	Joint Intelligence Sub-Committee
MI5	intelligence organization for national security within Britain
MI6	intelligence organization for Britain's security abroad
MI9	intelligence organization for prisoners of war
MI19	responsible for obtaining intelligence from prisoners of war

ABBREVIATIONS AND GLOSSARY

NKVD	People's Commissariat of Internal Affairs, Soviet intelligence organization (1934–46), successor organization to OGPU
OGPU	Soviet secret police (1923–34)
OSS	Office of Strategic Services (forerunner of the US Central Intelligence Agency)
POW	prisoner of war
RNVR	Royal Naval Volunteer Reserve
SA	Sturmabteilung, Storm Detachment, the Nazi Party's paramilitary wing
SD	Sicherheitsdienst, German security service, an intelligence-gathering agency
Sicherheitspolizei	security police
SIGINT	signals intelligence
SIS	Secret Intelligence Service
SOE	Special Operations Executive
SS	Schutzstaffel, Nazi Party security and policing organization
WRNS	Women's Royal Naval Service

AUTHOR'S NOTE

There are numerous challenges in trying to reconstruct the life of a man who, for almost 40 years, lived a very secretive life while working for the British Secret Intelligence Service (SIS, referred to as MI6 in the Second World War). SIS – the organization responsible for Britain's foreign operations and security abroad – did not publicly exist until its official history was published in 2010.[1] Its existence was presumed by the public, but from SIS/MI6 itself there was only silence for its first century. MI6 is the name by which it is commonly referred to today in popular culture by members of the public, but officially it remains the Secret Intelligence Service.[2] Even today, and with official recognition as an organization, precious little is known about its past or present operations and personnel. It is generally believed that all files of government departments are declassified after a set period of time, usually 30, 50 or 100 years. But this is not the case with SIS: the official files are never released by the service and historians have no access to its archives – except on extremely rare occasions, such as the writing of the organization's official history by the late Professor Keith Jeffery.

One of the major problems for any biographer and historian is the lack of sources both on the spies and agents themselves and on SIS, the organization. Few men and women who have worked in this closely guarded world leave any footprint.

Thomas Joseph Kendrick left no unpublished memoirs or interviews about his life. There were no obituaries to him in the national newspapers after his death – perhaps surprising, given his achievements; and yet perhaps not so surprising, given that he had worked for an organization that did not officially exist. The papers which Kendrick left after his death are known to have been destroyed. All that is left is a bundle of letters written to him between 1940 and 1946, the citation for his award of the Legion of Merit by the Americans in 1946 and a handful of photographs in the family album. I was able to interview Kendrick's grandchildren, Barbara Lloyd and Ken Walsh, about their memories of their grandfather. They gave me just a page and a half of sketchy notes, in the form of bullet points, to outline their grandfather's known movements. This was all I had to go on over 20 years ago, when I started the research.

The most extensive material available on Kendrick's work is to be found in the declassified files of his unit during the Second World War. These are in the National Archives at Kew, London, and amount to hundreds of files concerning the clandestine eavesdropping on the conversations of enemy prisoners of war, as well as the declassified Foreign Office files on Rudolf Hess. But even the files on the latter contain gaps, and not all papers concerning Hess have been released into the public domain.[3]

Working through hundreds of files for the period, looking for SIS reports that may have been sent to other departments which subsequently declassified their files, I have been able to gain some insight into SIS operations. I was eventually able to find relevant SIS reports in the declassified MI5 files. Like SIS, MI5 does not permit access to its archives; however, it does periodically release files into the public domain. It is true to say that today there is still a major gap in the National Archives about intelligence operations in Europe in the 1930s, including how far Britain penetrated Nazi groups and networks. Yet it is clearly not possible to reconstruct Kendrick's full network, nor is it desirable . . . some secrets have to be protected forever.

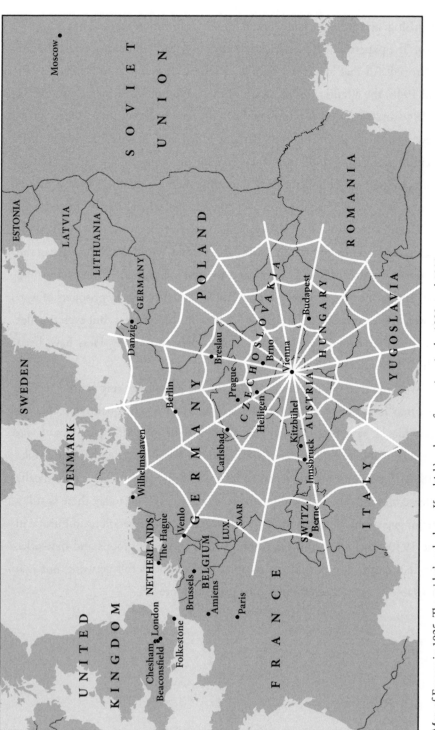

Map of Europe in 1925. The spider's web shows Kendrick's sphere of operations in the 1920s and 1930s.

PROLOGUE
COCKTAILS

Hietzing district, Vienna: March 1933
Imagine you are attending a cocktail party in one of the wealthiest districts of
Vienna. Your host is the charming Thomas Joseph Kendrick . . .

The smart apartment is on Wattmanngasse, just a five-minute stroll from the edge of the Schönbrunn park. On the far side of the park stands the grand Schloss Schönbrunn, once the imperial summer palace of the Habsburg ruling dynasty. Kendrick has just returned with his wife after hosting a concert at the embassy by Harriet Cohen, the British concert pianist, who is on a brief tour of Europe.[4] He is attached to the embassy as the British passport control officer, working on behalf of His Majesty's government.

This evening he is holding another of his famous soirées, which are renowned for their jovial atmosphere and high-society guests, who always arrive elegantly attired, the women in long dresses and fur wraps, the men in black tie.

The furniture is set around the edge of the room to allow for these occasions; the Kendricks entertain at least once a week. Pre-dinner cocktails are lined up in neat rows, almost military style, on a trolley in front of one of the bookcases. American expatriates are expected among the guests that evening, and he has chosen the Sidecar – a fashionable cocktail of cognac and orange liqueur, shaken together. Tiny silver dishes, with a selection of sweets in them, have been placed at various points in the room. Kendrick can usually be persuaded to lead the entertainment after dinner; this almost always consists of himself playing the piano (which he does by ear, as he cannot read a single note of music) accompanied by a virtuoso opera singer from the Vienna State Opera. He is a cultured gentleman whose jokes and old-fashioned humour entertain even the dullest of guests. Leslie Nicholson (SIS head of station in Prague) calls Kendrick 'a man of great charm, a keen sense of humour, with an air of middle-aged respectability'.[5] But Kendrick has a repertoire of political and historical jokes about the Austrian Chancellor Dollfuss – and even about Adolf Hitler – that is deemed quite risky. In years to come, this store of jokes will extend to the Nazi leaders in Austria.

This evening, Cohen is the last to make an appearance. Although it is only 6 o'clock, she looks weary and is desperately thin after a long battle with tuberculosis. Yet she is strikingly beautiful in her long, green satin gown; her only jewellery is a slim silver-and-diamond bracelet on her left wrist.

'Thank you for arranging this in my honour,' she is overheard to say to Kendrick. 'I've heard from diplomatic circles that your parties are becoming quite legendary, Captain.'

'Call me Tommy. All my friends do.' His eyes dance in his tanned face, his smile definitely mischievous. He passes her a cocktail.

Cohen cannot help but notice the interesting company in the room tonight – a few Austrian barons and their wives, a princess and a handful of counts and countesses. How has her host managed to gather together such an eclectic mix?

A shared love of opera and classical music has brought most of them together. Tonight, Kendrick considers whether he can broach a delicate topic with her. She has an impish look of innocence, but he has heard the rumours that she has seduced most of the leading British composers, including Edward Elgar, and is having a long-term love affair with Arnold Bax, a married man with a family.[6]

'The situation with Herr Hitler is serious,' he says to her. 'He's been in power less than two months and the region is becoming unstable. Vienna has seen fighting on the streets between the far right and the far left.'

She has already offered herself to the British government, but nothing has come of it.[7] With her frequent travel, she could be useful and she hates what Hitler is doing to her people, the Jews. Now she has witnessed the plight of

Jewish refugees fleeing into Vienna from Germany and this has awakened her own Jewish consciousness.[8]

'What would you do if Hitler invaded here?' she asks Kendrick.

'It could happen,' he replies. 'It's not a question of *if*, but *when*. But I promise you, I will do all in my power to save Austria's Jews. Of course, they are not the only ones at risk – most of my guests here and the greater part of the Austrian nobility will be in danger, too.'

Few guests, except for Kendrick's trusted secretaries, know that he has been placed in Vienna by 'C' – the head of the Secret Intelligence Service (SIS). How many people that evening are really working for him? His wife Norah, the perfect hostess, is unwittingly and unknowingly being drawn into his clandestine world. Her innocence of his true role will – just five years down the line – save her from a terrible fate at the hands of the Gestapo. Kendrick's desk job dealing with passports is a cover for his real work, running spy networks across Europe and gathering precious information for Britain about the threat from the Soviets – and the still greater threat it will soon face from the Nazis. Britain's secret service has placed him at the heart of its most important operations in Europe, for in Vienna he is at the crossroads of East and West, at the epicentre of the twin Soviet and Nazi threats.

INTRODUCTION
SOLDIER, SPY

Thomas Joseph Kendrick's life began in South Africa towards the end of the nineteenth century, at a time when the country was part of a vast Victorian British Empire, on which it was said that the sun never set. He was born in Cape Town on 26 November 1881, one of seven children of John Francis Kendrick, an American merchant; his mother was a South African woman named Katherine Redding.[1] The family was Roman Catholic, and he was educated at St Joseph's Academy in Cape Town and then at St Aidan's College, Grahamstown, where he was tutored by Jesuit priests. St Aidan's had all the traits of a traditional English public school, with its strong focus on sport and its own cadet corps, which gave the boys a grounding in military discipline. Photographs from this period show a school that could easily be mistaken for Eton or Harrow. Kendrick's time at St Aidan's was a defining period, providing him with a background that would allow him to slip later into the 'public school network' of the British secret service. As a formalized organization, the British Secret Intelligence Service had not yet been conceived. Indeed, neither SIS nor its predecessor MI1(c) even existed. Yet it was in South Africa that he would cross paths with men and women who would later become central and founding figures in the SIS. In a sense, South Africa could be described as the cradle of espionage.

In September 1900, Kendrick's father, John, purchased the grand five-storey Hotel Metropole in Cape Town for the sum of £16,000 – a fortune in those days. It was an imposing landmark, built in 1895 and designed in old German Renaissance style by the Dutch architect Anthony de Witt. The new family business exposed the young Kendrick to the highest social connections and gave him a taste for socialite life. But his relatively carefree youth was disrupted by the Second Boer War, which from 1899 was fought between the British Empire and two Boer states – the Republic of Transvaal and the Orange Free State. The Boers (white settlers in South Africa since 1652, with Dutch, German or Huguenot ancestors) were engaged in guerrilla warfare. In response, the British partitioned the region and undertook a scorched-earth policy of destroying farms, cattle and small-holdings.

On 15 January 1901, aged 21, Kendrick volunteered for the British forces in South Africa. He swore an oath of allegiance to Queen Victoria and her successors and enlisted in the Cape Colony Cyclists' Corps as a private.[2] The Cape Colony Cyclists' Corps had been raised at the end of December 1900 to defend Cape Town against enemy forces that had penetrated to within threatening distance of the town.[3] Bicycles were used in order to save the horses for combat duty while still allowing men to move quickly with messages between the cavalry and the infantry; cyclists could also be sent out as scouts to gather intelligence on the enemy's strongholds and positions.[4] Service with the Cyclists' Corps provided Kendrick with his first experience of intelligence work, tactical manoeuvres and reconnaissance behind enemy lines.[5]

The Boer War gave Kendrick the basic tools for field intelligence operations that would enable him to become a major player in espionage in the future. It was an important period for the British in the hitherto relatively unstructured world of military intelligence.[6] The small intelligence section in Cape Town ran intelligence courses which covered interrogation techniques, field intelligence work and how to secure intelligence from enemy prisoners of war. A section had been established to translate and extract intelligence from documents captured from the Boers, and pigeons were introduced as carriers of secret messages. The Boer War laid the foundations for military intelligence in wartime – foundations that have survived to this day. It taught the British that no future war could be fought without a professional body of military intelligence.[7]

On 18 July 1901, after 197 days of military service, Kendrick was discharged from the British forces and returned to Cape Town.

Diamond mines and spies

Having been demobilized, Kendrick settled into civilian life, initially pros-
pecting in the diamond mines of South Africa and Rhodesia. His life in the
years between the end of the Second Boer War (1902) and the outbreak of
the First World War (1914) is sketchy and lacks detail. However, it is known
that between 1901 and 1911, he moved around the different mining regions
and built up contacts that would lead him to a life-long career in espionage. He
undertook field intelligence work, gathering information for the British:
although the Boer War had formally ended in 1902, a four-year conflict ensued,
with numerous uprisings by native Khoikhoi (then known as Hottentots) and
German forces. The social hierarchy of key characters in the diamond mines
provided an opportunity for international spy networks and connections to be
forged that could serve Britain well in times of danger to its empire.

By the turn of the twentieth century, South Africa was a land of hope for
many young men seeking their fortune in the diamond and gold mines. It was
an exciting period that saw men travelling from abroad to make their fortune.
The diamond-mining industry was a tight-knit, closed world, where important connections could be made. Against the backdrop of political instability
involving the Khoikhoi, German forces in South Africa were secretly rearming
with newly developed weapons. The British needed to discover what these
were, in order to understand the German capability and potential threat to any
region, including Britain itself. Kendrick's work in the diamond-mining
industry (and a spell as a stockbroker) offered him – and indeed others – the
perfect cover to travel the region and gather intelligence for the British.

Kendrick appears to have worked at the Lace Diamond Mine, near
the town of Kroonstad in the Orange Free State (200km south-west of
Johannesburg).[8] The mine was owned by a wealthy Jewish émigré, Henry Atkins
(originally Etkins), who had fled the Russian Empire's Pale of Settlement, where
many Russian Jews had been forced to settle in the nineteenth century. Like
many European Jews, Atkins went to South Africa in search of a better life, free
from persecution, and he soon assimilated into society. Aspiring to become a real

Englishman, he anglicized his name from Etkins to Atkins and successfully masked his Russian-Jewish roots. Atkins started a new business exporting luxury ostrich feathers and took advantage of the unexpected commercial opportunities provided by the Boer War, supplying the British army in South Africa with large quantities of canned meat, flour and oats. His accumulated wealth from these new businesses enabled him to purchase the Lace Diamond Mine and acquire a number of other properties. Digging for diamonds at the mine began in 1901 and led to an immediate surge in interest. Atkins soon became one of the biggest and wealthiest property developers in the Cape, giving him entrée into the circle of the wealthy diamond magnate Cecil Rhodes. Atkins was known to Kendrick's father (John), who, as well as owning the Hotel Metropole, had shipping interests in the region. John Kendrick and Henry Atkins became close business associates, which is how the young Thomas Kendrick secured a job at the Lace Diamond Mine.

South Africa in the early 1900s offered fertile ground for Britain to recruit agents and intelligence officers for espionage. Kendrick crossed paths with a number of personalities who would rise to the upper echelons of SIS later in the twentieth century. His circle of friends included Hilda (the daughter of Henry Atkins), who was married to Max Rosenberg, a Jew who had migrated to the region in the early 1890s. From this time, the connections between Kendrick, intelligence and the Atkins/Rosenberg family would run deep for decades. Henry Atkins was described as a staunch British patriot, ready to help the British in their intelligence gathering in the region.[9] Max Rosenberg went on to become an agent for Kendrick in the 1920s; his daughter, Vera Atkins, who had been born in Romania, spoke several languages and often accompanied her father as an interpreter. It is believed that, as early as the 1920s, Vera was working for the intelligence services under the direction of Kendrick. In any case, she remained part of his close circle of friends for decades, until his death in 1972. When Vera later applied for British naturalization, Kendrick provided one of the references on her official application form.[10] Such was the closeness between Kendrick and the Atkins/Rosenbergs that in 1931 Vera was principal bridesmaid at the wedding of Kendrick's only daughter, Gladys.

The Atkins were not the only diamond-mining family in the region to provide valuable international trading connections and intelligence for the British. The Jewish diamond millionaire brothers Solly and Jack Joel were also involved in diamond mining in South Africa and went on later to have offices in 54 Broadway Buildings, the headquarters of MI6 in London; they are known to have worked for British intelligence.[11] There were important connections, too, between Kendrick and other key figures in the diamond-mining industry, most especially the Baring-Gould family of the Kimberley Mine in South Africa. The Baring-Goulds had been in South Africa since the late eighteenth century and had a large stake in the Kimberley Mine with Henry Atkins.[12] The connections between Kendrick, the Atkins and Baring-Gould families and the intelligence work continued from that period until the Second World War. Vera Atkins was taken up by British intelligence in the Second World War as head of F Section of the Special Operations Executive (SOE).[13] At least one member of the Baring-Gould family worked in Kendrick's intelligence unit in England in the 1940s.[14] And another member of the family had been used by British intelligence in the 1920s.[15]

Another key figure whose path crossed with Kendrick's in South Africa immediately after the Boer War was Claude Dansey, who, decades later, was to become the deputy head of MI6. He and Kendrick formed a life-long relationship while they were both conducting intelligence duties for the British in South Africa.[16] Throughout his life, Dansey was a controversial figure, colourful and dogmatic.[17] Weakness was not a characteristic that could be ascribed to him. He could be hard and tough, yet he could also be very persuasive: his dictum 'every man has his price, and every woman is seducible' pretty much defined his outlook on life. It was said that later, as deputy chief of MI6, he had the real power in the service.[18] Kendrick would not have been intimidated by Dansey. Although with a very different personality – relaxed, a natural charmer and joker – Kendrick was an equally strong character and would not have shied away from challenging Dansey. He would disarm the latter with old-fashioned humour, rather than by direct confrontation. Kendrick enjoyed socializing and parties, probably a legacy of the time when his parents owned the Hotel Metropole. By contrast, Dansey preferred to remain in the background, quietly meeting and recruiting an intelligence officer alone, over lunch. It was a different approach, yet both men contributed to the intelligence world and would go on to become high-ranking members of British intelligence. Dansey was also in contact in South Africa with another of Kendrick's contacts, Henry Atkins. But the wealthiest of Dansey's business friends there were the diamond-mine owners Solly and Jack Joel, the brothers again already known to Kendrick.[19]

It is possible to see how the intelligence community was extremely tight and closeted. As time progressed and different threats to Britain's security emerged, what was needed were men and women who could be trusted. These would be drawn from an intimate circle of intelligence personnel in early-twentieth-century South Africa. By connecting up these characters – joining the dots – we can gain a fresh understanding and see how the nascent British intelligence service that would later become SIS had some of its roots in the diamond-mining regions of South Africa. The spy world was extremely close-knit and has continued to be so.

East Africa and South West Africa

In 1903, Kendrick travelled to East Africa for new work. The precise details are unclear, but it is believed that he worked in Rhodesia for two years. It was there that he first met Rex (Reginald) Pearson. The two men would become friends (and brothers-in-law), both eventually working for SIS/MI6. Pearson arrived in Cape Town from England on 20 May 1902.[20] The 24-year-old mining engineer from Gateshead, Tyneside, had gone to South Africa in search of engineering work in the gold and diamond mines. Years later, he would give Kendrick an engraved ring fashioned from gold that he had reputedly unearthed himself.[21]

In 1905, Kendrick moved to Lüderitzbucht in German-occupied South West Africa (now Lüderitz in Namibia). Located some 1400km from Cape Town, this was a remote, hot and hostile region, but an important one for the diamond-mining industry. Many of the diggers lodged nearby in the town of Kolmanskop, and after work they could be found relaxing in a beer hall or enjoying a game in one of the bowling alleys. Kendrick consolidated his connections there and engaged in scouting for information on German forces in the region and other useful intelligence for the British. In 1909, Pearson also arrived in Lüderitzbucht, as a consultant mining engineer.[22]

In Lüderitzbucht, Kendrick worked for Frederick (Fritz) Wecke, a German businessman and manager of a diamond mine. He also worked as a stockbroker. Living in this region, he and Pearson came to master the German language, which would prove crucial for the future direction of their intelligence careers. It was at a social event that they met two of Frederick Wecke's daughters, Norah and Olga. Kendrick and Pearson courted the young sisters: Kendrick walked out with 19-year-old Norah (who was 10 years his junior), while Pearson preferred Olga.[23] Norah was short in stature, but physically strong, an accomplished horsewoman who was an unusually good shot with a rifle. On 29 March 1910, Kendrick married Norah by special licence, in front of a magistrate in Cape Town.[24]

Towards the end of 1910, Kendrick and Pearson left Lüderitzbucht and purchased Paardekop Farm near Standerton in the Transvaal, in what was then the Free State, not German-occupied territory. This coincided with the period when their father-in-law left the diamond mine to become a trader and co-founder of the firm Wecke & Voigts.[25] Life seemed idyllic on Paardekop Farm, even if it was geographically remote. The farmhouse was a wooden bungalow with a veranda standing beside a small plantation of tall trees and a few farm buildings.[26] The two families settled into a life of farming on the vast plain, with no other buildings for miles around, except for the characteristic round, thatched mud huts inhabited by the farm servants. The farm was reasonably self-sufficient, with items occasionally purchased at a makeshift store at Paardekop station. Kendrick's only child, Gladys, was born on New Year's Day 1911. Kendrick worked and travelled as a stockbroker; meanwhile Pearson worked, first, as mine manager for the Rhodesian firm of Schists Syndicate Ltd, and then, from 1913, in northern Nigeria for W. Mertens & Co., a German company with land leases in tin-mining areas.[27] With the men away from home, the day-to-day work of the farm was overseen by the wives.

The German threat

At the turn of the twentieth century, Germany was emerging as an aggressor with imperialistic, expansionist ambitions. It had a strong economy and was increasing its military power, including through the secret development of new weapons. It was fast overtaking Britain as an industrial and naval power, which caused grave concern for the British Empire. Between 1902 and 1907, Britain made agreements with Japan, France and Russia in an attempt to ally with them against the growing threat from Germany. British military intelligence closely monitored the situation in German South West Africa, where evidence of Germany's new guns and weaponry could be observed. By now, Kendrick and Pearson both spoke fluent German and already had a decade of experience in intelligence work for the British. They mixed in German business circles through their father-in-law's connections and gathered information for the British on German interests and military activity in the region.[28]

A friendship and working relationship began at this time with British-born Alexander Paterson Scotland, who had arrived in South Africa shortly after the Boer War. Scotland was drafted into intelligence activities and stationed at Ramons Drift, between Cape Colony and German South West Africa.[29] From there he travelled widely on horseback, gathering intelligence on German troop movements and rearmament. His work took him close to the protected diamond region of Lüderitzbucht at the same time that Kendrick and Pearson were there. Kendrick became acquainted with Scotland, and the two men went on to work together for British military intelligence, interrogating German prisoners of war in both the First and the Second World Wars.[30] It is interesting how many of Kendrick's intelligence colleagues – throughout his life – can be traced back to friendships forged in South Africa at the turn of the twentieth century.

Back in Britain there was 'spy fever' and fear fuelled by the popular books of William Le Queux in *Spies of the Kaiser* (1909) and *The Invasion of 1910*

(1906). Rumours spread that German spies were working in underground networks across London, ready to support Germany if it ever invaded Britain. These rumours have since been shown to have been exaggerated.[31] However, the wider threat of Germany to peace in Europe and South Africa was not exaggerated. In consequence, Britain decided to formalize its intelligence service on 4 July 1909 with the establishment of the Secret Service Bureau.[32] This began with two sections: a military branch (MO5) under Captain Vernon Kell; and a naval branch under Commander Mansfield Smith Cumming. A year later, the bureau split into two distinct organizations that were renamed MI5 and MI1(c).[33] The former continued under the directorship of Kell, and the latter under Cumming. In 1919, MI1(c) was to become the Secret Intelligence Service (SIS), otherwise known as MI6.[34] However, events in Europe had no direct impact on Kendrick's life, or on that of his family, until the outbreak of the First World War on 4 August 1914.

The First World War

The eruption of the First World War had consequences in South West Africa as dominion forces mobilized against their German neighbours there. Kendrick and Pearson went to the army recruitment office in Pretoria to re-enlist in the British forces and by 9 September 1914 Kendrick was back in army uniform. He was drafted into the Field Intelligence Scouts to collect military information about the enemy.[35] Of particular interest was intelligence on the formations of German troops, the position of machine guns, ammunition dumps and trench mortar, the condition of wire defences, patrol tracks and the use of particular arsenals by the Germans. Kendrick was now fluent in several languages: German, Dutch (Cape), Dutch, French and Kiswahili. Before the end of 1914, he was transferred to the South West African Central Force on unspecified intelligence duties.[36] His brother-in-law, Pearson, had joined Botha's Natal Horse Regiment, which was part of the irregular South African mounted forces.[37] During 1915, Pearson suffered a non-fatal gunshot wound which meant he could not serve in a fighting regiment. He was transferred to the European theatre of war for duties with the Intelligence Corps in France.[38] Just prior to his departure, the decision was taken by Kendrick and Pearson to sell Paardekop Farm and move their wives to Cape Province.

On 9 July 1915, the first major Allied victory in South West Africa was secured when German forces surrendered to the Union Defence Force under General Louis Botha. Kendrick's colleague, Scotland, had been interned as a prisoner of war by the Germans in August 1914 on suspicion of being a spy. The allegation of espionage was never proved against Scotland, but he spent 11 months in Windhoek Prison. He was released in July 1915 and left for England, where he joined the Intelligence Corps. Scotland was posted to general headquarters (GHQ) at Le Havre, on the French coast, where he was in charge of the interrogation of German prisoners of war (POWs). This brought him back into contact with Pearson, who was working for British military intelligence, sending pigeons behind enemy lines with secret messages under cover of darkness.[39] The use of pigeons in the First World War, as in the Boer War, was to prove indispensable as a means of communication when battalions lost wireless contact with each other on the front line.[40]

In South Africa, Keetmanshoop came under British military control after the German surrender in July 1915. The region saw the internment of thousands of German soldiers in special camps. Kendrick was seconded to Keetmanshoop as officer in charge at the Department of Native Affairs.[41] This was a judicial post that required him to process German prisoners of war for intelligence purposes – something at which he would become extremely adept. It was a defining period in his military career, as it trained him in interrogation work.

Towards the end of 1917, for reasons that are unclear, Pearson suggested to Kendrick that he seek a transfer to military intelligence in France.[42] Kendrick took up the suggestion and wrote to the administrator in Pretoria, requesting a commission overseas. His request was approved a few days later in a letter from Government House in Windhoek, in which it was acknowledged that his knowledge of the German language would prove invaluable in the European operations. The letter concluded with best wishes for 'every success and come through the war safely'.[43]

Although Kendrick would technically be working for MI1(c), it was necessary to have a parent military unit – in his case, the Intelligence Corps. But transfer was not automatic: he required three personal recommendations from people already serving in MI1(c) who were also attached to the Intelligence Corps. The references were provided by his brother-in-law Pearson, Colonel F. Pritchard (GHQ in France) and Alexander Scotland, his former colleague in South Africa.[44] Kendrick's original application form shows that he was actually applying to work for MI6(c), the section responsible for the Intelligence Corps in the war.[45] However, he remained within the auspices of MI1(c), and both branches of military intelligence are referenced in his personal army record for this period. Kendrick was accepted, left South Africa and formally transferred to the Intelligence Corps. For now, his wife and daughter remained in South Africa.

The move to intelligence work in Europe was a significant moment in Kendrick's military career, as it placed him among senior army officers in MI1(c) and at the heart of the embryonic British secret service. It also dramatically and irrevocably changed his life, for he (and, once they joined him, his immediate family and the Pearsons) would never again live in South Africa. Kendrick would be at the heart of European operations for British intelligence for the next three decades.

PART I
Europe

1
THE SLOW WAR

The war in Europe was entering its final year when Kendrick arrived in Britain in early 1918. The defeat of Germany and the Kaiser and the victory of the Allies – Britain, France and the United States – were still uncertain. German forces had been held back from advancing across France to Paris by Allied forces, but bloody battles had led to unprecedented numbers of casualties and huge loss of life. Over 415,000 British troops were dead, missing or wounded after the Battle of the Somme, which had lasted for four months from the summer of 1916. The trenches, the deep mud and the horror of so many young lives lost became the defining images of this war. The fighting at Verdun in 1917 had been equally ferocious. This was a war that had seen small military advances for both sides, with periods of stalemate. But a final German offensive could win the war. Intelligence on the enemy was as crucial in 1918 as at any point in the war; without it, the war would be lost by the Allies.

In spite of the importance of intelligence, the early years of the First World War had seen recruits receive only basic training in military intelligence. That had changed by 1918, and the range of subjects taught would form the basis for training in military intelligence for the rest of the twentieth century. Kendrick attended a four-week training course that built on his existing experience in reconnaissance and intelligence gathering in South Africa during the Second Boer War. The formal training covered the deciphering of German documents, the history of the German army prior to 1914, the political geography of Germany and its strategy and tactics, German military terms and recruitment system, the German Air Service, recognition of German regiments and uniforms, and the expansion of the German army during the war. Also on the syllabus were the principles of intelligence, aerial photography, how to plot information on maps, communications in the field, German ruses and 'booby traps', information on German shells and fuses, deciphering German script (for the translation of documents), the debriefing of escaped Allied POWs and the interrogation of enemy prisoners of war.[1] On the same course was Eric Gedye, a soldier who, after being wounded on the Somme in 1916, had transferred to military intelligence.[2] The two men's lives were thereafter to be linked in intelligence for decades. Gedye, who was 10 years younger than Kendrick, would go on to work for him as an agent in Vienna in the 1930s.

In early June 1918, Kendrick and Gedye were dispatched to British GHQ at Montreuil in France, which came under the overall army command of General Sir Walter Kirke, one-time director of military intelligence.[3] The intelligence work there fell under the umbrella organization MI1(c), the forerunner of SIS. Kendrick was promoted to the rank of lieutenant and joined Field Intelligence Security as Agent 2nd Class. Intelligence Corps personnel were formed into special groups and sent out to scout for intelligence.[4] This was familiar work for Kendrick, who had conducted similar operations behind enemy lines with the bicycle brigade in the Boer War.

Gedye was appointed political intelligence officer in the intelligence branch of GHQ. He and Kendrick joined an already far-reaching military intelligence operation which saw intelligence personnel also based in Paris and Rouen. Working alongside them during this period were officers who would later form the core of SIS after the war. These included Stewart Menzies (later the third head of MI6), Frank Foley,[5] Charles ('Dick') Ellis (the man who was always believed to have betrayed the SIS network in 1938) and Albert ('Bertie') Acton Burnell.[6] All were to remain part of Kendrick's close circle for the rest of his career with SIS/MI6, with Menzies becoming his boss in 1939. Meanwhile, Claude Dansey, from his South Africa days, had been tasked by Cumming with instigating structural changes to MI1(c).[7] Thus it can be seen that there was a close-knit circle of military intelligence officers with Kendrick at its heart – an insider who was part of the emerging 'old boys' club' of British intelligence officers who had served together in the First World War.

Clandestine operations

The precise nature of Kendrick's work during his first four months in France is unclear, except it is known that he conducted field intelligence and counter-espionage work related to the MI1(c) networks behind enemy lines. His career closely mirrored that of Frank Foley, who was also an Agent 2nd Class, engaged in counter-espionage and the recruitment of informers and enemy spies to work for the Allies.[8] In their work, the paths of Kendrick and Foley crossed with that of Stewart Menzies, who had been given the job of liaising between MI1(c) and the Directorate of Military Intelligence; for a while he was based at the War Office in Paris, shuttling back and forth to British GHQ.[9] Menzies would go on to head SIS/MI6 in the Second World War.

Paris had become the centre of espionage, with many foreign civilians and spies passing through on their travels across Europe. It was an ideal city for British intelligence to observe and track enemy agents; but intelligence was also required from behind enemy lines. Major Robert Bruce was in Paris to track German spies for MI1(c) and to establish clandestine networks into occupied Belgium and Luxembourg. From a discreet town house, at 41 Rue St Roch in Paris, he recruited and 'ran' a Belgian woman, Madame Rischard, for MI1(c).[10] Whether Kendrick had any direct contact with Bruce's work into Luxembourg is not known; however, he did have links to a network that operated in occupied Belgium, known as La Dame Blanche (The White Lady), and was run by Captain Landau of the Intelligence Corps.[11] In much the same way as Bruce's network in Luxembourg, La Dame Blanche gathered intelligence on the movements of German troop trains across Belgium, the intelligence being passed back by clandestine means to British GHQ in Montreuil. By careful observation of German troops and military manoeuvres, their direction and destination, the British could work out which part of the front line the reinforcements were heading for, and hence anticipate the next German offensive.

The operations were all connected. Bruce's centre in Paris was one of four that worked together to run various areas of intelligence work. The other three were the War Office (London), SIS at 4 Whitehall Court (London) and an office at Folkestone, on the south coast of England.[12] Major B. Wallinger operated out of London and recruited Sigismund Payne Best (who would become an SIS officer, later betrayed to the Nazis in 1939 in the infamous Venlo incident). The centres supplied intelligence to General Sir Walter Kirke, whose units were monitoring German train movements, running agents and sending pigeons over the front line (under the direction of Kendrick's brother-in-law, Pearson).[13] The Folkestone section was run by Major A. Cameron, who handled intelligence to and from Holland.[14]

After the Allied attack on Amiens in August 1918, British forces captured over 15,000 German POWs, who had to be processed and carefully interrogated in order to derive intelligence.[15] It was when the movements of the armies slowed down that the greatest progress was made in intelligence work. Because of Kendrick's fluency in German and his previous experience with German internees and POWs in Keetmanshoop, Bruce assigned him to work with his former colleague Alexander Scotland on the interrogation of German POWs. Prisoners and deserters were deemed a primary source of intelligence: they were interrogated about the movement of troops by train (many of them in retreat); about trenches and wire defences along the front line; and about the distribution of enemy forces and their locations.[16] It was from these interrogations that Kendrick and Scotland secured a vital and detailed picture of the German army and its fighting condition in the final stages of the war.

By 1918, British intelligence networks in France and Belgium had become reasonably sophisticated, and certainly better organized than earlier in the war. Their mechanism of collecting intelligence on German train movements, troop movements and aircraft (from the surveillance of aerodromes) was smooth and well oiled.[17] The meticulous gathering of intelligence – often masses of snippets of information – was mundane and slow, but vital, because it built up a comprehensive picture of the enemy and its fighting capability. It laid the foundations for intelligence methodology in the future. The major challenge for

British intelligence in this war had been to create an intelligence organization capable of operating between London and France on an ambitious scale and under war conditions. There had been no previous experience of any such thing: although the basic intelligence guidelines from the Boer War could be used as a starting point, the circumstances of the European war necessitated the creation of a larger and more efficient operational organization.

However, a bitter rivalry had developed between the London offices and Folkestone. This hampered the intelligence work, wasted time and required an unnecessary expenditure of energy in trying to sort out the tensions.[18] The First World War was, arguably, a defining moment in the development of British intelligence, as lessons were learned from the hostility that could develop between offices and that could result in inefficiency. It meant that when a major new inter-services intelligence-gathering unit was established in the next war, the man chosen to set it up and run an efficient operation was Kendrick. Level-headed, with an analytical handling of any situation and considerable interpersonal skills, he could navigate the egos of heads of departments and bring them together. These were skills that he developed during and after the 'slow war' of the First World War. During it, Kendrick had been immersed in an environment where military intelligence officers such as Bruce, Wallinger, Cameron and Pearson had to use ingenuity to develop novel ways of gathering intelligence. They had created new networks of agents behind the lines and had developed ingenious new methods of gaining intelligence (such as Pearson and the pigeons being sent behind enemy lines). The operations had not necessarily run smoothly, and nor were they particularly sophisticated in the beginning; however, the First World War had taught British intelligence that it needed the right people to adapt the service to new challenges and circumstances.

The 1918 Armistice and the Bolshevik threat

The Armistice on 11 November 1918 ended the First World War; but victory for the Allies came at a huge cost. Human life had been squandered on an unprecedented scale and the apparent futility of it would be felt for decades.

The immediate priority for the Allies was to disarm Germany, so that it could not wage another war on its neighbours. The Europe that emerged from the devastation of the bloody war was one in which 27 heads of state (royal and non-royal) had fallen. New political forces vied to fill the power vacuum, one of them being Soviet Russia. Russia had undergone immense political change in the 1917 Revolution, which culminated in the murder of Tsar Nicholas II and his family. The Bolsheviks and communists seized power and ended the rule of the Romanov imperial dynasty. The priority for the British Secret Intelligence Service was to monitor the new communist threat, tracking its spies across Europe and those agents who sought to enter Britain in order to destabilize democracy.

GHQ in France moved to Cologne as part of the British occupying forces in Germany. The headquarters opened there with 44 officers, including Kendrick, and 209 soldiers.[19] Its personnel were engaged in various intelligence duties, counter-espionage, postal censorship and combating German propaganda and sabotage.[20] Still officers of MI1(c), Kendrick, Foley, Acton Burnell and Pearson worked first for Major Bruce, then Colonel Tangye, and were engaged in tracking Bolshevik insurgents who were infiltrating the defeated German armies and trying to foment instability.[21]

After six months of negotiations with the Allied powers, Germany signed the Treaty of Versailles in Paris on 28 June 1919. The treaty restricted Germany's army to 100,000 men and effectively made its air force defunct. The Austro-Hungarian Empire was divided up to form new countries, including Austria, Czechoslovakia and Hungary. Large parts of West Prussia were conceded to Poland. The Allies imposed huge reparation costs on Germany in an attempt to prevent any future rearmament. The signing of the treaty was marked in Cologne with the firing of 101 guns across the Rhine. Trams ran again, the opera house reopened and the ban on Allied fraternization with Germans was lifted. While the Allied occupying forces could enjoy periods of relaxation in the city, a bigger threat was emerging. The dividing up of the Austro-Hungarian Empire impacted directly on political developments in Eastern Europe and, instead of providing security, had the opposite effect – of creating instability in the region. Communism sought to overthrow democratic rule in the newly created countries of Eastern Europe, as well as in the Balkans and Greece. A new organization called the Comintern had been founded in Moscow in March 1919 by the Soviet leader, Vladimir Lenin, to expound the ideals of communism, foster a wave of civil wars across Europe and kill any opponents, and establish an international Soviet republic in the countries of Europe, by means of a coup if necessary. Monitoring the Comintern became the urgent priority for SIS.

Towards the end of 1919, it became possible for Kendrick and Pearson to bring their wives and families to Germany. They sailed from South Africa via England, and Kendrick took temporary leave from Cologne and travelled to England to escort them to Germany. The party arrived in Cologne on Christmas Eve. Kendrick's daughter, Gladys, recalled that:

> The Christmas tree reached to the ceiling with real candles and decorated with gold and silver baubles, spicy biscuits and pretty ornaments. I remember all the wonderful presents, especially a big doll's house fully furnished with lights that turned on, and all the mod cons.[22]

The Kendricks were billeted with a German family called Sturm, in a house overlooking the Stadtwald forest in Cologne. The Pearsons and Colonel Tangye lived nearby. Gedye was posted to Cologne as private secretary to H.S. Ryan, the deputy high commissioner, and then to the economic section of the military governor of the occupied territories.

By 1920, the staff at GHQ in Cologne was reduced to just 10 officers and 62 soldiers.[23] SIS's tactics were changing: it started to install some of its key officers in British passport control offices, as a cover for their SIS work. This cover enabled them to continue to monitor communist spies operating across Europe. It would define much of SIS's work up to 1939 – and beyond 1945, into the Cold War. Frank Foley was posted to the passport control office in Berlin;[24] Sigismund Payne Best was sent to The Hague as British passport control officer there;

and Hanns Vischer, another intelligence officer, who had worked out of Berne in the war, was sent to Prague to fill the same post there.[25]

By the 1920s, Vienna, once the centre of the Austro-Hungarian Empire, constituted the main crossroads for spies of different nationalities to move in and out of Czechoslovakia, Hungary, Germany and the Soviet Union. It had replaced Paris as the centre of espionage and it is therefore understandable why SIS considered it the most important station in Europe. In 1922, Alban Ernan Forbes-Dennis retired as British passport control officer in Vienna and, together with his wife, the British novelist Phyllis Bottome, returned to Kitzbühel in Austria to establish a language and psychology school in the Tyrolean mountains.[26] He handed over command to an unnamed deputy – who turned out to be disastrous. This successor was totally unsuited to the job and spent more time attending a clinic for venereal diseases than carrying out intelligence duties.[27] The Vienna station was too important for SIS to leave to an inefficient officer: it needed someone who could establish high-level diplomatic, military and social contacts.

Attention turned to Kendrick, the outgoing military officer who enjoyed socializing, was known to have impeccable discretion and yet was relaxed and jovial. His openness in his dealings with people, coupled with his personal political discretion, marked him out as an ideal candidate to replace Forbes-Dennis's inefficient successor. In 1925, Hugh Sinclair, the new head of SIS, posted Kendrick to Vienna as the British passport control officer there. This was a cover for Kendrick's real work as head of the SIS station, running spy networks across Europe and gathering precious information for Britain about the threat from the Soviets – and later on, in the 1930s, about the still greater threat from the Nazis. The head of Britain's Secret Intelligence Service had placed him at the heart of its operations in Europe, monitoring the political threats posed to Britain by the struggle between East and West.

The soldier turned spymaster . . .

2

RED VIENNA

Kendrick arrived in Vienna on New Year's Day 1925 for his first day at
the British passport control office at 6 Metternichgasse. This was a time when
SIS officers had to figure out for themselves the best way of operating.[1] With
no formal SIS training, Kendrick had to set his own rules and boundaries of
operation; and there was no diplomatic immunity if he was caught spying in a
foreign country.[2] SIS was still an inexperienced organization that relied on the
gentleman amateur rather than trained intelligence professionals. 'It was not a
particularly sophisticated network', recalls Prudence Hopkinson, daughter of
Kendrick's SIS secretary, Clara Holmes. 'You backed your own judgement and
were thrown into the intelligence work with no rulebook. It had to be worked
out on instinct.'[3]

The skill lay in 'discovering the thing you should pay a spy to ferret out for
you – that is among the more vital, fascinating long-term tasks of true security
work'.[4] Kendrick would prove adept at this. Intelligence can be a slow game,
and its modus operandi was rather basic in those early days. SIS consisted of
gentlemen from the elite Etonian world of private education, many of whom
had been officers in military intelligence in the First World War. Until this
period, spying had largely consisted of the traditional 'old-school' style of culti-
vating members of the aristocracy, rather than those in power.[5] Kendrick
continued to mix in aristocratic, diplomatic and political circles, but he also
extended his network to build new friendships among Austrian intellectuals –
musicians, artists and journalists, who were more likely to be communists
or socialists. They were SIS's primary target in the 1920s. Kendrick's ability to

adapt to intelligence requirements already marked him out as a valuable spymaster. He was a charismatic personality who understood the importance of interpersonal relations that could be cultivated for human espionage (HUMINT). By forming strong friendships and acquaintances over several years, Kendrick built a base for intelligence gathering – as well as one that could provide help and sanctuary in a future crisis. One of the best ways of doing this was through hosting and attending dinners, cocktail parties, concerts and cultural events. His wife, Norah, saw nothing unusual in their very active social life or frequent appearances at exclusive parties.[6]

Most importantly, Kendrick understood the complexities of the Austria in which he had arrived. Historically, its capital, Vienna, had been 'red' – politically left wing, either socialist or communist. The rest of the country was right wing and clerical, and supported the Roman Catholic Church. The left was anticlerical and was seen as a threat to the Church. The recent dismantling at the end of the First World War of the vast Austro-Hungarian Empire had created an identity issue on the right. The more conservative wing of the right clung to its distinct, Austrian character, while the more radical right looked for a solution in the creation of a Greater Germany. Kendrick's early years in Vienna would be taken up with the left and communist groups. His Roman Catholic background may have been a possible reason for sending him (rather than an Anglican intelligence officer, say). In spite of the political turmoil, the capital displayed a culture that was arguably unrivalled in Europe. It was home to some of the finest musicians, artists, intellectuals and scientists, including its most famous inhabitant – Sigmund Freud, the founder of psychoanalysis.

The SIS secretaries

Three secretaries at the passport office were on the payroll of SIS and were an integral part of Kendrick's inner intelligence circle: Clara Holmes, Evelyn Stamper and Betty Hodgson. All were fiercely loyal, educated, highly efficient and feisty characters who worked from a back room of the passport office, secretly helping Kendrick to run the spy networks. They gathered intelligence, decrypted messages received in invisible ink and compiled reports for London on Czechoslovakia, Hungary and Italy.[7] Details are scant on the backgrounds of Stamper and Hodgson. It is known that Hodgson never married and lived in Vienna with her father (a retired officer of the Indian Army). And both Hodgson and Holmes were expert skiers.[8]

Clara Holmes – known as 'Bill' by her closest circle – had already had an intelligence career. At the age of 19 and under her maiden name of Clara Bates, she had gone to Kiel to teach English to the daughters of a respectable German family.[9] When war broke out in 1914, she returned to England to avoid internment and took up work in the Ministry of Munitions. An unnamed visitor arrived at the premises and enquired about German speakers. Holmes put her name forward and, in 1916, was sent to Berne on secret intelligence work, the nature of which she never disclosed. Her daughter, Prudence Hopkinson, recalled: 'The only mention she made was that it was all unofficial and not based in an embassy. My mother stayed in Berne for two years and worked for a man by the name of Vischer.'[10] This was Swiss-born Hanns Vischer, who worked in Berne and (as mentioned above) later transferred to the British passport control office in Prague.[11] Clara worked in Berne for six months and then transferred to Vienna. In 1926, she met her future husband, Reginald (Rex) Trayton Holmes, at her sister's wedding, soon returned to Britain and married him the same year. They started a new life in Kenya, but three years later he caught malaria while on safari and died. Clara returned to England with their one-year-old daughter, Prudence. The following summer she was invited to return to Vienna to work for Kendrick again.

Agents and officers

The nature of Kendrick's work means that the identity of most of his agents will remain unknown. Rare glimpses of his world occasionally surface in auto-biographies, biographies and the official MI6 history. During the 1920s and from Vienna, he continued with much the same type of work as he had undertaken in post-war Cologne – tracking communist spies and agents. One country of interest for SIS was Czechoslovakia, where communist agents and Russian spies were believed to be operating. Kendrick formed his own networks to penetrate them. At the head of one of these was an unnamed ex-officer of the Imperial Austrian Army, employed by the Czechoslovak Ministry of Defence; to this day he is only known by his SIS codename 44084. He was an ethnic German who became a Czechoslovak national when the Austro-Hungarian Empire collapsed in 1918 and the borders of Europe were redrawn. Agent 44084 had valuable contacts inside the military, civil service, police and banking and industry sectors in Czechoslovakia, and recruited sub-agents for Kendrick. These sub-agents included an electrical engineer who was engaged in military service and was able to provide information on call signs, wireless sets and military codes. He sent messages to Vienna in invisible ink which the secretaries deciphered. Agent 44084 recruited another (unnamed) sub-agent who was on the list of the army general staff and provided vital information on mobilization maps. Another worked for the firm Škoda and reported on its aircraft production.[12]

Two SIS intelligence officers working for Kendrick were his own brother-in-law, Rex Pearson, and Charles (Dick) Howard Ellis. They arrived in Vienna in 1926 and worked undercover in journalism.[13] Ellis had been born in Australia in 1895, to British parents. He had served on the Western Front during the war, been posted to the Caucasus with British forces at the end of the war and then taken up studies at Oxford University. He had abandoned his degree in 1921 to take up an SIS post in Istanbul. His marriage to a White Russian brought him valuable contacts for British intelligence, and he became the main contact for Russian agents.[14] Although Ellis spoke no German and had no training, in 1923 he was posted to Berlin – a city that was seen then as the centre of international Bolshevism. But there were many dangers for spies like Ellis as the White Russians had been penetrated by the Soviets. Ellis soon requested a transfer to Vienna, from where he worked on German and Russian targets for Kendrick.

Another agent was Eric Gedye, who had served with Kendrick in military intelligence in the First World War and then in Cologne.[15] During his time in Cologne, Gedye had gathered surplus material that was not classified by military intelligence and was therefore available for public release. He offered the stories to *The Times* and on the strength of these the newspaper employed him in the Rhineland region of Germany. Gedye was politically astute. He recognized that the financial reparations placed on Germany under the Treaty of Versailles would eventually have an impact on political developments in the country. He foresaw that Vienna would become the most important place from which to monitor changes in Europe and asked for a transfer there. *The Times* denied his request, so Gedye decided to take the risk and voluntarily resigned to work as a freelance journalist in Vienna. This gave him the freedom to cover the political stories that he believed to be important.[16] This all came at a time when he was feeling trapped in an unhappy marriage to a German Rhinelander, and by moving to Vienna he ended the relationship (although they did not divorce until after 1945).

Gedye described the Vienna in which he had arrived as politically stagnant. The city had been 'a playground for the aristocracy, plutocracy, the officer and the higher castes, with the Catholic Church ruling almost as co-equal with the Habsburgs. Could this highly desirable state of affairs ever be restored in what was now Red Vienna?'[17]

His reference to Red Vienna was to a capital inclined more towards communism than nationalism; a capital that was no longer the centre of the vast and powerful Austro-Hungarian Empire, which had been carved up after the war. Instead, it was the capital of a reconstructed Austria that was a political mix of nationalists and communists; it was not possible to predict with any certainty which way the balance of power would shift. This was the world in which Kendrick operated. Communism was believed by SIS to be the primary threat to democracy and hence the importance of tracking its activities and progress in the region was paramount. After a short period of freelance work, Gedye was engaged by the *News Chronicle* and then re-employed by *The Times*.[18] He travelled in and out of Austria, providing political assessment through his articles and gathering intelligence for Kendrick.

In the region, Kendrick found other old contacts and friends from his South Africa and First World War days whom he could draw into his network. Max Rosenberg had moved back to Romania to work in the family business; he travelled between ports on the Danube, passing information back to SIS via both Kendrick and Claude Dansey. Rosenberg became an important agent who was able to watch shipping interests and the movement of supplies in the region. He could monitor whether Germany was adhering to the Treaty of Versailles or illegally importing weapons or materials to manufacture armaments. The Danube was also the main route for Romanian oil. Concern was mounting about a possible German expansion to the east to take in the oilfields and granaries of Romania. If successful, nothing would then stand in the way of Germany's taking the oilfields of Iraq. Rosenberg was connected to the wealthy Mendl family of Romania, which already had links to British intelligence. Rosenberg's sister-in-law, May Atkins, had married into the Mendl family, placing her in high society within a family that had strong ties with Britain.[19] In 1910, Charles Mendl and Rosenberg expanded the family business to form a global shipping company called Dunarea. Its fleet was concentrated along the Danube and meant that the family was in a geographically influential position to serve as a key part of Kendrick's wide network.[20]

Russian penetration in Vienna

Kendrick's primary brief in Vienna during the 1920s was to uncover Russian, communist and Comintern activities in Vienna and the wider region.[21] The bulk of his work consisted of counter-espionage against Russian and communist spies, building up a picture of personalities, networks and organizations that were operating for Russian intelligence in the region.[22] SIS believed that Russian intelligence might infiltrate communist groups in Vienna, such as the Vienna Centre of the Communist International, and use them as a cover for espionage. This proved accurate – within four months of first taking up his post in Vienna, Kendrick's agents had successfully provided him with full details of the personnel structure and organization of the Vienna Centre.[23] This had been achieved with the help of 'an insider', an unnamed communist official who was in personal contact with various members at the centre and who had been befriended or 'turned' to gain intelligence for SIS. Importantly, Kendrick uncovered the fact that the Vienna Centre had become the headquarters for communist activities in Italy, Bulgaria, Greece, Romania, Czechoslovakia, Hungary, Switzerland and, from 1929, Yugoslavia.[24] It is possible, therefore, to appreciate why Kendrick's post in Vienna was so pivotal to SIS in terms of tracing and tracking Soviet intelligence agents and spies.

It is clear that Vienna had become the operational centre for much of the Comintern's work in the Balkans, too. Kendrick wrote in his report to SIS (which was then passed to MI5): 'The Vienna Centre is responsible for the whole of the revolutionary work in the Balkans and through it all instructions and money pass to the various Balkan communist parties.'[25] A precise and detailed picture of Russian agents and communist activists functioning in and out of Austria was being efficiently tracked by Kendrick. The importance of this lay in being able to monitor their movements if they sought entry into Britain to carry out subversive activities. The chairman of the Balkan committee at the Vienna Centre was a man by the name of Miliutine. He was discovered to be a member of the Russian Communist Party and responsible for the Balkan work. Although he lived in Vienna and frequently travelled to Moscow, he was not attached to the official Soviet diplomatic mission there and was therefore termed an 'illegal' in spy jargon.

Another member of the committee (known only as 'Yoffe') was discovered to be the head of the Soviet diplomatic mission in Vienna. The committee was thought to consist of 18 to 20 members. Kendrick's informant revealed that Moscow periodically sent specialists to Vienna to advise the committee, including an ex-officer of the general staff of the Russian Imperial Army, who was one of the Centre's highly trusted agents. The Comintern did not trust the various Balkan communist parties to maintain a network of reliable and secure agents and therefore preferred to run its own separate agents into the Balkans from Vienna. Kendrick reported that one success of the Comintern from Vienna was its penetration of the Internal Macedonian Revolutionary Organization. He found that there were nearly a hundred Comintern agents working in Yugoslavia. In addition, he learned that the foreign section of the OGPU (Soviet secret police at that time) in Moscow had its own intelligence branch in Vienna. It was administered by a man called Anderson, who had recently become chief of Soviet intelligence in the Balkans. Anderson employed two agents who worked solely for him, in absolute secrecy, to provide exclusive intelligence reports on the military forces of the countries into which they were sent.

Another Soviet agent and trusted source working for the Comintern was Victor Ivanovitch (sic – according to his MI5 file), an ex-captain in the Russian Mercantile Marine, who worked undercover as William Tikstone. His movements were watched by Kendrick's network and he was found to visit Marseille, Naples, Salonika, Constantinople and Genoa frequently, in the guise of a businessman in shipping. His real work was to report back to the Comintern and provide intelligence and information on naval matters in the region. This was achieved by organizing communist 'spy cells' to infiltrate the various naval and merchant ships using the Mediterranean ports.

Such was the intelligence coming Kendrick's way that he secured information about meetings between the Soviet diplomatic and commercial missions in Vienna and the Comintern. These meetings were conducted in complete secrecy, usually in private houses, and therefore harder to gain intelligence, so there must have been an 'insider'. Kendrick had another informant who had already met most of the agents working for the Vienna Centre, and so he became particularly significant.[26] Three travelling agents and couriers are named in Kendrick's report.[27] One was aged around 30, spoke many languages and was about to be transferred to the Soviet embassy in Rome. The second one travelled regularly between Vienna and Salonika on a Polish passport, via Bulgaria and Constantinople. And the third had gone into the Balkans on a German or an Estonian passport.

The Soviets reduced the activities of the Vienna Centre during 1925, and even considered closing it down; but by the following January its duties had increased. Comprehensive measures were put in place to deal with espionage in the countries of Eastern Europe, the Balkans and Greece. A directive came from Moscow that the Greek Communist Party should have a representative on the Committee of the Vienna Centre as a 'special and general delegate' of the Comintern.[28]

SIS was interested in operational details, such as how the Vienna Centre received its funds from Moscow. Kendrick's agents discovered that the mediator between Moscow and Vienna was a man called Klimov, described as a 'special and general delegate of the Comintern for the Balkans'.[29] He was an experienced Soviet agent and diplomatic representative who operated out of Vienna. Funds from Moscow for the Balkan work came via Klimov, who used a Russian-Jewish banker in Vienna – one Mr Landau.

Kendrick's extensive report for SIS was able to name each of the sections within the Vienna Centre and the head of each section, including the military intelligence wing. A check could then be made at SIS headquarters against its own list of known communist activists. Kendrick established that part of the press bureau of the Vienna Centre was attached to the Soviet embassy in Vienna as a cover. All liaison work between the Vienna Centre and the Soviet government in Moscow (including military intelligence operations) was handled by the Soviet embassy in Vienna. With this information, SIS could map the network of Soviet intelligence in Czechoslovakia, Hungary and the other target countries, and also gain confirmation of the operational process and communications being used by the Comintern. The level of Kendrick's penetration of the Comintern was quite extraordinary. Copies of his reports were dispatched to the Foreign Office, MI5, Scotland Yard and the War Office.

Perhaps the most serious concern for SIS was Kendrick's discovery that a military operations section at the Vienna Centre was coordinating the supply and transport of arms and ammunition to various communist groups in the Balkans and South-East Europe. Propaganda was coordinated from this centre, too. Vienna had become a major centre of clandestine Comintern and communist activities. Kendrick was even able to name the four heads of the propaganda sections responsible for Germany, Hungary, Poland and the Balkans.[30] His own agents were soon on the trail of two new Comintern agents who were to direct their operations against British intelligence. Nadia Zachariova posed as a Russian refugee, but in fact she was an agent from the counter-espionage section of the Comintern in Moscow. Another agent, known in the files simply as Swagens, was from the same department and had been dispatched to Vienna to uncover British intelligence organizations and networks in the capital.[31] A picture emerges of spies of different countries moving silently through the streets of Vienna, penetrating social circles and watching each other from the shadows, probably unaware of how far they themselves had been unmasked. But it is not clear whether the Comintern successfully uncovered Kendrick.

Kendrick went a step further and secretly tapped into the telephone cables of Russian intelligence in Vienna, thereby gaining for SIS a relatively complete picture of Soviet espionage operating from there into Czechoslovakia.[32] He was able to gain information about the NKVD (People's Commissariat for Internal Affairs), an internal intelligence organization based in Russia that was responsible for the secret police, the penal camps (gulags) and border control. However, although responsible for internal state security, it periodically carried out work abroad, such as the assassination of enemies of the Soviet State. The NKVD believed that Russian communist activity in Czechoslovakia was being undermined by other foreign communist groups and that this had resulted in Russian communists losing control of the political situation.

One of Kendrick's unnamed agents penetrated the 'collegia' of the NKVD and discovered tensions between the Comintern and the NKVD. A representative of the NKVD was reported as saying that its centres abroad still made use of local communities to secure secret information on the defence forces of a country.[33] Employees of the NKVD operating abroad were instructed not to have any contact with foreign communists, but to operate independently. In turn, the Comintern blamed the NKVD for espionage failures in Czechoslovakia – a country that was perceived to be hostile to the Soviet Union. This type of information gave SIS knowledge of friction between the different organizations of the Russian secret service and important insight into the thinking, operational methods and activities of a rival, possibly enemy, foreign intelligence organization.

RED VIENNA

Béla Kun, Hungarian revolutionary

Another figure being tracked in the 1920s was Béla Kun, a Hungarian revolutionary and friend of Lenin.[34] Kun had fought for the Austro-Hungarian Empire in the First World War and had been taken prisoner by the Russians. As a POW, he fell under the influence of communist ideology. Freed after the 1917 Russian Revolution, he travelled in Russia before returning to Hungary, where, in 1919, he led a Bolshevik-style party in an insurrection to overthrow the Hungarian government. He petitioned Lenin for help, but none was forthcoming. Kun was arrested, but continued to direct clandestine communist activities from his prison cell. On 21 March 1919, a new Hungarian Soviet Republic was established and Kun was released from prison to join a left-wing coalition government in Budapest. He was sworn into office as People's Commissar for Foreign Affairs, but in reality power in Hungary lay with him. A period of terror was soon witnessed across Hungary that became known as the Red Terror. It led to terrible atrocities, discovered by SIS to have been authorized by Kun. Hungary found itself at war with its neighbours, Romania and Czechoslovakia. Kun expected support from the Soviet army, but this did not materialize, as the Soviets were preoccupied with fighting in the Ukraine. Nor did Kun secure the support of the peasantry, because he had failed to redistribute power, land and wealth. The industrial proletariat also refused to fight. Kun was forced into exile in Austria, from where the SIS station in Vienna tracked his movements and intercepted his mail.[35]

Kendrick took over the counter-espionage work against Kun, who, while in Vienna, was working as a Comintern operative with responsibility for Austria, Czechoslovakia and Germany. Kun was discovered to be living under an assumed name and using a rented shop in the Neubau district of the city as a cover for his activities. From there, he gave orders for the assassination of two unnamed Ukrainian officials, who were thrown into the Danube near the Hungária Hotel in Budapest, which at the time was the Bolshevik headquarters. Numerous other killings were said to have been committed on Kun's orders.[36] He was finally arrested in Vienna in April 1926 and expelled.[37] He returned to Russia and continued his political activities for the Comintern into the 1930s. However, during Stalin's Great Purges of the 1930s, he was arrested and executed on 29 August 1938. His fate was kept secret in Russia until the 1950s, but was known to SIS.

Tracking Russian agents

By the latter half of the 1920s, Kendrick had become an expert for SIS on Comintern and Bolshevik activities. Such was his successful penetration work that, by the autumn of 1927, he had compiled a complete list of Bolshevik sympathizers and activists for MI5 to track if they entered Britain.[38] He discovered that the Soviets had engaged a German (or Austrian) named Comrade M. Schmidt, whose task was to track Sonia Alberovaya, an agent engaged by the Italian secret service on anti-Soviet espionage. Not only was Soviet intelligence following Alberovaya, but Kendrick was monitoring the Soviet tracking of her. Other Soviet agents who were being monitored by Kendrick included Comrade Fritzi, whose real surname was Loewe.[39] She was resident in Vienna and had worked for the Soviet OGPU since 1926. In another case, the Vienna representative of OGPU asked Moscow whether it had already employed the services of a German/Austrian woman by the name of Amalia (or Adele) Singer, who had visited Moscow twice and had a good knowledge of Russian.[40] It became clear that OGPU wished to use her for espionage in White Russian circles in Austria. This specific intelligence was thought to have originated with Kendrick's colleague Dick Ellis, who had been penetrating White Russian circles in Vienna since 1926.[41]

There was a little intelligence on other Soviet agents, such as one 'Comrade Kis', who reported to OGPU in Vienna. He was on the verge of securing a direct connection for OGPU in the Hungarian embassy in Vienna. As to his identity, he was thought to be a Hungarian, Joseph Kiss, described by SIS as 'a notorious anarchist deported from Hungary in 1920 and arrested by Italian authorities in Trieste'.[42]

The interception of mail continued throughout the 1920s and, in early June 1928, Kendrick's network gained access to a letter written by Stanislas Kalina of the 'special section' of the Soviet embassy in Vienna. This section was of particular interest to Kendrick, because it was believed to be directing espionage on behalf of the Soviet Union. The letter was written to the special section of the NKVD in Moscow and revealed that the Soviets had paid 120 dollars for material about secret instructions given to the commandant of a Bulgarian garrison for a planned armed uprising against the government.[43] It is also now clear that at this time Kendrick was sending intelligence back to Sinclair in London about other activities of the Soviet secret service in Vienna.[44] It became apparent that the Soviets were spying on Czechoslovakia through their agent Comrade Dikman. Of concern was the fact that Dikman had collected exhaustive material dealing with the status, organization, concentration and orders of the Czechoslovak army. Within a fortnight of this information being received, Kendrick sent another report to Sinclair that Russian agents were conducting surveillance of the Austrian far-right group Front-Kämpfer.[45] Kendrick's report was forwarded to MI5, the information in it gleaned from a letter that had been sent from the Soviet embassy in Vienna to the NKVD in Moscow. The Soviet handlers in Vienna requested reinforcement by agents with specialist military training, as their existing agents did not have sufficient military knowledge for the tasks they were required to undertake. This information in itself gave SIS an insight into how experienced (or otherwise) some of the Soviet agents were. Three other Soviet men were named in that original letter as also tracking the Front-Kämpfer for Soviet intelligence.[46] Kendrick ran a trace on them and reported that one was unidentifiable, a second had been head of a Military Topographical Commission and had left for Mongolia under the guise of a commercial agent and the third had been identified by one of SIS's own representatives in the Baltic.[47]

In the summer of 1929, one of Kendrick's agents secretly attended a session of the 'Council of People's Commissaries' in Vienna and was able to monitor the political tone and content of the speeches. A speech by the deputy of the council boasted that the Soviet Union had a well-organized intelligence apparatus in Persia, and could

boldly compete with the British who are very proud of the exemplary organization of their intelligence organizations in the Middle East. In

Austria and the Balkans and in Italy, our intelligence service fully satisfies the requirements and tasks set before it.[48]

A translation of the full speech was sent back to London.

Undoubtedly, the above information provides only a fraction of the intelligence that Kendrick was gathering for SIS, and this is only available because some of the security files have been declassified. It constitutes only material in MI5 files; there is nothing from the MI6 archives, which potentially could reveal so much more of the achievements of the Vienna station.

Chemical warfare

Communist groups operating in Eastern Europe, the Balkans and Greece in the late 1920s continued to seek to undermine the new democratic countries of Europe by stirring up political instability and encouraging subversion. An ideological battle between communism and democracy emerged that would last for most of the twentieth century and into the twenty-first. Against this backdrop in the 1920s, Austria's immediate neighbours were suspected of developing new chemical weapons to protect themselves in the event of another war, and Italy was believed to be supplying chemicals to Czechoslovakia and Hungary.[49] Chemical warfare is often assumed to be a relatively modern threat; however, it had started with the use of chlorine gas by the Germany military in the First World War. This was the first killing agent used against Allied soldiers in the trenches, and it caused severe burning of the throat and death by asphyxiation. By the late 1920s, intelligence was badly needed by SIS on new chemical weapons that had been, or were being, developed, and by which countries.

From at least 1927, and possibly earlier, Kendrick was sending agents into Italy, Czechoslovakia and Hungary to gather information on these armament programmes. It was discovered that the Chemical Warfare Service in Czechoslovakia had expanded and been strengthened over a 12-month period, and intended to use three kinds of bombs in warfare: explosive, incendiary and gas. The gas bombs contained yperite and phosgene, and were being manufactured at the Military Technical Institute in Bystrovany.[50] Yperite was used in the manufacture of mustard gas, while phosgene was another gas used in time of war. A report sent to Sinclair in the summer of 1928 informed him that: 'The Ministry of National Defence [in Czechoslovakia] has been making feverish endeavours to discover arsenic on Czech territory in such quantities as to render the country autonomous in this respect for chemical war requirements.'[51] Large strata of arsenical pyrites were discovered in the vicinity of the state mines, near the town of Smolotely, and contained 80 per cent arsenic. The mines had been placed under military (not civilian) control, which alerted SIS to the fact that the extracts were being used for military purposes.

One of Kendrick's agents identified a list of the country's chemical engineers who could be appointed to certain posts by the Czechoslovak government during a war. A number of factories had been earmarked for the production of toxic substances if Czechoslovak forces were ever mobilized. Although training appeared to be currently inadequate, gas chambers existed in all large barracks. The intelligence report stated: 'Phosgene and Mustard Gas are now produced and loaded onto aeroplane bombs, shells and grenades at the Military Chemical Institute. The output and stock now accumulated are not known ... Collective defence of the civilian population is receiving consideration.'[52]

During the same period, Hungary was discovered to be preparing for a probable chemical war. A technical intelligence report provided SIS with the precise formulae for the different gases being developed for offensive and defensive operations. A gas suitable for use against infantry units in the field was said to cause vomiting and weakness, but 'the disablement inflicted is temporary'.[53] Kendrick's reports informed London that one of Hungary's battalions had received a consignment of 150 German-manufactured gas masks. Made of rubber and covering the head completely, the masks were designed in such a way that the mouth and nose could be opened to facilitate breathing, without the mask being taken off. They were said to be tested 'on people in gas chambers and had good results'.[54] The gas masks were soon issued to other units of the Hungarian army.

The Romanian government covertly passed information to Kendrick's spies about new hand grenades being manufactured at a factory in Csepel, a district of Budapest, Hungary. There were two types of grenade: defensive and offensive.[55] The report was quite detailed: the defensive grenades weighed 1 kg, and the force of the explosion was described as considerable, but with no smoke; the offensive grenades weighed 700 grams and produced smoke over a radius of 5 metres.

The military attaché for Vienna, Budapest and Berne reported in July 1928 that the Hungarians were undertaking defensive and offensive gas measures, although precise details had not been successfully obtained. Experiments were known to be conducted in Hajmáskér, a village some 100 kilometres south-west of Budapest. To understand the extent of Hungary's capability in chemical warfare and its potential threat, Kendrick and his network sought to establish the amount of funding being allocated to it by the Hungarian government. By late autumn 1929, Italy was sending instructors to Hungary to train local officers and soldiers in defence against poison gas attacks. One of Kendrick's reports stated that Italy was already manufacturing poison gas, 'the secret of which will be communicated to Hungary'.[56]

There is now some clear insight into Kendrick's espionage and counter-espionage work from Vienna in this period, showing that he secured detailed and relevant intelligence on a range of subjects for SIS. However, it is not known either whether Soviet intelligence knew about Kendrick or to what extent it might have penetrated the SIS networks in Europe. It does appear that Kendrick managed to operate successfully in the shadows with tight security, so that he only ever briefed those in his inner circle. The likelihood is, therefore, that he was not compromised.

Socialite Vienna

As the 1920s drew to a close, Kendrick and his wife continued to lead very active social lives, with regular attendance at the theatre, concerts and the State Opera House. Their apartment continued to be a hub of cultural luncheons and dinners. A natural charmer, Kendrick's charisma was infectious and magnetic, but there was another factor. Though he was not a practising Roman Catholic, his background enabled him to move in the highest circles of Austria and be accepted there, because this was a conservative, Roman Catholic society. A Protestant would have found it harder to penetrate these high-level contacts, and Kendrick was seen as the perfect 'insider' for SIS's work there. He was described by one source as an 'organiser and life and soul of gatherings of the "colony" [British and American expatriates in Vienna]'. For many years, he was president of Vienna's famous Beef Steak Club and was reputed 'to have known more of the once famous night life of Vienna than is the good fortune of most foreigners'.[57] With complete discretion, he moved at ease in Viennese aristocratic and diplomatic circles, as well as among the Americans who were living in the capital. His wife, Norah, was accepted as a member of the American Women's Club there, even though she was not American. It was a club that frequently held cultural events and musical and intellectual lunches.

A rare insight into Kendrick's social circle comes from the guest list for his daughter Gladys's wedding to Geoffrey Walsh, at a civic ceremony at the British consulate in Vienna on 29 March 1931. She had met Walsh at a cocktail party; he was chief accountant of the firm Deloitte, Plender & Binder & Co. in Vienna. A religious ceremony followed in the Roman Catholic Maria Geburt Kirche in the Hietzing district. Gladys looked every part the bride of a society wedding, attired in a draped gown of panne velvet and wearing a veil of old Brussels lace. The four bridesmaids were Baroness Ilse von Lichtenberg, Norah Walsh (sister of the groom), Phyllis Pearson (a cousin) and Vera Atkins, whose family had worked for Kendrick since his South Africa days.[58] During the service, English opera singer Marjorie Wright performed. A close friend of the Kendricks, she moved in the same circles of the expatriate community in Vienna, having arrived after the First World War to train as an opera singer.

Among the 150 wedding guests that day were diplomats, military attachés and European nobility.[59] Staff from the British passport control office and American friends also attended, as did some of Kendrick's agents: Mr Doughty (a dealer for Standard Cars) and journalist Eric Gedye. The guest list reflects the background against which Kendrick had been operating in the region – aristocrats who were quite poor, having lost land after the First World War, alongside a growing Jewish bourgeoisie who had been successful in business and had often married into Catholic families. These Austrian Jews assimilated and hid their Jewishness.[60]

The guests attended an extravagant reception afterwards in Kendrick's apartment, where a lavish dinner party had been held the evening before. The days leading up to the wedding had been busy, as Kendrick and Pearson showed one of the bridesmaids around the city. As Phyllis Pearson recalled:

> Vienna was as exciting and romantic city as I had imagined. Rex [Pearson] and Tommy [Kendrick] gave us a wonderful time, showing us the sights and feeding us on delicious pastries and coffee piled with whipped cream. They were both great practical jokers, and on one occasion, having hailed the same taxi from opposite sides of the street, they then set up a furious argument about whose it was, till the poor driver became really worried. They suddenly bundled us all in together through both doors and happily gave the same address. The driver's face was a picture when he understood at last that we were all the same party.[61]

The anecdote offers a rare glimpse into Kendrick's mischievous character and the pranks he liked to play. Family and social life was not taken too seriously by him, and this contrasted starkly with his double existence with SIS.

After a honeymoon in Italy, the couple moved into an apartment in the Hietzing district, not far from Kendrick's apartment, and within three years had two children.[62]

Murder of communist spy

Within a few months of the wedding, in July 1931, a German communist spy was fatally shot in his apartment in Vienna.[63] Georg Semmelmann was about to sell secrets of the Soviet espionage system to the Yugoslav authorities.[64] He was murdered by a Yugoslav subject, 27-year-old Andreas Piklovitch, operating under the pseudonym Egon Spielmann and travelling on a Swiss passport. It appears that Piklovitch was working for Soviet intelligence. He was detained while trying to smuggle communist propaganda literature over the border to the Yugoslav army, at which time his real identity was established by the police and he was linked to the murder. Piklovitch did not deny his actions and during interview explained that he had visited Semmelmann and shot him after a brief and stormy exchange. Another unnamed source had overheard Semmelmann complaining to Piklovitch that he had been left to starve for three months by those who had been furnishing him with funds. The case underlines the dangers of espionage and an age-long trait of selling secrets or turning double agent for money. Semmelmann's wife was interviewed, and she confirmed that she knew nothing of his clandestine work, although she knew he had had close relations with the Soviet trade delegation in Vienna and Berlin. She had not suspected him of being a Soviet spy.

Viennese police had searched Semmelmann's flat during the investigation and found extensive communist literature. A watch was placed on the premises for several weeks, and this uncovered it as a clandestine communist headquarters that was receiving propaganda literature for espionage outside Austria. Christian Broda was discovered to be the agent dispatching the literature. He was a communist, whose father, Dr Ernst Broda, and elder brother, Engelbert, were already being monitored by Kendrick in Vienna and by MI5.[65]

The Semmelmann affair led to the Viennese police searching a number of properties and cracking down on communists in the city. That August, they raided the apartment of a Croat, Friedrich Hlavac, at 89 Kreuzgasse, where he lived with his Russian mistress, Kohut. They were arrested, along with three other communists on the premises. Documents were seized, including old army orders dealing with Austrian troop movements and communist propaganda leaflets and brochures. MI5 asked SIS if reports of the raids were accurate. SIS asked Kendrick, its representative in Vienna, for a report on the episode. SIS replied to MI5: 'We asked [name redacted] to let us have a report of this affair. He states that the Times report is, in the main, correct.'[66]

Because British intelligence deemed Hlavac to be of below-average intelligence, he was believed to be merely a pawn in a wider Soviet espionage network. SIS believed that the key figure was his mistress, Kohut. The SIS report highlighted the fact that further investigations by the police had led to another address: Schloss Fünfturm in Styria, southern Austria. The castle belonged to Dr Ernst Broda, who denied any involvement in communism. None of the family was arrested, but investigations continued into the eldest son, a scientist named Engelbert. He was found to be a registered member of the Austrian Communist Party.

Hitler's rise to power

The political landscape of Europe was changing. Rather than the Soviet Union, it was Germany that was emerging as a growing threat to peace. Since the Treaty of Versailles, Germany had struggled with the huge financial reparations and military restrictions imposed by the Allies. The country's loss of pride and its desperate economic position laid the foundations in Germany for a radical political change and for the rise of Nazism. Adolf Hitler, as the founder of Nazism, promised to restore Germany's fortunes and pride. A 'stab in the back' myth had been created, according to which the undefeated German army had, in fact, been undermined by dark forces – Jews and communists. Hitler's rallying speeches and powerful rhetoric inspired the nation, which saw in him a leader who could rebuild Germany. On 30 January 1933, German President Paul von Hindenburg signed a declaration appointing Hitler chancellor of Germany.[67] It gave Hitler the authorization and power he needed to turn Germany into a self-styled Nazi dictatorship.

The Nazi regime sought a scapegoat for Germany's misfortunes during the first half of the twentieth century and found it in the Jews. Anti-Semitism and the hatred of Jews that had been so deeply embedded in western culture for 2,000 years provided the perfect framework: Hitler's new regime targeted the Jews as enemies of the state and the originators of Germany's ills.[68] This was in spite of the fact that thousands of Jews had fought with pride and loyalty for

Germany in the First World War. Jewish intellectuals were the first to be targeted: they were legally forbidden to hold public office in Germany. This was a racial policy that, by 1936, would lead to the Nuremberg Laws and the denial of all civil rights for Jews and 'non-Aryans' – all of whom were seen as opponents of the regime. Germany witnessed a 'brain drain' and cultural disintegration, as Jews, political opponents and those the Nazis called 'degenerate artists' sought ways to emigrate. Austria witnessed a wave of Jewish refugees crossing the border and heading for the cultural capital, Vienna.

Reports coming out of Germany were disturbing. On 10 May 1933, Joseph Goebbels, the Nazi minister of propaganda, ordered the burning of 'undesirable books' written by leading Jewish intellectuals. On Bebelplatz, the square in front of Berlin's Humboldt University, German academics and students publicly incinerated approximately 20,000 books, including the works of Karl Marx and Sigmund Freud, whose books had already been banned. When news of these developments reached Kendrick, he knew that Austria would not be immune from developments in neighbouring Germany. Now his task for SIS was to monitor not only communist organizations and Soviet spies, but also the fast-changing situation in Germany and the growing support for right-wing ideology in Austria. Across Europe, the political and ideological demarcation lines became extremely polarized.

3

TANGLED WEB

The British Secret Intelligence Service had focused its attention almost exclusively in the 1920s on the communist and Soviet threat, but it failed to grasp early enough the dangers of the rise of Nazi ideology and its threat to democracy.[1] The 1920s witnessed the rise in Austria of new political factions, both left wing and right wing. The social democrats pursued a fairly left-wing course, known as Austromarxism, and from 1921 dominated the city administration in 'Red Vienna'. The city became a stronghold of paramilitary forces – the right-wing Heimwehr (Home Resistance) and the left-wing Republikanischer Schutzbund (Republican Defence League), both of which came into being in this period. Unemployment began to rise in Austria and, as economic pressures worsened, so political tensions rose. Austrian Chancellor Ignaz Seipel sought to prevent communist and Nazi ideologies from taking root in the population by bolstering Austria financially. He encouraged financial investment from nationalists and foreign investors from other European countries, in order to provide a buffer against the threat of both the 'Reds' (communists) and the Nazis. In persuading financiers to invest in the country again, he could not foresee the disastrous move for Austria in the re-creation of a privilege system. Ironically, in crushing communism, Seipel rendered powerless any political opposition in the country and undermined democracy itself. While the serious effects of this may not have been immediately obvious in 1934, in the long term it meant that Austria was powerless against the formidable threat of Hitler and the Nazis and could muster no opposition to it.

After Hitler came to power in Germany in 1933, Austria swiftly became a physical battleground between the opposing ideologies of the social democrats (communists) and the fascists. Ugly and violent skirmishes broke out on the streets of Vienna and threatened to develop into civil war. Journalist Eric Gedye continued to monitor the situation, moving in and out of Austria to provide regular reports on Czechoslovakia, Hungary and Bulgaria. His monitoring of the situation was invaluable to Kendrick and SIS. His articles exposed the political tensions that were developing in Europe, as he witnessed them, and he was frank in his assessment of the situation.[2]

With a serious situation developing in Germany, Kendrick expanded his network of spies and agents to include Samuel Denys Felkin.[3] Working under-cover for Kendrick, Felkin took up a job as manager of the Ideale Radiator Gesellschaft in the capital, a position that was believed to be a cover for his intelligence work, as he had no relevant technical knowledge.[4] He had served in the Artists Rifles from 1914 to 1915 and as a pilot in the Royal Flying Corps towards the end of the war. He acquired fluency in German during a posting to Berlin in 1918 with the Reparations Commission, working alongside the British diplomat and economist Sir Andrew McFadyean. Felkin arrived in Vienna in 1933 with his American socialite wife, Charlotte (Warner Burchard), whom he had married in Paris two years earlier. She was the cousin of Princess Heinrich XXXIII of Reuss and already had an influential social network. The Felkins fitted easily into Viennese intellectual and cultural society and joined Kendrick's intimate social circle. It marked the beginning of a life-long friendship that would see Felkin and Kendrick working together in intelligence during the Second World War. During the 1930s, Felkin travelled around Europe for his work, enabling him to monitor for Kendrick the Nazi regime in neighbouring Germany and other countries of the region. Like Kendrick, Felkin hosted cocktail parties at which usually around two thirds of the guests were European nobility. This social life firmly cemented relationships for Kendrick's intelligence network.[5]

The coffee houses of Vienna – Café Louvre, the Herrenhof and Café Atlantis – also became important places of intelligence gathering for Kendrick's agents, Gedye, Ellis and Pearson. These cafés were favourite meeting places for British and American journalists, workers, socialists, artists, actors, musicians and politicians. And the turbulent, shifting politics and society trends of the day were discussed there and analysed over copious amounts of coffee. American journalist Dorothy Thompson, who returned to Vienna in 1933, having lived in the capital in the 1920s, wrote: 'Coffee in Vienna is more than a national drink. It is a national cult . . . These palaces [coffee houses] are the centre of Vienna's social, intellectual and spiritual life, and coffee-making remains one of Vienna's most preferred cultures.'[6]

Among the journalistic circle that met at Café Louvre was Frederick Voigt, correspondent for the *Manchester Guardian*, who used his journalism from the mid-1930s as cover for his espionage activities on behalf of Claude Dansey.[7] Voigt worked out of Vienna into Germany and neighbouring countries until the Vienna SIS station was blown by Kendrick's arrest in August 1938.

Philby: Spy of spies

Twenty-one-year-old Harold Adrian Russell (Kim) Philby arrived in Vienna in 1933. He had completed his studies at Westminster School and Trinity College, Cambridge, and wished to pursue a career in the Foreign Office, for which he needed a foreign language. A visit to Berlin earlier that year had left him appalled by the brutality of the brown-shirted stormtroopers (from the SA) towards the Jews, and he was dead set against returning there to improve his German. He decided on Vienna instead. It is not clear whether Kendrick ever met Philby during this period, or whether Philby attended one of Kendrick's soirées, but Philby becomes important to Kendrick's story.

While at Trinity College, Philby had been influenced by Maurice Dobb, a lecturer and member of the British Communist Party. Dobb suggested to Philby that he make contact with the International Organization for Aid to Revolutionaries (IOAR) in Vienna, and gave him the number of the organization's Paris office. Philby telephoned the Paris branch and was given the details of Alice ('Litzi') Friedmann, leader of the IOAR in Vienna's ninth district. At this time, the IOAR in Vienna was actively helping communist refugees who had fled Nazi Germany and were living in Austria. Litzi was two years Philby's senior, a divorcee living with her parents, and an ardent communist who had spent two weeks in prison for her beliefs. Philby lodged with the family and swiftly embarked on a relationship with Litzi. They moved into a small, sparsely furnished flat in the same district and geographically at the heart of the political tensions between the communists and fascists. On 4 March 1933, Chancellor Dollfuss suspended the Austrian parliament, to outmanoeuvre both the Reds and the Nazis, and invested parliamentary power in himself. This was a serious erosion of democracy that saw Dollfuss confiscate 22 million Austrian Schillings the following month from the socialist municipal government in Vienna. The courts took no action.

That autumn of 1933, Dollfuss survived an assassination attempt. As he recovered from his injuries, he put in place a number of measures which gradually eroded Austria's democratic liberties. The regime hunted down communists as enemies of the state, and many of them went into hiding in the underground sewers of Vienna. Influenced by Litzi, Philby took up the communists' cause against the oppressive Dollfuss regime and joined them in the sewers of the Floridsdorf district. His British nationality was a major asset, because he could cross the border without suspicion and could carry messages for the IOAR to its networks in Czechoslovakia. He travelled to several European capitals, smuggling out money, documents and letters, and undertook six illegal missions into Czechoslovakia and two into Hungary, each time carrying special packages.[8] At personal risk, he aided communists in escaping Vienna and petitioned his friends to donate clothes for them. As one historian has written: 'Philby showed courage in his open identification with the resisters. Although his British passport would probably have saved him if he was captured, it offered no protection against stray bullets.'[9]

Philby frequently visited the Café Louvre and it was there that he came across a young Austrian socialist by the name of Edward Spiro.[10] They became friends and mixed with foreign journalists, who regularly gathered for updates on the political situation and to pass discreet messages to each other. Spiro worked for the *Daily Herald* and *Daily Mirror* until the papers' offices were closed down by Dollfuss's regime, then found employment with the small publishing house of Oesterreichische Monographie as an editorial adviser. Its office in Hörlgasse, in the ninth district of Vienna, became a focal point for Philby's activities and 'one of several clandestine centres of the illegal socialist movement'.[11] Spiro went on to have a career in military intelligence in the Second World War, after fleeing Nazi-occupied Austria, and penned a biography of Philby under the pseudonym E.H. Cookridge.

It was at the Café Louvre that Philby first met Kendrick's agent Eric Gedye, who was an occasional visitor there.[12] Philby and Gedye had much in common, as Gedye's son has commented:

My father and Philby were both highly educated. Neither was the kind of Englishman to sit on the fence. The political choice for them was simple: communism or fascism. They aligned themselves with the communists, but this in itself would not have immediately placed them on a suspect list.

Philby arrived at Gedye's flat one day and asked for spare clothes for the communists hiding in the city. Gedye – who at the time sympathized with Philby's communist stance – told him that he could search through his wardrobe and take a couple of suits. Gedye's attitude would later change, when he witnessed the brutal Stalinist regime and the purges in Moscow.[13]

February 1934 uprising

In February 1934, civil war erupted on the streets of Vienna and there were violent clashes between socialists and communists and fascists and right-wing groups. The unrest actually began in the town of Linz, but it spread to Vienna and other regions of Austria. Although lasting only a few days, it had serious consequences. On 11 February 1934, there were visible signs of a military crackdown, as the government constructed machine-gun positions in the capital. Soldiers in lorries entered the city and occupied the streets outside the Vienna State Opera. Communists and social democrats were outlawed, pursued and arrested. Members of the Schutzbund barricaded themselves in the city's housing estates and workers' flats – already strongholds of socialist supporters. The army used artillery and gunfire on workers' flats, killing some civilians and endangering the lives of thousands more.

Police searched the homes of social democrats for weapons and this resulted in further violence. Social democrats attacked Dollfuss's provincial party head-quarters in response, and Koloman Wallisch, the national secretary of the Austrian Socialist Party, called for a general strike. Dollfuss retaliated by imposing a curfew and martial law, and declaring the Social Democratic Party illegal. Nine members of the Schutzbund were subsequently executed. Wallisch himself was arrested on 18 February and executed on the orders of Dollfuss. As Prudence Hopkinson recalled: 'Kendrick and his secretaries, that included my mother, discussed the expectation that Hitler would take advantage of the volatility and invade at any moment. These were very uncertain times.'[14]

Arriving in Vienna from Britain at this time of violent unrest was another Oxbridge graduate: 27-year-old Hugh Gaitskell, a future chancellor of the exchequer in a Labour government. Gaitskell was educated at Winchester College and New College, Oxford. He went to Vienna on a Rockefeller schol-arship to study economic theory at the university there.[15] Whether he had any connections to SIS in this period is not known, but he would go on to work for British intelligence during the Second World War. Kendrick invited British students at the University of Vienna to small dinner parties at his apartment and Gaitskell is believed to have met Kendrick in this way.[16] From Vienna, Gaitskell petitioned a number of socialist and Labour figures in Britain to send aid to the communists. W.T. Rodgers, who was a contemporary witness to Gaitskell's work and who later wrote a biography of him, had this to say of the period: 'We raised all the funds we could, tried to wake up the slow-moving Socialist International . . . the fight against Fascism failed as it had already in Germany.'[17]

On 11 February, Gaitskell was attending a party of Vienna socialists and witnessed the start of the military crackdown at first hand. He placed himself at the forefront of helping the communists and risked arrest. In spite of the dangers, he organized clandestine meetings to coordinate humanitarian efforts;

he could also be seen on street corners where, as in any spy novel, he would wait for a courier to walk past him twice before slipping him a letter. He was frequently followed by the Austrian secret police but was never detained.

Gaitskell telephoned Naomi Mitchison, journalist and wife of his friend Dick Mitchison (a Labour activist), and induced her to come to Vienna to file a report for the British newspapers on the plight of the socialists. Mitchison arrived in Vienna on 25 February, bringing money for the socialist cause that would be used for the legal defence of those arrested and would pay for couriers to smuggle messages to networks in Czechoslovakia.[18] Mitchison wrote a number of newspaper articles and kept a diary every day. Witnessing the Dollfuss clampdown on the socialists, she wrote: 'They are trying to break and destroy Austrian Socialism. They will not be able to do it. The Red flag will fly again in the pine-woods under the snowy mountains.'[19] The diary was published later that year, with the names of people and places changed to protect them; thus, 'Sam' is Gaitskell.[20] This device unwittingly gives the entries a mystery, almost as if she were operating in the world of espionage.

In fact, Mitchison did come close to the spy world, even if she was not part of it – she visited the British embassy, anticipating support and a sympathetic hearing for those who had been arrested during the uprising. Instead, she found the mission 'curiously part of another world' as she entered a room with a large coloured map on the wall. She soon learned that the staff could not intervene on behalf of the prisoners. As she wrote in her diary:

> I was met with a political and economic lecture . . . of course it was all very sound, but oh dear, we were talking different languages. And somehow I seemed to have forgotten the kind of public school and university language which Legations talk. It was all from the head, and I had been living from the heart.[21]

Instead of a sympathetic understanding, she found Kendrick and staff offering an intellectual response to the situation, unable to get involved in local politics. This was not surprising, as throughout his life Kendrick never gave any hint of his own political views. The diary makes clear Mitchison's idealistic and emotional reaction to the fate of the communists and socialists, with her high expectations that they would ultimately succeed, in spite of the Dollfuss repression.

In the coming days, Mitchison retreated to Vienna's cafés for ice cream and coffee with English and Viennese friends and Anglo-American correspondents. Sometimes she sat and read *Vie Parisienne*, a popular women's magazine. She frequently met Gaitskell, who passed her information about communists and socialists being beaten up and imprisoned. He helped three socialist leaders to escape Vienna for Prague, and established escape routes with the aid of professional smugglers and a young socialist called Josef Simon.[22]

Gaitskell is credited with saving 170 Austrian socialists, many of whom used false papers secured with the money brought over by Mitchison.[23] It was dangerous for Gaitskell and Mitchison to gather evidence against the Dollfuss regime to publish in British newspapers. Mitchison discreetly met political dissidents in cafés on the Kärtner-Ring, in one of the most expensive areas of the city, with its luxury hotels and shops.[24] She returned to the British embassy on 9 March and met an unnamed official, who – from her description – sounds like Kendrick: 'a check tie, wavy hair, and a nice clean, scarcely lined public-school face'.[25] He listened to her tales of the brutal suffering of the socialists and said that he would look into the matter. But with the British policy of non-interference, there was nothing he could do. He asked for Mitchison's views on the political situation. She explained how Dollfuss was fiercely hated and sketched examples of the brutality that she had witnessed. The official's response was interesting. He said it would be nice if journalists could bring him their facts as soon as they had them. This was the spymaster talking. Kendrick may have then started to use an unwitting Mitchison as a source of intelligence.

One lunchtime, she arrived back at her hotel to find an urgent and anonymous note. She took up the story in her diary: 'After lunch, the unknown man turned up, a nice young Cambridge Communist, all het up about some of the Reichstag prisoners, and wanting to know if I or anyone I knew could fly at once to Berlin to see about it.'[26]

That nice young man was Kim Philby.[27] The reference to the Reichstag (the German parliament) was to a fire there the previous year. Those who had allegedly been involved in the arson attack had been put on trial in a process that lasted for several months. Eventually, van der Lubbe, supposedly one of the ringleaders, was sentenced to death for arson and attempting to overthrow the Third Reich. He was beheaded in a German prison yard in January 1934. Although it is now accepted by historians that he was acting alone, the Nazi regime pinned the blame on the communists.[28]

Philby linked up with another Englishwoman, known simply as 'Mary'. This was Muriel Gardiner, the ex-wife of a rich American. She had arrived in Vienna in 1927 as a medical student. She owned many properties in Vienna, including a villa in the Vienna Woods, and she offered her apartments as safe-houses for meetings. The shed in the garden of her villa was stacked with pamphlets and clandestine propaganda literature, which placed her life in potential danger. She was described as 'a brave and kind woman' who paid the expenses of some messengers, when the socialists and communists found they did not have sufficient funds to reimburse them.[29] Philby claimed that he had recruited her to the cause; but in fact that came about through another Austrian socialist, Ilse Kulczar.

Socialists, communists or spies?

Austria's social democrats and communists – many of them Jewish – became refugees from a regime that had brutally turned on its own people and treated them as enemies of the state. They remained active to their cause in the countries of Europe to which they subsequently escaped and therefore continued to be tracked by SIS and MI5. Within this mix were a number of communist spies who worked on behalf of Moscow and who would use some of the refugee socialists to infiltrate subversive propaganda material into the various armies of European countries. The aim was always the same – to foment unrest in those armies, undermine democracy and bring about regime change.

Among those who had gone into hiding after the Austrian civil war was an idealistic young Austrian journalist, Richard Hugo Schueller. Kendrick had been tracking him for SIS since the late 1920s.[30] Schueller was a suspected Soviet spy (later confirmed) and an active communist. He had been leader of the 'Communist Proletarian Youth Movement' and studied a course in political agitation at the Lenin Academy in Moscow in 1919. Afterwards he was sent to Vienna with the task of reorganizing and tightening the Austrian Communist Party. From 1925 to 1926, Schueller was attached to the Soviet mission in Berlin, placed there as a spy by the Soviets; there he soon became a member of the Comintern.[31] He subsequently travelled to Paris, Brussels, London, Palestine, Moscow and China. Schueller spoke several languages, including perfect English, and was known to have attended at least three secret meetings in England and Scotland, all monitored by Special Branch.[32] His letters to communist friends in Britain were written in the international language Esperanto and were intercepted by MI5.

Schueller was expelled from France in 1928 for spying on behalf of Moscow and on charges of trying to connect various communist cells and influence the French army. He returned to Vienna, where he lived with his wife at her mother's address.[33] From there, he continued to distribute subversive literature to various military units, this time with the aid of Polish communists.[34] A new (unnamed) source in Vienna provided Kendrick with information that Schueller was using premises in the small Polish town of Miloslav (Miłosław) to distribute propaganda, in an operation headed by a man called Peretz. Another man by the name of Masovietski acted as the point of liaison between Peretz and Schueller. The level of detailed information and penetration by Kendrick can now be appreciated.[35] Little had changed in Schueller's methods from when Kendrick and his colleagues were monitoring this type of subversive activity from Cologne at the end of the First World War.

During 1931, Schueller was under surveillance when he delivered a speech at a communist convention in Vienna, along with two colleagues who were also being shadowed by SIS.[36] He also addressed the central committee of International Workers' Aid (Austrian branch) that year. He was now chief editor of the anti-fascist communist newspaper *Die Rote Fahne* (*Red Flag*). Special Branch intercepted his mail on behalf of MI5 and discovered that he frequently wrote from Vienna on headed notepaper to communist figures in Britain. Schueller was caught up in the unrest in Vienna in 1933 and was arrested because of his position at *Die Rote Fahne* at the same time as 61 other communists were seized.[37] Police raided his home, but found only papers and literature about Austria, with no evidence to link him directly to Moscow or communist networks outside Austria.[38]

By April 1934, the Viennese authorities had issued another warrant for Schueller's arrest; but he had already fled in secret to Prague. He is believed to have been helped out of Vienna by either Kim Philby or Hugh Gaitskell. Schueller then came under suspicion of spying in Czechoslovakia and was arrested by the Prague police on 8 November 1934.[39] After serving a prison sentence, he was freed the following year.[40] MI5 and MI6 continued to monitor Schueller and his wife into the 1940s and 1950s.[41]

Intelligence on the movement of other political activists and agents was secured by secretly tapping their messages between Vienna and Moscow. This happened in the case of the young Viennese communist spy Johann Taeubl (aka 'Robert'), also an editor on *Die Rote Fahne*.[42] The interception of messages to and from him during 1934 provided Kendrick with details of his movements, along with information that 46 party members and 24 regional deputies had attended the Vienna conference. Information was also picked up this way about another leading communist, Basia Stern-Grünberg, who operated under the names Margarethe Fraenkl and Dr Maria Leitner (aka 'Steffi'). She acted as the central financial point for the Austrian Communist Party and was a known associate of Taeubl's.

Other information collected on Taeubl for SIS and MI5 included details that he had attended political and military courses in Moscow and Germany, carried out numerous unspecified missions and illegal work for Moscow, and stayed in Moscow in August and September 1928.[43] He also became the liaison officer between the Balkan Centre of the Comintern and the Soviet mission in Vienna. Taeubl became secretary of the Austrian branch of a new paramilitary organization called the Roter Frontkämpferbund (Alliance of Red-Front Fighters), which was affiliated to the Communist Party in Germany. By the 1920s, Austria had become a political centre for new revolutionary movements, and Taeubl led an Austrian delegation to Berlin in May 1928. In 1929, he came to the attention of the Vienna police while distributing communist pamphlets and newspapers. Kendrick is known to have had an informer inside the Vienna police: it is highly probable that he was Kendrick's source of this information. Taeubl turned out to be a serious political figure for SIS to monitor, because during 1931 he became a functionary of the Vienna Arbeiterwehr (a workers' party) and then representative of the Soviet Red Army in Austria. That same year, he was appointed assistant secretary of the Communist Party in Vienna.[44] At a meeting in Vienna on 28 August 1932, Taeubl advocated the formation of an anti-fascist united front. Intercepts picked up by Kendrick's network two years later gave advance warning that Taeubl had been selected again for illegal work for Moscow, to start in March 1935.[45] Taeubl was finally arrested by Vienna police and imprisoned for six months.[46] Also arrested at the same time was Theodor Malcher, president of the provincial committee of the Schutzbund, the paramilitary organization that had been banned by Dollfuss.

While in prison Taeubl fell ill and was transferred to hospital, from where he escaped. Kendrick was still tracking him and believed him to be in Prague, engaged by the counter-espionage section of the Communist Party.[47] Kendrick informed SIS that Taeubl had crossed the frontier into Czechoslovakia on a passport in the name of Stefan Neubauer. For several months, SIS had been unable to read traffic between Moscow and Prague, but it had now regained its capacity to do so. Kendrick established that leading members of the Austrian Communist Party had subsequently moved to the USSR.[48]

Kendrick was also monitoring two sisters, Suzanne and Eva Kolmer, who were believed to be communists.[49] Suzanne was arrested on 23 March 1935 at a communist meeting in a private house at 20 Berggasse, the same street as Sigmund Freud's residence.[50] She was sentenced to 14 days imprisonment. On her release, she travelled to Switzerland and Paris, and by November was intent on entering Britain, although she was no longer involved in communist activities.[51] Her elder sister, Eva, had taken part in a communist conference in December 1930 and was active in the communist movement in Vienna. Eva Kolmer was imprisoned for six weeks in August 1934 for illegal communist activities.[52] She sought to enter Britain in 1936 for temporary work at a London hospital specializing in cancer research.[53] MI5 was alerted to her intentions and, although she could not be prevented from entering the country, Special Branch was asked to watch her.[54] She was kept under constant surveillance while in the UK.[55] Although she returned to Vienna, she was forced to flee as a Jewish refugee on 19 March 1938 and found sanctuary in Britain; her entry was guaranteed by her friends Professor Robert Seton-Watson and Lady Layton.[56] Kolmer worked as a journalist for the *Spectator*, discreetly observed by MI5 to ensure that she did not use her role for communist propaganda.

Another glimpse into Kendrick's work in the 1930s can be found in the MI5 file on Samuel Hochstedt, which contains reports from SIS, MI5 and later the FBI.[57] Hochstedt was in Vienna from 1922 until 1934 and was an active member of the Austrian Communist Party. He became a Soviet agent and was employed in Vienna by a Russian organization called Ratao. His operational areas were Bulgaria, Yugoslavia and Hungary – the same countries covered by the SIS station in Vienna. His file contains an SIS report 'from our representative in Austria' (i.e. Kendrick), and provides details of Hochstedt's two visits to Russia and information about his passport.[58] The source and means by which Kendrick obtained this intelligence is not disclosed in the file.

Kendrick's reports for SIS on the movement of Wilhelm Scholz, a communist and Jew, have survived.[59] Scholz was secretary of the Communist Party in Graz and leader of a communist organization in the southern Austrian province of Styria. He was responsible for getting propaganda into neighbouring Yugoslavia, and travelled regularly from Graz to Vienna.[60] He was said to be well trusted by Moscow.[61] After the February 1934 uprising, he fled from Graz and went into hiding in Vienna under the name of Wilhelm Perner. He was found by police in early 1935 and arrested.[62] For his illegal communist activities, he was sent to a detention camp by the Dollfuss regime and then disappeared from Austria. Kendrick's network tracked Scholz's movements to Moscow, where he attended the Comintern school for 18 months. He spent a short time in Czechoslovakia before returning to Vienna with his wife.[63] He applied for a visa to the UK in October 1938 and this was granted, in spite of objections from MI5. He and his wife came to the UK on 7 December 1938 under the auspices of the News Chronicle Refugee Committee. His communist activities did not cease, and in 1940 he attended a meeting organized by Eva Kolmer.[64]

Another Jewish socialist was Frau Geiringer, part owner of a café in Vienna. Although deemed not to be a communist by British intelligence, a number of illegal socialists and communists patronized her (unnamed) café in the 1930s, including Willy Scholz.[65] She became the object of surveillance, as did her café. After the German invasion of Austria in March 1938, Geiringer had to leave on racial grounds and came to Britain on a domestic permit, almost certainly aided by Kendrick. While these refugees may not have been a security threat to Britain as anti-Nazis, they continued to be monitored in case they became active communists or spies for Moscow. Even though Nazism was arguably the greater menace in the 1930s, communism was still very active; as a threat to western democracy, it was therefore within SIS sights.

Edith Suschitzky

Edith Suschitzky (later Edith Tudor-Hart) was a prominent Austrian socialist. Her story is pivotal to understanding Kendrick's penetration of communist networks at this time, and she also crossed paths with Philby in Vienna in 1933–34. Suschitzky was born in Vienna into an affluent, assimilated Jewish family.[66] Her father, William (Wilhelm) Suschitzky, and his brother ran a bookshop in the tenth district of Vienna, selling books that advocated equal rights for women and the right to abortion – subjects that were then controversial in that society. This brought accusations that they were exerting a pernicious influence on the youth of the district.[67]

Edith Suschitzky was already involved in communism in the 1920s. A photographer by profession, her social conscience led her in 1930 to shoot a series of black-and-white photographs, which, controversially, depicted extreme poverty in parts of Vienna. She was ahead of her time in making social poverty the subject of the photographer's lens.[68] She first visited England as a governess in 1925. On a later visit, she met a Cambridge graduate, Dr Alexander Ethan Tudor-Hart, himself an active communist. MI5 began to track him from 1929.[69] On 26 October 1930, Suschitzky and Tudor-Hart took part in a communist demonstration in London's Trafalgar Square, where Suschitzky was observed talking to prominent communists.[70] This brought her to the immediate attention of both MI5 and Guy Liddell of Special Branch (later head of counter-espionage at MI5). She was placed under surveillance in Britain, and her movements were tracked between Britain and Austria. MI5 alerted Valentine Vivian (head of counter-intelligence at SIS) and asked whether SIS could make enquiries about Suschitzky abroad.[71] Vivian contacted Kendrick and was able to reply to Liddell without revealing Kendrick's identity:

> Our representative in Vienna states that . . . the local authorities reported that Edith Suschitzky has not come under the notice of the Police in any way. Like her parents, this woman is stated to be a Social Democrat, but she has shown no political activity in Vienna. There is nothing on record to show that she has Communist tendencies.[72]

Suschitzky may not yet have come to Kendrick's attention, but during the 1930s she became increasingly involved in communism, and in January 1931 was formally expelled from Britain for communist activities. She returned to Vienna and corresponded regularly with Tudor-Hart. His mail was intercepted by MI5 and his telephone line tapped from then until the 1950s. MI5 eventually concluded that he was not a threat as a communist.[73]

After Vivian's original tracing request, Kendrick placed Suschitzky under surveillance. Two months later, in March 1931, she took up employment as a photographer with the Soviet press agency Tass at 24 Bauernmarkt, in the first district of Vienna. SIS and MI5 believed that this was a cover for her espionage activities for the Soviets. MI5 immediately informed SIS:

It might be of interest to your representative in Vienna [i.e. Kendrick] to know that this woman who is still in Vienna, has now been appointed the official photographic reporter of the 'Press Cliché' [sic] in Moscow for Austria. Her appointment has been obtained through the Director of Tass in Vienna.[74]

Suschitzky was indeed working as a Soviet spy. Klara Modern, a Viennese-born Jew, had a strange encounter with her in 1933. Modern was working as an assistant at a bookshop managed by Paul Sonnenfeld, on the corner of Liechtensteinstrasse and Berggasse, which stocked scholarly books and was patronized by Sigmund Freud. Her son Richard Deveson takes up the story:

In March 1933, a man came into the shop and asked whether it could be used as an unofficial *poste restante* for a political refugee from Germany. Sonnenfeld agreed to help, not realizing the reality. A week or so later, a young woman who called herself Fräulein Braun collected the post on behalf of the supposed refugee. This continued every two or three days for about two months. In May, the Austrian police arrived and informed Sonnenfeld that they believed the shop was being used as a drop-off point by the Austrian Communist Party. This was a serious allegation which carried equally serious consequences. My mother and Sonnenfeld were taken to Federal Police headquarters and questioned at length and a watch kept on the shop. Fräulein Braun returned a short time later but, sensing that something was amiss, ran out of the shop.[75]

There is a postscript to this story. Modern came to Britain in 1936 and returned only twice to Vienna before the Nazi invasion of Austria in March 1938. At the end of the war, she was married to Charles Deveson, one of

Kendrick's intelligence officers, and was living with their new baby in south London. Their son explains:

> The encounter in the bookshop in Vienna was the last my mother saw of 'Fräulein Braun' until twelve years later. In 1945, in the back pages of the *New Statesman* my parents found an advertisement by a photographer called Edith Tudor-Hart [Suschitzky]. She came to the house in Dulwich to photograph the baby and it was the woman from the bookshop in Vienna. She and my mother looked one another in the eye. Nothing was said, but both women knew the truth.[76]

Modern's story about Suschitzky using the shop as a 'dead letter box' is confirmed elsewhere. The letters which Suschitzky had been couriering contained detailed reports on the communist situation and a call for more political action.[77]

Suschitzky continued her contact with Tudor-Hart and in April 1933 he visited her in Vienna. They were now in a relationship, even though Tudor-Hart was involved with another woman and details of that were being picked up by MI5.[78] In August 1933, Suschitzky married Tudor-Hart in Vienna.[79] As in the case of Litzi Friedmann (Philby), Suschitzky could not be denied a British passport or residence in the UK, even though SIS and MI5 had files on her. A British passport was issued to her on 18 August 1933 by Kendrick.[80] While Kendrick may not have been able to deny a passport to the new Mrs Tudor-Hart, MI5 continued its surveillance of the couple. Details survive in Alexander Tudor-Hart's MI5 file showing that, within two years of their marriage, the relationship was over and they had separated.[81]

It is immediately evident that there are parallels between the cases of Edith Suschitzky and Litzi Friedmann. Suschitzky was politically active in Vienna during the 1920s and 1930s, and the women knew each other as friends, not mere acquaintances. They worked for Soviet intelligence as scouts and recruiters, and both women married Cambridge graduates in Vienna during the period of unrest of 1933 and 1934. Both separated from their English husbands within a couple of years of marriage. It was through the friendship of these two women, who had known each other since the Vienna of their youth, that Philby was to be recruited as a Russian penetration spy.

Philby returns to Britain

On 24 February 1934, two weeks after civil war erupted in Vienna, Philby married Litzi Friedmann in Vienna Town Hall. He informed his parents that the marriage was only temporary and that he had married her to protect her. Vienna was too dangerous for her as a leading member of the IOAR and in April Philby smuggled himself and Litzi out of Vienna, through the sewers, from Karl-Marx-Hof on the Donaukanal. The novelist Graham Greene, a friend of his, used this historic escape by Philby as a basis for the plot of his novel *The Third Man*. The main character, Harry Lime, is known to have been based on Philby. The film version was produced by the Hungarian Alexander Korda, another SIS intelligence officer recruited by Claude Dansey.

Once in Britain, Litzi introduced Philby to her friend Edith Tudor-Hart. Tudor-Hart saw potential in Philby and arranged for him to meet an anonymous Soviet agent. This was Arnold Deutsch, an illegal NKVD agent operating in Britain on forged papers. Deutsch had been born in Vienna in 1904 and was described in his MI5 file as a research student who had been issued with an Austrian passport on 9 April 1931. He arrived in England on 4 April 1934 and thereafter operated as a recruiter and controller for Soviet intelligence for two years. Deutsch (aka 'Otto', aka Stefan Lang) was confirmed as an active agent for the OGPU (renamed NKVD in 1934), with a brief to acquire intelligence on British naval and RAF matters. His handler was Paul Hardt ('Theo'), whose MI5 files have also been declassified, but offer no relevant insights into this period.[82] Within a few weeks of returning to Britain, Philby was recruited by Deutsch as a Russian penetration agent, following a meeting on a park bench in Regent's Park.[83] A copy of Philby's own account of their first meeting survives in Deutsch's MI5 file, in which Philby describes Deutsch as 'a man of considerable cultural background'. Philby knew Deutsch as 'Otto' and only later learned his real name when he had sight of Deutsch's MI5 file and recognized his photograph in it.[84]

Deutsch had known Edith Suschitzky (as she then was) in Vienna, which has led one historian to conclude that 'Edith Tudor-Hart was as dangerous as Scotland Yard had suspected.'[85] Deutsch also knew Litzi Friedmann from the period in Vienna, before she married Philby. Did SIS and MI5 fail to notice that Edith Suschitzky (Tudor-Hart) and Litzi Friedmann (Philby) were the link in the Vienna–London–Moscow triangle from the 1930s?

MI5 files show that, as far back as October 1930, Special Branch and MI5 had known Suschitzky/Tudor-Hart to be 'an extremist and an associate of leading members of the Communist Party of Great Britain'.[86] During her questioning by MI5 in 1951, Tudor-Hart finally confessed that she had formerly operated for Soviet intelligence in Austria and Italy in the early 1930s.[87] She also admitted working for a Russian colonel and running a photographic studio in Vienna as a cover for her intelligence work. In her file, the colonel is known as the Hungarian-born Arpad Haaz, although there is currently no separate declassified MI5 file for him.[88] How likely is it that Kendrick also missed Haaz and his network? MI5 concluded of Edith Tudor-Hart that she remained in contact with top-ranking communists and known Russian spies for 25 years.[89]

Hans Peter Smollett, another of Litzi's communist friends in Vienna, was a Jew who had to flee Austria after the Nazis confiscated his father's buckle and metalware business in 1938. Litzi remained in contact with him after that date. Her husband, Kim Philby, allegedly recruited Smollett (aka Peter Smolka) as a Russian agent once he was in Britain.[90] He and Smollett together set up a press agency – London Continental News Ltd – during Smollett's brief stay in London in 1934, although the details once in Foreign Office files have been weeded out.[91] Smollett's MI5 file has now been released and there is nothing in it to suggest that he was a Soviet spy, although he was a friend of Philby's Cambridge friend and defector Guy Burgess.[92] After Philby's defection to Russia in 1963, Smollett was interviewed by MI5 and admitted to a life-long friendship with Philby.[93] Interestingly, during the Second World War Smollett served in a British labour unit in North Africa, before transferring to the Ministry of Information. After the war, he became a correspondent for *The Times*, working in Vienna until 1950.[94] The picture of Smollett in MI5's KV files seems incomplete, and it is possible that not all files have been released.

Philby: The unanswered questions

When Philby brought his wife to England in April 1934, she needed either to be added to his British passport or to obtain one in her own name. In either case, she was required to register at the British passport office in Vienna. Litzi applied for her own British passport, as historian Edward Harrison writes:

> Lizy's [sic] application for a passport was made to the Passport Control Officer in the Vienna Embassy. Passport Control Officer was of course the cover used by the local SIS representative and provided him with an opportunity to check applicants for counter-espionage purposes.[95]

Litzi was issued with a British passport by Kendrick in April 1934. This raises a number of questions regarding Philby and Kendrick that also impinge on questions surrounding Philby's later recruitment to MI6. How could Kendrick – the efficient and shrewd spymaster, with an excellent memory for names – have overlooked an upper-middle-class Englishman from Cambridge who had just married the leader of a major communist organization in Vienna? The day after Philby had arrived in Vienna, Litzi had persuaded him to donate a quarter of his allowance to the cause. Philby was rewarded by being appointed treasurer of the IOAR by Litzi. Effectively, he was whisked to the heart of an important left-wing organization within hours of arriving in the city. Was none of this known to Kendrick? Why was Kendrick not tracking Litzi in the period up to 1934? It is possible that Kendrick had missed her, but this is unlikely given that he was one of SIS's most competent spymasters and adept at penetrating communist networks. His role was to penetrate every known communist organization and network. The IOAR should have been on his list for surveillance. It is interesting that there are currently no declassified MI5 files for Litzi, a leading communist, who ought to have been in the sights of both MI5 and SIS.

Kendrick may not have been able to prevent Litzi from receiving a British passport as the wife of an Englishman, but the point is – given that she was a leading member of the Communist Party in Austria, why was he not already tracking her? Gedye, one of Kendrick's closest agents, had already encountered Philby in Vienna. Of course, one explanation is that Gedye could have been sheltering Philby from discovery by Kendrick. But Philby was not the only young person caught up in the political turmoil of 1930s Vienna. There, too, were Gaitskell (already mentioned); his future wife, Dora Frost; Muriel Gardiner; Elwyn Jones (a Welsh lawyer who later served Prime Minister Harold Wilson); Emma Cadbury (a Quaker); and Stephen Spender.[96] It is possible, though not proven, that some or all of these may have been involved in intelligence work alongside their humanitarian efforts.

According to Spiro (E.H. Cookridge), Philby's friend and an eyewitness to the Vienna days, Philby was operating as a go-between for the communists, but was also in close contact with two figures at the Russian embassy in Vienna, one of whom, Vladimir Alexeievich Antonov-Ovseyenko, was suspected of being a Russian spy.[97] Spiro began to suspect that Philby was working as a Soviet agent and therefore distanced himself from him. But, given that Kendrick was to penetrate Russian intelligence in Vienna, could the spymaster have instructed Philby to get close to members of the Russian embassy there? Was Philby, in fact, one of Kendrick's agents?

From Philby himself there was only silence about how and when he was recruited to work as a Soviet agent. According to a chronological timeline at the back of his autobiography *My Silent War*, he was recruited as a Soviet agent in Vienna in February 1934. But there is no reference to this by Philby himself in the main body of the text.[98] Furthermore, with the exception of a fleeting mention of Vienna in a footnote on page xxvi and the chronological timeline on page 203 – both of which were added by the publisher – there is a total absence of any mention by Philby of his time in Vienna. This is odd, given that it was the time and place in his life which, arguably, defined his future. He does not mention meeting his first wife, Litzi Friedmann, or his recruitment by the Soviets – whether it happened in Vienna or on a park bench in London sometime after April 1934.[99]

It is my belief that the Vienna period raises broader questions about Philby and holds the key to understanding much of what follows in his life. Why was Philby accepted into MI6 just a few years later (in 1940, according to his own memoirs),[100] given that he had a wife who was a high-level threat to Britain as a Soviet agent, described in an MI5 document as 'an extremist'?[101] It is, however, possible – though not yet definitively proven – that Philby went to Vienna in 1933 to penetrate the communist network for SIS and was, in fact, working for Kendrick. Philby's closeness to the IOAR would have placed him in an extremely useful position for SIS, and he may even have been recruited by Kendrick on an ad hoc basis.

Of relevance, too, is the case of Hugh Gaitskell, who worked in the same small quarters as Philby in their humanitarian efforts in Vienna. Both smuggled messages to Czechoslovakia on behalf of the underground communist network. Given that Philby and Gaitskell later worked for British intelligence, their arrival in Vienna in 1933 might not have been coincidental; they could in fact have been penetrating the networks for SIS, under the direction of Kendrick. Gaitskell returned to Britain in 1934, just a few months after Philby, and abandoned his revolutionary socialist rhetoric that had been born out of the fight against fascism. This meant that he was dead set against any appeasement policy towards Germany, and he started to petition for the rearmament of European countries against the very real threat to peace from Hitler.[102]

On the surface, it would initially appear as if Kendrick missed the majority of the prominent, potentially dangerous, communists in Vienna. He would also appear to have overlooked the young British figures there who would later become pivotal characters in the history of British intelligence. But how likely is this? Though limited, the currently declassified files do show that Kendrick was sending back intelligence to London on some of these figures. In a twist of fate, many of the socialists of pre-war Vienna fled to Britain as Jewish refugees when Hitler invaded Austria in March 1938 and their escape was aided by Kendrick. Many lived around Hampstead, Swiss Cottage and Belsize Park in north London and created a continental intellectual social hub in those areas.

Some were tracked by MI5 after entry into Britain, including Austrian scientist Engelbert Broda, who was in constant communication with Tudor-Hart in London. Broda went on to cause security concerns during the Cold War for allegedly handing scientific secrets to the Russians.[103]

Even with the currently limited declassified files, it is possible to see that Kendrick was extraordinarily successful in penetrating communist organizations and the Comintern for SIS, and in identifying and tracking Russian agents operating in and out of Vienna and the region. Because of his slow, methodical clandestine operations, SIS had a clear and comprehensive picture of the movements and activities of the Comintern in much of Eastern Europe, and was thereby able to assess the ongoing threat to western democracy. It is therefore possible to see why Vienna was considered the most important SIS station in Europe in the 1920s and 1930s.

But this period continues to leave unanswered questions about Philby's own recruitment to MI6 and his operations as a Soviet double agent and spy in a betrayal that would haunt MI6 for decades – even up to the present day. It is possible that he, along with Gaitskell, were already working loosely for British intelligence at this time and had been sent out to Vienna to gather intelligence at one of the most politically unstable periods for Austria. This would also explain why they were so easily taken up by British intelligence in 1939–40 – in Philby's case, rising to the highest echelons of MI6.[104] In the end, it was not the communism that they sought to defend during the civil unrest of 1934 that would destroy Austrian democracy. Within just four years, the cultured world of Vienna – the city of classical music, baroque architecture, art, science, medicine and literature that Kendrick so loved – would be crushed under the Nazi jackboot.

4

A DANGEROUS GAME

Tensions continued between the socialists and the fascists, even after the end of the civil war in February 1934. Anger bubbling below the surface in the Austrian population threatened to erupt into further violence. Any periods of calm were short-lived, with more violence breaking out as different factions continued to vie for power and influence. On 25 July 1934, a group of Nazi activists broke into Chancellor Dollfuss's offices on the Ballhausplatz. Dollfuss was shot dead by Otto Planetta, a 35-year-old ex-soldier and Nazi. Dollfuss's Patriotic Front had succeeded for a long time in frustrating the Nazis in Austria, but the consequence of this policy was his assassination. The long-term dangers were understood by Eric Gedye, who reported at this time that Austria would be dominated by the Nazis within a matter of weeks. Although the timeline of his prediction was inaccurate, ultimately he was proved correct as Austria capitulated to Nazi forces just four years later, in March 1938.

Mussolini, although a fascist dictator himself, had signed a treaty with Britain and France to guard Austrian independence against Germany. He now intervened to protect Austria, by mobilizing Italian troops across the Brenner Pass. Mussolini's intervention at this time is believed to have averted Hitler's plans to invade Austria in 1934. On 2 August, German President Hindenburg died at the age of 86, paving the way for Adolf Hitler to gain a tighter hold on power and be proclaimed 'Führer and Reichskanzler' (chancellor) of Germany.

On 9 October 1934, King Alexander I of Yugoslavia and French Foreign Minister Jean Barthou were murdered in Marseilles by Bulgarian and Croat terrorists. Kendrick's mind must have been cast back to the outbreak of the

Great War, which had been sparked by the assassination of Archduke Franz Ferdinand. With its sparse financial resources, SIS was stretched to the limit, as bemoaned by its chief, Sinclair.[1] However, there is no evidence that the lack of funds hampered or compromised Kendrick's operations. By the mid-1930s, his reports included information about foreign agents working within Yugoslavia for the intelligence services of three major European countries: France, Germany and Italy.[2] With growing concern within SIS about Mussolini's threat to the region, Kendrick's portfolio expanded to include intelligence on the Italian secret service, which was very active in Yugoslavia.[3] It was undertaking military, political, financial and economic surveillance and counter-espionage, and it boasted that no other country had such an effective intelligence service. Operating from two insurance companies to mask its real activities, it claimed that it 'could easily bring about a revolution in Croatia and Macedonia through their agents in the Yugoslav Communist Party who could cause social disorder in all parts of the Kingdom'.[4]

Kendrick wrote:

The service has contact with individual informers in various commercial and society circles from whom they pump information . . . Hungarian, Bulgarian and Albanian agents carry out, under Italian instructions, intelligence services of a local nature, each in the frontier region of their own country.[5]

German military intelligence – the Abwehr – began to operate on the territory of Yugoslavia, independently of its allies (the Italians). It sought to establish a branch in Zagreb, making use of its commercial connections and representatives among the German minority in the country. It had as its main objective 'the propagation of Hitler ideals among Germans abroad but, in point of fact, it is an Intelligence Service and its headquarters are in Hamburg'.[6]

Although these reports offer a limited view on SIS work, the information does provide an insight into the scope of Kendrick's work, and further adds to our understanding of why SIS considered its station in Vienna to be its most important in the inter-war period. Kendrick's greatest asset was his ability to organize and run his networks with competence and efficiency. It places him as one of the most important, yet undiscovered, characters in SIS's history.

The Abyssinian war

In October 1935, Mussolini mounted an invasion of Abyssinia (today's Ethiopia). With its rich fertile land, Abyssinia lay between the two Italian colonies of Eritrea and Somaliland. Mussolini succeeded in creating an Italian East African Empire, as part of his vision of bringing greatness to the Italian people. Kendrick's brief now included the monitoring of Italian naval vessels leaving their bases in Italy during the Abyssinian war, which lasted from October 1936 until February 1937.[7] He ran agents into Italy and became SIS's predominant source of Italian intelligence during the crisis. At the same time, he undertook surveillance of Italian fascist activities.[8] The lack of funds during the Abyssinian crisis again caused Sinclair to complain that SIS was carrying out work in peacetime that was not its usual activity. It had caused him to divert money away from other operations and to spend funds on covering Italy and Abyssinia.[9] Kendrick dispatched one of his own SIS secretaries from Vienna into Italy. Clara Holmes was instructed 'to get close' to an unnamed Italian naval officer, to whom she was giving English lessons. It was one of the oldest tricks in espionage tradecraft. Holmes was successful in gaining 'pillow secrets' for Kendrick, although the precise details of that intelligence are not known.[10]

Kendrick's colleague Claude Dansey was stationed at the British passport control office in Rome, working under the same cover for SIS. The Rome SIS station was beset with its own problems when it was discovered in 1935 that an Italian official there, Secondo Constantini, was a 'mole' in the station, stealing papers and documents and passing them back to the Italians. Against the background of these difficulties, Dansey had to leave Kendrick to cover the Abyssinian crisis. Dansey ran his own part-time agents from Italy into Germany.

Still on the scene was Vera Atkins, whose father's trade had enabled him to penetrate Nazi society. Vera often accompanied him in his work to act as a translator. After his death, the family moved to Vienna, before returning to England, where Vera's mother, Hilda, had been born. With relatives still in Vienna, Vera and her mother visited the Kendricks whenever they returned to the capital.[11] Another of Kendrick's trusted agents at this time was an Austrian Jew named Edmund Pollitzer, who will come back into focus after the annexation of Austria in 1938 (see chapter 6). Also in Vienna and working on unspecified intelligence was Bernard Edge. While little is known about his precise work for SIS, it is believed that he was working along similar lines to Kendrick. Edge remained in SIS and later acted as a referee for Kendrick's granddaughter when she joined the service.[12] Kendrick built up contacts with British expatriates living in Vienna. One of these was the British-born pianist Alfred Kitchin, whose talent took him to Germany. He studied in Leipzig under Robert Teichmüller in the period immediately after the First World War. When, years later, the Nazis tore down a statue of Felix Mendelssohn-Bartholdy, Kitchin left Germany in protest and went to Vienna, where he studied music under Karl Steiner and Paul Weingarten. Kitchin enjoyed the same musical circle that was to bring him into contact with Kendrick, who recruited him in Vienna and later – on account of his being a fluent German speaker – drafted him into his secret unit in the Second World War.

Kendrick's manager in Vienna for operations was Fred (Siegfried) Richter. On the surface, he carried out routine paperwork at the British passport office; but, in reality, he was tasked with finding suitable agents to send into Italy. He became the man who recruited most of Kendrick's agents and who acted as intermediary, enabling Kendrick to remain in the shadows. Although born in Vienna, Richter grew up in Rechnitz (then part of Hungary). His father was a Jewish horse-trader; his mother a Roman Catholic. In 1908, Richter applied for naturalization as a British subject, having married an Irish woman whom he had met on a visit to Ireland. Returning to Vienna in 1912, he managed a set of stables for the Schlesingers, the famous Jewish family of horse-breeders. During the First World War, he served in the Imperial Austrian Army, even though he had dual nationality. Sometime from the mid-1920s, he began to work for Kendrick. Richter was a verger in the Anglican church in Vienna and a colleague of another SIS operative, Revd Hugh Grimes. It is thought that Grimes may have introduced Richter to Kendrick. During the Abyssinian crisis, Kendrick asked Richter to find agents to send into Italy. Richter knew a corvette captain in the German navy – one von Gatterer. Although he failed to recruit von Gatterer for Kendrick, the captain suggested another contact – Rudolf Koren, who was secretary of the Navy League. Richter persuaded Koren to travel to Italy to spy on the Italian navy. Much of what was passed back to Kendrick was in the form of verbal reports and therefore precise details of the intelligence gained are not known.

The news from Germany continued to cause concern, with Hitler actively rearming his forces, in direct contravention of the Treaty of Versailles. In March 1935, he formed the Luftwaffe (German air force) and on 16 March introduced conscription for men between the ages of 18 and 45. In July 1936, Hitler reoccupied the Rhineland in a further erosion of the Treaty of Versailles. Austrian Chancellor Schuschnigg was forced to take two Nazi sympathizers into his government and to lift the ban on Nazi newspapers. The situation facing Germany's Jews deteriorated even further with the passage of the Nuremberg Laws that summer: these denied Jews any civil rights and ostracized them from all areas of society. By now, the SIS network had spread extensively across Europe. From the 1920s, it had had Frank Foley – functioning as the British passport officer – to run the SIS station in Berlin.[13] Foley operated his own networks in Germany, but left Kendrick to dispatch agents to German naval bases, such as Wilhelmshaven, to monitor the new battleships that were being constructed. Bertie Acton Burnell, who had served with Foley and Kendrick in France during the First World War, and then in Cologne in 1918, was posted to Berlin in 1936 as assistant passport officer under Foley.[14] Kendrick's brother-in-law, Rex Pearson, had left Vienna, along with SIS colleague Dick Ellis, to undertake intelligence work out of Switzerland.

The Z Organisation

With the increasing menace from Nazi Germany, Claude Dansey was tasked by 'C' with creating a new top-secret organization to carry out espionage – especially industrial espionage in Europe. It was called the Z Organisation and was to gain intelligence on Nazi Germany and fascist Italy. It is not clear whether the Z Organisation was intended to replace the SIS if the latter ceased to be able to operate – for example, if Hitler invaded Britain.[15]

Dansey recruited Kendrick's own brother-in-law, Rex Pearson, into this new organization (with operational cover from Unilever in Switzerland) and also Sigismund Payne Best, who worked out of The Hague as director of the pharmaceutical firm Menoline Ltd. Payne Best's marriage to a Dutch painter gave him important social contacts, including access to royal circles, and he was an ideal recruit for Dansey. He was also an old colleague of Dansey, Kendrick and Pearson from military intelligence in the First World War.

Although the two main centres of operation were Holland and Switzerland, the Z Organisation was headquartered in offices on the eighth floor of Bush House on Aldwych in London. Dansey used a hidden back entrance, through offices next to those of an old friend, the barrister Geoffrey Duveen.[16] On the floor below were the Joel brothers, the wealthy diamond magnates from South Africa who had been part of the Kendrick/Atkins circle since the Boer War. The Joel brothers provided a respectable facade for the Z Organisation, as part of its diamond-exporting business, and funded it together with another major diamond company from South Africa, De Beers.

Hungarian Jewish film producer Alexander Korda, who set up the London Film Productions company in 1932, also provided funds for Dansey's new network.[17] In 1937, Dansey dispatched a young Cambridge graduate named Andrew King to Vienna, under cover of the film business, as part of the Z Organisation. King was also drafted into the SIS. From Vienna, he travelled the region to send back information on the German order of battle and other military details. He reported to Dansey, possibly via Kendrick.[18] The extent to which Kendrick was involved in running agents in Vienna for the Z Organisation is an open question. Remembering that his own brother-in-law worked for both SIS and the Z Organisation, it is plausible. Especially since the new Z Organisation was also tasked with gaining intelligence on Italy, which fell within Kendrick's SIS domain. Lieutenant Commander Kenneth

Cohen (later working closely with Kendrick in SIS and MI9) recruited operatives for Dansey, but found that, with only rudimentary training and no proper instructions, they only sent back low-level intelligence.[19]

Working out of Kitzbühel in the 1930s for Dansey's Z Organisation as Agent Z3, Conrad O'Brien-ffrench had links to Kendrick. He had been recruited into SIS by Stewart Menzies in 1918, and his cover was as a tour operator and playboy.[20] It is understood from an unnamed source that O'Brien-ffrench worked closely with Kendrick, reporting back to Dansey. Later, in 1938, O'Brien-ffrench observed German troop movements just prior to Hitler's annexation of Austria and reported on them for SIS. The future author Ian Fleming was another principal figure living in Kitzbühel in the early 1930s, attending Forbes-Dennis's finishing school there. Fleming is believed to have been recruited into SIS at the school and was linked personally to O'Brien-ffrench, Kendrick and Dansey, as well as Forbes-Dennis.[21] These men moved in the same intelligence circles in that region of Austria and all worked for SIS. Fleming spent time in Vienna, where he met one of his Austrian girlfriends, Edith Maria Thonet (née von Morpurgo). They spent time together in Kitzbühel in 1934 and embarked on a tempestuous relationship. When Fleming returned to London, Thonet visited him there; but the relationship did not last and she went back to Vienna. Kendrick and Fleming worked closely together during the Second World War, with Fleming recruiting the naval intelligence section at Kendrick's 'M Room' operations.[22]

The Z Organisation had numerous other agents and officers, but a complete list of their names is difficult to reconstruct today without access to the MI6 archives.[23] A picture emerges here of SIS and the Z Organisation, in which the leading spymasters and operatives were known to each other in military intelligence from either the Boer War or the First World War.

The Benton memoirs

Kenneth Benton was 26 when he arrived in Vienna in 1935 to take up a post as an English teacher at the Theresianum College, a Catholic institution.[24] Two years later, he met a lady who changed the direction of his life and introduced him to Kendrick. Peggy Lambert worked as a secretary in the commercial department of the British embassy, compiling economic reports and linking up with local intelligence agencies. She invited him to accompany her to one of Kendrick's parties, where he also met the two SIS secretaries, Clara Holmes and Betty Hodgson. Nothing was revealed that evening to suggest that any of the guests were involved in clandestine work. Kendrick took an immediate interest in Benton when he learned that he spoke Italian. Kendrick needed a fluent Italian speaker for his intelligence work on fascist Italy and he dispatched Benton to London for an interview with Maurice Jeffes, head of the Passport Control Department. The interview took place in an office on the first floor of Broadway Buildings, the SIS headquarters. Benton was unaware that the Passport Control Department shared the same building as SIS. The interview was brief because, though Benton had no inkling of it, the real reason for his interview was not passport work, but intelligence. He was escorted to the back of the building, through a door, and into another building at the rear, which was in Queen Anne's Gate. There, in an apartment, sat a short, red-faced man with a bowler hat. This was Benton's first encounter with Hugh Sinclair, 'C' and head of SIS. Benton was quizzed about his degree in languages and knowledge of other foreign countries.

On Kendrick's recommendation, Sinclair engaged Benton with SIS on a tax-free salary of £500 a year, with the warning that if he was not up to the job, he would be dismissed without any right of appeal. Benton agreed, still unaware that he had been engaged by SIS. He returned to Vienna with the notion that he would be dealing with visas. On the first morning, he learned the truth that Kendrick carried out very few passport responsibilities because he was engaged in intelligence work with the help of Hodgson and Holmes. Benton's reminiscences offer a rare glimpse into Kendrick's clandestine world: nothing has ever been released about it by MI6. He was taken into a rear room, where Holmes passed him a letter with a Czech name on it and asked him to translate. He opened the letter, and then called Holmes back into the room.

'Look, I can't do this. It is in Czech,' he said.

'Oh, I'm sorry,' she replied. 'How stupid. Hang on for a moment.'

At the back of my desk there was a little open bottle of colourless liquid with a brush, and she dipped the brush in the liquid, passed it over the whole of the front of the letter and to my amazed eyes, red writing appeared at right angles to the Czech text and it was in German. Then she turned the letter over and did the same on the rear side, so that I had two sides of what was in fact a German report. I began to translate – it was obviously from somebody in Czechoslovakia reporting about events in the Sudetenland where the Germans were already planning to take over. After that, almost all my work was of this kind.

Holmes and Hodgson were corresponding with agents in various parts of Europe, using invisible ink. They wrote to agents in Czechoslovakia and Hungary; but there was a particular focus on southern Italy and Sicily. The agents had been recruited by Kendrick's intermediary, Richter, to send back reports from the region on military and naval activity by the Italians. The reports were mostly in German, but sometimes Italian – hence Benton's recruitment by Kendrick. Benton recalled that some of the reports were from Augusta in Sicily and gave details of Italian battleships and other vessels in the naval base:

We received quite a number of reports about the Tenth Flotilla MAS (*Decima Flotilla MAS*), the special naval unit headed by Prince Borghese, which employed the E-boats in which our Admiralty was very much interested. They were very fast boats, each with two torpedo tubes, and the idea was that they would penetrate our naval ports like Alexandria and Gibraltar, loose off their torpedoes under cover of night, and escape by sheer speed from the immediate response of our guns and aircraft.[25]

As Kendrick gathered vital intelligence for Sinclair back in London, he seemed too extrovert an 'English gentleman' to be suspected of being a spymaster. As he carried out his duties with utter loyalty to the British Crown, he was prepared to go to the edge of the precipice to gain secrets for his country. Unwittingly, and with approval from London, he entered a dangerous game of double agents and Nazi spies. The world of SIS was about to be beset with double agents and traitors, who placed Kendrick himself at direct personal risk.

Agent Tucek

One of those agents was an Austrian-born inventor, Karl Tucek. His work and his encounters with Kendrick are known today and can be reconstructed here, because the details survive in Abwehr reports that were captured by the Allies at the end of the Second World War.[26] Fred Richter, who was working for Kendrick, first met Tucek in June 1937. Tucek appeared to have great potential as an agent for SIS. He wanted to offer two inventions to an English firm: one was a concrete-breaking machine and the other was a hand-operated concrete rammer.[27] Tucek needed a translator in the negotiations and thought of approaching Richter at the British embassy. During their initial discussion, Richter thought of Kendrick, knowing that his boss was always seeking to cultivate potential espionage opportunities in the industrial world. Tucek had revealed enough information to convince Richter that he would be a valuable asset for Kendrick. He had served in the Austrian navy and had a vast amount of technical knowledge. He also spoke fluent Italian – coming to the attention of Richter at a time when Kendrick still needed fluent Italian speakers for operations against Mussolini and fascist Italy. Richter made an educated guess that Tucek was probably short of money – he had a wife to support and needed cash to finance his inventions and pass them through the appropriate channels. Richter made him an offer: he would provide cash for Tucek's inventions, if the latter agreed to travel to Italy.

Tucek immediately recognized the offer for what it was – and refused. He told Richter that spying was a dangerous game and he would 'pay with his head' if discovered. Richter failed to persuade him to travel to Italy. However, during the conversation it emerged that Tucek had significant connections with two companies in Germany, Demag in Düsseldorf and Knorr-Bremse AG Berlin. He also had a close friend in construction at Schichau in Elbing (today Elblag, in Poland). and business contacts in Hungary. The headquarters of Demag in Germany had already disappointed Tucek by turning down his inventions, even though Johann Kroschel (Demag's representative in Vienna) had shown an interest and had offered to pay from his own private funds. Tucek desperately wanted to succeed with his inventions and realized that, if he handled Richter with care, he might secure all the funds he needed. In spite of his original reservations about spying, he did agree to take a solo trip to Knorr-Bremse in Germany, in exchange for a cash advance of 1,000 Schillings. Richter reported back to Kendrick that Tucek would not spy in Italy, but was prepared to travel to Germany, as he felt that his existing contacts with Knorr-Bremse would place him above suspicion. During the time that he worked for Kendrick, Tucek never knew his real name: he always referred to him as 'the elusive Englishman', and all correspondence between them was conducted through Richter.

Tucek hid from Richter his close friendship with another leading constructor, Johannes Kroetice, at Schichau-Werke in the port of Danzig (modern-day Gdańsk). The company was firmly loyal to the Nazi regime. Tucek was also imbued with the ideology and was an illegal member of the National Socialist German Workers' Party (NSDAP) in Austria. Unknown to Kendrick and Richter, he was a personal friend of top-ranking Nazi SS Führer Ernst Kaltenbrunner, one of the architects of the Holocaust and later chief of the Gestapo and the Sicherheitsdienst (SD – the security service). Kaltenbrunner would stand trial at Nuremberg as one of the leading members of Hitler's government. Born in Austria, he had studied law at the University of Graz, and by 1929 was practising law in Linz, not far from Hitler's birthplace of Braunau. During the 1930s, he had friends at the German mission in Vienna and was engaged as the Nazi Party's legal representative in Austria. In 1933, he was appointed commander of the 37th SS Regiment in Upper Austria and was said to have taken part in the 1934 Nazi putsch in Vienna and the murder of Dollfuss.[28] Although arrested several times in Linz for illegal Nazi activities, no evidence could be found against Kaltenbrunner and he was always released. Ignoring the ban on Nazi activities, by 1937 he had become head of the Austrian SS in Upper Austria and had organized an illegal SS formation in the region. He would go on frequent secret trips to Berlin.[29] He then became head of the SS in Vienna at a dangerous time for Kendrick, was promoted to chief of the Sicherheitspolizei (security police) and eventually of the RSHA, the umbrella organization that covered the Gestapo, the security police and the SD.[30]

Tucek already knew where his loyalties lay – and that was not with either SIS or even his homeland of Austria. He believed in Hitler's vision, and Kendrick could not have crossed swords with a more dangerous man. Tucek was shrewd enough to realize that the real spymaster was not Richter, but the 'elusive Englishman'. He immediately told Kaltenbrunner about the British offer of espionage. Kaltenbrunner informed the German embassy in Vienna and that led to a devastating chain of events over the next 12 months. For a year, the Abwehr laid a trail to uncover the identity of Kendrick and trap him. Tucek was twice invited to the German mission by the military attaché, known only by his cover name of Karl Mueller. During one of the meetings, Tucek was recruited by Mueller as an agent for the military section of the Abwehr, enabling Hitler's secret service to begin its penetration of SIS in Vienna. The Abwehr exerted pressure on Tucek to meet Kendrick and establish his identity.

Richter successfully convinced Tucek that Kendrick lived in England and only visited Vienna every two to three weeks. He arranged a number of meetings between Kendrick and Tucek, but Kendrick always cancelled at the last minute, while he waited for clearance from London. At no point did Tucek suspect that Kendrick worked in Vienna. As Tucek waited to meet the elusive Englishman, events were about to take a dramatic turn for Austria with regard to Nazi Germany.

Last waltz in Vienna

The new year of 1938 dawned on arguably the darkest chapter in Austrian history. Hitler was intent on pursuing his vision of creating a united

Austria–Germany, as set out in his book *Mein Kampf*, which had been published in 1925. His gaze was firmly fixed on Austria, which would not escape his maniacal obsession with absolute power and expansion of the Third Reich.

Prudence Hopkinson, daughter of Clara Holmes, commented:

Staff at the British Passport Control Office in Vienna knew that an invasion was imminent. No one was under any illusion of what was about to happen, except perhaps the Jews of Austria themselves. It was not a question of *if* Germany invaded Austria, but *when*.[31]

A measure of how seriously the threat was taken by the Foreign Office is the fact that it asked the British embassy to draw up a list of leading public figures in Austria who would be at risk after a Nazi invasion, and a list of those who could turn Nazi.[32] The list of those at risk contained 93 names, including Sigmund Freud, Alfons Rothschild, Louis Rothschild and Dr Otto Bauer (a prominent left-wing social democrat).[33]

On 4 February 1938, Hitler dismissed his generals and appointed himself supreme commander of the German armed forces. A solution to 'the Austrian question' was uppermost in his mind. Less than a week later, Austrian Chancellor Kurt von Schuschnigg was summoned by Hitler to his private mountain retreat in Berchtesgaden to meet Minister of State for Foreign Affairs Dr Guido Schmidt. Back in Vienna, talk within the small expatriate British community centred on the uncertainty over Austria's future. Knowing that times would soon change, Kendrick, Holmes and SIS secretary Evelyn Stamper held a dinner party and cabaret in Holmes' apartment on Bernbrunngasse in the Hietzing district. As Prudence Hopkinson recalled:

They knew matters were coming to a head and the party would be one of the last times they could celebrate in a free Austria. In the privacy of the apartment over dinner, the adults discussed the developing crisis. In 1938 they knew about the concentration camps, but not the full extent of the death camps.[34]

Although the party was overshadowed by a sense of unease for Austria, Kendrick played the piano, accompanying the New Zealand singer Winnie Fraser, who was in the capital for voice training. Together they performed pieces from *The Merry Widow*. Also present at the party was James Joll, a history don from the University of Oxford. Joll was a cousin of Stamper's and lodged with her during his sabbatical at the University of Vienna, where he was trying to improve his German. He was an outstanding pianist and played a duet with Kendrick. Joll is known to have been working for British intelligence, possibly already in Vienna. During the Second World War, he served in the German section of the Special Operations Executive, before transferring to the Foreign Office. In 1964, he gave shelter to his old friend Anthony Blunt after Blunt went into hiding immediately before confessing to being one of the famous Cambridge spy ring passing secrets to the Soviets.

Kendrick was immersed in the musical world of Vienna. Among his close friends and acquaintances were the eminent conductors Arturo Toscanini, Hans Knappertsbusch, Otto Klemperer and the British conductor Adrian Boult and the Jewish violinist Yehudi Menuhin, cellist Alexander Rosdol of the Vienna Philharmonic Orchestra and his son Sandy Rosdol (a violinist), and the Czech composer Oskar Morawetz. Morawetz had arrived in Vienna from Prague in 1937 to study piano, and would witness Hitler's entry into Vienna the following year. He would have to return to Prague because he was Jewish.[35] He had to escape a second time, when Czechoslovakia was invaded by the Nazis in March 1939. He later went on to compose the music for the film about Anne Frank. Violinist Sandy Rosdol worked for Kendrick and SIS in Vienna (although he never disclosed the nature of this work) and later served in intelligence in the Second World War.[36]

Although the concert halls continued to fill their seats during February 1938, and the annual carnival and state ball were attended by the new middle class and diplomats, under the surface there was fear and a quiet realization that the inevitable was about to happen. At the state ball the guests danced to the music of Johann Strauss late into the night; but it was a swansong to a country that was about to bid farewell to its freedom. On 20 February, Bruno Walter conducted the premiere of Anton Bruckner's Symphony No. 4 and Egon Wellesz's *Prosperos Beschwörungen* in the last concert before Hitler's annexation of the country.

With Hitler's plans well advanced, the Abwehr became increasingly impatient to snare the English spy and it instructed the German diplomatic mission in Vienna to bait a trap and break the SIS network. On 28 February 1938, Tucek received a telegram supposedly from Knorr-Bremse about a proposed visit. It had, in fact, been sent by the military attaché at the German embassy. Tucek met Richter and showed him the telegram. This gave Richter the written proof he needed to convince Kendrick to finally meet Tucek.

The Abwehr's snare

On 6 March 1938, less than a week before Hitler annexed Austria, a man described as 'over 1.80 metres, broad and heavy, with a heavy walk, hair combed back, thick upper lip and blue eyes' entered 52 Favoritenstrasse in Vienna. Hitler's secret service described the Englishman as 'well dressed, could be an officer and speaks extraordinarily broken German'.[37] Tucek had been given very little notice of the face-to-face meeting with Kendrick. He knew a meeting was scheduled with an officer from British intelligence, but not that it was Sinclair's top spymaster in Europe. This was to be the first and last time that Tucek met Kendrick.

Kendrick shook his hand and immediately put Tucek at ease with a few pleasantries. Then he gave him direct instructions to secure information and plans on Germany's U-boat and battleship construction, by travelling from Vienna to the German ports of Wilhelmshaven and Elbing. Of particular interest to Kendrick was the speed and power of the U-boats under construction. Kendrick handed Tucek a questionnaire, asking him to learn the questions by heart and then destroy it. He told him: 'You must carry nothing in writing across the frontier. You should travel via Prague to Germany.'[38] Tucek disagreed with Kendrick and insisted that he cross the border at Passau.

Kendrick conceded and responded: 'Business with Knorr-Bremse should be completed within three or four days. From there you should go on to Elbing, live with your friend if possible and try to get a job with Schichau-Werke.'

Tucek's tone was still challenging as he replied: 'When I was once in Stuttgart I discovered that the regulations governing the appointment of workers of foreign nationality in Germany industry takes 10–12 days to go through.'

'In that case,' said Kendrick, 'you must return to Vienna after three weeks and report to us on the pretext of your wife's illness. We will then see. While you are in Elbing you are to obtain as much material as possible to answer the questionnaire. Under no circumstances should you tell your friend about your true activity.'

Tucek nodded. Kendrick continued:

Any contact with people in Austria during your absence must be minimal and consist only of short postcards to your wife containing harmless private news, from which certain conclusions could be drawn. For instance, you might say that business is going well. You are absolutely forbidden to write to Richter, and neither are you to give a cover address.

The meeting lasted half an hour. Once Kendrick had left the premises, Tucek disobeyed instructions and committed Kendrick's instructions to paper. Kendrick walked down the street, not realizing that members of the Abwehr were watching him from the shadows of nearby doorways.[39] It is not known why they did not follow him to the British passport control office, which would immediately have blown his cover. The whole story raises questions about why Kendrick did not take more precautions. Until then, he had been so careful not to meet agents, except through an intermediary. This one meeting with Tucek was to have far-reaching consequences, not only for Kendrick but for SIS.

On 10 March 1938, just two days before Hitler annexed Austria, Tucek arrived at Knorr-Bremse in Berlin to meet its senior manager, Mr Reinhardt. The German attaché in Vienna had informed Tucek that members of the military branch of the Abwehr would also be present at the meeting. The two

Abwehr officers are named in the reports as Major Rohleder and Oberleutnant Brandt.[40] The meeting began at 10 o'clock, during which Tucek gave an account of his encounter with 'the Englishman' four days earlier. He handed Kendrick's questionnaire to Rohleder.

Rohleder told Tucek that he would be in touch again with a plan. Just over a week later, on 19 March, Rohleder and Brandt met Tucek in Café Berolina at the Alexanderplatz railway terminus in central Berlin. They discussed their strategy and instructed him to travel to the Schichau company in Elbing, as planned by Kendrick. Once there, he would be provided with one of the Abwehr men as 'a friend', in case the British were secretly observing his meetings.

Tucek subsequently arrived in Elbing, looked around the area and noted information which any member of the public could observe: this formed the basis of 'chickenfeed' to be passed to Richter for onward transmission to Kendrick. Chickenfeed is espionage language for information passed to an enemy intelligence agency that is sometimes accurate (and sometimes not), but would not be seriously damaging to the originating agency. Tucek remained in Elbing for a few days, then returned to Berlin to report back to Rohleder and Brandt. During the debriefing session, Tucek was told that from now on he was not to be seen anywhere near the German embassy in Vienna. If Kendrick engaged him on other espionage activity, he was to write immediately to the Knorr-Bremse company, which would act as an intermediary and inform the Abwehr.

Tucek left Berlin and arrived back in Vienna on 20 March; but he returned to a very different city. The streets were heaving with stormtroopers and military vehicles. Large swastika flags hung from buildings. Austria had been annexed by the Third Reich.

The Anschluss

In the last weeks of February and in early March 1938, events moved swiftly. On 9 March 1938, Austrian Chancellor Schuschnigg announced that there would be a plebiscite the following week, designed to safeguard Austrian independence: Austrians could vote for a free, independent, Christian and united

Austria. But Hitler was already calling for Schuschnigg's resignation. On Friday, 11 March, amid concerns of an imminent German invasion of Austria, the German War Office moved to reassure nervous European leaders. It informed the British military attaché in Vienna and the Foreign Office in London that no troop movements were being made, beyond ordinary spring training.[41] British intelligence knew differently, because the reassurances from the German War Office contradicted reports coming from the British consul-general in Munich, who had witnessed the general mobilization in Bavaria and German troop movements on the Austrian frontier. Considerable air activity was also observed over Nuremberg. Mobilization orders applied to 'all armed mecha-nised units and SS auxiliaries at Dachau. Reservists had been called up and confined to barracks. Troops were moving along all roads towards Czechoslovak and Austrian frontiers.'[42] The Lithuanian military attaché in Berlin reported that the German 3rd Armoured Division was being mobilized. On receiving this information, Kendrick knew it was already too late for Austria.

At 7.45 p.m. that evening, Schuschnigg called off the referendum. Kendrick and his staff stayed late at the office and listened on the wireless to Schuschnigg's resignation speech to Austrians in which he said he had no desire to see the shedding of Austrian blood. In a move to protect his own people, he urged Austrian forces not to oppose a German invasion. That night Hitler ordered a huge invasion force over the border.

By 5 a.m., three divisions of German infantry and one division of lorries had crossed the Austrian frontier between Passau and Salzburg. Two thousand German troops landed at Aspern airport, near Vienna, in 200 transport planes – which meant landing 50 planes an hour.[43] By the early hours of the morning, armoured vehicles and troops were occupying the streets of Vienna. As per Schuschnigg's appeal to the nation, Austrians offered no resistance. Field Marshal Hermann Goering assured Sir Nevile Henderson (the British ambassador in Berlin) that German troops would be withdrawn from Austria as soon as the situation had stabilized.

This dramatic turn of events led Vienna's most famous Jew, Sigmund Freud, to scrawl across the page of his diary *Finis Austriae* – Austria is finished.

5
FINIS AUSTRIAE

On Saturday, 12 March 1938, the Third Reich annexed Austria. The Anschluss, as it was termed, marked the beginning of seven years of incorporation into Germany and the destruction of Viennese culture and Jewish life. Austrians woke to the visible effects of the Nazi occupation: everywhere were military vehicles and there was a heavy presence of SS men and stormtroopers. Large swastika flags hung from the windows of apartments and buildings, reaching almost to the pavement below. Anti-Jewish slogans were daubed in black paint on the doors and windows of Jewish businesses. The sound was deafening as hundreds of German bombers flew low over the city, dropping propaganda leaflets onto the streets below. Brownshirts waved swastika flags and chanted, 'Ju-da-verr-rrecke!' (Perish Judah!). The fate of Austria's 200,000 Jews changed overnight as they became the immediate victims of Nazi racist policies. The anti-Jewish laws that had been gradually introduced in Germany over a period of years came into force immediately in Austria. Now Austria's Jews were in mortal danger and Kendrick was acutely aware of this as he left his apartment that morning for the British passport office on Metternichgasse. He arrived at the office to find it besieged by hundreds of Jews queuing along the west wall.

Kendrick faced the beginning of a human catastrophe of immeasurable proportions. Many of his Jewish friends were now at risk. The massive volume of applications from Jews seeking to emigrate was something for which the passport office was ill-prepared. In the coming weeks and months, he and his staff would be pushed to breaking point. Kendrick embarked on the path of a rescuer, becoming the 'Oskar Schindler' of Vienna.

Anti-Semitism was deeply ingrained in Vienna – partly because the working classes gave their support to the Nazi regime for economic reasons. However, the picture is rather more complex than that. Austrian anti-Semitism in this period was not initially directed against Vienna's highly educated, upper-middle-class Jewish intellectuals and successful businessmen who had become integrated into life in the country. But over 100,000 Eastern European Jews had left Poland in 1918–19, fleeing extreme Polish anti-Semitism and nationalism. Many of them had settled in Germany, but from 1933 they were forced to leave again because of Nazi persecution. These poverty-stricken Jews tended to move into Austria and Vienna's own Jewish population feared that these people would fuel wider anti-Semitism and jeopardize their own position. Their concerns were not totally unjustified. The situation changed rapidly after the Nazi invasion and all Jews, whether religious or assimilated, became the object of racial hatred and anti-Semitism. British businessman Arengo-Jones, who was married to an Austrian Jew, had engaged an Austrian lawyer named Arthur Seyss-Inquart to conduct their legal matters. But after the Anschluss, Seyss-Inquart turned Nazi and told them that he could no longer represent them.[1] Seyss-Inquart entered the cabinet as the new Nazi chancellor of Austria for just two days, before becoming a leading member of Hitler's government. He was joined by another Austrian lawyer, Ernst Kaltenbrunner, who was appointed leader of the SS in Austria. As secretary of state for security, Kaltenbrunner was head of the security police and commandant of the SS. In 1944, he was also head of the Gestapo in Vienna. These appointments gave him tight control over all aspects of state security. He was considered the right man because of his ruthless, fanatical adherence to Nazi ideology, and could often be seen entering his office at 7 Herrengasse in SS uniform.[2] Immediately after the Anschluss, he arrested all officials who were not supportive of the Nazi regime and struck their names off the lists of civic posts and establishments. They were replaced by his SS men, thereby tightening the Third Reich's authority and control over Austria.[3]

FINIS AUSTRIAE

A messianic welcome

Two days after the Anschluss, on 14 March 1938, Adolf Hitler arrived in Vienna to a rapturous, almost messianic, reception. Thousands of Austrians lined the route for a glimpse of the Führer in his open-top Mercedes, cheering as the entourage made its way towards the Hofburg (the imperial palace), where, it was rumoured, Archbishop Cardinal Innitzer was to give Hitler a blessing, thus ensuring the allegiance of Austrian Catholics. The city's Jews remained behind closed doors. On the balcony of the Hofburg, in front of a crowd of thousands, the blessing took place. Adolf Hitler – the Austrian who, as an impoverished youth, had once swept the steps of Vienna's Imperial Hotel – was ruler of all that he surveyed that day. He finished his rallying speech with a final proclamation: 'Long live national-socialist German–Austria!'

The military build-up continued in the days immediately after the annexation. By 15 March, the British embassy estimated that the total German military strength in the country was 100,000 men, 1,000 air personnel and 200 aircraft. Generals Milch and von Brauchitsch and Admiral Canaris arrived in the city. At 6 p.m. that evening, German troops were still entering the capital, including 7,000 from artillery, anti-aircraft artillery and other units. Surely there could be no justification for such a display of force in Austria? It caused concern in the British embassies in Austria and Germany, where intelligence staff based in those offices identified which German battalions were on the move and reported the results back to London.

The following day, 16 March, the Cabinet met in London to discuss the anticipated Jewish refugee crisis. The home secretary, Sir Samuel Hoare, said that he felt a great reluctance to put any further obstacles in the way of 'these unfortunate people' and reported that a curious story had reached him from MI5, to the effect that the Germans were anxious to swamp the United Kingdom with Jews so as to create a Jewish problem in the country.[4] A Home Office memorandum issued after the meeting noted:

The incorporation of Austria in the German Reich has made it essential to reconsider the arrangements for the control of aliens holding German or Austrian passports who may seek admission to this country . . . the future status of people holding an Austrian passport was now uncertain.

Jews who had fled Germany in the early 1930s and found asylum in Austria were among those now trying to flee Austria.[5] Decisions in London on visas and the status of refugees would directly impact on what Kendrick and other British passport officers across Europe could do.

The Jewish community in Britain had previously provided the Home Office with a written undertaking that no refugee arriving in the country would be a burden on the public purse.[6] The community would take care of their welfare. But matters changed after the Anschluss. The German Jewish Aid Committee could no longer guarantee financial assistance for newly arrived refugees. The Home Office instigated a new visa system for émigrés coming into Britain, something that had been abolished for the countries of Germany and Austria in 1928. Now all refugees needed a British visa, as well as other documentation required by the German authorities for emigration. It was recognized that the consequence of this decision would be extra work for British passport officers. That afternoon, a cypher was sent by the Foreign Office to the British embassy in Vienna, stating that if the German occupying forces reopened the Austrian borders, large numbers of refugees could seek entry into Britain.[7] The Foreign Office wished to be informed immediately by telegram if this was the case.

While the Cabinet and Home Office debated the Austrian crisis and new visa regulations, Kendrick faced the day-to-day practicalities of emigration for the hundreds of Jews cramming every available space at the embassy.

City of terror

Within days of the Anschluss, the Jews of Vienna were to experience the full brutality of the Nazi regime. Jewish males were rounded up by Brownshirts and SS and never seen again. Eric Gedye reported: 'From my window I could watch for many days how they would arrest Jewish passers-by – generally doctors, lawyers and merchants, for they preferred their victims to belong to the better educated classes.' Signs appeared on shop windows: 'No Jews or dogs here.' Gedye provided many examples of the degradation and brutality against Vienna's Jews:

> every morning in the Habsburgergasse the SS squads were told how many Jews to round up that day for menial tasks . . . The favourite task was that of cleaning the [toilet] bowls of the WCs in the SS barracks, which Jews were forced to do simply with their naked hands.[8]

Kendrick came out of the passport building to humiliating scenes of Jews scrubbing the pavement in front of his office, with acid solutions that burned their hands. Unintimidated by the jeering onlookers of stormtroopers and Brownshirts, he kicked over the buckets of acid solution and shouted at them: 'Not on my patch!' The *Argus* newspaper reported:

> The queue [around the British passport control office] sometimes extended into the street where the larrikin youth of the Nazi stormtroopers amused themselves by making the Jews who were waiting wash the pavement. Kendrick stopped that.[9]

Gedye also tried to reconcile the brutality and humiliation with the Vienna he knew:

> [It is] the fluffy Viennese blondes, fighting one another to get closer to the elevating spectacle of an ashen-faced Jewish surgeon on hands and knees before half a dozen young hooligans with Swastika armlets and dog-whips that sticks in my mind. His delicate fingers, which must have made the swift and confident incisions that had saved the lives of many Viennese,

held a scrubbing-brush. A Stormtrooper was pouring some acid solution over the brush – taking care to drench the surgeon's striped trousers as he did so. And the Viennese – not uniformed Nazis or a raging mob, but the Viennese little man and his wife – just grinned approval at the glorious fun.[10]

The greater part of the Jewish population had lost its livelihood. The despair could be measured by the number of suicides. In the first four days after the Anschluss, there were 140 Jewish suicides – an average of 35 a day. Within the month, 500 Jews had taken their own lives – mainly intellectuals from the upper middle class. Franz Rothenberg, chairman of Austria's largest bank, Creditanstalt-Bankverein, was arrested and thrown out of a moving car by stormtroopers. Isidor Pollak, the Jewish director of the chemical company Pulverfabrik, was killed during an SA raid on his home. In a two-hour speech, Dr Goebbels, Hitler's minister for propaganda, attacked world democracy and the international press, and said that Jewish persecution and suicides in Austria were inventions, and that 'the Jewish problem would have to be solved'.[11]

Less than 12 hours after Hitler's triumphal procession through Vienna, the Gestapo arrived at the apartment of Sigmund Freud at 19 Berggasse and raided it.[12] A week later, Freud was subjected to a second raid, during which his daughter Anna was taken away for hours of questioning. His eldest son Martin was placed under house arrest. A flurry of US and British diplomatic efforts ensued in the coming weeks to get the Freud family out of Austria. Concern mounted for the fate of Austrian scientists, particularly Otto Loewi, recipient of the Nobel Prize for medicine.[13]

Vice Consul-General Gainer reported back to London on the extreme anti-Semitism gripping the Austrian capital. He told London that the local German authorities believed they could solve 'the Jewish problem' by arresting hundreds of Jews on a daily basis, confining them for a short period and then releasing them on condition that they sign an undertaking to hand over all their possessions to the Nazi Party and leave the country within three to four weeks. It was but a temporary freedom, as they were often rearrested before they could organize all the paperwork to leave.

Intelligence work under strain

Hitler's annexation of Austria was the most serious crisis in Kendrick's career with SIS. For 13 years, he had been engaged exclusively in Vienna on intelligence work. The human catastrophe and urgency of visa work meant that he struggled to get any intelligence reports back to Sinclair in London. He wrote to Sinclair apologizing that his reports were 'somewhat scrappy and badly collated because of the pressure of passport work'.[14] The Foreign Office convened a meeting to discuss his future and whether he should leave Vienna, but it was decided to keep him in post. The passport work put enormous strain on Kendrick's SIS secretaries, who were employed on visa work while still trying to gather intelligence on Germany. Marjorie Weller, who transferred from the passport control office in Sofia, the Bulgarian capital, to Vienna, recalled:

> We had these queues outside and I used to say, I had this pile of passports here and a pile of secret ink letters there and I was doing both. It was terribly sad. Pregnant women would lay about in the consulate in the hope they would have babies on British territory. I remember one occasion when a couple went away and committed suicide. There was just nothing I could do for them.[15]

Amid the agitation in the corridors outside his office, Kendrick ordered his secretaries to destroy sensitive papers in the event of a raid on the offices by the Gestapo. A series of 'burnings' took place in the basement of the British embassy. Any documentation from this period which survives today consists of copies of correspondence, transcripts and telegrams that had already been sent to the Foreign Office.

Gedye was the first of Kendrick's agents to be harassed by the Gestapo. As a vocal anti-Nazi journalist, he was a priority on the Gestapo's wanted list. In the first few days after annexation, several unsuccessful attempts were made to expel him from Vienna. On 19 March, Gedye was called to the office of the police chief, Dr Zoffal, who had been instructed by Gestapo headquarters in Berlin to politely ask him to leave Austria.[16] No reason was given, but it was clear that his journalism did not meet with the approval of the Third Reich. Three days later, Ambassador Henderson in Berlin received a phone call from the German Ministry of Foreign Affairs to inform him that Gedye was being expelled from Austria because one of his articles was 'considered insolent and untrue particularly with regard to the number of persons imprisoned by the Nazis in Austria'.[17] In response the British government ordered the expulsion from the UK of Dr Karl Abshagen, a prominent German journalist for the *Hamburger Nachrichten*. This was followed by the expulsion of other German journalists whom the British suspected of conducting espionage in the UK.[18]

There was a more pressing concern for Gedye than his own personal safety. He had employed an Austrian, Litzi Mehler, as his personal secretary. She was also his mistress, and – as a Jew – her life was now in danger. How long before the Gestapo would come after her? Their son, Robin Gedye, recalled:

My father was called to the British embassy and told that he had to get out of Austria because his life was in danger. The Nazis hated the fact that he reported what he saw – all the brutality of a regime that was trying to hide it from the world. John Lepper [?] at the British consulate forged a marriage certificate to enable my mother to get a passport and thus hide her Jewishness. These forged papers enabled her to safely get out of Austria.[19]

Gedye left Vienna for Prague with his new 'wife'.[20] From the temporary safety of Czechoslovakia, he continued to write articles against the Nazi regime and the serious events in Austria. He and Litzi remained in Czechoslovakia until German forces invaded the country in March 1939, when they were forced to flee again. Gedye and Litzi went on to serve British intelligence abroad during the Second World War.[21]

One of Kendrick's friends who was at risk was opera singer, Marjorie Wright, who had married Stephen Eisinger, an Austrian Jew, in 1932.[22] She and Eisinger had met when they both attended a performance of *Carmen* at the Vienna State Opera. During the 1930s, they were invited to supper with the Kendricks – until Eisinger breached etiquette and correctness by his informal attire. Marjorie wrote: 'he [Stephen] has been a communist and he would never dress up when we were invited out. He refused to wear a dinner jacket on a visit to my friends the Kendricks and was never invited there again.'[23] Despite his disapproval, Kendrick helped them out of Austria in March 1938. On marrying Eisinger, Marjorie had lost her British nationality, because dual nationality was not permitted (one reason why Kendrick had objected so strongly to his own daughter, Gladys, being first engaged to an Austrian, before she married Geoffrey Walsh).

The Eisingers and their children were at risk and needed to get out of the country. Of the scenes during the first day of the annexation, Marjorie Eisinger wrote: 'Already Vienna was full of anguish with sights such as Jews scrubbing the pavements.' That same day (or shortly afterwards), Stephen Eisinger fled for Prague, because his life was at immediate risk from the Nazis. From Prague he took a flight to safety in London. It took longer to secure an exit for his wife and their two children from Austria. Marjorie had already met the British diplomat Michael Palairet, minister to Austria, through their expatriate circles, just prior to the Anschluss. He advised her that matters were becoming so serious that she should acquire a false British passport from Kendrick. Palairet was himself recalled to London at the time of the Anschluss and honoured with a knighthood shortly afterwards.

Marjorie Eisinger duly visited the British passport control office and was told to return at 4 o'clock. She then telephoned Kendrick for help, because she had to make the journey twice. He gave her the money for the taxi fare. He ensured that his staff issued a false passport in her maiden name as Marjorie Wright. He also coached her in a cover story in the event that she was detained and questioned by the authorities: she was to pretend to be the wife of a British Indian Army officer, Major Wright, and she was on holiday in Vienna with their two sons. Marjorie obtained the false passport and noted in her diary: 'At 9pm I arrived at Westbahnhof [railway station] with the children. I went to telephone Tommy Kendrick to ask him to come and help but I never got through.' By this time, Kendrick was inundated by the events surrounding him. Nevertheless, he was always ready to help any British citizen living or passing through Vienna who needed his assistance.[24]

Gedye and the Eisingers were not the only ones in Kendrick's inner circle who were at risk. His subordinate, Fred Richter, had a Jewish father who could be subjected to the anti-Jewish racial policies of the regime. Although Richter had dual nationality, it was unclear whether his British nationality still held, because he had served in the Imperial Austrian Army in the First World War. As a measure of protection, the British ambassador in Vienna issued him with a new British passport in March 1938. In the end, it would afford Richter no protection against the Gestapo. In the background to these events, Richter was still in contact with agent Tucek, whom Kendrick had met just prior to the Anschluss. On 22 March 1938, Tucek met Richter for a debriefing in the Mondl pub in Favoritenstrasse. Tucek seemed nervous and less sure of his position. Richter wondered if the annexation had affected him. Tucek informed him that his appointment with the shipyard had not materialized; however, he had been able to obtain some material for the 'Englishman' from his own observations and friendly conversations with friends who completely trusted him. 'I couldn't stay in Germany any longer because I ran out of money,' he told Richter.

Tucek indicated that he would be willing to undertake espionage work again, depending on the rate the 'Englishman' was willing to pay, but matters had changed. Tucek felt he could no longer spy in Germany, because as an Austrian (and now a German citizen), if he was caught he would be executed for treason. He considered it too dangerous to hand over drawings and to answer any questions in Austria, but he was prepared to meet a British representative in neutral territory. Switzerland was suggested. Tucek insisted that the representative must be a member of British intelligence.

Kendrick contacted London for advice. While Kendrick waited for a reply, Richter met Tucek again – this time in the Anglican church where Richter was a verger. Tucek had important news for him. He had received an offer of employment at the port of Wilhelmshaven and had details of construction work for the German navy that was under way at Danzig, Elbing and Königsberg. Richter could not have hoped for a better result. Kendrick received a telegram from London with instructions that Tucek was to travel to the Berner Hof in Interlaken, where a British agent would be waiting for him. Tucek was given 600 Schillings in expenses to hand over information to an Englishman called Albert Acton Brandon and a return train ticket to Zurich. Brandon was, in fact, Albert Ernest Acton Burnell, SIS's man in Switzerland and a close colleague of Kendrick's.[25]

Tucek met Burnell on 28 May and told him how he had masqueraded as a technician and had successfully gained access to Wilhelmshaven, where he had observed work on U-boats and torpedo boats. Of particular value to SIS were his verbal reports on the construction of the German battleships *Scharnhorst* and *Tirpitz*, their fuel consumption and capabilities. Over the ensuing months, Tucek met Richter in Vienna and continued to feed information to the British from his Abwehr handlers, most of it accurate. At no point did Kendrick suspect that anything was amiss. He was swamped by a humanitarian crisis unparalleled in Austrian history.

British subjects arrested

Nazi harassment quickly extended to British subjects of Jewish origin who were living and well settled in Vienna. A hotelier, Captain Edmund Pollak MC, who had served in the Royal Air Force in the First World War, was arrested on 13 March – the day after the Anschluss.[26] Four stormtroopers with revolvers and rifles entered his house at 22 Gloriettegasse. He protested that he was a British subject and demanded to be allowed to contact the British consul-general, John Taylor. His demand was refused and he was bundled into a taxi. Pollak's wife immediately telephoned Taylor, who alerted the Foreign

Office. Pollak was driven to the police prison on the Rossauer Lände. He later recounted:

> On the way there, my foot inadvertently touched one of the Stormtrooper's feet, whereupon he turned to me saying, 'I'll show you how to keep your feet in order', and stamped on my feet with his heavy field boot . . . They also regaled me with stories of how they had seen prisoners beaten up that morning.[27]

Pollak was ushered into a small room with a Nazi in uniform and a number of police officers. The stormtrooper explained to him that, as a Jew, he was guilty of displaying a swastika flag outside his hotel and restaurant, Münchner Hof. After two and a half hours, Pollak was released without charge, following the intervention of Consul-General Taylor with the German authorities.[28]

Arriving home, his wife told him how the British flag had been torn off his Daimler car, confiscated and replaced by a swastika flag.[29] Questioning the servants, Pollak learned that they had taken a telephone call from an anonymous caller the previous evening while he and his wife were out, enquiring about Pollak's Jewishness. Sensing something was amiss, Pollak telephoned the Münchner Hof to be told that it had been confiscated. Fearing for his other business, a fish and poultry restaurant at 12 Fleischmarkt, he telephoned the manager and learned that it, too, had been raided by stormtroopers and seized.

Pollak headed straight to see Taylor at the embassy. The consul-general advised Pollak that he should leave the country immediately. Taylor and Kendrick organized the necessary papers and visas for Pollak, his wife and their child to escape Vienna that same evening. Pollak recalled:

> I thereupon called up Dr Paul Kaltenegger, the lawyer to the British Legation, who is also a personal friend of mine of long standing, and explained the whole position to him and gave him full Power of Attorney.[30]

This meant that Kaltenegger could act on Pollak's behalf in any matters relating to the confiscated businesses and assets.

While packing a suitcase that evening, Pollak received a telephone call from the Nazi authorities stating that he was not to enter his hotel under any circumstances, that it had been ransacked and cash amounting to £100 taken. That evening, Pollak and his family successfully escaped from Austria, but in so doing he left everything he had built up. He lost not only the hotel business, but approximately 400,000 Schillings in investments (equivalent to £15,000 in those days), his import business as sole agent for the whisky company James Buchanan Ltd, Gordon & Co. (gin) and others.[31] He also lost around 40,000 Schillings owed to him, all his stocks, the villa that he had leased on Gloriettegasse and had furnished at a cost of 60,000 Schillings, his silver and glass collections and his personal belongings. The Foreign Office was advised to make strong representations to the German government for compensation for Pollak, restitution to the value of the property confiscated and punishment of the offenders.[32] Pollak was advised not to contact the press for fear of a media frenzy or to have questions asked in parliament, as that could jeopardize representations made on his behalf by His Majesty's government.

Pollak and his family were successfully smuggled out of Austria. They arrived back in London and stayed temporarily at the Royal Air Force Club in Piccadilly. It seems likely that Pollak may have been working for Kendrick while in Vienna: they were close friends and Pollak went on to work for him in the Second World War, in charge of the air intelligence section at Kendrick's top-secret unit.

The Foreign Office in London began to receive calls for help in locating Jewish friends and relatives whose whereabouts in Austria were unknown after the Anschluss. Sir Philip Sassoon, owner of a 400-acre country estate at Trent Park in north London (which ironically would be requisitioned by Kendrick for secret purposes in the Second World War), enquired about the safety of the wife of the world-renowned Austrian glider pilot Robert Kronfeld, a close friend of his.[33] She had been living in Vienna with her mother, Isabella Jolesch. The latter owned several properties in the city and was rumoured to have been arrested by the Nazis. A cypher was sent to Vienna asking about their safety and that of Captain Hans Bauer, mayor of Lambach in Upper Austria, who was an anti-Nazi with an English wife and four children.[34]

Enquiries were made on behalf of a Mrs Wright, an Austrian by birth but British by marriage. Her mother, Ida Kohn, and aunt, Jenny Stern, were still living in Vienna.[35] The Wrights agreed to vouch for them if they were permitted to leave Austria. Arrangements were also made for Mrs Adele Fraenkel, sister of Sir Henry Strakosch, to leave Vienna as quickly as possible. She was described by the Foreign Office as 'of advanced years and extremely delicate', and a friend travelled from England to Vienna to help her on the journey. English friends of Dr and Mrs Hecht of 6 Stubenring were also anxious for news, because the couple were known to be Catholics with monarchist leanings. The British embassy was asked to establish whether the Hechts were still in the city.

One British subject at risk of arrest was violinist and amateur radio ham Katherine Olive Milne Myler. She was working undercover for Kendrick in Vienna and is one of the very few female SIS operatives known to have been working in the region. Known to everyone as Olive, she had been educated in Bath and was fluent in German and other languages. Like so many in SIS, she left no footprint of her clandestine work. She had arrived in Vienna in the 1930s (or possibly earlier) and as an accomplished violinist is thought to have played in the orchestra of the Vienna State Opera. This was a place frequented by Kendrick and his wife, who loved opera. There has been some suggestion that Myler played for the Vienna Philharmonic Orchestra, but no trace has been found in records.

Myler had to flee Vienna immediately after the Anschluss, because she was at risk. It is not clear whether she was Jewish or had to flee because of her work for SIS. When she returned to her bungalow in the village of Knowle, near Braunton in North Devon, she took up amateur radio again with the call sign G3GH. During the Second World War she became one of only three female voluntary interceptors (VIs) known to have worked for MI8, linked to Bletchley Park. She intercepted signals from German U-boats and marked their location; and she also identified the inland submarine pens near Brest on the French coast. For her contribution, she was awarded the British Empire

Medal. The snippets of information that are known about her have only emerged because of interviews with people who knew her.[36] She revealed nothing as such of her personal life, and remained a figure of mystery right up to her death in August 1948.

Arrest of public figures

Some of Austria's key public figures were arrested, among them former Chancellor Schuschnigg, Baron Louis Rothschild and the princes Hohenberg.[37] In the coming weeks, Kendrick and Taylor tried to establish the whereabouts of a number of public figures known to be missing. It was not only a matter of securing the safety of these figures: it also provided the Foreign Office and SIS with intelligence from the ground on what was happening. Reports that Kendrick and Taylor sent back to London included information that Schuschnigg was being held under house arrest in the Belvedere, where he was being forced to listen to Nazi political speeches.[38] This had annoyed Schuschnigg so much that he had smashed two wireless sets; a third had been installed by the Nazis in an inaccessible position.

Dr Schmitz, the former mayor of Vienna, was in prison in the city; Austrian President Miklas was confined to his house, but was permitted to attend daily mass under escort. By the end of March, there was still no news of Captain Hans Bauer, the mayor of Lambach. He had been arrested by the regime for being a member of an illegal anti-Nazi group, the Fatherland Front. Count Engleberg Arco-Valley was another member of the Austrian aristocracy to be arrested. He was a cousin of the brothers Count Nando and Tony Arco-Valley, who in 1919 had murdered Kurt Eisner, a Bavarian Bolshevik. The brothers were described by the Foreign Office as 'rather mad and apt to trail their coats before the Nazis'.[39]

Within hours of the Anschluss, a number of public figures and Austrian aristocrats were transported to Dachau concentration camp. Among them were the duke of Hohenberg and his brother Prince Max Hohenberg; a 72-year-old former imperial ambassador, Prince Karl Emil Furstenberg;

Colonel Adam of the federal chancellery; and around 50 police officials.[40] Furstenberg was eventually released on 8 April, with a stark warning that not recognizing the Nazi regime was treason, the sentence for which (he was informed) was decapitation. A direct appeal was issued to German Foreign Minister von Ribbentrop for the release of these figures, but to no avail. Jewish banker and philanthropist Baron Louis Rothschild was arrested at Vienna airport as he tried to board a plane to Venice.[41] He faced a possible trial on trumped-up charges of misappropriating money for political purposes. While he was being held at Gestapo headquarters at the Hotel Metropole, he befriended his jailers: 'His valet arrived at the prison in a van, which contained not only large amounts of luggage, but a bed and bed linen, lamps, carpets and tapestries as well as orchids from the Rothschild greenhouses, peaches, grapes and wine from the Rothschild cellars.'[42] The guards let the valet in. But Rothschild soon became so popular with the guards that they were replaced by brutal German Nazis and he was deprived of these luxuries. To annoy the Nazi guards, he quoted sections of Hitler's *Mein Kampf*, much of which he had learned by heart. For Rothschild, it was an attitude of defiance in the face of brutality and oppression. However, the situation could have turned out differently for him had the guards decided to beat him up for his provocations.

Arrested around the same time as Rothschild was Karl Seemann, director of a coal distribution company that had international connections within the coal industry. Given his connections abroad, it is possible that Seemann might have been working as an agent or contact for Kendrick. He supplied fuel to some of the biggest hotels in Vienna: the Metropole, Bristol and Regina, as well as to the company Sascha-Film.[43] This last had been started by Count Alexander 'Sascha' von Kolowrat-Krakowsky, a pioneer in films, friend of Alexander Korda and founder of the first studios in Vienna, located in the Sievering suburb.[44] One day after the Anschluss, Seemann disappeared, taken by the Gestapo while in one of the hotels. He returned a few days later (the details are sketchy), but the episode hastened the family's departure from Vienna. It is not known whether Kendrick was involved in his release from custody, but, as Jews, Seemann and his family were at risk. It was Kendrick in the British embassy who suggested that Seemann leave urgently: 'The place I would send you is East Africa.'[45]

As Seemann's granddaughter, Susan Gompels, recalls:

There has been a suggestion of a parallel between my grandparents' story and that of the Rothschilds. The Gestapo apparently allowed Jews to pack only one case. All other possessions were surrendered – and some might be packed by the Gestapo for 'shipping' out of Vienna. There was a suggestion that some goods could be chosen to accompany the refugees, but the Gestapo had the final decision; and there were trade-offs. My grandparents could list which items they would like, but these might not be sent on to them in East Africa. How any was sent remains a mystery – some members of the family today have items from the Vienna days that include a very large painting of Vienna Woods and a complete delicate set of Lobmeyr crystal.

Seemann and his wife Fredericke (Fritzi) fled Vienna with their sons, Robert and William, in July 1938, sailing for Mombasa, East Africa. With no money or possessions, they made a new life labouring on farms, in small manufacturing units and eventually setting up their own businesses. Circumstances eventually brought the family to Britain.[46]

Gompels discovered quite accidentally from her father, William, about Kendrick's role in saving her family from extermination in the Nazi death camps:

One day my father made a casual comment: 'Isn't it strange that Captain Kendrick ended up living just down the road from us here in Surrey?'

'So, who is Captain Kendrick?' I asked.

My father replied: 'He was the amazing passport officer who saved our lives.'

Growing up in Nairobi in the 1950s, almost all our friends had similar stories and were refugees from Vienna and Czechoslovakia. They included

Dr Eric Horowitz, the doctor who delivered me as a baby, and Hungarian/ Czech architect George Farkas, and musician Charles Petera.[47]

Many others who made their escape to East Africa and South Africa may well have been saved by Kendrick, but their stories have yet to come to light.

By 19 March, some 2,500 Austrian political prisoners had been taken from Vienna by road to Dachau concentration camp. Michael Creswell, head of the passport control in London, scribbled on the report that it was 'a far higher number than we had previously had any indication of'.[48] It was also noted that the accommodation at Dachau had been considerably increased over the previous six months to allow for more inmates. This caused some concern at the Foreign Office.

There was so much uncertainty and no one was safe, even among the Austrian aristocracy. And Kendrick's rescue efforts extended to them. He enabled Baroness Daisy Weigelsperg, who was Jewish, to get out of Austria.[49] She had attended Gladys Kendrick's wedding in Vienna in 1931. After fleeing to Paris, she changed her name to Daisy Carol. It was not only Austria's Jews who needed Kendrick's help. Members of the Habsburg family – the dynasty that had once ruled the vast Austro-Hungarian Empire – were in difficulties, with their wealth targeted and confiscated by the Nazi regime. A British officer and non-Jew, Captain Charles Piercy, whose wife was the daughter of Princess Beatrix Bourbon Massimo, was lunching with Princess Ileana of Romania (a great-granddaughter of Queen Victoria) and Archduchess Blanca of Austria at the Palais Toskana in Vienna, when the secret police burst in to confiscate their jewels and papers.[50] Piercy himself fell under suspicion, too, for allegedly trying to hide the Habsburg wealth from the Nazi regime. The British consulate in Vienna advised him to leave the country immediately. Although further details have not come to light on this, the story highlights the closeness between some British circles in Vienna and Austrian royalty. As has been seen already for the 1920s and 1930s, Kendrick himself tried to penetrate and build up social contacts in these circles – all part of his role as a spymaster to gain information and keep abreast of events for SIS.

However, not all remained loyal to Kendrick. One of his long-standing friends, Baron Lichtenberg, whose daughter had been a bridesmaid at Gladys Kendrick's wedding, turned Nazi immediately after the Anschluss. Kendrick's granddaughter, Barbara Lloyd, recalls:

My mother refused to visit Countess Lichtenberg if she knew that her husband was going to be at home. My mother was disgusted with the baron for changing with the wind. I think my grandfather may have had nothing to do with him either.[51]

These were dangerous times for Kendrick: any of his once close circle could turn and become genuine supporters of the Nazi regime. In such cases, he had to exercise caution and dissociate himself from them. Until the regime occupied Austria, it was difficult for anyone to judge who might become disloyal. His network had to be protected at all costs.

A crisis beyond proportions

By early April 1938, over 7,000 Austrian Jewish males had been arrested and sent to concentration camps. As Consul-General Gainer wrote:

The arrests are entirely haphazard. Jews walking in the streets are approached by SA or SS men, asked if they are Jews and then taken off to prison. The whole process is senseless and inhumane and the problem remains unsolved. For those who believe that the Germans are amongst the most cultured and highly civilised of the European peoples, I would recommend a short sojourn in Vienna.[52]

The Nazi regime forbade Jews to enter parks on the banks of the Danube or bathe in the river. Within a fortnight, this exclusion applied to any park in the city. In Salzburg, they were forbidden to wear Austrian national costume. Jewish lawyers were given three weeks to close their businesses. The offices of the Zionist Federation, the Palestine Office and other Jewish community organizations were closed and sealed by the German authorities, and their leaders and officials arrested.[53]

Months of chaos at the British passport office followed the Anschluss. The building was mobbed daily by Jews and intelligentsia seeking ways to leave Austria. With only sporadic directives from the British government, Kendrick and his staff muddled along as best they could. According to the *News Chronicle*, Kendrick was 'a tremendous worker, doing 15 hours a day for weeks when the Jewish rush to escape first began'.[54] He and his staff worked flat-out, but still it was not enough. As he confided to Gainer: 'My staff are so overwrought, they will burst into tears at the slightest provocation.'[55] One typist was at breaking point and had to take compassionate leave.

Gainer reported back to London: 'To conduct the work of the passport office as applicants desire . . . we should need a staff of 40 people and a building like the Albert Hall.'[56] Extra help came from staff transferred from the British passport offices in Sofia and Copenhagen, which doubled the number of visa staff at Vienna to 16.[57] Even this was insufficient to handle more than 175 applications a day. Each day, at least 700 applicants would be queuing in the hallway and outside the building.[58] Many left at the end of the day without being seen. For the sake of fairness, Kendrick introduced a ticket system, so that they would not lose their place in the queue the following day. Gainer admitted that 'some people have to be firmly dealt with . . . the ushers are pushed about and occasionally even struck and often insulted'.[59]

Throughout this, Kendrick had to contend with a number of bureaucratic changes. In April, the British embassy at 8 Wallnerstrasse was downgraded to the status of a legation, which meant that all directives now came from the British ambassador in Berlin, Sir Nevile Henderson. There were discussions about merging the legation with the passport office. Although no formal merger occurred, Kendrick had to move his staff from 6 Metternichgasse to the second floor of 8 Wallnerstrasse. The legation and passport office functioned in the same building, but remained separate.[60] Sir Philip Sassoon, in his role as first commissioner of works and responsible for requisitioning properties for the government, later faced questions in the British parliament about why 6 Metternichgasse was sold for less than its value.[61] Part of the answer given at the time was the slump in property prices, but another factor involved the restrictions imposed by the German government on how much money the British government could take out of German territories.

Structural alterations were made so that the passport control office had its own separate entrance and waiting room, in order to prevent serious congestion at the legation.[62] The issue of space for Kendrick was still being discussed several months later. As Gainer wrote to the secretary of state for foreign affairs: 'Owing to the abnormal conditions obtaining in Vienna, Captain Kendrick needs a minimum of twelve rooms in which to house his staff, but I found myself unable to offer him this accommodation.'[63] Kendrick became vice-consul at his own suggestion. From time to time he acted as consul-general in Gainer's absence.[64] Kendrick and Gainer were important eyewitnesses to events on the ground in Austria and the region. They sent regular reports back to the Foreign Office and oversaw cypher and decoding work, but their official duties meant that they often struggled to keep up. Gainer's own intelligence work was also suffering, and he wrote to Sir Robert Vansittart (permanent under-secretary at the Foreign Office) that he had had no time to maintain contacts or draft intelligence reports. Vansittart advised him that he should travel about his consular district periodically to keep abreast of the political situation.

May 1938: Czechoslovakia

After the Anschluss, it was widely anticipated that Germany would invade Czechoslovakia.[65] It did not in fact happen for another year, and yet the concern remained. Czechoslovakia was a target for Hitler because a quarter of the country's 12 million citizens were ethnic Germans. The vast majority of those 3 million people were German speakers and lived in an area known as the Sudetenland – the former regions of Moravia, Bohemia and Czech Silesia that had once been part of the Austrian Empire. These people looked to Vienna, not Berlin, as their cultural capital. It was not unusual for the cultured intellectuals and aristocracy of Czech society to travel to Vienna for concerts, theatre and opera. In these circles, Kendrick recruited 'contacts' who could observe events on the ground in Czechoslovakia. Because of the secrecy surrounding his work, their names have not been released.

By May 1938, the situation escalated further after the movement of German troops towards the Czechoslovak border in an action largely believed to be an imminent invasion. Kendrick's work with regard to Czechoslovakia assumed a pressing urgency, with concerns over possible German intentions towards Hungary, too. His agents, contacts and informers were embedded across both countries: reliable intelligence was vital.[66]

At this time, there was an interesting case of suspected espionage involving German military activity. On 22 May 1938, a Canadian couple, Mr and Mrs Bennett, were arrested by the authorities in Salzburg on suspicion of spying.[67] Stewart Gordon Bennett had been caught photographing the construction work of new military barracks at Hitler's Bavarian mountain retreat in Berchtesgaden, near the border with Austria. Details of the allegations were sent by the secret police to the British consulate in Vienna, where they were dealt with by Kendrick and Gainer. The Bennetts were, in fact, engaged not in tourism (as they claimed to the Gestapo), but in securing intelligence for Kendrick. The photographs were intended for Kendrick and then SIS in London.

Gainer issued an official response on behalf of the Foreign Office, in effect demanding an explanation for the arrest. The Gestapo replied that they had their suspicions that 'Mr and Mrs Bennett had a special interest in military buildings and camps, and that they had already prior to this case photographed objects to which it was not desired to give publicity, either in Germany or elsewhere.'[68] The camera was confiscated and, when opened, was found to have rare colour film inside that could only be developed in Berlin. The Bennetts remained in custody while the Gestapo waited for the film to be processed. It provided no incriminating evidence against them and they were released without charge. The photographs were returned to the Bennetts via the British legation in July 1938 – a month that would see a re-emergence of fears over a German invasion of Czechoslovakia.[69]

Kendrick's own staff now came under the suspicion of the German authorities, possibly as a result of this incident. Clara Holmes became aware of a Nazi couple being unexpectedly billeted in the basement of her apartment block. Her daughter Prudence commented:

> We were conscious that this couple were watching us. I was told not to fraternize with them because anything Nazi was bad. We had to be very careful who visited us and our activities. They might have given information away to the Gestapo.[70]

These fears were not unfounded, as subsequent events would soon show.

The political situation within Austria was changing. After the appointment of Gauleiter Josef Bürckel, a Nazi politician, as the new governor of the region in July 1938, Nazi political propaganda flooded into Austria. Gainer noted that in Vienna the propaganda was received rather apathetically. In late July 1938, his report to London stated:

> A fresh wave of anti-Semite hooliganism has disturbed Vienna during the past week. It coincided with the absence of Gauleiter Bürckel [now governor] and immediately subsided on his return. The rank and file of the SA and Hitler Jugend [Hitler Youth] have a healthy respect for Herr Bürckel when he is on the spot but are uncontrolled during his absence which leads again to the conclusion that the Gestapo are not giving Herr Bürckel the support they should.

While Austrians outside Vienna continued to embrace the Nazi regime, the situation in the capital was becoming very different. The persecution of Jews began to affect perceptions of the Nazi regime, and the Viennese began to realize the wider impact of the persecution:

> In the provinces, the population is being speedily trained in a true National Socialist spirit. There is also some genuine enthusiasm for the cause in these

places. This cannot truly be said of Vienna ... That this city is at the moment not considered a particularly salubrious place for a prominent Nazi is proved by the fact that while leaders such as Goebbels and Herr Hess [the deputy Führer] are quite willing to visit Western Austria they take great care to avoid the chief city of the Ostmark.[71]

This report challenges long-held historical views that all Austria remained loyal to the Nazi regime because her anti-Semitism was more virulent than that in Germany. In fact, this report shows that, by July 1938, Vienna had become a city where the top Nazi leaders, such as Goebbels and Hess, were not welcome. It begins to shed a new light on the nuances regarding Austria and Nazism.

Conditions for emigration

At midday on 25 July 1938, the legation was stormed by hundreds of Jews, described as 'terrified hysterical', begging for a visa to go anywhere.[72] With great reluctance, Gainer intervened and telephoned the police to restore some order. The chaos outside the British passport control office now necessitated the permanent presence of a police officer. Every effort was made in the coming weeks to see people with minimum delay; but that did not prevent periodic outbursts of emotion from those waiting in the queue. Kendrick, on his own initiative, sent off numerous letters to as many officials as possible who could potentially help Austria's Jews. Jewish organizations added their own pressure on the British government. The World Jewish Congress implored the British government to use certificates for Palestine, available in Vienna for the period ending 31 March.[73] British policy on emigration to Palestine would soon become a trickier situation for Kendrick. In an attempt to avert a refugee crisis on British soil, the Home Office, in consultation with MI5 and SIS, announced that passport officers could no longer issue temporary visitor visas to refugees.[74] All visas had to be for full emigration and accompanied by the name of a guarantor, who would vouch that the refugee would not be a financial drain on the state. British consuls-general in several European cities were informed that valid Austrian passports would be temporarily acceptable for entry to the United Kingdom, so long as the passport holders could satisfy immigration officers on arrival that they met the requirements. The government soon tightened this legislation.

Prior to the Anschluss, there was an agreement that German and Austrian citizens did not need a visa to enter Britain. On 2 May 1938, Britain had imposed visas requirements on all German and Austrian refugees entering the United Kingdom, including those wishing to go on to the British colonies that were not fully self-governing. The ruling also applied to territories under mandate, such as Palestine. Visas were not required for entry into the British dominions or self-governing colonies. Kendrick looked to those countries to take more Jewish refugees. The standard fee for a visa was stipulated at 10 gold francs for an ordinary visa and 1 gold franc for a transit visa, both valid for a year. Kendrick made an appeal to the dominions and received a reply via the Foreign Office. It outlined in regards to Southern Rhodesia that émigrés must have sufficient funds to support themselves:

The precise sum required is not stated as it is understood that the Southern Rhodesian Government is not anxious to encourage the immigration of aliens . . . The Secretary of State assumes that, as far as the Dominions are concerned, the Passport Control Officer at Vienna is in possession of full instructions as to how to deal with applications for admission into those countries.[75]

Kendrick became increasingly frustrated, and fired off letters to any country that might take in Jewish refugees. In theory, there was no restriction on entry into India and Burma, or any of the British colonies, so long as emigrants had the necessary passport, complied with the visa regulations of the country of immigration and had sufficient financial support.[76] In practice, however, it worked out very differently. The Colonial Office told Kendrick:

Climatic and economic conditions and the existence of large native populations make it extremely difficult to suggest any area in which large scale settlement would be practicable. No such area has yet been found, although certain enquiries are still proceeding.[77]

The high commissioner of the League of Nations for German refugees supported Kendrick and petitioned a large number of colonial governors to consider openings for Austrian refugees holding professional, business or agricultural qualifications. It soon became clear that there were no opportunities for them either. At the end of May, the Passport Control Department in London instructed Kendrick actively to discourage refugees from going to the colonial dependencies, unless they had definite offers of employment.[78] Austrian Jews discovered that it was becoming hard to enter other British colonies. In April, Kendrick wrote to the secretary of state for India, appealing for Jewish refugees to be admitted into India on humanitarian grounds.[79] The reply, six weeks later, from the India Office in Whitehall was not favourable:

> The government of India feels that, in view of the difficulties in the way of foreigners from Western European countries finding employment in India, only such Jewish refugees should be granted visas for India as are found after careful investigation to be not politically undesirable, and who have friends in India who will accept responsibility for finding them employment or further support.[80]

During parliamentary questions in the House of Commons on 23 June, Prime Minister Neville Chamberlain was asked about the number of applications that had been processed in Vienna since the beginning of April for those fleeing on grounds of political or religious persecution. Maurice Jeffes, head of the Passport Control Department, reported that approximately 1,250 visas had been issued during May: 'I know that staff, both at Berlin and Vienna, are after office hours working on into the night to try to cope with the enormous rush of applications they are receiving.'[81] Kendrick estimated that the visa figures for June would be much higher.

John Back of the Passport Control Department in London returned from a visit to Vienna, where he had been struck by the patience and good temper of all members of staff under exceptionally trying circumstances. Prime Minister Chamberlain reported to parliament that Kendrick's staff had been increased from 4 members before the Anschluss to 15, including clerical assistants, examiners, secretaries, clerks and messengers.

By July, Kendrick was still struggling to deal with applications from refugees who sought emigration to Australia. He wrote to Jeffes outlining the impossibilities of his office taking applications for Australia and the Commonwealth. He put forward a solution to the grim situation by appointing a local Jewish committee to vet cases in the first instance

> under the supervision of an Englishman from a Jewish organization in the UK . . . who would act as liaison between the said committee and the Passport Control Officer here, who would then make the final recommendations at his discretion to the Commonwealth Government.

When Jeffes received this recommendation from Kendrick, he scrawled across it: 'We must take a firm line with the Australians in this connection – 15,000 application forms have been issued in Vienna alone and several thousand more in Berlin. To take on the job as proposed would drown Kendrick entirely.'[82]

Kendrick found himself in an impossible situation, with his options becoming severely limited.

Palestine and illegal transports

In the first few weeks after the Anschluss, the emigration of the country's Jews was supported by Adolf Eichmann, who became one of the infamous architects of the 'Final Solution' for the systematic eradication of European Jewry. The policy led to the murder of 6 million Jews and 5 million others by 1945. Eichmann was dispatched to Vienna in March 1938 with orders from the Führer to 'rid Austria of her Jews'. He set up an office in the Austrian capital called the Central Office for Jewish Emigration and was prepared to use his own funds to finance the exit of around 20,000 Austrian Jews to Palestine. Kendrick visited Eichmann's office in Vienna for discussions on ways in which Eichmann could help him with the exit of Jews from the country. Eichmann was keen to work with him, because Kendrick was providing a solution to the problem of how to get Jews out of the Third Reich.

Of all the possible destinations for émigré Jews, Palestine became a thorn in the side of Kendrick's rescue efforts. It seemed an obvious sanctuary for Europe's Jews, but it was under British mandate, with strict quotas for emigration. Between 1936 and early 1938, immigration quotas into Palestine were limited by the British to 12,000, after the Arabs demanded that the British government cease any quota for Jews entering there. In 1937, Kendrick's office issued 214 legal permits for Austrian Jews to enter Palestine.[83] After the Anschluss, that number rose to 2,964; Kendrick and his staff worked indefatigably to enable them to enter Palestine legally. Then Eichmann struck a deal with Kendrick, under which a thousand Jews were given *illegal* visas to enter Palestine. The paperwork was executed by Kendrick's secretary, Evelyn Stamper.

As Kenneth Benton recalled:

They [Jewish émigrés] used to fill up the courtyard by about nine o'clock in the morning and I used to stand on the steps and give them a lecture on what chance they had of getting away. 'Your only chance of getting to Palestine now is either if you've got relatives or a capitalist visa. But you might be able to get to Grenada. You might be able to get to Jamaica' . . . But the stories were so terrible. The regulations were very, very limited. There were very few chances of giving anybody a visa for Palestine in those days. It was all trying to keep the numbers down because they knew the Arabs were going to revolt at some time; and of course they did.[84]

Wherever possible, Kendrick worked within the law on emigration. When those efforts were frustrated by British bureaucracy, he turned a blind eye to illegal transports to Palestine. By July 1938, it was known that 381 illegal migrants had made it into Palestine. Visas were issued to enable a thousand young immigrants to enter Palestine to attend a sports camp. When he sanctioned these temporary visas, Kendrick knew that the youngsters would not return to Austria; and they did not. Kendrick faced daily dilemmas and difficult choices which sometimes determined whether a Jew would survive the Holocaust or not. Sometimes he turned a blind eye to illegal transports to Palestine; but his efforts were frustrated when he was called to account by the Foreign Office. Publicly, Kendrick was forced to disavow these transports on the orders of the British government: 'he showed understanding in a difficult situation, but the law was the law'.[85] Because the British government had issued such orders to him, he did not wish to jeopardize the ongoing legal emigrations; he therefore now had to place pressure on Yugoslavia to annul any illegal visas from other sources that granted permission to cross its territory.

By the end of July 1938, borders in Greece and Yugoslavia were effectively closed to Jews. It was probably the most controversial and painful issue that Kendrick had to deal with as the British passport control officer.

6

THE SPY WHO SAVED A GENERATION

From March 1938, Kendrick embarked on a humanitarian mission that was rooted in a sense of social justice. While he had no qualms about stealing secrets from the enemy and using surreptitious methods to gain them, the persecution of innocent people was different. It is now emerging that Kendrick and his staff saved a generation of Austrian Jews, with official records placing their rescue efforts at between 175 and 200 Jews a day.[1] In a two-month period, this could have been as high as 10,000 saved. It included many of the Viennese intelligentsia: prominent doctors, surgeons, musicians, artists, psychoanalysts, architects and businessmen. Nor was he held back by his Roman Catholic background. This was a period when the Roman Catholic Church, and Christianity in general, was still entrenched in two thousand years of anti-Jewish teachings. He and his wife had many Jewish friends, and in fact his father-in-law was Jewish.

One Jewish doctor whom Kendrick helped was Erwin Pulay, an eminent skin allergy specialist and close friend of Sigmund Freud. Pulay was the grandfather of a well-known British actor, the late Roger Lloyd-Pack (famed for his part as Trigger in the TV comedy series *Only Fools and Horses*). As Lloyd-Pack recalled:

My grandfather's name was on the Black Book – the list of prominent Jews to be rounded up by the Nazis – along with his friend Sigmund Freud. He had to get out of Austria, but that proved not so easy even for someone with a prominent medical position. He tried unsuccessfully to escape illicitly over the border into Switzerland, but eventually came out of Austria on a false passport. My grandfather was the first of the family to come out of Austria, leaving behind his wife and two children (my mother and uncle, George).[2]

Erwin Pulay was able to emigrate to Britain with help of the British liberal politician Lord Reading, himself a Jew. It was Kendrick who secured the necessary visa. In discussions with Lloyd-Pack, it became clear that the family always felt that Erwin had abandoned them, and they never really forgave him. They harboured a sense of betrayal, as he had left them to the horrors that were unfolding in Austria. Later, Lloyd-Pack came to realize just how difficult it was for Jews to emigrate. His grandfather was at immediate risk after the Anschluss and therefore his emigration was the most urgent. It took time to bring Lloyd-Pack's grandmother Ida, mother Uli (Ulrike) and his uncle George out; but by 1939 they, too, had left Austria, aided by the British passport control office. Ironically, just a few years later, during the war, George Pulay was drafted into the Intelligence Corps and served as one of Kendrick's secret listeners. Having escaped Austria, Erwin Pulay separated from Ida and continued as a specialist in his field, gaining respect for his work. The children were raised in England by Ida. Uli went on marry English-born actor Charles Lloyd-Pack.

Those who managed to flee with Kendrick's help included his own physician, Dr Bauer. Bauer was later interned on the Isle of Man during the British invasion scare of 1940. Also Hans Schick, a Jewish lawyer, and his wife Mary; the famous pianist Peter Stadlen and his family; and Trude Holmes, who was born Gertrud Falk. It is believed that Kendrick knew Trude's mother, Olga, who sang with the Vienna State Opera Chorus.[3] Trude's father, Berthold, was a familiar figure in Vienna, as he played chess at the Café Central, a place frequented by Freud and Trotsky. In 1935, Trude had completed a doctorate in psychology at the University of Vienna and studied under Professor Charlotte Bühler. Active in the socialist youth movement in the city, she was a close friend of Wolf Speiser, whose father Paul had been deputy mayor of Vienna. It was not until 1947 that Trude received confirmation that her parents had been deported to the Łódź Ghetto in October 1941 and had perished there in spring 1942.

Some of Europe's finest musicians felt the full impact of the Nazi discrimination against Jews and 'undesirable' artists. Conductor Bruno Walter had already fled the Nazis once – in 1933, from Berlin to Vienna; and now he found himself in potential danger again. He was recording in Paris when news of the Anschluss came, and he took the decision not to return to Vienna. His daughter Lotte was arrested by the Gestapo in Vienna and held in custody until Walter used his influence to secure her release and get her out of the country. From the Vienna Philharmonic Orchestra, a number of Jewish musicians lost their jobs. They included first violinist Josef Geringer, second violinists Berthold Salander and Leopold Föderl, principal clarinettist Rudolf Jettel and oboist Armin Tyroler.

Another public figure who was helped to England by Kendrick was the distinguished Austrian musician, writer and conductor Erwin Stein, along with his wife Sophie and daughter Marion. Stein worked as an editor for the music publishers Boosey & Hawkes in London. Daughter Marion, a concert pianist, studied at the Royal College of Music in London, went on to marry the seventh earl of Harewood and became the countess of Harewood. The marriage eventually ended in divorce, after her husband's extramarital affairs, and she married the Liberal politician and MP for North Devon, Jeremy Thorpe.

Leaving Austria was not easy, as Eric Sanders recalled:

I needed permission to leave Austria. For this I had to provide evidence that I was a Jew, that I was a legal resident in Vienna and had no criminal record. I had to obtain proof that I did not owe any taxes and was not liable for military service. For each of these documents I had to queue at least three times at the competent authority, first to obtain the application form, then to submit it duly filled in and finally collecting the approved document – if it was ready. At each office, I was one of hundreds standing for hours in kilometre-long queues.[4]

Kendrick soon found himself making discretionary decisions to save Jews when they did not meet emigration requirements. One of his future wartime interrogators, Derrick Simon, wrote in his unpublished memoirs that, during this period, Kendrick smuggled Jews and political opponents of the Nazi regime over the border by putting a sign in the back of the car 'Corps Diplomatique'.[5] This meant that the car had diplomatic protection and should not be searched at checkpoints or temporary roadblocks.

Bending the rules

The majority of the Jews whom Kendrick helped received their visas within the boundaries of British immigration laws; but he became increasingly frustrated by the number of Austrian Jews who could not be helped through legitimate means. There was a large number to whom it was proving hard to issue legitimate exit papers. With the pressure of émigrés queuing daily in the corridors outside his office, Kendrick faced a dilemma – how could he help them? Now he began to bend the rules and issue visas on the flimsiest of evidence, and for Jews who did not meet the criteria.

Although Hitler's full-scale programme of annihilation of European Jewry – the Final Solution – was not formulated until 1942, even in 1938 it was clear to the SIS staff working across Europe that Jews and opponents of the Nazi regime were disappearing. There was knowledge, too, of the concentration camps. Pressure mounted on Kendrick to save more Austrian Jews and he faced difficult decisions. Within a fortnight of Hitler's annexation, one of the first cases to pass across his desk was that of a seven-year-old Jewish boy. The Foreign Office had received a request that he be allowed to travel out of Austria on the passport of a British national, Mr Farquharson, of the Institute of Sociology. There was no question that the young boy would be returning to Austria after his 'visit' to England. The endeavour relied on the consent of his parents, the endorsement of Kendrick and someone to act as guarantor in the UK. Although the boy is not named in official documents, he came to Britain successfully, accompanied by Mr Farquharson. His was not an isolated case. A memo from Creswell at the Passport Control Department in London stated: 'We have had several inquiries about the trick of adding the name of an Austrian child to a British passport.'[6]

When the noted Austrian black-and-white portrait photographer Lotte Meitner-Graf came into Holmes' office, the latter exclaimed: 'What are you doing here?'[7]

'I'm Jewish,' she replied. Meitner-Graf was a close friend, but Holmes had not realized that she was Jewish. Meitner-Graf and her husband, the scientist and chemist Walter Meitner, escaped Vienna in August 1938, certainly with the help of Kendrick and Holmes.[8] Philip Franz Meitner recalled:

> One night the British military attaché in Austria turned up at our house and informed my father that the British government wanted him to come to England. He was told a job awaited him. An RAF aircraft was waiting at the airport to transport him and my mother Lotte, and he had only two hours to get his stuff together.[9]

Walter Meitner was provided with a flat in south London and continued his studies at Manchester University, subsequently joining Imperial Chemical Industries. Lotte built up a successful career as a renowned photographer: 10 of her portrait photographs survive in the National Portrait Gallery, including famous figures such as Benjamin Britten, Yehudi Menuhin and Hollywood actress Elizabeth Taylor. Philip Meitner escaped from Vienna a few weeks before his parents. Aged just seven, he was escorted out by an unnamed Frenchwoman, who had already taken a number of children out of Vienna by adding them to her passport as her own.[10] She was a friend of the Meitner-Graf family, visiting the house to teach French to Philip's father. On 16 June 1938, Philip's parents took him to Vienna railway station to meet her. He recalled that she was probably in her twenties, but he did not know whether or not she was married. She sat Philip on her knee during the journey – that much he remembers. They arrived at Calais the same day, disembarked from the train and took a boat to Dover, then a train to London. Philip was taken into the care of the Frankels, who were family friends. The unnamed Frenchwoman returned to Vienna and went on to save two more children in this way. She was later discovered and shot by the Germans.

There was concern, too, for Dr Paul Koretz, an Austrian Jewish lawyer working for the Hollywood film-makers Twentieth Century Fox. He was deemed to be at sufficient risk for the Foreign Office to send a telegram to the passport control office in Vienna. Twentieth Century Fox had made an appeal on behalf of Koretz, a leading employee in the firm's European representation. It requested Koretz's presence at an important consultation, adding that 'he should now live outside [Vienna] and continue in their employ'.[11] Kendrick was asked whether, in view of Koretz's value 'to British commercial interests, if you would do anything possible to facilitate his journey'. It was decided that the easiest way to bring him out of Vienna was to issue a temporary visa, despite the certain knowledge that Koretz would not return to Austria.

Another person who did not qualify for emigration was 19-year-old George Weidenfeld, later founder of the publishing house Weidenfeld & Nicolson. In 1938, he was studying law at the Diplomatic Academy in Vienna.[12] His father was arrested by the Gestapo on 15 March and imprisoned for no other reason than that he was Jewish and his name was on a list of prominent Jews to be rounded up immediately. With emigration to Palestine or the United States impossible, Weidenfeld's English teacher at the academy, Mr Parry-Jones, gave him a letter to take to Kendrick. Weidenfeld recalled the one and only meeting he had with Kendrick that saved his life. With a non-committal letter from a distant relative in England, Weidenfeld arrived at the British passport office with his mother.

'It was doubtful that I had enough support in England to stay there,' he recalled. 'We were shown into Kendrick's office. My mother pleaded with him for a visa.'

'I'm terribly sorry – there's nothing I can do,' said Kendrick. 'You don't have the right papers. You need further support.'

Weidenfeld's mother burst into tears. Kendrick swiftly grabbed Weidenfeld's passport from his hand and stamped it. Kendrick could not grant a permanent visa for Weidenfeld to emigrate, because the fact that he did not have the right papers could easily have been detected. Instead, he issued a three-month temporary visa – something that by now the passport offices had been told not to do by the British government. It was enough to enable Weidenfeld to exit Austria and Kendrick knew that, once in Britain, it would be difficult to send him back. Weidenfeld entered England on 8 August 1938, via Switzerland, on a transmigration visa. Decades later, when speaking about it, Lord Weidenfeld was absolutely clear that, without Kendrick, he would have perished in the Holocaust. After coming to England, he took up a scholarship at King's College London. Just over six months later, after the German occupation of Prague, he noticed that the BBC was advertising for foreign linguists. Being fluent in five languages, he was successful in joining the BBC Monitoring Service, eventually became a news commentator in 1942. He wrote a weekly column about foreign affairs in the *News Chronicle* and was introduced to some of the influential politicians and thinkers of the day. In post-war Britain, he established his own publishing house and became phenomenally successful.

Seventeen-year-old Eric Sanders (original name Ignaz Schwarz) had a similar experience. He presented himself at the British passport office, writing in his diary: 'Fri 20 May. 10 a.m. British Consulate with my course enrolment. Huge queue as usual.' After queuing for hours, he was told by Clara Holmes that he had insufficient papers to emigrate. He recalled:

> She scanned the enrolment details and shook her head. 'That's not continuing your studies. This is just a short course.' She looked at me and whatever she saw in my face was enough to influence her decision. She said, 'Oh, never mind,' and stamped *Approved* on the application form . . . Watching her sign her signature across the 'Approved' stamp, I had no reason to expect that our paths would ever cross again. But cross they did during the war and she would play an important part in my life.[13]

During the war, Sanders first enlisted in the Pioneer Corps, and then transferred to the Special Operations Executive, where he was trained to be dropped behind enemy lines into Austria. He arrived at an address in London to be kitted out for his mission. The lady who opened the door and who issued the kit was Clara Holmes, who was by then working for the Austrian section of SOE. Holmes is also known to have helped Freda Mary Rhein, a governess to English families in Vienna. Rhein was known to the legation because she attended many of Kendrick's social occasions. As a Jew, she had to flee Vienna; and with the help of Kendrick's staff, she emigrated to England and settled in Cambridge. Holmes' daughter Prudence commented:

I remember one occasion when I was told not to go into the salon of our apartment. They didn't want me to see that we were sheltering a Jewish friend of my mother's and Miss Stamper. They smuggled her out of Austria. I am terribly proud of what my mother did to save Austria's Jews.[14]

Another former refugee, Francis Steiner, vividly remembered the day in their family apartment when his mother pleaded on the telephone with Kendrick to get his brother Willi out of Vienna: 'These are things you don't forget.'[15] Steiner's brother had been accepted as a pupil barrister at Gray's Inn in London, but did not have the correct paperwork:

I remember my mother's impassioned pleading for my brother that the necessary documentation had been submitted and the visa should be granted. While the basic conditions were set by the Home Office, ultimately the power was left to the Passport Office to admit or refuse entry. The real discretion lay with him [Kendrick].[16]

Willi Steiner visited the legation and commented:

The consulate premises then were much too small. There were, of course, enormous numbers of people who applied for visas and went there. The result was that the queues sometimes extended into the street and there was a danger that people might be arrested arbitrarily out of the queues.[17]

That summer of 1938, Kendrick stamped a temporary visa for Steiner for three months – knowing it was against the rules to issue temporary visas, and in the certain knowledge that Willi Steiner would not be returning to Austria. His brother Francis also came out of Vienna. [18]

There is the unusual case of two brothers who fled Vienna – Georg Andreas Schwarz and Johann Hans Schwarz. They both changed their surname to Kendrick, in tribute to the man who had saved their lives. Georg Schwarz thus became George Kendrick, and when war broke out in September 1939 he was studying at Lille University in France. The French authorities offered him a choice between internment as an enemy alien and volunteering for the French Foreign Legion. He chose the latter and served with the legion at Oran in Algeria. His unit was then disbanded and he travelled to Portugal to spend some months there, while his mother, Hedwig, arranged for his entry into Britain. As George Kendrick, he enlisted in the British army's Pioneer Corps. [19] His brother, Johann, became John Kendrick and served in the Royal Armoured Corps, then as an interpreter at the interrogations in Munich of Nazi war criminals. Hedwig also changed her surname to Kendrick after her arrival in England.

Other Jews known to have been saved by Kendrick were his family's friends, Ibby Koerner and Poldi Bloch Bauer. While nothing is known today about Ibby Koerner, Poldi Bauer was Kendrick's golfing partner. Kendrick made it possible for Bauer to settle in Vancouver, where he started a timber business called Canadian Pacific Veneer and gained an international reputation. Some years later, Kendrick's grandson Ken Walsh worked for the company for three years. The business was eventually handed over to Bauer's sons and is now called Canfor. While in Canada, the family changed its surname from Bauer to Bentley. It remains extremely grateful to Kendrick.

Viennese-born Klara Modern – whose path had crossed with that of Soviet spy Edith Suschitzky in Vienna in the early 1930s – was working in England at the time of the Anschluss and did not return. Her family, however, was still living in Vienna and was at risk. It was thanks, in part, to the efforts of Kendrick and his staff that they were able to flee. Her brother, Ernst, obtained a visa signed by Betty Hodgson in May 1938. Their sister, Alice, had already left via Switzerland on 23 March 1938 with her husband Franz Alt, and they later went to New York via England.[20] Kendrick was known to have contacts in Switzerland and he may well have been the one to help Klara Modern's family out via Switzerland, through the British author Bryher, who was living there. Bryher, whose real name was Winifred Ellerman, was the daughter of wealthy shipping magnate Sir John Ellerman and was a long-time friend and companion of the American poet H.D. (Hilda Doolittle). Bryher travelled several times to Vienna and Prague to interview applicants for visas.

She later wrote about her rescue efforts, which saved 105 Jews and political refugees from Germany, Austria and Czechoslovakia:

> We were tough. We made loans for travel expenses and retraining on condition that as soon as the borrowers found work, they repaid us back even if it was a small sum each week. In this way our funds were continually employed and as the loans came back we could rescue another person from our long waiting list.[21]

Klara Modern, her sister Alice and brother-in-law Franz were active in 1938 and 1939 in getting other refugees out of Austria. In this, they were helped by Bryher, who sent them money from Switzerland for the purpose.[22] Franz and Alice managed to rescue 30 individuals between 1938 and the outbreak of war the following year. It is not known how many were saved by Klara. In 1944, she went on to marry Charles Deveson, one of Kendrick's intelligence officers.

There were some who did not manage to escape the Nazis. One such from Kendrick's circle was Colonel Grossmann, an unmarried officer who had served in the Kaiser's army in the First World War. He played the piano at several parties held by Kendrick or his secretaries. Prudence Hopkinson recalled:

> After the Anschluss, Grossmann was urged by my mother and the staff to get out of Austria. They promised him: 'We will get you to England.'

Unfortunately, Grossmann went to the equivalent of the British Legion in Vienna and was told that as a distinguished war veteran (even though a Jew) he would be safe.

He remained in Vienna, because he believed that his service to the Kaiser and his decoration for bravery would protect him. But the Nazis were indiscriminate in their targeting of Jews, including those who had fought for their country. The tragedy of his story is that he stayed in Vienna and perished in the Holocaust.

The count, the countess and the aristocratic art dealer

Kendrick had mixed in the highest social circles of Vienna for nearly a decade and a half. Now he drew on these contacts to help the city's Jews.

Thus far, there has been little recognition of (or little information on) the part played in the rescue of Jews by Austrian aristocrats, who brought those Jews at immediate risk from the Nazis to Kendrick's attention. One such person was Countess Cecilia Sternberg, who had been born Cecilia Reventlow Criminil into an aristocratic family in Schleswig-Holstein. At the age of 17, she had married a Bohemian nobleman, Count Leopold Sternberg, and found herself the mistress of two castles and a palace in Vienna. She moved in new circles and by chance met Count Kari Wilczek when they both attended a party at the house of Coco Chanel in Paris. Countess Sternberg found Wilczek quiet and reserved. He was an art connoisseur, described by her as 'a confirmed bachelor and rather eccentric'. He agreed to show her Paris and impart his considerable knowledge of the city's famous landmarks. It marked the beginning of a life-long friendship. Once back in Vienna, Wilczek introduced her to his friends, including the art dealer Count Antoine Seilern.

After the Anschluss, at great personal risk Wilczek sheltered Jews in Palais Wilczek. He had many friends either with Jewish wives or with part Jewish ancestry. Although Wilczek was not rich, his Jewish friends came to him for help in 1938. There is little surviving information about his bravery and personal sacrifice in helping Austrian Jews, except what Cecilia Sternberg wrote of him:

> He protected their property and later their lives as best he could. His became a strange household. He had been forced to dismiss his valet because he believed him not entirely trustworthy. He had to go and forage for food himself, paying high prices for discretion. He had to carry heavy loads back to his flat to feed his hidden guests. There were always two or three, even more, who found at least temporary refuge there.[23]

Wilczek was questioned several times by the Gestapo and his home was searched. But no evidence was ever found against him, because, ahead of any raid, he was warned by a former female student whose boyfriend worked for the Gestapo. In the end, Wilczek was betrayed by a distant relation, in return for an exit visa from the Nazis to visit her lover in Spain. The Austrian aristocracy – including some of the pro-Nazi clique – came to Wilczek's defence and he was released. Wilczek looked to Kendrick to help smuggle his Jewish friends out of Austria. This is known because

> a note found by chance by a friend who has family links with that circle indicates that Count Wilczek knew Kendrick in the summer of 1938, and was referring people to him a couple of months before Kendrick was arrested. Wilczek forwarded to a friend the name and address of Captain Kendrick, for the sake of a Fräulein Steiner who needed to get out with a Kendrick-passport.[24]

There is a postscript to the Kendrick–Wilczek–Sternberg story. Count and Countess Sternberg were able to return to their estate at Častolovice in Czechoslovakia and entertained in a style reminiscent of the pre-war period. Wilczek lived out the war in Austria in poor health; he had a frugal existence, as he had spent his money helping others. At the end of the war, with fears over the Russian treatment of Austrians, a young British officer stationed in Vienna was sent to ascertain that Wilczek and Sternberg were safe.[25] The person who sent that young officer was Kendrick.

Closely connected to this aristocratic circle was the art historian and collector Count Antoine Seilern. He had been born in Farnham, in the English county of Surrey, the son of Count Carl von Seilern und Aspang and the American-born Antoinette Woerishoffer. His mother died five days after his birth and he was raised by his grandmother in Vienna. Between 1933 and 1939, he attended the University of Vienna to study art history. There, Seilern became close friends with the notable art collector Count Karl Lanckoronski. Seilern was known to Kendrick as he was part of the social scene in Vienna in the 1930s. Within a year of the annexation of Austria, Seilern had left Austria for Britain, taking with him his collection of art and drawings. Because he had British nationality, his exit posed no problem. In England, he continued to support his Jewish émigré art colleagues, one example being the financial help he gave the Austrian art historian Ludwig Münz. He also helped his friend Johannes Wilde, an expert on the drawings of Michelangelo, to bring his collection of books out of Austria. Wilde's wife was Jewish and it was therefore essential to get both of them out of the country.

In 1939, Seilern purchased Hogg Lane Farm, near Chesham in Buckinghamshire, just a few miles from Latimer House, one of Kendrick's top-secret wartime listening stations. Seilern enlisted in the Pioneer Corps, transferred to the Royal Artillery and, in November 1944, was commissioned into the Intelligence Corps on the recommendation of Kendrick, his old acquaintance from Vienna.[26] The nature of Seilern's work in the unit is unknown, but is thought to have involved a mysterious secret mission abroad.

Bribes, accusations and favouritism

The tension and stress of passport work was intensified by accusations against Kendrick and his staff of bribery and favouritism towards those who received visas. Gainer told London:

The wildest accusations are made daily against Kendrick, myself and all of the staff. We are accused of favouritism and even of accepting bribes. It is admitted that some people have to be firmly dealt with because if discipline were relaxed, it would be quite impossible to handle the large crowd which flock to the offices.[27]

The allegation of bribes in exchange for visas was a serious one. Kendrick and Gainer undertook an exhaustive investigation and concluded that none of their staff was guilty of such activity either during or outside working hours. Even so, the accusations did not go away. Miss Felner of the German Jewish Aid Committee in London visited Vienna in early August and complained to the Home Office that she found conditions chaotic, with corruption rampant in official circles; there was, she reported, nothing that could not be bought – including forged passports.[28] Kendrick's investigations were severely hampered by the fact that the Viennese police were implicated, so he could not ask for their help: it was reported that the police were taking buses full of Jews over the border at night into Czechoslovakia and Switzerland in order to rid Austria of some of its Jews.[29]

There were other problems for Kendrick. Mary Ormerod, secretary of the Co-ordinating Committee for Refugees from Austria, was offering proof that certain Jews had the financial means to support themselves, in the form of assets held outside Germany to aid their emigration from Austria. She argued to the Foreign Office that the refugee work of her committee was being seriously hampered by the lack of confidential communications with Vienna.[30] She suggested that details of these assets could be sent via the diplomatic bag, which would not be intercepted and its contents not disclosed to the Nazi regime. The details could then be given to Kendrick in person at his office.

Ormerod said she had definite proof that:

Letters and telegrams sent through the ordinary channels were sometimes never delivered and as a result, in several cases already, Captain Kendrick had refused visas to people some days after the Home Office had instructed him to grant them. In one such case, the person concerned had been rearrested before confirmation of an undelivered telegram came by bag.[31]

In May 1938, Ormerod lodged a formal complaint against Kendrick's secretary Evelyn Stamper, accusing her of mistreating Jewish visa applicants. Apart from her secret SIS duties, Stamper's job at the passport control office during 1938 was to categorize émigrés and assess whether they were genuine or persons who might become a drain on Britain's resources. Ormerod complained that Stamper was asking emigrants whether they were Jewish, as a way of categorizing them; in her eyes, this amounted to anti-Semitism. The allegation was taken seriously, but it was not the only one. Stamper was accused of telling someone in an abrupt tone: 'We cannot have any Jews in England.' And 'no visas for the United Kingdom will be given to people of Jewish origin'.[32] Ormerod was quick to add that, during her visits to Vienna, she had always found Kendrick and his staff to be 'helpful and sympathetic to the situation of Vienna's Jews'.[33] Stamper defended herself by saying that she had done everything possible to help Jews and that many thousand could bear witness to that. Today there is insufficient evidence to assess whether the accusations against Stamper were true, but Kendrick investigated the allegations at the time. He and Consul-General Gainer took the view that asking whether someone was Jewish was not incivility on the part of Miss Stamper, and nor was it anti-Semitism.[34]

The stress became too much for Stamper and she tendered her resignation, requesting a month's sick leave, in lieu of working out her notice. It was granted. Kendrick continued to investigate and concluded that Ormerod's complaints had been exaggerated. As Gainer wrote: 'if certain instances appeared to be rudeness, it could be ascribed entirely to the overwork and nerve-strain resulting from the enormous pressure under which his staff were working'. Gainer went on: 'No one who has not first hand knowledge of the conditions in Vienna can fully understand the strain which the Passport Control Officer and his staff are undergoing.'[35]

The Passport Control Department in London received testimony from an official at the World Zionist Organization in London, which was headed by Dr

Chaim Weizmann (later first president of the State of Israel). It endorsed Kendrick's work and that of his staff, and expressed

> the great gratitude of the Jews for the extreme courtesy and consideration with which applicants for permits and visas were treated by the Passport Control staff at Vienna . . . going to the British Consulate was for the Viennese Jews like passing from hell to heaven.[36]

Known for his fairness and objectivity, Kendrick defended his staff in difficult times, without denying the challenges they faced on a daily basis. At the end of a long day under extreme emotional strain, his staff were overtired, having had to deal with hundreds of hysterical Jews, some of whom had to be turned away. By August 1938, Maurice Jeffes, head of the Passport Control Department in London, estimated that there were still approximately half a million non-Aryans in Vienna and admitted that it was not possible to grant a visa to them all. According to another passport official in London, Kendrick's staff faced 'an unprecedented and almost intolerable situation'.[37]

The accusation of favouritism was the hardest allegation to counter. Gainer was accused of favouring non-Jewish businessmen who sought to travel to Britain. He dismissed such allegations, saying 'knowing how difficult it is to get through the crowds they apply to me or members of my staff by letter or in person and they are given a card which allows them to pass through the crowds'.[38] Members of the British diplomatic and consular services in other countries occasionally tried to get visas for their Viennese friends. Gainer admitted that he felt bound to honour the stream of personal letters which he received from them and recommended to Kendrick that he give them priority.

Jews and fake baptisms

With increasing pressure from London to limit immigration, Kendrick started to issue false passports to Jews. Revd Hugh Grimes, chaplain of Christ Church (the Anglican church in Vienna) and pastor to the British legation, was also working for Kendrick and SIS. Grimes has been described as 'a shadowy figure, an intellectual priest, a former Cambridge scholar who taught at university before taking Holy Orders'.[39] The triangle of Kendrick–Grimes–Richter (of the passport control office) was involved in a number of humanitarian efforts for Austria's Jews. In his capacity as a clergyman, Grimes issued false baptism certificates with the help of Richter, who was a verger at the church. They used a loophole in the emigration rules to issue false baptism certificates to Jews without a real baptism ceremony taking place.[40] Jews were required to pay for one of these baptism certificates, and this money then appears to have been used by Richter to supplement SIS's meagre finances for operations in the region.

While Christ Church was undergoing repairs that summer, Jews queued outside Grimes' apartment on Metternichgasse and entered there to learn the Lord's Prayer and the catechism, so that they had some basic knowledge of Anglicanism if they chanced to be questioned by the German authorities. It was a political baptism, solely to enable them to leave the country. There was no immersion in water and no intention that they should become practising Anglicans. They were issued with a backdated certificate and prayer book as evidence of their baptism. Between 13 March and 25 July, Grimes baptized some 900 Jews, including 93 on 24 July and as many as 224 the following day.[41]

By July 1938, Grimes had come under suspicion as a British spy, possibly because of his association with Richter and the fact that Richter was still meeting Tucek. Or perhaps Tucek had merely presumed that Grimes also worked for SIS. Either way, it meant that Grimes was forced to make a swift exit from Vienna, on pretence of a holiday. The Foreign Office debated whether or not to send him back to Vienna later that summer, but this was deemed too risky. In fact, the Gestapo were waiting to arrest him if he re-entered Austria. Instead, 66-year-old Revd Fred Collard arrived in Vienna as Grimes' replacement. The choice of Collard may not have been totally coincidental: having served in the Royal Army Medical Corps in the First World War, he had been posted in 1918 to the British army of occupation in Cologne, where Kendrick was stationed. Thus, the two men may have known each other from then.

Collard continued with Grimes' humanitarian rescue work and with issuing false baptism certificates. The workload was so heavy that he looked for help with the paperwork. Edmund Henry Pollitzer, a 46-year-old Viennese Jew, presented himself with a recommendation from Grimes. He wrote out the baptismal certificates, ready for Collard to sign. From time to time, Pollitzer was given donations for the church by grateful 'Jewish converts'. Pollitzer was in fact a close friend of Kendrick's and one of his agents. He himself managed to escape later on a false baptism certificate, but not until the Gestapo had significantly harassed him.

Protecting the family

Vienna became a city where allegiance to Hitler and Nazism was a non-negotiable absolute. Those who were not overtly on the Nazi side were viewed with extreme suspicion. These were dangerous times – and not only for the city's Jews. Communism was banned and a thousand communists were arrested in the early days of the Anschluss. The danger came closer to home when Kendrick's daughter and son-in-law were suspected of being Jewish for not draping a swastika flag from their apartment. Kendrick immediately provided them with a Union Flag from the legation, which they promptly hung from the roof of their house. As his granddaughter Barbara recalled:

> The flag was so large that it almost reached the pavement. We had to wear tiny Union Jack brooches on our coats, otherwise we would have been mistaken for Jews. We already saw what was happening to Jews. One day, we returned from the park with our nanny Deta, wearing tiny swastika brooches, which we proudly showed our mother. Our friends had been wearing swastika brooches, but preferred our Union Jack ones so we had swapped them. Of course, the swastika brooches were swiftly confiscated.[42]

Even the homes of foreign nationals were not exempt from Gestapo raids. Kendrick's grandson, Ken Walsh, recalled:

Things got difficult for us. The Gestapo turned their attention to our household. They banged on the door one day and searched the place to see if we had any Jewish connections. They pulled out all our books and stamped them inside with a swastika. Our pictures and carpets were also stamped.[43]

By June 1938, Kendrick deemed it no longer safe for his family to remain in Vienna and began arrangements for their travel to the United Kingdom. Their exit from Austria was precipitated by wider threats in the region, with concerns that a German invasion of Czechoslovakia was imminent. That would have impelled the whole region towards war. Son-in-law Geoffrey left for Glasgow, ahead of his wife and family. On 19 July, Gladys and the children (Barbara and Ken), accompanied by the family cook Poldi, said their farewells at Vienna's main railway station. On the platform to see them off was Edmund Pollitzer, the trusted family friend and one of Kendrick's agents. Barbara recalls:

For my mother [Gladys], the departure was a terrible wrench because she had spent her formative years in Vienna. We children had only known Vienna for a few years and were embarking on a strange new life. But the Vienna we loved had gone.[44]

There was no question of Kendrick leaving with them. As far as his family knew, he had essential duties as the British passport control officer. Even in summer 1938, they did not realize his true role in SIS. Kendrick remained in Vienna with Norah until personal danger the following month decided his fate.

Agents at risk

Events surrounding Czechoslovakia continued to escalate and every diplomatic effort was made that July to prevent an invasion by German forces. Kendrick continued to meet agents and contacts working out of Czechoslovakia who were bringing him intelligence. One of them is believed by his family to have been Willi Bondi. He lived in Brno in Czechoslovakia, a relatively quick train journey from Vienna, which he and his family used to visit regularly on business and to go to the theatres. As great-nephew Peter Barber comments:

Willi's occupation had always been very vague up until 1938. We did not really know what his work was, and he was regarded by his nieces as benevolent but not particularly bright in comparison with the rest of the family. This may have been subterfuge however, since later the family came to understand that he was a skilful wheeler-dealer.[45]

Bondi's two sisters also lived in Brno and were married to two brothers – the Fleischers – who ran a successful import-export business. Leo Fleischer had assets (and presumably contacts) in London.[46] Sometime during or after 1938, Bondi began to work for the Fleischer business in Brno, probably as a cover for his undercover work. His passport, which survives among family papers, shows repeated border crossings between Czechoslovakia and Austria on 21, 28 and 30 July, and finally on 4 August 1938 – the crucial period, when it was believed the Germans might invade. During these day trips, it is believed that he was passing urgent intelligence to Kendrick.[47] As Barber recalls:

A clue to my great-uncle Willi's clandestine work may be ascertained from events which unfolded for Bondi in 1941. He and other members of my family had already been arrested more than once after the Nazi occupation of Czechoslovakia in March 1939. They were accused by the Germans of being communists, but they were, in fact, social democrats. Willi spent four months in prison in 1940 and was subjected to two sets of interrogations again in 1941: one because he had befriended a German soldier who was homosexual, although he did not have a relationship with him. The Germans may have suspected that Bondi was gaining military intelligence from the soldier. The second political interrogation could have been due to German suspicions that Bondi was working for British intelligence, probably for Kendrick in 1938. The interrogation reports make it quite clear that he had been arrested, not because of his Jewish background, but because of other activities. A telling point is that Bondi was shot in Auschwitz on 30 August 1941 for political reasons, and not as a Jew. For us as a family, it is difficult to be sure about certain aspects of his life. There is a sense that something was going on because of his travels. Finding a paper trail has been elusive because of the nature of his undercover work, believed to have been conducted from Brno and passed through meetings with Kendrick or an intermediary in Vienna.[48]

It is highly probable (but not certain) that other members of the Fleischer family had contact with Kendrick, too.

On 2 August 1938, a case was reported to Kendrick that related to an Australian couple, Mr and Mrs Cecil Rhodes-Smith, who had been stopped at the frontier town of Neu Bentschen (today, Zbąszynek in Poland) because the border guards mistakenly thought they needed a special visa as British subjects.[49] When it was made clear to the authorities that, as Australian citizens, they did not legally require a visa to travel, they were permitted to cross the border and continue on their journey. Although they were both Australian by nationality, Cecil Rhodes-Smith had been born in Cape Town, South Africa, circa 1896 and was of the same generation as Kendrick. While the couple were not detained on suspicion of espionage, it is possible that they had connections to Kendrick and may have been one of his contacts. For this Australian couple to have been travelling in parts of Nazi Germany on holiday seems perhaps more than mere coincidence. Rhodes-Smith was the managing director of Felt and Textiles of Australia Ltd, was a pioneer in wool carbonizing in the country and a wool exporter.[50] The nature of his business at that time would have provided legitimate cover for him to occasionally pass information back to the British.

A German invasion of Czechoslovakia was averted by the signing of the Munich Agreement a few months later, in September 1938, by British Prime Minister Neville Chamberlain and Adolf Hitler. To appease Hitler and avoid a war with Germany in autumn 1938, for which Britain was ill-prepared, Chamberlain conceded the Sudetenland to Germany, in return for the non-invasion of Czechoslovakia. In the weeks prior to Munich, however, as the diplomatic wheels were turning behind the scenes, a crisis was brewing that would place the whole SIS network in Europe at risk.

Betrayal

In the months following the Anschluss, Karl Tucek continued actively to gather damning evidence against Richter and Kendrick. Although he still did not know Kendrick's real name, he continued to meet Richter regularly, and Richter had no suspicions that anything was amiss. By June 1938, Tucek was working for another Abwehr agent, Captain Sokolowski of the German navy and head of the Abwehr station at Wilhelmshaven, although ultimately he was still with the Abwehr station in Vienna (Ast. Wien) under Major Rohleder. Tucek used a number of aliases, including Touceck, Tull and Tullinger.[51] His role was now exclusively to provide 'chickenfeed' to the British on the naval shipyard at Wilhelmshaven and the Schichau-Werke. Abwehr correspondence between a German naval officer named Otto Schulz and Lieutenant Colonel Bamler referred to 'a GV-Mann [secret service man] belonging to Ast. Wien who was passing chickenfeed to the British on the German battleships *Scharnhorst* and *Gneisenau*'.[52] These two battleships were high on Kendrick's list for intelligence. The 'GV-Mann' mentioned was certainly Tucek/Tullinger. Bamler signed off all chickenfeed on behalf of Admiral Canaris (the head of the Abwehr) as the highest ranking of Canaris's staff. Bamler endorsed the information that was passed from Tucek to Richter for Kendrick. Construction was under way at Wilhelmshaven on another German battleship, *Tirpitz*. Kendrick expected to receive information from Tucek on its strength, armour and capacity.

On 17 July 1938, Richter met Tucek for what turned out to be their final encounter. Afterwards, Tucek filed his report with his Abwehr handler, with devastating consequences. The Abwehr held onto the information, so that it could strike at Kendrick at a time of its choosing. The Tucek affair would soon have ramifications for Kendrick's whole network and for SIS agents in passport offices across Europe. For decades, speculation was rife that it was Kendrick's colleague Dick Ellis who had been the double agent who had betrayed him and the SIS network.[53] Ellis always denied this, and it has never been proved. Ellis later argued that a lack of formal intelligence training had led him to inadvertently give away the SIS network to Berlin-based Russian agents, who (unbeknownst to him) were working for German intelligence. However, new research undertaken for this book clearly demonstrates that Kendrick was betrayed by Tucek, not Ellis.

At this time, Kendrick received notification that the British legation and passport control office in Vienna would close, because Austria was now part of the Third Reich and visa business was to be transferred to Berlin. In the end, it did not close that summer. As Prudence Hopkinson recalls:

My mother and other staff at the passport office started to pack because they understood that it was about to close. We prepared to leave Vienna. It was suggested that they all have a last holiday with the Kendricks in Austria before everyone left the country. They agreed to meet instead at Amiens in France, rather than remain in Austria, which was becoming too dangerous. But events overtook their holiday plans.[54]

On Saturday, 13 August, the secret police arrested Richter on the Elisabeth-Promenade, just after he had locked up the British passport office. He was found to be carrying a large sum of cash, amounting to 1,000 Reichsmarks, in an envelope marked 'Capt. Kendrick, Brit. Passport Office'. News of Richter's arrest did not reach the British legation until the Monday morning.

Gainer made immediate enquiries and was informed by the Gestapo that Richter had been arrested on suspicion of contravening currency regulations by being in possession of an extraordinarily large amount of money for a minor official of a passport office.[55] Possibly suspecting that he could be at risk, Kendrick made preparations to leave Vienna on the pretence of a three-week holiday to England with his wife. They planned to leave by the end of the week because, had they left immediately, they would have aroused suspicion.

The Gestapo provided reassurance to Gainer that Richter's case would be dealt with quickly and their investigations concluded by the end of the week. Gainer established from private discussions with the Gestapo that Richter had been under suspicion for some time for allegedly undertaking dishonest financial transactions, by extracting money in return for visas. The Gestapo said that this money was rightfully due to the Third Reich and that Richter would face criminal charges. Gainer realized that this explanation was untrue, as Richter had been arrested specifically by No. 3 Section of the Gestapo, which was responsible for counter-espionage. Gainer now feared that this was not, in fact, a criminal investigation, but that Richter's activities as an agent for SIS had been uncovered.

Richter's nationality was a further complicating factor. Shortly after the Anschluss, Gainer's predecessor had issued Richter with a British passport to protect him from arrest, because of his Jewish background. Richter's original application form for the British passport was found to have been incorrectly completed and his claim to British nationality was based on his apparent naturalization in Great Britain in 1908. Gainer wrote to Ambassador Henderson in Berlin that there may have been special reasons why his predecessor had granted Richter a British passport: 'I consider it advisable to regard him as of dual nationality and while keeping in touch with the police on the matter to allow the case to take its natural course.'[56]

It was clear from Gainer's approach of leaving Richter to his fate that the Foreign Office was not going to jeopardize the SIS network by raising further objections to Richter's arrest. John Back of the Passport Control Department in London arrived in Vienna to relieve Kendrick during his three-week holiday. En route back to England, Kendrick had originally planned a two-day break in Salzburg, stopping briefly at the ski resort of Kitzbühel, before travelling to Amiens in France to meet up with his secretaries, Holmes and Stamper. The secretaries had already left Vienna for Kitzbühel, where Kendrick's predecessor Alban Ernan Forbes-Dennis and his wife Phyllis Bottome were running a finishing school at the Tennerhof.

On the afternoon of Tuesday, 16 August 1938, tired and strained from months of intense work at the passport control office, Kendrick left his apartment in Vienna with Norah. The arrest of Richter just days earlier had made Kendrick edgy. His long-serving and loyal chauffeur, Herr Bernklau, drove them to a hotel near Innsbruck for an overnight stop. That same evening, the Gestapo called at Kendrick's apartment in Vienna to find it empty. They learned that Kendrick and his wife had already left the city. All frontier posts were immediately notified.

Kendrick and Norah left the hotel at Innsbruck at dawn the following morning, Wednesday, 17 August. It was a two-hour journey and 180km to the border town of Freilassing. On the way, an unidentified vehicle swerved at the car and tried to force it off the road. This unsuccessful assassination attempt confirmed to Kendrick that his life was in danger. He ordered Herr Bernklau to drive non-stop to the border.

It was 8 a.m. as they finally neared Freilassing.[57] An unexpected checkpoint blocked the road. Sitting in the back of the car, Kendrick strained to see ahead.

'Damn!' he muttered to Norah.

The guard's hand went up and the car slowed to a halt. Kendrick was ordered out and the car was searched thoroughly. Norah was allowed to return to Vienna with Bernklau, while Kendrick was escorted separately back to Gestapo headquarters in Vienna.

The Gestapo finally had the elusive SIS spymaster.

7

AT THE MERCY OF THE GESTAPO

The arrest of 57-year-old Kendrick made headline news around the world. 'Secret Police arrest British Passport Chief' was one heading in the *News Chronicle*.[1] The events in Vienna caused panic in Whitehall, with fears that the whole SIS network in Europe may have been compromised. Kendrick was considered by SIS to be 'one of their best heads of station'.[2] British Foreign Secretary Lord Halifax was attending a shooting party at Garrowby, in the north of England, when he was interrupted with the news. It was not the first time that Kendrick had got into difficulties with the authorities in Austria. Prior to the German annexation of Austria, he had come under suspicion from the political police for alleged espionage activities against Mussolini in Italy. He had been forced to leave temporarily, smuggled to the border in the back of a diplomatic car by Sir Dudley Forwood, honorary attaché at the British legation.[3]

The Abwehr had taken so long to penetrate the SIS because of the belief that the British secret service abroad was run under cover of the military attaché at the British embassy, rather than through the passport offices.[4]

Kendrick was taken into a room with bright lights, a single table and chair. It was the first of many 'Soviet-style' eight-hour interrogations by Franz Huber, head of the Gestapo in Vienna, during which he was shocked by how much the Germans knew about SIS's European network.[5] Aside from long interrogations at night, he was also subjected to sleep deprivation.

The first question Huber asked him was: 'Where are the secretaries?'[6]

Kendrick said nothing. The question confirmed in his mind that, while his secretaries had not yet been found, they were also being implicated in the espionage. Unknown to him, Holmes, her daughter Prudence and Stamper had already got to the border. Although the frontiers were on alert, the guards were watching out for two lone secretaries, rather than two women with a young girl. As they crossed the border, they attached themselves to two other British families, so that the guards thought they were all travelling together. When they arrived at Amiens two days later, they expected to meet Kendrick and his wife. Prudence, a teenager at the time, recalled:

> Getting to Amiens within two days was a bit tight for us. We arrived at the hotel very late in the evening to find the Kendricks were not there. It was only when we reached Boulogne and bought an English newspaper that we saw the headlines that he had been arrested. Our reaction was one of shock. We genuinely worried for his safety because one could never predict what the Nazis might do.[7]

There is no evidence that Kendrick was tortured while in custody, or that he gave anything away.[8] The Abwehr was traditionally anti-Nazi and had a respect for SIS, since they were both military intelligence organizations composed of gentleman officers.

'One of our best rooms'

The gravity of Kendrick's arrest led to a series of urgent telegrams between London and the British ambassador in Berlin, Sir Nevile Henderson.[9] Henderson told the Foreign Office that Kendrick's treatment 'differed in no way from the practices usually observed in Moscow'.[10] The Gestapo reassured the British government that Kendrick was being well treated, permitted such items as tobacco and newspapers, and had been given 'one of our best rooms'.[11] He was held in an attic room next to former Chancellor Schuschnigg and Baron Louis Rothschild. Rothschild's business assets had already been seized by the regime. He survived the Holocaust, but the majority of his belongings were never recovered.[12]

Kenneth Benton supported Norah Kendrick at the apartment and helped her to contact the appropriate British officials. Consul-General Gainer telephoned Gestapo headquarters immediately and was told that no information was available and anything of relevance would be passed on. He then phoned Henderson in Berlin. The concern about Kendrick's safety was compounded by the fact that passport control officers had no diplomatic immunity at this time.[13]

The morning after the arrest, Henderson visited Ernst von Weizsäcker, the German state secretary for foreign affairs in Berlin, and lodged a formal protest. Von Weizsäcker told him: 'Information from Vienna suggests the police had brought charges of very serious anti-German espionage activities against him [Kendrick] and that under international law Consular Officers did not enjoy diplomatic immunity in cases of such gravity.'[14]

'I am wholly aware of Kendrick's reputation and he is incapable of incorrect behaviour of the kind alleged,' replied Henderson.

Von Weizsäcker went on: 'May I remind you that only a few days ago one of Kendrick's staff was arrested on the same charges.'

Henderson went back on the defence: 'The German government has the right to undertake enquiries about Kendrick but in the meantime, he should at least be allowed to return to his apartment.'

'I'm afraid I cannot allow that,' responded von Weizsäcker.

Henderson left without making any progress. In a long cypher to the Foreign Office, he concluded: 'I fear that Richter's arrest has complicated this unfortunate affair, since Captain Kendrick's attempted departure on leave immediately after it will certainly be regarded as inspired by guilty conscience.'[15]

In Kendrick's absence, Benton took over as the British passport officer. Gainer dispatched him and the temporary vice-consul, Cecil King, to the Hotel Metropole to talk directly to Huber.[16] Gainer issued clear instructions to them to 'protest energetically against Captain Kendrick's arrest, to enquire the reason for it and to request permission to see him'.[17]

They were received personally by Huber and informed:

He is being charged with actions detrimental to the German Reich, committed in Germany. He has not been arrested without good reason. His arrest was carried out on my personal orders and the details immediately reported to Berlin. The situation is all the more grave, gentlemen, because Captain Kendrick has an official position. The matter is now down to Berlin, I will not act further without instruction from Berlin.[18]

'Can we visit him?' asked King.

'Not without permission from the Berlin authorities. I personally guarantee that Captain Kendrick will be well looked after and properly treated. He can have papers, cigarettes and food or anything else sent to him,' said Huber.

Benton asked if Kendrick could be released immediately, but was given a firm 'no'. He handed over a parcel of Kendrick's pyjamas and shaving things. At no point did Benton come under suspicion of espionage himself, although it is now known that he was on the payroll of SIS. While he and King were at Gestapo headquarters, Gainer sent a strongly worded protest by dispatch messenger to Seyss-Inquart, state governor of Austria. He received an immediate reply that an investigation was under way into the case and, as soon as full particulars were received, a further communication would be sent to him personally.

Once back at the legation, Benton was ordered to burn papers and documents as a precaution, in case the Gestapo mounted a raid. Stewart Menzies, who would become the new head of SIS in 1939, reassured the Foreign Office that there was not the slightest possibility of any compromising material being found there.[19]

That evening, Gainer cabled a long cypher to the Foreign Office outlining the day's events. The reply he received told him to inform the German Ministry of Foreign Affairs that he took a very serious view of the arrest of an officer of His Majesty's government:

In arresting Kendrick, the Germans may be technically within their rights, but even supposing there were sufficiently serious grounds to justify an arrest, they cannot be absolved from the charge of grave discourtesy in acting without prior communication with yourself.[20]

The German government used the excuse that Kendrick had been arrested for spying in a German military zone close to the border, where army manoeuvres were taking place. But this was a cover for the fact that he had been betrayed by an Abwehr agent. That evening, Ambassador Henderson attended a soirée at the French embassy in Berlin. In conversation with Joachim von Ribbentrop, the German foreign minister, he raised the subject of Kendrick. Von Ribbentrop's attitude was conciliatory and he admitted that, 'whilst espionage was an unpleasant affair, the matter must be bridged over'.[21] It became clear from the conversation that the secret police had acted without his knowledge. Christopher Andrew, author of the official history of MI5, writes that Kendrick's arrest may have been timed to prevent him from discovering the plans for Operation Green, the German invasion of Czechoslovakia (which finally came in March 1939).[22] German military manoeuvres for the operation were already taking place near the Austrian border and Kendrick had allegedly passed nearby on his way to Freilassing on 17 August.

Reverend Grimes revisited

Kendrick was not the only British subject to be attracting attention from the Gestapo. London was contemplating sending Revd Grimes back to Vienna.[23] He had left Vienna in July and was still suspected by the Germans of having links to British intelligence. On 16 August, the Gestapo raided his flat in Vienna and found Revd Collard occupying it. A number of Jews were congregating there, waiting for Edmund Pollitzer to distribute their pre-dated false baptism certificates. After a search of the premises, the Gestapo confiscated the baptismal registers and declared the baptism certificates illegal. Collard defended Pollitzer and argued that, because of the large volume of certificates being processed, Pollitzer had signed many without reading them. His explanation made no impact. Collard, Pollitzer and an unnamed woman were arrested and taken to Gestapo headquarters for questioning.[24]

It was no coincidence that the raid occurred on the same day the Gestapo arrived at Kendrick's empty apartment to arrest him. The Gestapo were linking Grimes and Pollitzer to Kendrick. Their raid was portrayed as concern over forged baptism certificates, but in reality they were breaking up a spy ring. Grimes and Pollitzer were both working for Kendrick.

After interrogating him at the Hotel Metropole, the Gestapo decided that Collard was not engaged in espionage. The baptismal registers were returned and he was released, but Pollitzer was detained. Two days later, on 18 August, the Gestapo appeared again at Grimes' apartment with questions about money that Pollitzer was alleged to have left there. They were handed cash found on the premises.

The situation continued to cause concern in Whitehall and SIS. Henderson persisted in trying to secure Kendrick's release. Benton recalled that it was 'very unlikely that Kendrick disclosed any information. But what is certainly true is that he was told a great deal about what they knew of his work and of our work in general throughout Europe.'[25]

Kendrick was held for less than four days. If the Abwehr and Gestapo had seriously wanted to 'break him down' to gain information, they would have held him for longer.

Release and expulsion

On the morning of Saturday, 20 August, Henderson received a request from von Weizsäcker for an immediate face-to-face meeting. The two men exchanged brief diplomatic and civil pleasantries before von Weizsäcker said that the German government 'took a very serious view of Captain Kendrick's intelligence service activities and intended to raise with His Majesty's government the whole question of functions of Passport Control Officers'.[26] It was proof – if proof were needed – that other passport officers in Europe were falling under suspicion, too. Henderson was then informed that Kendrick would be released at noon that day, on condition that he left Austria within 24 hours. He was also told that Kendrick had admitted to being engaged in spying activities against Germany.

'That is quite inconceivable,' protested Henderson.

'I am quite sure of the facts,' replied von Weizsäcker. 'Captain Kendrick will explain everything on his return to London.'

'What proof do you have?' asked Henderson.

'The German Government prefers not to produce them. In my opinion the British Intelligence Service is the best in the world, but they have been extraordinarily stupid in Vienna. To avoid further trouble, I must tell you that it would be better if vice-consul Walker does not return to Vienna. He is similarly implicated.'[27]

A tired and badly shaken Kendrick was released at noon, as the German government issued a brief public statement that proof had been obtained of his espionage activities.

Today, in interpreting the events of over 80 years ago, it is true that the Third Reich could have taken far more severe measures against Kendrick than expulsion. It is probable that, with the Munich Agreement coming up the following month, the Germans wished to remain on friendly terms with Britain. The expulsion was intended to send a strong warning to Britain about its spying activities. Henderson telephoned the Foreign Office and reported that

the worldwide activity and methods of the British Secret Service are not unknown in Germany. Captain Kendrick's case is not the only one about which the authorities have information, it was only in view of its exceptional gravity that it was in his case considered necessary [by the Germans] to take action.[28]

SIS had been compromised in Europe at this time. Just how much the German secret service knew about SIS activities is revealed in declassified Foreign Office files. On his release, Kendrick was able to inform SIS and the Foreign Office that the German intelligence service had 'the fullest information regarding his whole organisation'.[29] This was supported by evidence about exact dates and places, and even photographs.

Kendrick returned to his apartment in Hietzing under police escort.[30] SIS was taking no chances with their spymaster and intended to smuggle him out of Austria quietly and swiftly before the Germans changed their minds. Gainer arrived at Kendrick's apartment to discuss the best route out. He instructed Vice-Consul King simply to inform any press correspondents who called at the legation or who telephoned that Captain Kendrick was to be released at some point that day: it was feared that any interviews by the press would delay Kendrick's departure. In the short time that Gainer spent with Kendrick that afternoon, he established from him that the secret police had full information on all his agents, including Richter, Walker and Grimes.[31]

Kendrick and his wife left Vienna at 2.30 p.m. that day. The aim was to get them over the border within two hours. The Swiss and French frontiers were deemed to be too far and there was the risk of substantial delay in the event of a mechanical breakdown or accident. No seats were available on any flights out of Vienna, and the train departure times did not allow for getting Kendrick out within two hours. Only the border posts of Czechoslovakia and Hungary could be reached by car in under two hours. Gainer's chauffeur smuggled the Kendricks over the border into Hungary at 4 p.m. in his car. While they were en route to Budapest, the press gathered outside the legation in Vienna for news. Seeing Gainer arrive at the legation in a chauffeur-driven car, they believed Kendrick to be still in the building. Only when Kendrick was safely in Hungary were reporters informed that he had already left Vienna. Kendrick and his wife arrived in Budapest at 8.30 p.m.[32] He spent the following day in the city with Mr A. Gascoigne at the British embassy, as Gascoigne made arrangements for the flight back to England.

On 22 August, Gascoigne accompanied Kendrick and his wife to Budapest airport to board a flight at 9.30 a.m. for London, via Prague and Rotterdam.[33]

Kendrick's expulsion was prominently reported in the world's media, under headlines such as 'Captain Kendrick was a Spy' and 'Alleged Confession/Then Release'. The *Sunday Express* reported that the 'bluff, hearty Kendrick was suddenly released from custody yesterday and ordered to leave German territory immediately'.[34] The *Deutsche Allgemeine Zeitung* ran a story that Kendrick had confessed to military espionage against Germany. The *Hamburg Fremdenblatt* noted that there was good reason to believe that 'the Kendrick affair is not necessarily an isolated case'.[35] The *Daily Telegraph* rebutted the accusations and said the charges were 'regarded in British quarters as extremely unlikely'.[36]

The plane touched down at London's Croydon airport just before 5 p.m. Kendrick descended the steps of the aircraft wearing a trilby hat, his trench coat thrown over his left shoulder and diplomatic bag in hand. He declined to comment to the waiting reporters, who immediately surrounded him. He was ushered to a waiting car and driven to the Foreign Office. His lengthy debriefing was summarized in a coded telegram to Ambassador Henderson in Berlin:

Captain Kendrick has arrived and been interviewed. The treatment to which he was subjected in Vienna prison appears to have differed in no way from the practices usually observed in Moscow. On three consecutive days he was cross-examined by relays of police for eight hours on end. He himself denies that he made any admission of guilt.[37]

Contrary to speculation, then, he had given nothing away in interrogation.[38] He was a professional and did not admit to espionage. The following day, 23 August, he telephoned SIS headquarters.[39]

There is no doubt that the German government's desire to maintain good relations with Britain ahead of the Munich Conference saved Kendrick from a more serious fate.[40] Within a month, Adolf Hitler would sign a mutual accord with British Prime Minister Chamberlain – the Munich Agreement.

The Kendrick affair

Kendrick's expulsion continued to have ramifications throughout the late summer and early autumn of 1938. His former chauffeur, Herr Bernklau, arrived at the British consulate in Lyons at the end of August 1938 and sought assistance, having escaped from a German prison.[41] During his escape, he had been fired at and been grazed on the knuckle. He told Consul-General O'Meara at Lyons that he had been offered a bribe of 5,000 Reichsmarks if he would confess that he and Kendrick had taken illicit photographs. After refusing to cooperate, he was beaten. O'Meara contacted London to see whether Bernklau should be sent to Britain and received an unexpected reply from the Foreign Office: 'This man is an impostor. The real Bernklau was in Glasgow on Aug 31 last.'[42]

The German authorities were edgy about foreign businessmen travelling in the Third Reich, possibly undercover and with ulterior motives. That autumn saw a series of arrests of British nationals by the Gestapo on allegations of espionage. British merchant Walter Becker was apprehended in Vienna on 15 September, having entered the Third Reich the previous week.[43] Gainer and Ambassador Henderson sought permission to visit him in prison, but their request was denied. Becker was investigated by the Gestapo and his case passed to the prosecution.[44] The outcome of his case is unknown.

The detention of British nationals following the Anschluss, and especially after Kendrick's arrest, was an ongoing concern for the British government. Michael Creswell commented on a Foreign Office memo: 'since the Kendrick affair, the Vienna authorities have been very easy with their charges of espionage against British subjects'.[45]

Nor had the Revd Grimes matter died down. He arrived at the Foreign Office on 24 August to see diplomat and politician Hubert Gladwyn Jebb (later Lord Jebb). During the debriefing, Jebb said to him: 'I've heard rumours that the German authorities in Vienna suspect you in connection with the Kendrick affair. Tell me frankly, what were your relations with Captain Kendrick?'

'I knew Captain Kendrick quite well,' replied Grimes. 'But did not see him very often because he was a Catholic and did not come to the British [i.e. Anglican] Church.'

'What about your official relations with him?'

'On nine or ten occasions, I sent Jews to Captain Kendrick and asked him to obtain visas for them. Otherwise I had no dealings with him at all.'

Jebb then said: 'As far as I know, Richter has been arrested. His exact fate is unknown.'

'Richter was a slippery customer, and though very useful, has always been treated by me with considerable reserve,' said Grimes.

'On the matter of your return to Vienna,' said Jebb, 'I suggest we write to Consul general Gainer and ask whether he thinks it wise for you to return. He will reply promptly.' Grimes was, in fact, never given clearance by the Foreign Office to return to Vienna.[46]

But, at the end of the first week of October, Grimes penned a letter to a friend mentioning the Kendrick affair. In an error of judgement, he sent it by ordinary post. It was intercepted on the orders of the Foreign Office. Grimes' indiscretion caused concern in secret service circles, because it was believed that he had also given some interviews to the press.[47]

Grimes had continued to press Gainer to be allowed to return to Vienna and had asked Gainer to take up his case with the Austrian authorities. Gainer's frustration at Grimes is clear in correspondence with A.E. Hutcheon at the Foreign Office:

I wonder if it would be possible to make Grimes understand that the authorities cannot be approached in any way. Does he suppose that either I, or my legal advisor, can tell the Secret Police that Kendrick had an organisation but that Grimes did not belong to it and ask them if they are now satisfied about him? The only way of dealing with this matter is to let it die a speedy and natural death, which it will probably do when Richter is tried.[48]

While Kendrick and Grimes had been lucky to get out of Austria alive, the fate of Kendrick's former agent handler Richter was far from certain. He remained in custody, and questions about him began to circulate in the Foreign Office.

The fate of Richter

Richter's case was complicated by the fact that he had dual British and German nationality.[49] The Foreign Office was reluctant to intervene because, as a German national, Richter came under German law; but also Richter was being linked to Kendrick. Richter's wife visited the legation to petition for his release. On leaving, she was arrested by the Gestapo and held for a short time. Maud Richter later claimed that the Gestapo knew exactly whom she had visited at the legation and what had been said during her meeting. The Richters' son, Richard, who in 1938 lived in Coventry and had British nationality, claimed that an insider at the British legation had leaked information to the Gestapo. His suspicions were rejected by both the Foreign Office and the Passport Control Department in London, both of which believed it more likely that Mrs Richter had inadvertently given away information when the Gestapo gave the impression that they knew everything.

Revd Grimes did not return to Vienna in September 1938 as he had hoped, because of the arrests of Richter and Kendrick.[50] He was staying at the Connaught Club, near Marble Arch in London, when he wrote to Richard Richter acknowledging that he had received an appeal from his mother.[51] Grimes promised to raise Fred Richter's arrest with the Foreign Office. Shortly after sending this letter, Grimes met Kendrick at an unknown location in London to discuss the Richter case. They agreed that the responsibility for any appeal to the German government rested with Gainer in Vienna, because Richter had been employed by the legation. Although the Richters had been granted a three-month British visa, allowing them to leave Austria via Switzerland, the government could not make formal petition to the German government for Fred's release because of his German nationality.[52] The Foreign Office wrote to the son: 'It is therefore greatly regretted that, in spite of every desire to assist your father in his present difficulties, there is no possibility of instructing His Majesty's ambassador at Berlin to take action on his behalf.'[53]

In spite of working for SIS, Richter was left to the mercy of the Gestapo. He was soon to be placed on trial for treason.[54] Richard Richter asked the

Foreign Office whether he would be protected if he travelled to Vienna for the trial, but the Foreign Office advised him not to go. As the son of a man of dual nationality, he might not have sufficient protection from arrest by the Gestapo.

Maud Richter had been released from custody and made a direct appeal to the Foreign Office to intervene, because her husband was facing charges as 'a traitor in connection with Captain Kendrick's arrest'.[55] Michael Creswell at the Foreign Office wrote an internal letter to Sir Walford Selby:

I am afraid Richter's prospects are very gloomy indeed: but we have had to turn a deaf ear to them all, and the whole situation connected with Kendrick's departure was so difficult that Gainer has had to have as little as possible to do with the whole affair.[56]

On 20 January 1939, Richter appeared before a magistrate in the mid-level Landgericht court, offering a plea that he had no idea that he had been recruited for espionage by the British. Nine months later, on 15 September 1939, he was tried before the infamous 'People's Court' in Berlin, where Karl Tucek testified against him. A senior detective, Kriminalrat Preiss, who had been one of those who had interrogated Kendrick, acted for the prosecution and produced his own personal evidence against Richter. The testimonies of Tucek and Preiss corroborated each other. In the final verdict, the People's Court concluded that Richter had been lying, and he was sentenced to 12 years' imprisonment for acting as Kendrick's accomplice. He was escorted back to Austria and incarcerated in Stein prison. On 15 June 1942, he was transferred to Marburg (now Maribor in Slovenia) and a few months later to Graz. In February 1943, Richter was transported to Auschwitz, where he perished within 24 hours of arrival. The official cause of death was given as heart disease. The British government's non-intervention sealed Richter's fate. The suspicion is that he had to be sacrificed to protect Britain's wider intelligence operations.

Very little is known about what happened to the double agent Karl Tucek, except that during the Second World War he was engaged in hunting down and torturing Austrian communists in Paris.[57] After the war, he returned to

Vienna, where he was arrested as a war criminal and extradited to Paris. He was subsequently tried by a French military court and sentenced to five years in prison.

The subject of Kendrick's expulsion refused to go away. On 30 November 1938, a question to Prime Minister Chamberlain was tabled in parliament about whether he had any statement to make about the circumstances under which Kendrick had been expelled for spying. A non-committal reply was given, to the effect that the issue had been taken up with the German authorities and disposed of: 'I do not think any useful purpose would be served by a discussion of the circumstances under which Captain Kendrick was expelled from Germany and I am consequently not prepared to make any statement on the subject.'[58]

Kendrick remained within the sights of the Nazi regime. His name was included in the 'Black Book' of prominent figures to hunt down and arrest, if and when Germany invaded Britain.[59] His entry in the book says that he was wanted by Amt IVE 4 – Gestapo Counter-intelligence Scandinavia, the section under which Britain was listed.

Consequences of Kendrick's arrest

Kendrick's arrest had consequences beyond his immediate detention and expulsion. It had ramifications for the whole European network of SIS officers. Staff at the passport offices in Berlin and Prague were recalled to Britain, including Kendrick's colleague in Berlin, Frank Foley.[60] The remaining female staff in the legation at Vienna were also evacuated.[61] Kendrick's in-depth knowledge and experience of Soviet and communist spy networks outside Russia, as well as Nazi Germany, placed him as one of SIS's most valuable spymasters of this era and that experience was lost in the region. But the consequences went much deeper. Kendrick had been in charge of gaining intelligence on Italy, including during the Abyssinian war, and of running agents into Italy. Even though information provided by the pre-war SIS station in Vienna was described as 'far from complete', intelligence gathering on Italy was broken when its cover was blown.[62] Penetration into Italy thereafter was extremely difficult, and SIS was unable to establish port-watchers in the country. This meant that SIS had no real intelligence coming out of Italy.

The ramifications were felt even into the Second World War itself. In the first few years of the war, intelligence on Italy was extremely disorganized. Frederick Winterbotham (an MI9 officer) described the lack of British intelligence on Italy as 'lamentable'.[63] There is no doubt that Kendrick's arrest was the most serious mishap to befall SIS until the Venlo incident the following year, when two SIS colleagues were picked up by the Abwehr on the Dutch border and the whole SIS network was compromised to the Third Reich.

Back in England, Kendrick disappeared from the public eye, but not from the ranks of the British secret service. In an office in MI6 headquarters in Broadway, he was planning the biggest deception plan against Nazi Germany – but this time from within Britain's borders.

PART II
Britain

8

SECRETS OF THE TOWER

In mid-September 1938, Kendrick arrived at MI6 headquarters at 54 Broadway Buildings to hectic scenes, as MI6 prepared for war.[1] Hugh 'Quex' Sinclair, 'C', assured him, 'I have your future under consideration.'[2] Sinclair was convinced that war with Nazi Germany was inevitable: it was just a question of when.[3] He asked Kendrick if he would train operatives and agents for SIS to send on missions abroad. This is as much as is currently known about Kendrick's work in this respect, because no files have been released that contain the names of the agents or their missions. That same month, Prime Minister Neville Chamberlain signed the Munich Agreement, in an attempt to avert imminent war with Adolf Hitler, who continued to threaten to annex the Sudetenland and Czechoslovakia. In later years, Chamberlain was to come in for fierce criticism over his appeasement policy; but a very different picture is now emerging about why he signed it. Britain was wholly unprepared for another war, just 21 years after the Great War. In a rare move, Sinclair intervened in government policy, telling Chamberlain that unless he signed the Munich Agreement, Britain would be at war with Germany immediately – at a time when Britain was ill-prepared both militarily and in terms of British intelligence structures.[4] He advised Chamberlain to accept Hitler's demands over Czechoslovakia and the Sudetenland.

Although the Munich Agreement did not avert a war, it did buy enough time for MI5 and MI6 to set up key intelligence units to fight the war when it came. It has been said that the intervention of the head of MI6 at this time demonstrated that Sinclair had emerged as 'a policy advisor as well as intelligence supplier and analyst'.[5] At no point did Sinclair or his successor, Stewart Menzies, even contemplate the notion that Britain would lose the war. Sinclair believed that a war was won on the basis of early and good intelligence, and therefore he planned a sweeping strategy that would leave no stone unturned. The plans included the establishment of a new section of SIS, known as Section D, to disseminate propaganda and conduct acts of sabotage.[6] In 1938, Sinclair had also purchased the estate of Bletchley Park, in Buckinghamshire. During the war, it was there that the codebreakers cracked the German Enigma codes and intercepted enemy communications and signals.[7] The history of Bletchley Park is well documented.

British intelligence believed that one of the most important sources of intelligence in any war was prisoners of war. Major General Sir William Thwaites once said in a training lecture: 'The information of greatest value to the intelligence section of General Staff is that derived from the interrogation of prisoners and deserters, and the documents found on them.'[8] Kendrick knew that to be true from his experience in the First World War. As another war loomed in the late 1930s, Sinclair had Kendrick in mind to establish a new unit that would spring into action as soon as war broke out. It would involve, for the first time, the mass recording of the unguarded conversations of German prisoners of war at secret locations under Kendrick's command. In early 1939, alongside his training of SIS agents for the field, it was Kendrick's task to find a suitable location for a wartime bugging unit. He earmarked rooms in the Tower of London for a hush-hush unit initially known as the Prisoners of War Collecting Centre, within fell under the auspices of MI1(h).[9]

Sinclair's judgement that Kendrick was the right man to establish this new far-reaching intelligence-gathering unit was, in the end, proved correct. Kendrick could draw on his experiences in dealing with German prisoners in the Boer War and the First World War, and he was a past master at running a complex bureaucratic system and networks. But there was another reason for choosing him: from the outset, this would be a tri-service unit, featuring army, navy and air intelligence – the first such inter-services unit in the history of British intelligence. The smooth working of such a combined centre depended entirely on the breadth of mind and cooperation of the chiefs of the three service departments. This could not be taken for granted, as the services were used to working autonomously and had a history of rivalry and jealousies. Sinclair judged that Kendrick's strength of character and his skill in managing interpersonal relationships and fostering cooperation meant that he could navigate the egos and agendas of individuals within the services. The success of the unit was to lay the foundations for intelligence work and tri-service co-operation right up to the present day.

The idea of listening into enemy conversations in war was not new. There is a fleeting reference in a military lecture to the tapping of enemy telephone lines in the field during the First World War – a development described as 'pioneering'; but there are no further details in military sources.[10] It is not known whether Kendrick had been involved in this, but it seems highly probable. The extent of what was unleashed by Kendrick's skills can be gauged from the over 75,000 declassified transcripts and intelligence reports in the National Archives at Kew, London.[11] These provide a unique record of the unguarded conversations of over 10,000 German prisoners of war. The files, which were only declassified in the 1990s and have remained largely untapped by historians, reveal an extraordinary volume of intelligence and are relevant to every campaign of the war.

Prisoners of War Collecting Centre

On 1 September 1939, the day Hitler invaded Poland, Major Kendrick (as he now was) opened the Prisoners of War Collecting Centre in a special area of the Tower of London.[12] He had already arranged for a team from the Post Office Research Station at Dollis Hill, north London, to enter the site in late August in order to install microphones in the light fittings and fireplaces of the rooms.[13] This had not been an easy task in the thousand-year-old fortress. Kendrick wrote that the team at Dollis Hill 'helped us over a difficult stile at the outset at the Tower where conditions were about as unfavourable as can be imagined', while the surveyor undertook 'difficult work, demanding fine craftsmanship without which it would have been difficult to obtain the very satisfactory results'.[14] The existence of this clandestine operation had to be closely guarded: if it became public knowledge, or if the German prisoners suspected anything, that would jeopardize one of the most important sources of intelligence collecting in the war. To protect the top-secret nature of this unit, Kendrick was given the freedom to choose his own staff. He selected his closest, most-trusted colleagues from his pre-war life to become part of a team that initially comprised no more than eight officers.[15] They included Samuel Denys Felkin, who soon headed up the air intelligence section of the unit; Arthur Rawlinson (an interrogator from the First World War); and Edmund Pollak, the British businessman whom Kendrick had smuggled out of Vienna in March 1938.[16]

The centre could hold up to 120 prisoners at any one time. The first German POWs arrived in the latter half of September: 43 U-boat officers and other ranks from U39, the first enemy U-boat to be sunk in the war (off the coast of north-west Ireland, on 14 September).[17] On 20 September, a further 38 German POWs were brought to the compound. All had to be interrogated and processed for intelligence. At this stage in the war (and even later on), prisoners were reluctant to divulge any information in interrogation, believing that Germany would emerge victorious. Kendrick's staff kept strictly to the rules of the Geneva Convention, permitting no violence or unorthodox methods of interrogation: prisoners were only required to give their name, rank and number, as per the Geneva Convention. Kendrick had a clever ruse to get POWs to spill what they knew. The prisoners were subjected to a 'phoney' interrogation. Then, back in their cells and rather irritated by the incompetence shown during the interrogation, they would brag to each other about what they had not told their interrogators, little realizing that there were hidden microphones. These were connected to an M Room ('M' for 'miked'), where secret listeners worked in 12-hour shifts, recording the conversations.

There was no easy or quick way of gleaning intelligence from prisoners. Throughout the war, it would remain a question of patiently gathering snippets of information to build a bigger picture of the enemy. Kendrick knew that the steady, painstaking, methodical collection of data – which was to increase with the influx of POWs as the war progressed – would gradually yield results. The results of the listening programme in September and early October 1939 were disappointing, partly because the prisoners had little to say, and partly because many of them were U-boat petty officers, who were found not to be as talkative as officers. The bugged conversations at this early stage yielded only fragments of information. But that would soon change.

Secret recordings

In the first two months of the war, the prisoners were primarily U-boat survivors, with the first German air force prisoners only arriving towards the end of October 1939. There were two U-boat prisoners, brought to the Tower on 1 October 1939, who believed that they had successfully deceived their interrogators, boasting repeatedly to one another in their room: '*Herrgott, was haben wir die verkackert!*' ('My God – what shit we served them up!'). Kendrick wrote that he found them 'crude and incapable of deceiving anyone'.[18]

Occasionally a prisoner evinced some suspicion. Petty Officer Hochstuhl was overheard to say: 'I don't trust the quietness of it here . . . They will use all sorts of means here to get information out of us. I think it is despicable when they put English officers into German air force uniforms.'[19] Clearly, he suspected the British of using 'stool pigeons' – British officers masquerading as German prisoners to guide private conversations in a particular direction. Although it was never admitted, Kendrick did indeed use stool pigeons, a technique used in the First World War with which Kendrick would have been familiar.[20] As the war progressed, he would use Czech refugees as stool pigeons, as well as deserters, German Jewish refugees and German prisoners willing to operate against Germany, because they no longer believed in the German cause.[21] The names of most of the stool pigeons used in the war have not been released; however, one of those used in the Tower was Brinley (Brin) Newton-John, the father of British-Australian actress Olivia Newton-John;[22] Ernst Lederer, a Czech refugee and grandfather of comedienne Helen Lederer, was another (although later, at Trent Park in north London).[23]

Kendrick already had over two decades of expertise in HUMINT, gathering human intelligence. His life in Vienna in the pre-war period had taught him the value of befriending persons who could provide valuable intelligence. The POWs coming through his wartime unit were no different; and if a prisoner was believed to have a large amount of valuable information, he could find himself being accompanied on a nice trip to the theatre, cinema or lunch in central London by a member of Kendrick's team. This was as much about 'political deconditioning' as it was about using blandishments to loosen a prisoner's tongue: he could observe for himself that London was functioning well, with plenty of goods on sale in the shops. This revelation would undermine Third Reich propaganda that Britain was short of supplies and on the verge of surrender. Or, in another technique, a British officer might talk about politics to try and gauge the prisoner's opinions on certain matters. This might cause the prisoner to give something away inadvertently. A prisoner's disillusionment with the Nazi regime might only be temporary, but it was usually long enough for an interrogator to gain the information required.[24]

One of the most remarkable pieces of intelligence recorded in the M Room at this early stage of the bugging operation came on 28 October. As Kendrick wrote in his summary for that day: 'They [the prisoners] think the war will end when the Führer comes out with his secret weapon.'[25] At this stage, it was not known what the secret weapon was – or indeed whether the prisoner merely *hoped* that Hitler would come up with a super-weapon that would win the war for Germany. Subjects discussed by prisoners at this time included the synthetic fuel used in German aircraft, combat reconnaissance tactics, torpedoes, the manufacture of Heinkel and Junkers aircraft, U-boat production and U-boat strength and losses. This last topic of conversation was particularly helpful, as it was difficult for Britain independently to verify the number of operational U-boats and the strength of the German navy.[26] By the end of January 1940, prisoners were unwittingly divulging information about the testing of new aircraft at Travemünde, on the Baltic coast. One prisoner exhorted his comrades: 'They [the British] mustn't find out anything about it and we mustn't talk about it in the camp. It is still being kept dark, even in Germany.'[27]

Needless to say, the secret listeners pounced on this with glee and sent the information to various departments, most especially the Air Ministry. The intelligence gleaned and a more detailed account of the bugging operation in the Tower are discussed in my book *The Walls Have Ears*.[28]

While Kendrick and his team were successfully harvesting information from the POWs in the Tower, a disaster was about to beset SIS on Dutch soil. This would have serious ramifications for the whole SIS network across Europe, and would mean that Kendrick's operation back in Britain gained fresh urgency.

The Venlo incident

In mid-October 1939, Richard Stevens, Kendrick's colleague and the British passport control officer in The Hague, was approached by German army officers who hoped to instigate a coup in Germany and bring down Hitler.[29] If successful, they wished to negotiate with the British government. It is now clear from declassified files that 'C', the head of MI6, was involved behind the scenes, and that the negotiations involved SIS. 'C' made it clear that, if the coup succeeded, the British government would be prepared to consider peace proposals, as the British had 'no desire to wage a vindictive war'. In return, the government would require some kind of autonomy for the Czechs and the restoration of Poland.[30] The two figures who acted as intermediaries abroad were Stevens and his SIS colleague Sigismund Payne Best. Both men were working for Dansey's Z Organisation and were reporting to him on clandestine negotiations with the anti-Nazi officers organizing the coup against Hitler.[31] Colonel Teichmann reported that 'only a small impetus was required to set the ball rolling and get rid of the Nazis'.[32] Clandestine meetings were set up on the Dutch–German border, but frequently had to be rescheduled.

On 9 November, ironically the anniversary of Hitler's attempted putsch in Munich in 1923, and also the first anniversary of *Kristallnacht* ('The Night of Broken Glass', which had seen the windows of synagogues and Jewish businesses smashed across the Third Reich), Stevens arrived at Venlo with his colleague Payne Best. But the whole thing was a sting operation. They were met by unknown Gestapo men and arrested. Payne Best was originally thought to have been fatally shot, along with their driver Dirk Klop. But in fact he was still alive. He and Stevens were taken to Gestapo headquarters in Berlin and interrogated, before being transferred to Sachsenhausen concentration camp. Stevens was later transferred to Dachau; Payne Best went to Buchenwald and then Dachau. They survived the war.

The Venlo affair was the most serious catastrophe to befall SIS since its foundation and the repercussions would be felt for years to come. What is not clear is how much information Payne Best and Stevens gave up in interrogation; but SIS certainly feared and believed that its whole network in Western Europe had been compromised. This blindsided SIS, because it could not verify how much the Germans knew about its agents and operations. In retrospect, it would appear that Payne Best and Stevens only gave away the names of those involved in the Z Organisation network (leaving SIS otherwise unscathed), but SIS did not know that. Kendrick's name subsequently appeared on the Black Book's list of names of those who were to be rounded up following a German invasion of Britain.

The Venlo affair was a real failure of professionalism, especially on the part of Kendrick's colleague Claude Dansey, head of the Z Organisation, of which Payne Best and Stevens were members. Venlo badly damaged the unique position of SIS in Britain – for reasons that relate to the intense rivalry between SIS and MI5 (Britain's security service responsible for security on British soil). Historically, SIS – like its parent, the Foreign Office – recruited mainly from certain exclusive public schools in the UK and from the universities of Oxford and Cambridge. Its objective was to create sources to provide the best intelligence from abroad so as to defend the realm; it was therefore not interested in seeking justice, and it used questionable people with suspect backgrounds. MI5, on the other hand, was all about security and therefore was made up primarily of police officers and non-senior army officers. Some of its staff were recruited from private schools – but not the same ones that supplied SIS. MI5's brief was to bring to justice anyone who threatened the realm from inside the borders of the UK. And although SIS and MI5 worked together up to a point, there was intense hostility and different emphases.

Within six months of Venlo, Britain had a new prime minister, Winston Churchill, who was prepared to countenance a new type of foreign intelligence and operations – ungentlemanly warfare – which broke the mould of the public-school ethos. By 1942 – albeit under pressure from Labour coalition members – he had sanctioned the creation of the Special Operations Executive (SOE). Because of Venlo, SIS and SOE, as well as the new branch of military intelligence MI9, tried to function independently, especially in their escape lines during the Second World War.[33]

How could the British secret service survive the catastrophe of Venlo?

The answer was to be found nearly 350 miles away, in north London. Kendrick had just requisitioned an estate near Cockfosters and was about to expand his eavesdropping operations. The Combined Services Detailed Interrogation Centre (CSDIC) at Trent Park would allow him to process far more enemy prisoners. The rather clunky name of this unit obscured its real purpose: it was to become the biggest bugging operation ever mounted against an enemy of Britain. Kendrick would go on to orchestrate the greatest deception against Hitler's generals – a slow subterfuge that would ultimately help shorten the war and enable SIS to survive Venlo.

9

EAVESDROPPING ON THE ENEMY

The prospect of a swift end to the war via a military coup by a clique of Hitler's generals had turned out to be a ruse by the Abwehr that targeted SIS. Kendrick was astute enough to know that the long, slow intelligence game was now Britain's only hope of eventually defeating Nazi Germany. Experience had taught him that battles are won by intelligence and the quality of intelligence. His unique knowledge of Germany and his understanding of German psychology since the First World War, as well as his experience of Nazi Germany in the 1930s from his years in Vienna, made him a highly experienced and successful intelligence officer. His foresight in understanding that his new eavesdropping unit could produce intelligence capable of substantially altering the course of the war, and his expertise and determination in turning the M Room project into a major intelligence-gathering operation, arguably saved MI6 in the end. The key points of the M Room operation are outlined here; but a much more detailed and comprehensive history can be read in my book *The Walls Have Ears*, the first such account by a British historian and featuring unique interviews with veterans.

From October 1939, Kendrick focused on substantially increasing the bugging programme and making the site at Trent Park fit for purpose.[1] A specialist team from Dollis Hill Research Station installed state-of-the-art eavesdropping equipment in five interrogation rooms and six bedrooms in the mansion house, as well as in rooms in the stable block. This work took five months to complete.[2] The installation team was required to sign the Official Secrets Act, and Kendrick witnessed and countersigned the declarations. False panels and double ceilings were installed inside the house, in part to help with the soundproofing. Tiny microphones were concealed in the fireplaces and light fittings, with the wiring well concealed behind the wall panels and skirting boards. Temporary buildings were erected next to the main house, to accommodate interrogation rooms and an M Room.

The operation was dramatically scaled up as Kendrick increased his staff to just over 500, a third of them women.[3] This marked the beginning of a highly efficient, methodical intelligence-gathering 'factory' organized by Kendrick. He kept a tight rein on it, and it was no coincidence that his office was set up in the Blue Room of the mansion house – directly above one of the M Rooms. On his desk he had special equipment that enabled him to plug into any of the bugged bedrooms and interrogation rooms and to listen in via headphones or on a loudspeaker. The scale of the operation that was beginning to unfold is staggering. Kendrick – the spymaster – was orchestrating a superbly efficient spy network – targeted at the enemy, but on British soil.

Technology and HUMINT

Between January 1940 and the spring of 1942, over 3,000 German and Italian POWs were processed through Trent Park; at this stage in the war, the majority comprised Luftwaffe officers and U-boat crew. It became one of the most successful and far-reaching technology-driven HUMINT deception operations in the Second World War.

A prisoner expected to be interrogated after capture; but, as Kendrick discovered, this was most fruitful when used in conjunction with the listening operation and stool pigeons. As he wrote in a memorandum to Norman Crockatt (head of MI9):

> Whilst direct interrogation may provide valuable information it cannot, as a general rule, reasonably be expected to provide the same insight into the prisoner's mind as is possible by the proper use of the listening method, which in addition to providing independent intelligence, often provides the interrogators with a check on statements made to them.[4]

It was his foresight in combining the three techniques – interrogation, stool pigeons and hidden microphones – that made the operation as an extraordinary success story.[5]

The state-of-the-art microphones used could pick up even a whispered conversation between prisoners, as former intelligence officer Catherine Townshend recalled:

After an extensive examination of the walls, floor and furniture of his room, a senior prisoner was heard to say to his cellmate: 'There are no microphones here.' But for safety's sake the two men decided that they could converse more freely if they leant far out of the window. Little did they suspect that in addition to a minute microphone attached to the ceiling light fixture, another was hidden in the outside wall beneath the window sill.[6]

The authorities always tried to ensure that prisoners shared a room with someone carefully selected. Thus, back in their cells after interrogation, each man would begin to discuss the war with his cellmate – and often mentioned new technology being employed by the German navy or air force. Idle chatter by prisoners before interrogation offered the interrogators advance warning of what a prisoner might know and could be trying to withhold from them. After interrogation, a prisoner would often boast to his cellmate what he had not revealed. Kendrick reported that the attitude of prisoners who were security conscious could be broken down 'by careful grouping of POWs and by devising ways and means of disarming suspicion'.[7] He held a weekly conference with the operations staff, and this proved extremely useful in promoting discussion of ways in which the modus operandi could be adapted to the changing intelligence needs of the day. He also issued a 'Weekly Personal Report', but these appear not to have been declassified into the National Archives.[8]

It was U-boat personnel, as early as January 1940, who gave Kendrick's unit one of its earliest intelligence coups of the war, when they revealed secrets about German naval Enigma. This was to have a direct impact on the work at Bletchley Park, and is a good example of where a bugged conversation had a direct impact operationally.[9] The information came from U-boat Petty Officer Erich May of U-35, a U-boat that had been scuttled at the end of November 1939.[10] May proved so valuable to British intelligence that he was still being held at Trent Park in January 1940.[11] Naval interrogator Richard Pennell (RNVR) gained the trust of May to such an extent that the latter began to discuss with him how German naval Enigma worked.[12]

He provided valuable information on naval codes and short signals, which confirmed that the German navy spelt out numerals in full, instead of using the top row of a keyboard.[13] The transcripts of conversations between May and Pennell, which had been recorded in the M Room, were sent direct to Bletchley Park's head, Commander Alastair Denniston, and to his cryptographers, Dilly Knox, Oliver Strachey and Frank Birch. The information was passed to Alan Turing and, as a result, he looked again at the German encryption for 28 November 1938 and came to the conclusion that British analysis of it had been fundamentally correct, provided the numerals were spelt out.[14] He and his colleagues turned to the unbroken cribs of shortly before December 1938 and, based on the new intelligence from Trent Park, they were able to break the code within a fortnight. The history of Hut 8 in declassified files at the National Archives confirms that naval Enigma was cracked using special intelligence garnered from prisoners of war at Kendrick's site.[15]

Throughout the war, Axis prisoners continued to provide intelligence on German codes, Enigma and communications that was of direct relevance to Bletchley Park. Indeed, in an indication of the close cooperation that existed between CSDIC and the codebreaking site, Kendrick placed suitable rooms at the disposal of personnel from Bletchley Park, so that they could come and interrogate any prisoners who had specialist knowledge of German codes and Enigma.[16] This close relationship continued throughout the conflict.

Intelligence from enemy POWs

The intelligence gathered by the combined services unit became increasingly detailed and of much greater significance. CSDIC disseminated vast quantities of information and snippets of intelligence about the enemy to those departments that needed to see it – from MI5, MI6 and MI14 to the War Office, Bomber Command, the Air Ministry, the Admiralty and – eventually, once the United States entered the war in December 1941 – to US intelligence. Kendrick's first intelligence summary of the unit's work, which covered September 1939 to December 1940, demonstrates the extensive and detailed information about Germany's military capabilities that was being harvested by eavesdropping on prisoners' conversations.[17] An appendix to his report provides a comprehensive list of the topics on which reports were available, based on interrogations and recorded conversations. The subjects included aerodromes in German-occupied countries, artillery, enemy aircraft equipment and navigational technology, the Gestapo, conditions in Germany, hand grenades, identification of German units and aircraft production, German paratroopers, Poland, rockets, weapons and torpedoes, U-boat movements and tactics, tanks, Jews, the SS and the strength of enemy armed forces.[18] Information had been gained on U-boat operations around Norway between April and June 1940, as well as on British submarines in the region – essential for assessing how much the Germans knew about British naval operations.[19]

Major General Francis H. Davidson, the new director of military intelligence, was impressed by Kendrick's first report, commenting: 'The general spirit of this Survey (and the weekly reports) shows the true spirit of attacking intelligence.'[20]

Airmen POWs not infrequently alluded in their conversations to technology on board their aircraft – often 'a considerable time before the emergence of such a weapon in operations'.[21] In February 1940, the microphones picked up the first mentions of new technology being used by the Luftwaffe, called *X-Gerät* and *Knickebein*.[22] The system functioned like an early radar system, enabling German pilots to conduct more precise bombing raids across Britain. It was the first inkling that British intelligence had of this new technology. Armed with information about *X-Gerät* from the special recordings, the Air Ministry was able to build a profile of the German war capability and to develop counter-technology.[23] As Professor R.V. Jones, scientific adviser to

MI6, confirmed, the British countermeasures resulted in the deflection of many bombs from their intended targets. Kendrick's close friend and colleague Denys Felkin (head of air intelligence at Trent Park) concluded that the discovery of the existence of *X-Gerät* and *Knickebein* had 'the most far-reaching consequences . . . [The developments were] reported in time for the British authorities to prepare countermeasures against a method of bombing which in the autumn of 1940 constituted a very real threat to British war industries.'[24] It gave Britain time to improve its defences, so that the German air force had to find new ways of attacking.

The uncovering of *X-Gerät* and *Knickebein* was so critical that Norman Crockatt, head of MI9, wrote to Kendrick to congratulate him and 'those officers under you who contributed so largely to one of the most successful pieces of intelligence investigation I have ever come across'.[25] Crockatt later reported that: 'The secret recordings produced some of the earliest information of the German experiments in Air Navigational aids [March 1940], and has played an important part in the successful development of the British counter-measures.'[26] German radar devices – both land and airborne – continued to be reported by prisoners throughout the war, in many cases ahead of their appearance in the various theatres of battle.

All transcripts of conversations and interrogations were filed in a newly compiled index library, so that if a particular subject became relevant or urgent as the war progressed, the appropriate transcripts could be pulled from the filing cabinets and consulted. To gauge the usefulness or otherwise of the recorded conversations, Kendrick sent a questionnaire to the intelligence departments. The response from Admiral John Godfrey, head of naval intelligence, was telling:

Without them [the Special Reports] it would have been impossible to piece together the histories of [enemy] ships, their activities and the tactics employed by U-boats in attacking convoys. The hardest naval information to obtain with any degree of reliability concerned technical matters . . . I wish to convey to the staff at the CSDIC my warm appreciation of their work.[27]

173

Stewart Menzies, 'C', reinforced the importance of the work from the MI6 angle:

> The reports are of distinct value, and I trust the work will be maintained and every possible assistance given to the Centre [CSDIC]. It is essential that the Service Departments should collaborate closely by providing Kendrick with the latest questionnaires, without which he must be working largely in the dark.[28]

The expansion of the bugging operation was proving successful. At moments of crisis in this war, Kendrick could be relied upon to deliver intelligence. He was confident in his methods, because he understood the prisoners: he understood human nature and how best to secure information. While it is true that the thousands of transcripts emanating from Trent Park offered screeds of information in piecemeal form, this could be used to corroborate intelligence coming in from other sources (such as Bletchley Park or the resistance movements in Europe). However, CSDIC could equally well provide the first source of intelligence.

The success of this almost mechanized, efficient system of intelligence gathering depended largely on the hard work of the personnel, day in and day out. In no small part, this was encouraged by the atmosphere that Kendrick – so adroit at interpersonal relationships – created at the site. It was his character that held the unit together, and he enjoyed the respect of personnel of all ranks and from all services. It was his vision and his skills that led to the establishment of the first wide-ranging operation combining HUMINT and technology. In this respect, he demonstrated his ability to set up and run an unprecedented, innovative and sophisticated organization from scratch, in very short order and at a time when Britain was fighting for survival.

The unit's work was so valuable to the outcome of the war that its existence had to be heavily protected. Charles Deveson, an intelligence officer, recalled that on his first day he was called into Kendrick's office and ordered to sign the Official Secrets Act.[29] Kendrick slid a pistol across the desk and looked Deveson

1. Thomas Joseph Kendrick in Vienna in the 1930s where he was posted as the British passport control officer, a cover for his real role as head of station for the Secret Intelligence Service. His post was considered SIS's most important station in Europe in the 1920s and 1930s, and it was from Vienna that he ran his own spy networks into Czechoslovakia, Hungary, Germany and Italy.

2. Kendrick with army colleagues in 1901 during the Second Boer War. Kendrick is the man driving the vehicle. In January 1901 Kendrick volunteered for the British forces in South Africa and with the Cape Colony Cyclists' Corps. It gave him the basic tools for field intelligence operations that would enable him to become a major player in British espionage for nearly 40 years.

3. Norah Wecke whom Kendrick married by special licence in Cape Town on 29 March 1910. Norah was the daughter of Friedrich Wecke, a German businessman and manager of a diamond mine who had settled in Lüderitzbucht in German-occupied South West Africa. Kendrick worked for Wecke from 1905 for five years.

4. Gladys Kendrick on her wedding day to Geoffrey Walsh, 29 March 1931. They married at a civic ceremony at the British Consulate in Vienna, followed by a religious ceremony in the Roman Catholic Maria Geburt Kirche. The high-society wedding included many guests from aristocratic and diplomatic circles. An extravagant reception was held afterwards in Kendrick's apartment.

5. Kendrick with granddaughter Barbara in Vienna, c. 1937.

6. Clara Holmes, an expert skier, with her daughter Prudence at an Austrian ski resort during the 1930s. Holmes was one of Kendrick's SIS secretaries who worked undercover at the British passport control office, communicating with agents across Europe using invisible ink.

7. Adolf Hitler making a triumphant entry into Vienna on 14 March 1938, two days after his forces annexed Austria into the Third Reich in an action termed 'the Anschluss'. It marked the beginning of seven years of incorporation of the country into Germany, a period which saw the Nazi decimation of Viennese culture and Jewish life.

8. Dr Erwin Pulay, an eminent skin specialist and close friend of Sigmund Freud. As a Jew, Pulay was at risk of arrest, and so Kendrick enabled him to flee Austria within days of the Anschluss. Kendrick went on to save thousands of Austrian Jews until his own arrest in August 1938. His humanitarian efforts have yet to be fully recognized.

9. Sigmund Freud, Austrian neurologist and founder of psychoanalysis, whom it is believed was helped out of Vienna in early June 1938 by Kendrick and the Americans. Freud is pictured here shortly after his arrival in England, a desperately ill man. He died the following year, on 23 September 1939.

10. Kendrick's daughter and grandchildren saying goodbye to Kendrick and Norah at Vienna train station, 19 July 1938. Kendrick deemed it no longer safe for them to remain in Vienna. Also there to see them off safely were Deti (the children's nanny), Kendrick's friends Mary and Hans Schick, and Edmund Pollitzer, a family friend and one of Kendrick's agents.

11. Gladys, Barbara and Ken leaving Vienna by train on 19 July 1938 for a new life in Scotland. Kendrick is pictured here, but only his trilby hat is visible.

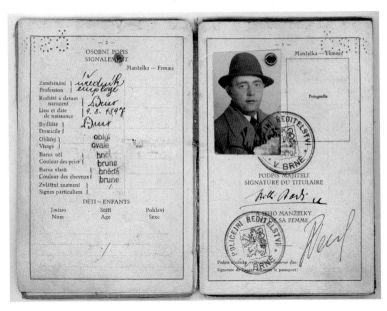

12. Passport of Willi Bondi who lived in Brno, Czechoslovakia, believed to have been one of Kendrick's agents. By 1938 he was working for the import-export business Fleischers, which was owned by his two brothers-in-law. His passport shows repeated visits between Czechoslovakia and Austria in June, July and August 1938 at a crucial time, against mounting expectation of a German invasion of Czechoslovakia. Bondi had visited Austria only once or twice between the years 1933 and 1936, so the frenetic activity of 1938 was atypical.

13. The entry stamps into Austria in Willi Bondi's passport. Blond and blue-eyed, Bondi chose not to escape the Nazi regime, but other members of his family were saved by Kendrick. Bondi was later arrested, not for being Jewish, but for political reasons. His interrogations made it clear that the Gestapo suspected him of passing intelligence to the British. He was shot in Auschwitz on 30 August 1941.

14. The wedding of Countess Marianne Szápáry to Günther von Reibnitz, December 1941. It was discovered during the writing of this book that the countess, who is the mother of Her Royal Highness Marie-Christine, Princess Michael of Kent, worked for Kendrick and SIS in the 1930s.

15. Kendrick's brother-in-law Rex Pearson who married Olga Wecke (sister of Norah Kendrick). Pearson first met Kendrick in South Africa after the Boer War. In the First World War Kendrick transferred to the Intelligence Corps on Pearson's recommendation and they served together in intelligence duties in France. They subsequently spent the rest of their careers in the SIS, commonly known as MI6, and were among the higher echelons of the British Secret Service.

16. Franz Bernklau, the chauffeur used by Kendrick in Vienna. Bernklau was driving the car with Kendrick and Norah in the back when it was stopped at the border town of Freilassing on 17 August 1938. The border police had been alerted that Kendrick was trying to flee the country. Kendrick was arrested and driven back to Vienna to face the Gestapo.

17. The Hotel Metropole, Vienna. After the Anschluss the hotel became the Gestapo headquarters. Kendrick was brought here from Freilassing and subjected to four days of 'Soviet-style' interrogations. He was held in an attic room next to the former Austrian Chancellor Schuschnigg and Baron Louis Rothschild. The German authorities sarcastically assured Sir Nevile Henderson, the British ambassador in Berlin, that Kendrick had 'one of their best rooms'.

CAPT. KENDRICK EXPELLED

EVENING NEWS

6.30

18. After intense diplomatic activity, the German authorities released Kendrick on condition he left the country within 24 hours. He was formally expelled from Austria on charges of suspected espionage, for which the Germans claimed to have reliable evidence. The expulsion was prominently reported in the world's media. Reporters waited outside his apartment in Vienna to speak with him, but Kendrick and his wife had already been smuggled by car into Hungary to avoid arrest.

THE DAILY TELEGRAPH
AND MORNING POST, TUESDAY, AUGUST 23, 19

CAPT. THOMAS KENDRICK, the British Passport Control Officer in Vienna, who was arrested by the German secret police, photographed on his arrival at Croydon Aerodrome yesterday.   P.T.O

19. Kendrick's arrival back at Croydon aerodrome on 22 August 1938. He refused to answer questions to waiting reporters and was taken off to the Foreign Office and MI6 headquarters for debriefing.

20. Stewart Menzies, who became the third head of MI6 in 1939. Kendrick and Menzies were colleagues in intelligence since the days of the First World War when both were engaged in counter-espionage activities for British intelligence.

21. Kendrick at Latimer House, one of his wartime eavesdropping sites. During the Second World War he set up and commanded a unit that secretly recorded the unguarded conversations of over 10,000 German and Italian prisoners of war to gain crucial intelligence for the Allies. The success of this huge operation was largely due to his character and masterful skills as a spymaster.

22. Trent Park at Cockfosters, North London. The house and estate were requisitioned in October 1939 and 'wired for sound'. Kendrick moved here from the Tower of London in December 1939. From 1942 until late 1945, the house held Hitler's captured generals and senior officers. The German generals were treated to a life of relative luxury in this house, little realizing that their conversations were being secretly recorded via hidden microphones.

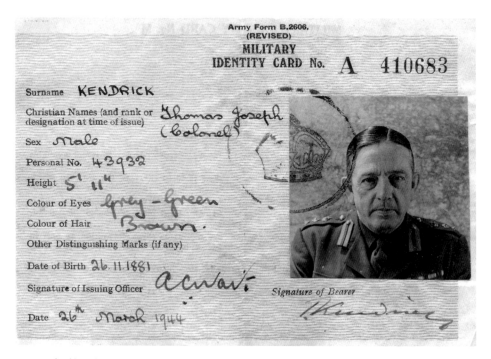

Army Form B.2606.
(REVISED)

MILITARY
IDENTITY CARD No. A 410683

Surname **KENDRICK**

Christian Names (and rank or designation at time of issue) *Thomas Joseph (Colonel)*

Sex *Male*

Personal No. *43932*

Height *5' 11"*

Colour of Eyes *grey-green*

Colour of Hair *Brown.*

Other Distinguishing Marks (if any)

Date of Birth *26.11.1881*

Signature of Issuing Officer *acwai.*

Date *26th March 1944*

Signature of Bearer *TKendrick*

23. Kendrick's military identity pass as the commanding officer of the Combined Services Detailed Interrogation Centre, as his clandestine unit was named. Although still a senior member of SIS/MI6, he was attached to the Intelligence Corps and back in military uniform from 1939 until 1945.

24. Rudolf Hess, Hitler's deputy and designated successor. Hess flew to Scotland on a peace mission on 10 May 1941, baling out near the Duke of Hamilton's estate, Dungavel. Hess was arrested and soon found himself in the care of three MI6 minders at Mytchett Place near Aldershot. They were Kendrick (aka 'Colonel Wallace'), Frank Foley and 'Captain Barnes'.

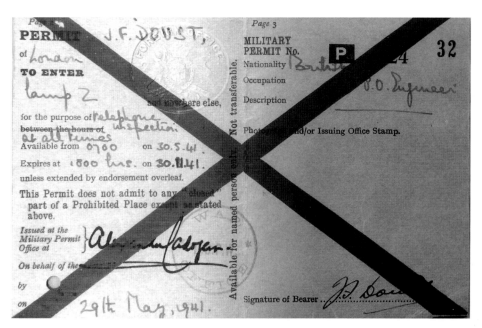

25. The identity pass of chief engineer J.F. Doust of the Post Office Research, Dollis Hill, North London. Doust and his engineers installed hidden microphones at Mytchett Place (also known as Camp Z) prior to Hess's arrival there. Doust was responsible for inspecting the secret equipment and dealing with any technical issues that arose on site. No entry was permitted into the camp without one of these passes – marked with a red cross – and had to be authorised by 'C', the head of MI6.

26. Latimer House, near Chesham in Buckinghamshire which became Kendrick's headquarters from July 1942 when he moved out there from Trent Park. By the summer of 1942, Kendrick had expanded the unit further and now commanded three eavesdropping sites for British intelligence at Latimer House, Wilton Park at Beaconsfield and Trent Park.

27. A view of the White House at Wilton Park, Beaconsfield in Buckinghamshire, Kendrick's third eavesdropping site, some eight miles from Latimer House. Until the end of the war, the site processed thousands of lower rank German POWs, especially a number of German generals captured after D-Day and before their transfer to Trent Park.

28. The naval intelligence team outside Latimer House, summer 1943. Recruited by Ian Fleming, it was part of the tri-services personnel operating at Kendrick's sites. They interrogated German POWs across the services, not only U-boat crews. Ralph Izzard (tall man standing alone at the back). From left to right (standing): unknown, unknown, Ian Fleming, Commander Burton Cope, Richard Weatherby, Donald Welbourn, unknown. From left to right (seated): Jean Flower, Evelyn Barron, George Blake, Esme Mackenzie, Gwendoline Neel-Wall.

29. Drinks party of the naval intelligence team on the terrace at Latimer House, summer 1943. Pink gin was the favourite cocktail, a somewhat exotic choice in wartime. Visible in the photograph are the same members as Plate 28, including George Blake (smiling, standing on the right in the foreground).

30. Lieutenant General Theodor von Sponeck and Friedrich von Broich, chauffeured to Trent Park after surrendering with the German army in Tunisia in May 1943. Little did they realize during their time at Trent Park that their conversations were being recorded by secret listeners from the three 'M Rooms' in the basement.

31. German generals landing at Plymouth, Devon, after capture on the battlefields of Normandy, June 1944. Thousands of German POWs were captured during the Normandy campaign and the most important transferred to Kendrick's sites for detailed interrogation and their conversations recorded in the cells. Kendrick's unit amassed tens of thousands of transcripts which survive in the National Archives, London.

32. Commanding Officer Colonel Thomas Joseph Kendrick (seated in the middle), pictured here with the army intelligence officers of CSDIC, Latimer House, c. 1944.

33. Christmas party for non-commissioned officers in a Nissen hut at Latimer House. Pictured here are male secret listeners who fled Nazi oppression, volunteered for the British army and later transferred to the Intelligence Corps and Kendrick's wartime sites. Here, too, are female German-Jewish refugees who carried out vital intelligence work, including translation and typing of the transcripts of bugged conversations.

34. In retirement, Thomas Kendrick with friends at his house in Oxshott, Surrey, c. 1960s. From left to right: Frederick Warner (Dental Dean of Guy's Hospital), Gladys Walsh, Kendrick, Kathleen Montague (Gladys Walsh's sister-in-law).

35. The Kendricks in England with their close friends from the Vienna days, *c*. 1960s. From left to right: Hans Schick, Norah Kendrick, Mary Schick, Thomas Kendrick. Kendrick managed to get Hans Schick, a Jewish lawyer, and his wife Mary out of Austria. They remained life-long friends.

36. From left to right: Thomas Kendrick, his sister Mary Rowlands and his wife Norah at Briarholme, Oxshott.

straight in the eye: 'If you ever betray anything about this work, here is the gun with which I expect you to do the decent thing. If you don't, I will.'[30]

Though a jovial military commander, who on the surface seemed like an amiable grandfather, Kendrick had a serious side – a deadly side that meant he would kill to protect his country. Betrayal of this operation had only one possible ending.

The Battle of Britain

The fall of Norway and Denmark in April 1940 to the German invading forces, and of the Low Countries and France in May 1940, left Britain standing alone against Nazi Germany. Now more than ever, it was up to Kendrick's unit to harvest intelligence in an effort to keep ahead in the war. Central to this was intelligence on the Luftwaffe, new technology and fighter tactics. Britain had to retain air superiority over the Luftwaffe in order to avert an invasion of its shores by Hitler's forces under cover of German aircraft. It is no exaggeration to say that the Battle of Britain, fought from July 1940 to October 1940, was a fight for survival. The conversations of Axis prisoners at this time were peppered with information on new aircraft being developed in Germany, including details of the new Focke-Wulf fighters, gleaned from German pilots shot down in the Battle of Britain:[31]

Prisoner A: The Focke-Wulf fighters ought to be out.
Prisoner B: We have been told they are already on their way, these birds – 700 or 720 [km/hour] cruising speed – at any rate, according to a friend of mine who has flown them.[32]

Those prisoners had just provided details of a new German aircraft in development and being tested, including details of its capability.

Other prisoners continued to talk about losses, as in the case of Prisoner A427 (true name unknown), who commented to his cellmate: 'Only five out of eight of our aircraft come back . . . We are losing too many aircraft . . . We have lost our best airmen.'[33] Such snippets of information were analysed by the British in an attempt to gauge the true losses of German aircraft and fighting capability.

There were eyewitness accounts of the Battle of Britain from the enemy perspective, as it was happening. On 2 September 1940, two prisoners being held at Trent Park watched a dogfight overhead between German aircraft and British Spitfires. Their bugged conversation captured a moment when the battle was actually taking place:

Prisoner B: You can see it from here, a Spitfire up there. Just there – underneath. It has flown in a sort of arc. There it comes again over here.
Prisoner A: Oh! There is a Zerstörer [heavy fighter] (More M.G. [machine-gun] fire and roaring of engines is heard). There it is again, the Spitfire, always following up.
Prisoner B: Yes!
Prisoner A: It seems to be coming down [the German ME 110]. It's already on fire.
Prisoner B: Now he's dropping incendiary bombs.
Prisoner A: Now you can see how fast it is [the Spitfire].[34]

Today, the transcripts are historically significant, as they preserve rare conversations of the Second World War and eyewitness accounts of the war from an enemy perspective. The dialogues are very natural and human: at one point Prisoner A437 described to his cellmate how, after capture, he had been given a really good meal of fried eggs and bacon, toast, jam and butter. His cellmate piped up: 'Well, you don't get a meal like that in the whole of our armed forces.'[35]

During 1940, most prisoners expected the invasion to be imminent. But by 1941, their hopes had waned and they were increasingly sceptical that there would be any invasion of England at all. Even so, there could be no let-up in the intelligence gathering. The eavesdropping programme continued throughout 1941, with prisoners starting to speak about the heavy U-boat losses suffered. The surviving crew from the *Admiral Graf Spee* and the warship

Gneisenau were brought to Trent Park, where they were monitored discussing the movements and tactics of their vessels. They also spoke about the German battleship *Scharnhorst* – the same ship whose construction in the 1930s had so interested Kendrick's agents dispatched from Vienna. Survivors of the *Bismarck* described its last voyage in considerable detail, including the damage inflicted on it by HMS *Hood* and HMS *Prince of Wales*. In all, 110 survivors were picked up (from a crew of 2,200) and brought to Trent Park. In their unguarded conversations, German seamen gave away the names of shipyards, their locations on the Baltic coast and details of their production of new U-boats and warships.[36] Some shipyards were already known to the British, such as Kiel and Wilhelmshaven – facilities that remained as important to Kendrick's intelligence work as they had been in the 1930s.

The most intense battles were being fought at sea, and vital information about the Battle of the Atlantic was being harvested from prisoners of war passing through Kendrick's site.[37] On technical matters, the most important naval information for this period was the development of a new magnetically fused torpedo.[38]

From Trent Park came the first confirmation that Hitler was shifting his focus away from invasion to a marine campaign and blockade of supplies into Britain.[39] It was vital for British commanders to anticipate the enemy's next move if they were to maintain supremacy of the seas through difficult battles that would last most of the war. For that, intelligence was needed – and a major source was the M Room transcripts.

Kendrick believed that Britain would win the intelligence war. But Trent Park was to prove inadequate to deal with the thousands of German prisoners who would be captured on the battlefields and at sea. In response, Kendrick scaled up his operations and expanded capacity yet further.

Secret houses

In early 1941, Kendrick requisitioned Latimer House, near Chesham, and Wilton Park at Beaconsfield, in Buckinghamshire. The sites were chosen because they were secluded and yet were within easy reach of London, only some 25–30 miles away. So valuable for the war effort was the intelligence that had already been generated at Trent Park that the Joint Intelligence Sub-Committee (JIC) in London authorized an unlimited budget for Kendrick to make Latimer House and Wilton Park operational. It concluded that Kendrick's unit was:

> Of the utmost operational importance, vital to the needs of the three fighting services and should accordingly be given the highest degree of priority in all its requirements; that the normal formalities regarding surveys, plans and tenders should be waived and that any work required should be put in hand at once and completed by the earliest possible date irrespective of cost.[40]

This endorsement was signed by, among others, Stewart Menzies ('C'), John Godfrey (head of naval intelligence) and Francis Davidson (director of military intelligence).

A declassified memo (marked 'To be Kept under Lock and Key') indicates the cost involved in expanding to these two sites: £400,000 (roughly £25 million today).[41] This involved the construction of a complex of temporary prefabricated buildings at both sites, known as the 'Spider'. It consisted of cells, an interrogation and administration block, M Room, a cookhouse, guard block and Nissen huts in the grounds. The rooms were fitted with bugging devices and wired to M Room. Kendrick increased his complement of staff across the sites to 967 army personnel (intelligence and non-intelligence);[42] the naval intelligence team there was expanded by Ian Fleming.[43] Within the year, Fleming himself had moved to Buckinghamshire to train his 30 Assault Unit at nearby Shardeloes House, Amersham. He was a frequent visitor to Latimer House and was photographed with the naval intelligence team on site and at a drinks party on the balcony of the mansion house.

Fleming's boss, John Godfrey, commented that he regarded the expansion of CSDIC as 'of such importance as to override normal considerations of cost and I hope that you will be able to use every endeavour to see that this expansion is given absolute priority'. The JIC decided that Kendrick did not need to go through the usual channels for the authorization of funds for any aspect of his unit's work.[44] It was an extraordinary situation and serves to emphasize both the importance of his operation and also the trust placed in him as commanding officer. The JIC also took the important decision to downgrade the new aerodrome at Bovingdon, just four miles away from Latimer House, to avoid noise interference with the listening work going on there. The aerodrome was nearly complete and had cost around £300,000. This underlines again the priority attached to intelligence gathering, which trumped even operational airfields for Bomber Command.

While construction continued at Latimer House and Wilton Park, Kendrick received a telephone call from his boss, 'C'. Kendrick's war was about to take an unexpected turn as he, with two other SIS officers – Frank Foley and a certain 'Captain R. Barnes' (whose identify has never been revealed) – was about to take charge of the most prized and highest-ranking German prisoner ever to be held in Britain.

10

THE HESS AFFAIR

At 11 p.m. on 10 May 1941, Kendrick was in his office in the Blue Room at Trent Park, waiting for a phone call from his boss, Menzies. At just that time, the Luftwaffe was starting its worst ever bombing raid on the capital. The secret listeners had finished for the night and had returned to their billets, unaware of the extraordinary events unfolding in the north of England.

A lone plane approaching the coast of northern England was being tracked by British radar, but had not been shot down.[1] A few minutes later, it ran out of fuel and the pilot baled out on the edge of Eaglesham Moors, a few miles from Dungavel House in Scotland. He was arrested by Major Graham Donald (Royal Observer Corps) and taken to Busby drill hall, where Donald asked the Home Guard to hold him until he had checked the wreckage of the aircraft.

The pilot had flown from Augsburg, Germany, in a Messerschmitt Bf 110 twin-engine fighter plane, on what had been logged as a cross-country test flight across Germany. He believed that his special mission was as important for Germany as it was for Britain. He had actually been heading for the duke of Hamilton's estate at Dungavel House, believing that Hamilton would be sympathetic to his peace mission.

The pilot initially concealed his true identity from Donald and presented his identity papers in the name of Alfred Horn. No one in the hall that evening recognized him as 46-year-old Rudolf Hess – deputy Führer of the Third Reich and Hitler's designated successor.[2] The events that unfolded in subsequent days begin to answer certain questions that were raised in my book *The London Cage* and clarify for certain that Hess was soon transferred to the jurisdiction of MI6.[3]

Who in Britain and Germany knew that Hess was flying to Britain that night? Where was he interrogated after his transfer from Scotland? And by whom?

The prisoner's identity

The wreckage of the ME Bf 110 was searched by Donald and Flying Officer Malcolm. Something seemed to be wrong: they noted that there were no guns or bomb racks, no cameras – and no drop tanks in place.[4] Thus the pilot had had insufficient fuel to fly back to Germany. This raised the immediate question of how he was expecting to get back home.

In Donald's absence, the pilot was interrogated by Roman Battaglia, a member of the Polish consulate in Glasgow. Battaglia did not recognize Hess at the time of the interrogation. Hess remained calm and gave little away, except to reiterate that he had a message for the duke of Hamilton and had once met Hamilton at the Olympic Games in Berlin in 1936. Battaglia asked the nature of the special message, but Hess merely replied: 'It is the highest interests of the British air force.'[5]

When Donald returned to the drill hall, Chief Inspector Gray was trying to question Hess with Battaglia. Gray repeatedly asked Hess how many men had been in the aircraft, and suggested to Hess that they had captured another pilot.[6]

Donald noticed that the pilot was wearing an expensively tailored uniform with three eagle stripes, and he tried to establish his name.

'Oh, we know his name,' interrupted Gray. 'It's Hoffmann.'

'Nein, nein,' replied Hess. 'Nicht Hoffmann – Hauptmann.'

Donald turned to Gray and corrected him, informing him that Hauptmann was not his name, but his rank: captain in the German air force. Hess seemed pleased that Donald understood him. He stood up with some difficulty, his ankle injured from baling out, and explained that he did not intend to go back to Germany. Battaglia interjected that therefore Hess was a deserter.[7]

Hess protested again that he was a special emissary with a message for the duke of Hamilton and that his name was Alfred Horn. Donald instinctively felt that he recognized the face. A reference to Löwenbräu beer in their conversation produced a sour expression from Horn: Donald knew of only two teetotallers in Nazi Germany – Hitler and Hess. Suddenly it came to him that the man in front of him was Rudolf Hess. Donald relayed a message to the RAF duty controller at Turnhouse, where the duke of Hamilton was serving with No. 602 Squadron RAF, as an air commodore. Hamilton did not believe it could be Hess and so he went to bed.

The following morning, 11 May – and much to his frustration – Donald was informed that Hamilton had not seen Hess during the night. In the interim, the German had been moved to Maryhill Barracks, outside Glasgow.[8] Hamilton finally arrived at 10 a.m. and spoke to Hess alone.[9] He told Hess: 'If we make peace now, we will be at war again within two years.'[10]

Even now, Hamilton was uncertain about Hess's identity and he telephoned Winston Churchill. Churchill ordered him to fly south and meet him at the prime minister's wartime country residence, Ditchley Park, north of Oxford. This he duly did.[11] Churchill listened to his account of events and decided to dispatch Ivone Kirkpatrick (a German expert at the Foreign Office) to Maryhill Barracks formally to identify Hess.[12] It meant that Hess was not positively identified until Monday, 12 May – 36 hours after he had landed in Scotland. By then, the Nazi regime had made a formal announcement that Hess was suffering from severe mental illness and was missing in a flight over the North Sea. This was followed by a BBC broadcast that Hess was safe in a Glasgow hospital.[13] After a medical examination by Lieutenant Colonel Gibson Graham (Royal Army Medical Corps), Hess was declared sane and in general good health.[14]

At Trent Park, Kendrick had already been alerted by Menzies of Hess's arrival. Hess was going to have to be treated as a special case and would need careful handling. Menzies told Kendrick that Hess would need to be kept apart from other German prisoners. Churchill decreed that Hess should be 'strictly isolated in a convenient house not too far from London, fitted by "C" with the necessary appliances [listening equipment] and every endeavour made to study his mentality and get anything worthwhile out of him'.[15]

The reports which were generated about Hess in the coming weeks offer a rare, detailed insight into the daily life of spymaster Kendrick at that time. It is clear from the declassified files that Hess was under the jurisdiction and care of MI6 at this time and decisions about him were made by 'C'.[16] This is also confirmed in the official history of MI6.[17] Hess was not to be treated as a peace emissary, or a defector, but as an enemy prisoner of war.[18] His three MI6 minders – Kendrick, Frank Foley and 'Captain R. Barnes' – were to gain intelligence from Hess about the Nazi regime. A secret report in the Hess files, previously overlooked by historians, was written at this time by Kendrick's colleague Denys Felkin (head of air intelligence at Trent Park): 'So far nothing can be ascertained about either the second occupant of the aircraft, or regarding the Canadian Bearer Bonds.'[19]

The reference to a second occupant is a potentially ground-breaking discovery, because inherited versions of the Hess story have always claimed that he flew solo to Scotland. Was there a second person on that flight? And if so, who was it? When he was captured, Hess was found to be carrying £140,000 in Canadian bonds, tied around his body. Were these real bonds? And if so, what was their significance or purpose? Or perhaps they were a coded term for the detailed peace plans that he brought with him. This report by Felkin is currently the only document written by Felkin in the declassified files. His comments in it leave unanswered certain questions about the Hess affair.

It has always been understood that Felkin interrogated Hess, but no report on such an interrogation has been released. Cynthia Turner (née Crew), who later worked for Felkin's air intelligence section at Latimer House, commented: 'It was generally understood that one of our senior RAF officers, I think it was Squadron Leader Spencsely [sic], was sent to interview him [Hess].'[20] Squadron Leader G.W. Spenceley was an interrogator with ADI(K), the air intelligence section attached to CSDIC, in 1941, and an official report of his interview with Hess does survive among the declassified files.[21]

Hess's mission remains shrouded in controversy and conspiracy theories. There are many unanswered questions. Who in Germany knew? Did he come with the knowledge of Adolf Hitler or Hermann Goering or both? He always claimed that he flew to Britain on his own initiative, without Hitler's authority or the knowledge of any member of the Nazi government.[22] He argued that Hitler did not want war with Britain, but a permanent understanding that would give Hitler free rein in Europe, while allowing Britain to keep its empire intact, with no interference from Germany. Hitler believed that Russia was the real threat, and therefore Germany and Britain should form an alliance.[23]

Historian Michael Smith has uncovered evidence of an MI6 sting operation to lure Hess to Britain, already being planned in 1940.[24] Kendrick's colleague Frank Foley had been dispatched to Lisbon for two weeks that year to assess the viability of such a plan. He had returned to London and advised 'C' that it was too risky. The 'Hess sting' was apparently abandoned. Or was it?

Hess and the Tower of London

During the night of 16/17 May, Hess was moved by train, under tight security and in the utmost secrecy, from Scotland to the Tower of London.[25] This was to be his temporary quarters, while Mytchett Place, near Aldershot, was made ready for him and 'wired for sound'. Churchill wrote that Hess was 'to be kept in the strictest seclusion, and those in charge of him should refrain from conversation'.[26] Churchill believed that Hess was an accomplice of Hitler's in

all murders, treacheries and cruelties by which the Nazi regime imposed itself first on Germany, as it now seeks to impose itself on Europe . . . the horrors of the German concentration camps, the brutal persecution of the Jews, the perfidious inroad upon Czechoslovakia, the unspeakable, incredible brutalities and bestialities of the German invasion and conquest of Poland . . . are all cases in which he [Hess] has participated.[27]

Whether Kendrick ever visited Hess in the Tower is not known. Hess was accommodated in the Queen's House overlooking the White Tower. He expected to be in Britain for only a few days, before returning to Germany; but

MI6 had other plans. What followed in the next 24 hours was recalled by Charles Fraser-Smith, who was already undertaking work for another branch of military intelligence, MI9, where he was sourcing and dispatching special gadgets to be smuggled to British POWs in camps to aid escape.[28] He received a phone call from MI5 and was asked if he could copy the uniform of a senior German officer. Fraser-Smith confirmed that he could. The following evening, he travelled with his men to the agreed location in an MI6 car. With him was an experienced tailor from the textile company Courtaulds. They were taken into a room where an immaculate uniform of an officer of the German air force was laid out on a table. One of the MI5 officers took Fraser-Smith to one side and said: 'We've given Hess something to ensure that he doesn't wake up until morning. But this is his uniform, and we must have it back to him in the next four hours.'

A duplicate of Hess's uniform was made within that time. 'What it was used for – if it was used, is something I shall be interested to know one day,' wrote Fraser-Smith.[29] It is possible that British intelligence had intended to send a 'double' of Hess back to Germany, but this did not transpire.

While Hess enjoyed attention in the Tower, believing he was about to return to Germany, Kendrick was organizing the Post Office Research Station at Dollis Hill to install bugging equipment and an M Room at Mytchett Place. Subsequent servicing of the equipment would also be carried out by engineers from Dollis Hill.[30] They were only permitted to enter the camp with the agreement of 'C', and their passes were held by Captain Howard at MI6 while they were not on site. Although a list of secret listeners for Mytchett Place has not been seen, documentation indicates that one was a Lieutenant H. Reade. He was a shorthand typist and was engaged in recording Hess's conversations.[31] He appears to have come and gone for certain periods of time and not to have been based in the camp permanently. Mytchett Place was given the codename 'Camp Z', and special conditions there were designed so that a study could be made of Hess and any worthwhile intelligence gained from him. He was to be held under the care of his MI6 minders, Kendrick, Foley and 'Captain Barnes'.

Camp Z

On 18 May, Lieutenant Colonel A. Malcom Scott was handed top-secret orders to proceed to Camp Z at midday that day and take command of the place as camp commandant, in charge of its strict security.[32] Hess was allowed books, writing materials and recreation items, but no newspapers or radio broadcasts. Any letters he wished to send to Germany had to be approved by the director of prisoners of war. No visitors were allowed into the camp unless prescribed by the Foreign Office and unless they carried a special military permit. Even Prime Minister Winston Churchill was not permitted into the camp without clearance from MI6.[33]

Kendrick, Foley and 'Barnes' were issued with special passes.[34] Kendrick was given the name 'Colonel L.G. Wallace', to avoid Hess recognizing him as the spymaster expelled from Vienna just three years earlier. Foley appears to have been the only minder who was not given a pseudonym. Hess was known in reports by a codename 'Jonathan' or 'Z'.

On 20 May, a military ambulance carrying Hess arrived at Mytchett Place. He was escorted to his room and then introduced to Kendrick, Foley and 'Barnes'. Although Hess never discovered Kendrick's identity, he did suspect that he was being held by the British secret service and frequently complained that he believed his minders were trying to poison him – something that was vehemently denied.[35]

It was expected that Hess would give away key information about the Nazi regime during the first few days. All conversations were recorded and transcribed in an M Room on site. Even though these transcripts have not been declassified, a few summary reports of the conversations have been released and provide sketchy material. Soon after his arrival, Hess began to display anxiety that his new private quarters were behind barbed wire and bars and within a 'grille'.[36] The grille – consisting of thick metal bars and a secure door – had been constructed around the main quarters upstairs to prevent Hess from wandering around the rest of the house. The door to this grille was always guarded and locked when necessary. Kendrick's bedroom was next to Hess's within the grille. With all this security, Hess again complained that he had fallen into the hands of a clique of the secret service.

Menzies ('C') wrote that Hess was very depressed and wished to be left alone, but his psychological state might be turned to MI6's advantage: 'We are of the opinion that this might be the psychological moment when he might change his attitude . . . Doctor says he is moody, like a spoilt child. His present mood should, if possible, be exploited.'[37]

On the first evening, Hess was served dinner in his room at 8 o'clock and appeared more settled. At 11 o'clock the duty officer, Second Lieutenant W. Malone, took up his position within the grille to guard him for the night. Hess woke at around 8 o'clock the following morning, having had only five hours' sleep. He asked for bacon and fish for breakfast. After being served the food in his room, he confided to 'Barnes' that he was being poisoned and suspected the guard, Malone. Hess then refused to eat or drink. At 1 o'clock, he finally came downstairs to take lunch with his three minders. He appeared in much better spirits and apologized for his suspicions at breakfast. After lunch, he returned to his room, because his ankle was still hurting from the crash. When he reappeared downstairs at 8 o'clock that evening, Kendrick looked up to see Hess in the full uniform of a captain of the German air force. This incident marked the beginning of increasingly strange and unpredictable behaviour by Hess.

Two days after Hess's arrival, on 22 May, he expressed the belief that the guards were planning to murder him. He spent the morning in his room and came down to lunch at 1 o'clock dressed in plain clothes. After lunch, he walked in the garden with Kendrick, Foley, 'Barnes' and Dr Gibson Graham. At dinner with them that evening, Hess was much easier in his mind and franker in his conversation. He remained convinced that Germany was going to win the war, and told Graham:

There is no oil shortage, Germany has more aircraft than she knows what to do with, and submarines are being made in every part of the country, even in Czechoslovakia. The Führer has no wish to destroy the British

Empire, but if we persist in fighting, we will be forced to launch a terrible air offensive. It will result in the killing of hundreds of thousands of people.

Hess still clung to the hope that he could negotiate a peace deal. Graham's report noted that Hess was

> in a high state of depression at the possible failure of his mission, and has hinted that it might be better for him to die. He is convinced that he is in the hands of a clique who are preventing him from daily access to the King, and that the only way for him to secure access to the King is through the Duke of Hamilton.[38]

At around 10.15 a.m. the following day, Hess went into the garden with Kendrick, Foley and 'Barnes'. He stayed only a few minutes before returning to his room with 'Barnes', and became increasingly suspicious of his three minders. In the weeks after his transfer from the Tower, he began to notice that his food and medication left him with a distinctly unusual sensation, and this may have been at the root of his belief that he was being given poison or 'truth drugs'. He alleged that

> a short time after taking it, a curious development of warmth rising over the nape of the neck to the head: in the head feelings which are similar to headache pains, but which are not the same: there follows for many hours an extraordinary feeling of well-being, physical and mental energy joie de vivre, optimism. Little sleep during the night but this did not in the least destroy my sense of euphoria.[39]

Hess observed withdrawal symptoms when the unknown substance was not being used. He felt a difference in his body after drinking a cup of milk.[40] Without any apparent cause, he was plunged into pessimism and felt on the verge of a nervous breakdown. This was followed by lengthy periods of exceptionally rapid exhaustion of the brain. Hess became convinced that his captors were trying to poison him and he accused Kendrick and Foley of drugging him with 'Mexican Brain Poison'; he is thought to have been referring to mescaline, which was supposed to induce talkativeness.[41] MI5 was encouraged by the War Office to give Hess the barbiturate evipan sodium.[42] A large selection of drugs had been confiscated from Hess when he landed in Scotland. These were subsequently analysed by the Medical Research Council and found to be harmless.[43]

On the morning of 25 May, Hess refused to speak to anyone. Outside, he silently watched the commanding officer's parade from a distance, with Kendrick, Foley and 'Barnes'. Without warning, he launched into a modified Nazi goose-step in front of them. Afterwards, he remained in his room all afternoon, except for a short walk with 'Barnes'. At 5.30 p.m., 'C' arrived at Camp Z for a private meeting with Kendrick, Foley and 'Barnes'. They discussed the lack of progress with Hess from an intelligence point of view. It is not known whether 'C' spoke with Hess.

The next day, 26 May, it rained so hard that Hess was unable to take a walk. Apart from eating his meals downstairs with his minders, he read in his room. Kendrick noted how depressed and dejected Hess had become; in his opinion, Hess was beginning to realize that Britain was very different from what he had been led to believe. The following morning was wet again and Hess was similarly unable to go out. He managed a walk after tea, with 'Barnes' and Graham. He seemed calmer and in a better temper, but complained of his food being over-seasoned. He was restless that night and woke at 5 a.m.

Nothing much by way of conversation was exchanged over breakfast on 28 May, and Hess went out for a long walk in the garden afterwards. In his absence, Kendrick and Foley discussed when to break the news to him of the sinking of the *Bismarck*, Germany's newest and finest battleship. They decided on that lunchtime. Hess had requested the same food as the previous day, and said he preferred to eat in the company of his minders than alone in his room. Over lunch, Kendrick broke the news of the *Bismarck*.[44] Hess displayed shock, swiftly complained of exhaustion and backache, and retired to bed. The sinking of the *Bismarck* provoked no comment from him, which was rather a disappointment for his minders. Kendrick and 'Barnes' were frustrated and bored with 'Death's Head', as they nicknamed Hess. Kendrick had a running wager with 'Barnes' and Foley about how many shillings Hess was worth in terms of intelligence. That day he piped up to 'Barnes': 'He's now worth thirty-five shillings a week – no more.'[45]

Elements of paranoia were beginning to haunt Hess. He feared that a member of the secret service would creep into his bedroom at night and cut an artery to fake his suicide. He said as much to Kendrick and told him that he was especially suspicious of 'Barnes', because of his ill-fitting uniform and because his badges had obviously been removed.[46]

Hess openly articulated again that the British secret service wanted him dead and the method would be to drive him to insanity and suicide. He drafted a letter stating that he would not commit suicide: if he was found dead, Hitler would know that he had not taken his own life. He complained of the endless sound of motorbike engines, loud voices and people clicking their heels – all designed, he said, to drive him mad.[47]

At the evening meal on 28 May, Hess seemed to have a good appetite. He insisted that Kendrick helped himself first to the fish. He then took the fish from Kendrick's plate, rather than from the serving dish. This was all part of his paranoia and his efforts to avoid being poisoned. Hess's delusion even extended to seeing Hitler's face in his soup.

That night Hess asked for a hairnet for bed. Malone wrote in his private diary:

I find it difficult to realise that this rather broken man who slouches into his chair, careless as to his dress, whose expressions are unstudied, who is capable of hiding his emotions, who swings in mood from cheerfulness to depression in a few hours, whose body reflects his mental pain and whose mind is clouded with delusionary ideas . . . that this man was the Deputy Fuhrer of the Reich![48]

Hess retired to bed at 10 o'clock on 28 May. An hour later, when visited by Dr Graham, he asked for a sedative because he felt confused and very anxious.

The next day, Hess was silent at breakfast. Kendrick submitted a report to 'C':

> The following are the latest developments in Jonathan's mental state. In view of their seriousness, it is considered urgent that you should read the Medical Officer's report and extracts from the night Duty Officer's report. We would point out that Jonathan has indicated, should he die, there would be terrible repercussions. The inference we draw from that statement is that Hitler would not believe in suicide and would take reprisals on British people in his hands.[49]

As a result of Hess's preoccupation with death and suicide, Graham recommended a psychiatric investigation, stating: 'this man shows definitive abnormal traits which have become suddenly acute and . . . the problem is one for a skilled psychiatrist.'[50]

Major Dicks and Colonel Rees

Graham was temporarily relieved of his duties at Camp Z, and Major Henry Dicks, a psychiatrist in the Royal Army Medical Corps, arrived on the afternoon of 29 May to make an assessment of Hess. Dicks was already working for Kendrick's unit CSDIC. Having been born in Estonia to a British father and German mother, he could speak several languages. At CSDIC, he provided analysis of the psychological profile of prisoners of war and assessed how best to obtain information from them. He also compiled reports on the state of morale in the German forces and recommended how to conduct psychological warfare and target propaganda for maximum effect. As far as Hess knew, Dicks was an ordinary doctor, but his presence at Camp Z would help to extract some useful information for MI6. Hess seemed very relaxed and chatted a great deal with him on Dicks' first day.

On the evening of 30 May, Scott joined Hess and his minders for supper. Hess remained silent throughout and refused to be drawn into conversation.

At the end of the meal, he asked to speak to Scott. Kendrick translated. Hess made a formal protest about being kept within the enclosure and asked for parole, giving an undertaking not to try to escape. He complained of being trapped with Dicks and 'the German-speaking companions', who were thwarting his mission to save the world from war. Kendrick telephoned 'C' and expressed concern that Scott was going to ask for a relaxation of restrictions on Hess's movements within the camp.

At the end of May 1941, Hess was assessed by Colonel Rees, consultant in psychological medicine to the army. Rees was a fluent German speaker. Before seeing Hess, he was briefed by Kendrick, Foley and 'Barnes'. Rees's assessment of Hess is contained in a three-page report, in which he commented:

> While this man is certainly not today insane in the sense that would make one consider certification, he is mentally sick. He is anxious and somewhat tense; he is of a somewhat paranoid type ... In my opinion, Hess is a man of unstable mentality and has almost certainly been like that since adolescence ... a psychopathic personality of the schizophrenic type.

Rees recommended that Hess be allowed edited news bulletins to prevent discontentment and to put him less on his guard: 'his reaction to the news, whichever way it went, ought to be of some value to the men [the minders] who are with him ... and it might assist in loosening his tongue'.[51]

Two days later, 1 June, Hess was still suffering from restlessness, particularly at night. He now began to treat Dicks with even greater distrust and suspicion. The following day, Hess stayed in bed until midday, after another restless night. He complained to Kendrick at lunch that his food was over-seasoned in a deliberate attempt to starve him. He went straight to his room and wrote furiously all afternoon. Kendrick and Foley discussed what to do about his periods of introspection, and suggested to Dicks that he persuade Hess to come down for a walk in the garden. This he duly did. That night, Hess requested something to help him sleep and was given the drug phanodorm, used to treat insomnia.

By 4 June, Hess was displaying symptoms of deep depression and was almost suicidal. He was observed sitting morosely under a tree in the garden, in a position that looked quite uncomfortable, and refusing to speak. From the window that evening, his minders observed him pacing up and down in the garden, very agitated. Hidden microphones in the trees overhead him muttering that he couldn't stand this any longer. When he came back inside, he refused the company of his minders. It was 10 o'clock when he turned to them and said 'goodnight'. He had never wished them goodnight before. Kendrick became uneasy. As the clock in the sitting room chimed half past 10, Kendrick went off to talk to Commandant Scott. He expressed concern that Hess could be planning to kill himself that night. It was a concern shared by Foley and 'Barnes'. Scott ordered Second Lieutenant Malone to be on duty inside the grille.

11

THE MADNESS OF HESS

By early June 1941, MI6 was becoming increasingly concerned about the sanity of Hess. His state of mind was of paramount importance, because, if he was declared insane, then according to the Geneva Convention he could not be treated as a prisoner of war. The doctors had concluded that he was not mad, but there was mounting concern at Mytchett Place.[1] Being in such close daily contact with Hess, Kendrick became cynical and increasingly impatient at the prized prisoner, who was still convinced that he was being poisoned by the British secret service. In later years, Kendrick spoke to his family of Hess only rarely, though he did comment to his grandson, Ken Walsh, that Hess had been mad.

Mealtimes turned into a battleground: Hess would frequently refuse to eat his food and would ask Kendrick to eat it instead. Hess was still not allowed contact with the outside world, and strict secrecy continued to surround his whereabouts. He wrote letters to his wife in Germany, but these were never sent by the authorities and survive now in the National Archives.[2] Menzies and the Foreign Office discussed what to do with the letters, because one day they might be evidence of Jonathan's decision to kill himself. It was decided that the letters were to be photographed and copies kept out of London, at Bletchley Park.[3]

Uppermost in the minds of Kendrick, Foley, 'Barnes' and 'C' was how to secure intelligence from their highest-ranking Nazi prisoner.[4] It was thought that Hess might be more open if he was sent a negotiator to discuss his peace plan.[5] Lord Simon (the lord chancellor) agreed to take on the task. He had a basic knowledge of German, was known to be an appeaser and had met Hess in Berlin six years earlier. Menzies discussed with Sir Alexander Cadogan at the Foreign Office how they could make a fresh attempt to trick Hess into revealing state secrets. Simon was shown all the transcripts of Hess's secretly bugged conversations and the accompanying notes, in order to provide guidance on the kind of information he might gain. These transcripts and notes have not been declassified.

Hess had been through several days of increasing, severe depression, and again it was feared that he might attempt suicide. But the news of a negotiator coming to Camp Z had a positive effect on him. He came downstairs to breakfast on 5 June in a highly excitable state. Although he calmed down as the day wore on, he continued to maintain that the staff were trying to poison him.[6] He stayed up later than usual that night and drank port until a quarter to midnight. Before sleeping, he asked whether he could be given a calendar showing the phases of the moon, professing himself to be a keen astrologer. Kendrick still occupied the bedroom next to Hess's quarters.

The following day, 6 June, Hess complained of a headache. He spent most of the day writing in his sitting room and preparing for the 'negotiator'. Kendrick delivered a report to 'C' over the secure green telephone, during which he said that Hess seemed 'somewhat dazed and not fully to understand the importance of my communication'.[7] Hess was complaining of severe head pains and thought he might faint. In the afternoon, he was still being uncommunicative. At 9.15 that evening, Kendrick went for a walk with him in the rain in the garden, later writing: 'he talked cheerfully and vividly of general matters, and of his flight to Scotland. He appeared to be a changed man.'

Then Kendrick discussed with him his health – Hess's favourite topic. Hess complained about pains in his back and head.

Kendrick suggested: 'Your nerves are probably responsible for your difficulty in finding sleep. After the meeting on Monday, you will no doubt experience relief.'

'Yes,' mused Hess, 'it will be a relief to me.'

'Are there others in high places in Germany who feel the same as you about peace?'

After some hesitation, Hess replied, 'Ja, Ich glaube schon' (Yes, I believe there are). Kendrick later reported to 'C' that Hess appeared reluctant to answer the question and that may be of some interest as 'it appears to indicate that there is some kind of internal dissension [in Germany]'.[8]

The negotiator

Hess did not surface for breakfast on the morning of 7 June. Lord Simon was due in two days and Hess spent the whole day in an agitated state. He ventured into the garden for a short time between the showers of rain. He did not sleep well that night and remained in bed until 1 o'clock the following lunchtime. He finally arrived downstairs and Kendrick enquired about his health.

'I can't concentrate,' replied Hess, extremely morose and hostile. 'I can't read Liddell Hart's *Dynamic Defence* that you've given me. It's too difficult and I can't find the German equivalents for the English words which I understand perfectly well.'[9]

'That's a pity,' replied Kendrick, noting that Hess appeared totally preoccupied with the special delegation that was visiting him the following afternoon. Hess helped himself to soup from the tureen, but refused to eat it. He then refused some plain boiled fish. Kendrick helped himself to the sliced roast beef, Yorkshire pudding, cabbage and potatoes. Foley reported the incident to 'C':

> Colonel Wallace [i.e. Kendrick], who sits at the head of the table, served himself first. Jonathan sits on his left and is served second. On this occasion, Jonathan asked Colonel Wallace whether he could have the food which he, Wallace, had already selected for himself. Wallace agreed and they exchanged plates. Jonathan remarked: 'You will probably think this as idea fixe and perhaps somewhat hysterical.' He helped himself to apple pie, but refused pastry and custard. This is the most demonstrative instance of his fear of poisoning, which we have experienced.[10]

After lunch, Hess refused to take the air in the garden and retired to his room. The deterioration in his mental health caused further concern and 'C' was given an update by Foley, who suggested that 'C' might wish to warn the delegation visiting Hess the following day that it might be difficult to converse sensibly with him.[11]

That evening, Kendrick, Foley and 'Barnes' sat down to discuss what to do about Hess's lunch prior to the arrival of the 'negotiator' the next day. They contemplated having Hess eat in his bedroom with an officer, but then decided that Hess should dine with the visitors and his minders, because otherwise 'he may imagine that his food has been specially selected and doped, with the object of dulling his mental powers'.[12] After Hess had gone upstairs to his quarters that night, Scott commented in his diary that he had 'retired to bed like a spoilt child' and 'it seems unlikely he will be in a fit state for tomorrow's conference'. Kendrick agreed with Foley and 'Barnes' that they would all be glad when the meeting was over, as the tension inside Camp Z was continuing to mount.

On the morning of 9 June, Lord Simon reported to Churchill that he had read the bugged conversations and his chief preliminary deductions were: Hess had come here without the prior knowledge of Hitler; while not 'psychotic' (i.e. 'mad' in the medical sense), he was a highly neurotic man who was not involved in the inner councils of Hitler or his generals on high strategy, but may unwittingly possess knowledge of which he himself was unaware; and he genuinely believed that he could bring about a rapprochement between Britain and Germany.

As far as Hess understood matters, he was about to meet a high representative of His Majesty's government. Officers from MI5 were to form part of the delegation. Hess insisted on the presence of a German witness and this was to be Kurt Maas, a senior Nazi official being held in a POW camp in England. Under the cover name of 'A. Benson', Maas was transferred in the utmost secrecy to Camp Z for the three-hour meeting.[13] Lord Simon arrived, disguised as 'Dr Guthrie' to mask his true identity from the camp guards.

Hess took lunch in his room with 'Barnes', but ate nothing, except for some glucose tablets. An hour later, the stenographer arrived. Hess was waiting for the delegation in his upstairs drawing room in the full Luftwaffe captain's uniform and regalia in which he had set off from Augsburg four weeks earlier. He had prepared assiduously for the meeting by writing out and signing Hitler's peace terms as he knew them. Fearful of the tactics of his minders, Hess asked to see Lord Simon alone. However, the hidden microphones picked up every word of the three-hour meeting, all recorded by Kendrick's secret listeners. Part of this has survived in declassified files.

'I would not deceive you for any purpose at all,' said Simon, concealing the real reason why he had been sent. 'You have got the idea that clever people might be interfering with your food – it is fantastic nonsense!'

Hess interpolated a polite 'yes'.

'It is really fantastic nonsense,' Simon said again. 'You have got the impression that there is mixed up here some sort of Secret Service with the officers! It makes me wonder what happens in Germany but it does not happen here.'

'I have the impression,' explained Hess in awkward English, 'that the soldier who always sleeps with me had the intention to give me something different. I always eat from the common stand and drink from the common water . . . But mornings, I get the milk – milk [meant] only for me – and I get a feeling, pains, in my –'[14]

'It's perfect nonsense!' Simon interrupted.

'If you will not believe me, I will go off my head and be dead,' said Hess.

'It is ridiculous because nothing of the sort happened,' said Simon.

'But there are in England surely some [people] who don't desire an understanding between England and Germany?' said Hess.

'I am sure I don't know.'

'May I show you my wife and son?' pleaded Hess, taking a photograph out of his pocket.

'I shall be very pleased to see them,' said Simon.

Kendrick was listening from the M Room. Through the microphones, Hess was heard to shriek: '*Please, save me for them!* Save me for peace, and save me for them [my wife and son]!'[15]

That evening, a summary of the conference was telephoned to 'C'. Simon reported to Churchill that Hess believed that noises were deliberately made at night to prevent him from sleeping and that he might be assassinated. He considered that he had risked his life to fly to Britain, but it was all in vain. Churchill wrote:

> I have read the [Simon–Hess] transcripts which seem to me to consist of the outpourings of a disordered mind. They are like a conversation with a mentally defective child who has been guilty of murder or arson. Nevertheless, I think it might be well to send them by air in a sure hand to President Roosevelt . . . and meanwhile [Hess] should be kept strictly isolated where he is.[16]

The meeting with Simon did, nevertheless, have a positive effect on Hess, as he had a better night's sleep. He woke only once – at 5 a.m. – to open his window, draw the curtains and slam the door.

The following day, 10 June, Hess was observed in the garden with a spade, attempting to dig one of the flower beds. It was clear to Kendrick that he was not used to wielding a spade. The exercise seemed to exhaust him, and he retired to his room to lie down. In the following days, Hess's moods fluctuated. On the morning of 13 June, he did not come down for breakfast, but asked for milk and biscuits in his room. He spent the whole day there until 6 o'clock, when he went for a short walk in the garden. He took another long walk after dinner, not retiring for bed until 11 o'clock. The only incident during the day was a short battle with one of the guards over his underclothes. But the tension continued to rise, and on 14 June Commandant Scott noted in his diary:

> Z was in a difficult mood all day and paced the terrace like a caged lion, refusing to answer when spoken to. His only request was for an enema which was duly purchased for him by 'Captain Barnes'. He retired to his bathroom with his treasure but emerged eventually without apparently having received any consolation from his new toy and spent the afternoon in his room in the deepest gloom. After dinner, however, he condescended to go into the garden and play dart bowls with Capt. 'Barnes' and even went so far as to make a joke.[17]

A dramatic crisis broke during the early hours of 15 June.

Inside the grille

Just before 1 a.m. on 15 June, Lieutenant Jackson woke the commandant to say that Hess was in a greatly agitated state of mind and was demanding to see Lieutenant Malone, but Malone was on duty outside.[18] Dicks was sent upstairs to see Hess, but Hess had developed an intense dislike of Dicks. At the sight of him, Hess flew into a rage. With fists clenched, he screamed: 'I am being undone and you know it!'[19]

'How do you mean – undone?' asked Dicks.

At the sound of shouting, Lieutenant Stephen Smith, the adjutant, rushed upstairs to find Hess in his sitting room in dressing gown and pyjamas, looking very drawn and pale, his eyes sunk deep in his head. Dicks withdrew from the room.

Smith said quietly: 'I heard you've asked for an officer of the Guard.' Hess's garbled reply in English made little sense.

'I speak German,' said Smith. Hess appeared to relax as he told Smith that he trusted Malone, that he feared that he might not live through the night and he wished to give certain letters to Malone.

Smith replied, 'Malone is a soldier like the rest of the Guard. He's on duty and cannot leave his post. I can do anything for you that Mr Malone can do. You can trust me.'

'I trust all members of the Guard,' said Hess. 'But I am in the hands of the Secret Service. I'm being poisoned and there is nothing you can do to stop them.'

Smith adopted a formality which, he believed, Hess would relate to:

Your life and security are in the hands of the Brigade of Guards and are *ipso facto* secure. I am the adjutant and I do know that Germans are not the only efficient soldiers. We, the Guard, have the fullest control over all that goes on here.[20]

Smith talked to Hess for over an hour. Hess gave him a sample of his whisky to be analysed for secret dope.[21]

Foley sent an urgent message to 'C' that Hess's mental state had

> deteriorated seriously during the last 48 hours. During the night, his fear of poisoning became more acute than it has ever been . . . It is obvious, even to us laymen, that he is very ill. Under these conditions, we are precluded from doing any useful work from our angle.[22]

Forty-five minutes later, Kendrick made a telephone call to 'C' to inform him that Hess had put on his uniform and had asked to speak to the commandant. He was making three demands: to be allowed to speak to Malone; to be removed without delay to hospital; and that the commandant procure luminal and phano-dorm for him without the knowledge of the medical officer.[23] Kendrick, Foley and 'Barnes' watched as their charge deteriorated. Back at MI6 headquarters in London, 'C' tried to work out what to do with Hess and went to visit Sir Alexander Cadogan, permanent under-secretary at the Foreign Office. The latter wrote in his diary:

> 'C' came in about Hess, who's going off his head. I don't much care what happens to *him*. *We* can use him. There's a meeting tomorrow between Winston and [Lord] Simon about him, at which I hope to be present and to get decisions on how to treat and how to exploit him – alive, mad or dead.[24]

Hess went to bed early and was given a sedative. He became angry and tried to snatch the box from Scott. That evening, he left two very brief notes on his table. In translation, they read:

> Please give my uniform to the Duke of Hamilton, who may be good enough to send it to my family in peace time. 15.6.41.
>
> I shall win the pure war of nerves (special sirens etc.); I cannot win the chemical war against my nerves, especially as its end is not to be foreseen. The means of defence are lacking to me.[25]

At five minutes to four on the morning of 16 June, Hess walked in his pyjamas into the duty officer's room inside the grille. He told the officer on guard, Lieutenant Young, that he could not sleep and had taken some whisky.

A few minutes later, Hess was heard back in his room, calling for a doctor. Roused from his bedroom on the far side of the landing, Dicks put on his dressing gown and rushed to the grille with more sleeping tablets. The warder unlocked the gate and stood aside to let him through. Hess's bedroom was directly opposite the gate. Hess rushed out of his bedroom towards the open gate, no longer in pyjamas but now in full Luftwaffe uniform. His flying boots thudding across the floorboards, a look of despair in his eyes, he pushed passed Dicks. An army sergeant came running up the stairs and drew his revolver.

Dicks screamed: 'Don't shoot him!'

Kendrick rushed out of his room just as Hess leapt into the air, clearing the stairwell balustrade like an Olympic hurdler. Still conscious, even after the fall, Hess lay in the stairwell surrounded by ashen-faced officers – Kendrick, Scott, Dicks and now Malone.

Now in agony, Hess groaned: 'Morphia. Give me morphia!'

Malone bent down to Hess and asked: 'Surely you didn't mean to kill yourself?'

'I certainly did, and I still will,' replied Hess. He went on:

I cannot face madness. It would be too terrible for me to bear and for others to witness. By killing myself, I will be acting like a man. I know that of late I have been behaving like a woman, *daemlich*. When I first came here, I got up at eight each morning. But then came that period of no sleep, no sleep, no sleep. I began to go to pieces under the influence of drugs.

By now, Foley had arrived. He took in the scene and hurried off to phone 'C'. Dicks was insisting on a specialist surgeon to attend to Hess's injuries. An hour and a half after the suicide attempt, Kendrick gave an update over the green telephone to the War Office, to explain that Hess had broken through the grille in a deliberate attempt to injure himself. He then telephoned a report to 'C':

The crash came at 4 a.m. The upper thigh is broken and there is contusion of the shoulder. The Camp Commandant has spoken to Colonel Coates and asked him to make arrangements for an X-ray van and other apparatus to be sent here within twelve hours, when the bone will be set. As far as I know there is no immediate danger.[26]

While Kendrick was on the telephone, the surgeon, Major Murray, arrived. He temporarily splinted Hess's leg until it could be X-rayed. Once the X-ray van had arrived, it confirmed that Hess had fractured his thigh, with some splintering. Murray injected an anaesthetic of sodium pentothal to enable him to perform the necessary surgery. Hess's leg was put in traction, with a large 'Steinmann pin' through the shin bone. The pin had weights attached to maintain steady traction on the thigh and to straighten the fragments of bone.[27] It was the beginning of four months of immobility for Hess, during which time he was confined to bed and was frequently difficult and demanding.

After the failed suicide, Commandant Scott informed 'C':

Z's case has now definitely become one that can only be dealt with by trained mental specialists from an asylum ... I cannot subject young officers to the strain and responsibility of sitting with a patient who is insane. Apart from the two medical orderlies now arrived, there is no one in this camp who is used to the diabolical cunning shown by a patient of this sort, or who is trained in the various methods whereby we can defeat the object of a madman determined to commit suicide.[28]

The day after the attempted suicide, 17 June, Hess remained quiet all day and ate lunch with 'Barnes' next to his bed. That evening, he sent a message downstairs to say that he would refuse any meals unless accompanied by an officer. The fear of poisoning had returned. Although still held in total isolation from the outside world, Hess was now permitted to read *The Times* newspaper.

Camp Z after the failed suicide

It was clear that changes would have to be made at Camp Z for Hess's own protection. Colonel Rees, consultant in psychological medicine to the army, who was in Ireland at the time of the attempted suicide, flew back to Camp Z immediately on a special plane. In his subsequent assessment for MI6, he confirmed that Hess was a 'constant suicidal risk and precautions must be taken'.[29] He recommended the installation of armoured glass in all windows within the grille, as well as in the sitting room and the mess room downstairs. These were the only rooms accessible to Hess. The stairwell was to be furnished with wired grilles. A new type of toilet without a chain was installed and changes were made to the toilet door – all in an effort to prevent further suicide attempts once Hess became mobile again.[30]

Hess had become totally withdrawn, so that any conversation with his minders was impossible. He told Dicks that he thought Rees and Scott were under the influence of a 'Mexican drug' and were not responsible for their actions.[31] 'I can see it in their eyes,' he said. 'I feel sorry for them. If I knew the antidote, I would be only too pleased to give it to them. I will take no more medicines from the doctor.'

On 19 June, 'Barnes' received orders to return to MI6 headquarters and left that same afternoon. Kendrick received instructions from 'C' to return to Trent Park the following day. Kendrick left Hess in the care of Foley, and Colonel Scott penned in his diary: 'Colonel "Wallace" left today to return to his duties at Cockfosters. Major Foley is now alone as representative of MI [military intelligence].'[32] Kendrick is said to have been relieved to have finally left Mytchett Place.[33]

By the end of July 1941, Hess had prepared a paper requesting an enquiry into his treatment and 'full powers to release witnesses from their pledge of secrecy and to question them under oath'. On his list for questioning were Dicks, Foley and 'Wallace' (i.e. Kendrick). Hess wrote:

> I have asked myself over and over again how it is possible to reconcile their
> thoroughly likeable natures with their treatment of me . . . I have no real

proof of course for the suspicion that they are acting under duress . . .
Major Dr Dicks, Major Foley and Colonel Wallace made it a practice to
suggest to me that all my sufferings were attributable to a psychosis. All my
attempts at lodging an official complaint with higher authority through
these gentlemen failed.[34]

During the first week of August, Hess spent long periods in his room, fran-
tically writing pages and pages. His new document was intended for the duke
of Hamilton; in spite of his psychosis, Hess constructed a logical and coherent
argument. He laid out how Britain could only lose by continuing the war and
argued for a second Versailles. He warned Britain not to underestimate the
Russians, as Bolshevik Russia would be the world power of the future.

On Saturday, 9 August, Kendrick visited Camp Z again to read this new
document. He admitted to Scott and Foley that it 'contained some items of
interest'.[35] This visit was not the end of the Hess affair for Kendrick. He covered
the camp during Foley's period of leave in late August and September 1941.
Only one of his reports survive for this period of approximately six weeks:

Jonathan appears to be in very elated mood at present. The medical officer
believes this state of mind is to a great extent due to the belief that he has
circumvented his oppressors . . . J is now working out his grandiose plans
for his future dwelling houses. He intends to build one in Scotland, another
in Sussex and a third in Germany. The accommodation in one of them
provides for a dining room to seat 180 persons. The medical officer states
that such grandiose ideas are part and parcel of the form of mental distur-
bance from which J is suffering. J's leg now rests in a normal position and
the medical officer states he is making a remarkable recovery. He takes an
immense interest in the surgical treatment he is receiving to the exclusion
of almost everything else.[36]

During September 1941, Kendrick's intelligence staff were withdrawn from
Camp Z. The official MI6 history notes that 'Kendrick's skilled interrogation

officers were withdrawn during September and the recording apparatus removed.'[37] 'C' had decided that there was little point in bugging Hess's conversations any further. The secret recordings of Hess's conversations are believed to have been destroyed. However, given Hess's importance as a prisoner, there may be hope that the transcripts or acetate discs were kept and may yet come to light.

Hess as an intelligence asset

An interesting question to emerge from Kendrick's time with Hess was the extent to which Hess was an intelligence asset. According to one report, Hess provided the following information:

> As regards the Battle of the Atlantic, submarines were now being constructed in large numbers all over Germany. Submarine parts were even being built in occupied territory and the waterways of Germany were being used to transport the parts for assembly on the coast. Along some waterways, completed submarines were being delivered to be commissioned. At the same time, crews were being trained on a huge scale. We must, therefore, expect that very shortly we should have to deal with a vastly increased number of submarines, working in cooperation with aircraft against our shipping.[38]

The Admiralty doubted Hess's claim about the large-scale production of U-boats.[39] Reports from Foreign Office files suggest that he gave no useful information that could help Britain in the war. However, transcripts of bugged conversations at Trent Park enable a reassessment of this. These show that the situation was more nuanced and German prisoners spoke about an increase in U-boat production of up to one new U-boat a week. By early 1942, details were overheard from the prisoners about the major German construction programme of U-boats at the ports of Danzig, Kiel, Wilhelmshaven, Rostock, Lübeck and Flensburg. Hess appears, therefore, to have provided accurate information.

Hess also spoke about large-scale German aircraft production. But, in this respect, he appears to have been exaggerating. He also said there was not the slightest hope of bringing about a coup in Germany, because of 'the blindest confidence of the German masses' in Hitler. Prisoners at Trent Park confirmed this in 1941, when they were overheard speaking about high morale and blind loyalty to Hitler.[40]

The question of atrocities and the concentration camps – and how much he knew – was raised with Hess. 'C' wrote to Churchill: 'He [Hess] has a request to be provided with evidence of our contention that atrocities have been committed in concentration camps, as he denies hotly that anything of the sort has taken place.'[41]

One might say that Hess's military knowledge and his usefulness to MI6 were patchy. He did not give away anything that British intelligence did not already know from its other clandestine sources. His possible exploitation for British propaganda purposes was discussed at the Foreign Office, and it was suggested that rumours about him could be sent out as whispers or secret broadcasts.[42] One official at the Foreign Office wrote: 'whispers have made, and no doubt will continue to make, great use of the case . . . In general, the best theme for whispers to play is: *Hess came because he knew Germany could not win the war.*' The report concluded that 'the undiluted truth about the Hess case does not make good propaganda'. The propaganda that was released about Hess for ears in Germany was along the lines that Hess was sane; he had given important information on various subjects; he was anxious for peace because he had lost his confidence in Germany victory; and he was not an idealist or a refugee, but a Nazi who had lost his nerve and his faith in Hitler. The report conceded that none of the latter points was true: 'It may be repugnant and disagreeable to distort the truth. But if we are to use the case of Hess to inflict the maximum damage on the morale of the enemy, I think we must do so.'[43]

Hess's flight was, naturally, the subject of speculation and curiosity in prisoners' bugged conversations at Trent Park.[44] In one conversation, Prisoner A891 commented to A881: 'Hess is said to have been helped by several people. He got away in spite of having been forbidden to fly.'

Prisoner A881 replied: 'I expect Professor Messerschmitt placed an aircraft at his disposal.'

Prisoner A891 responded:

It is perfectly clear that everyone knows quite well what is going on. Hess was often at the Messerschmitt works. Now he appears to spend his time writing. In my opinion, there was something particular he wanted to do. He went to the Führer, but the Führer turned him down.

A881 did not believe that Hess was mad. A891 agreed and commented: 'But that the Führer's Deputy should fly to England!' The conversation concluded with A881 pointing out that Hess could only fly to Britain, and not back to Germany.[45]

As late as 1943, Kendrick's secret listeners were still picking up prisoners' reactions to Hess's flight to Britain.

Hess's failed mission to broker peace between Germany and Britain, undertaken just six weeks before Hitler's invasion of Russia in Operation Barbarossa, continues to be cloaked in myth and mystery. As mentioned in the previous chapter, the drama of the weeks immediately following his capture are still being debated by historians. Now, to such controversies as whether Hess flew to Britain with the knowledge of Hitler or Hermann Goering can be added the tantalizing question – suggested by recently declassified files – of whether his was a solo mission or whether there could have been another person on board.

Hess's symptoms continued to baffle the medical officers and psychologists. His health took an unexpected turn for the worse in March 1942. Foley's reports to 'C' had curious references about Hess, blackouts and a period of unconsciousness, which appear not to have been subsequently picked up by historians. As Foley wrote: 'On the evening of 3.3.42, after [my] report was dispatched to London, Jonathan [Hess] emerged from his black-out.'[46] Within a fortnight, he would write again:

Jonathan has come out of his coma or blackout which lasted several weeks. To a casual observer he would appear normal . . . He has apparently been considering his headaches, loss of memory, and is again obsessed with the idea that drugs have or are being given to him to cause his brain to weaken.[47]

The professionals could reach no consensus on his condition.

Conspiracy theories continue to circulate, too, as to whether it was the real Hess who stood trial at Nuremberg or whether he committed suicide in Spandau Prison in 1987. It is worth reflecting that in the months and years before Hess flew to Britain, he was not as close to Hitler as he had been during the early years of the Nazi Party. He appears genuinely to have flown to Britain in the belief that those figures who were opposed to war would accept his peace terms. He appears to have disagreed with Hitler over the plans to invade Russia (believing that that would prove a military disaster). In the end – for all his madness – Hess was proved right: the invasion of Russia ultimately did cost Germany the war.

12

A VERY SECRET PLACE

In July 1942, Kendrick moved his headquarters to Latimer House in the Chess Valley, a few miles from Chesham in Buckinghamshire. He now had three sites under his command, all so well hidden that they could preserve total secrecy about what was going on. Trent Park was now reserved exclusively for the long-term internment of German generals and senior officers. Latimer House and Wilton Park processed lower-ranking Axis prisoners of war for intelligence.[1] Wilton Park initially held captured Italian generals and some lower-rank Germans. Later, it housed German generals for a few days of interrogation before they were transferred to Trent Park. To the outside world, Latimer House masqueraded as a supply depot – No.1 Distribution Centre; Wilton Park was known as No. 2 Distribution Centre. Even the local villagers knew nothing of their true functions.

'Latimer was a very secret place,' wrote one former interrogator, John Whitten. 'The prisoners entered and left in closed vans, so they never knew where they were.'[2]

The Latimer estate was surrounded by a barbed wire fence, with two check-point entrances. Photography was strictly forbidden and no one could enter the site without a special permit. At the far end of the estate, a purpose-built complex known as 'the Spider' housed the interrogation rooms, cells, an M Room and administration block (see Chapter 9). The clocks and calendars were all changed in order to disorient the prisoners. Just below the Spider, a path called King's Walk led to the red-brick mansion house, which served as the officers' mess. Only the tall mock-Tudor chimneys of the mansion house could be seen from the Spider. The house also became a hub for coordinating and discussing intelligence operations in confidence.

At the west end of the house, a temporary building provided living quarters for the female officers and also accommodated the naval intelligence section. One of the upstairs rooms in the mansion house was Kendrick's office, while the other rooms there were used by female staff for typing up classified reports. Kendrick walked back and forth to the Spider when necessary, but, as commander in chief, he did not conduct any of the interrogations. Recordings from the M Room and interrogation reports were brought across to his office. There he compiled summary reports for distribution to the relevant departments of the War Office, the Admiralty and the air force, with frequent liaison with MI5 and MI6.

Most of the women in the unit performed clerical and typing duties; however, there were some female officers who were responsible for assessing the material coming out of the M Room in terms of its intelligence value and importance. Furthermore, German-Jewish émigré women had the task of translating prisoners' conversations and keeping prisoners' records on site: most of them had been transferred to the unit from the Auxiliary Territorial Service (ATS) on account of their fluency in German. Interrogation reports, M Room transcripts and intelligence summaries all had to be dispatched as swiftly as possible, otherwise they risked becoming old intelligence. Day and night, dispatch riders worked in and out of Latimer House (and indeed the other two sites at Wilton Park and Trent Park).

A substantial body of reference material was held in a library at Latimer House and could be accessed by interrogators and intelligence officers: technical intelligence files, industrial reference works, airfield intelligence reports, aerial intelligence, maps, technical dictionaries and a quarterly index covering all reports from home and abroad. All of this was supported by a card index that linked to intelligence reports, as well as an index of 80,000 names of enemy air personnel and a log book that recorded daily details of enemy aircraft compiled by ADI(K), the air intelligence section. The unit shifted vast amounts of paperwork and distributed tens of thousands of transcripts of recorded conversations, intelligence reports and memos. This level of output increased after D-Day and would continue until the end of the war.

The operational template of CSDIC, masterminded by Kendrick, was so successful that it became the model for additional CSDIC stations set up abroad to process POWs for intelligence. These included listening stations at Cairo and Rome, and in Greece and Austria.[3] They, too, generated transcripts of interrogations and bugged conversations which warrant further analysis by historians.

No roughing up of prisoners

The technique of befriending the prisoners lay at the heart of Kendrick's vision for subtly gaining whatever information the British needed. There was no contravention of the Geneva Convention during an interrogation.[4] Derrick Simon, an interrogator with expertise on German anti-aircraft technology and rocket-propelled shells, recalled:

> Discipline and the behaviour of interrogation officers should be of the highest standard but this can only be ensured if the Colonel in charge is fully aware of every activity that is going on within his centre. Colonel Kendrick was such a man.[5]

Lower-rank prisoners could find themselves on a quiet walk with a British officer in the grounds of Latimer, usually within earshot of a microphone hidden in a tree. The accompanying officer was issued with a .32 pistol, hidden in a trouser pocket and never seen by the prisoner, as a precaution in case the prisoner tried to escape. As Matthew Sullivan, a former interrogator, recalled, the general method was 'a sophisticated mixture of cunning and bluff, of softening a man with kindness and wearing him down, and, if necessary, hinting at or threatening other possible methods'.

Denys Felkin (head of the air intelligence section) was known by the prisoners as 'Oberst King' (Colonel King). As Sullivan recalled:

His favourite time of day was at night. Over a glass of whisky in a room fitted out as a sitting room, he would slowly convince a POW that Germany had lost the war. This he proved by taking the prisoner for a night out in London to show the German that the city, far from being in ruins, as Goebbels claimed, was bustling with activity and night life.[6]

Female naval interrogator Claudia Furneaux was known to have accompanied U-boat officers on a pub-crawl in London as a reward for their cooperative behaviour.[7]

The methods used to gain intelligence from lower-rank prisoners involved several layers of deception and relied on both formal and phoney interrogations. Furneaux's colleague Colin McFadyean commented:

We didn't regard them [U-boat prisoners] as Nazi swine but as fellow naval officers. The interrogators knew more about the U-boats than the prisoners realised: microphones had been hidden in the light sockets of their cells and much valuable information was gained that way. The dirtiest it got was when German *stool pigeons* were placed in the cells to get prisoners talking. This gentlemanly style of interrogation paid off and much that was useful filtered through.[8]

Army interrogator Derrick Simon concluded: 'Through humane sympathetic treatment, far more valuable reliable information was obtained than could have been brutally extracted.'[9]

The combination of interrogation and M Room worked like clockwork. The scale of the listening operation provided intelligence at every stage of the war – from survivors of six U-boats and two E-boats in the first six months of 1942, to prisoners captured during the commando raids into Norway.[10] Their unguarded conversations inadvertently yielded information about the German order of battle, new shelters that were being built for E-boats at St Nazaire and other French ports, and the construction of new warships, including details of the new German battleship *Tirpitz*, which was ready for action in 1943.[11]

Details emerged of U-boat construction at Danzig, Kiel, Wilhelmshaven, Rostock, Lübeck and Flensburg,[12] and of Germany's ability to make up its U-boat losses relatively quickly. This was vital intelligence if the Allies were to win the Battle of the Atlantic. German pilots spoke of the impact that the devastating RAF raids were having on Hamburg, Essen and Cologne. From these prisoners, too, came information about the war on the Russian Front, and about the disposition of Russian and German troops. It was possible to track a shifting attitude of pessimism about the outcome of the war for Germany.

Even the smallest of details from prisoners' conversations could be used in subtle ways against other POWs. A file was prepared from different sources, including the bugged conversations, of the names and nicknames of restaurant staff and waiters in German towns and cities, as well as the names of girls working in brothels. On one occasion, an interrogator asked a prisoner about the well-being of a certain Lulu, who worked in an establishment where he lived. When he returned to his cell, the prisoner admitted to his cellmate that he had been shaken by the fact that the interrogator even knew Lulu – it was not worth hiding anything from the British.[13]

The transcripts could offer useful snippets of information for wider propaganda purposes. Kendrick began a close collaboration with the political intelligence department (PID) of the Foreign Office and, from January 1943, held joint meetings at Latimer House once a month to aid the work of PID. Any stories of scandals were collected from the M Room and could be particularly useful when deployed against the enemy. As Norman Crockatt, head of MI9, commented: 'although such material which dealt with Party scandals, local colour, erotic stories and low-class jokes had no Service value, such material is of great propaganda value'.[14] Copies of relevant reports were sent to PID, providing information that could not be obtained any other way. The effectiveness of the PID propaganda was not known until the secret recordings confirmed that BBC programmes were being widely listened to by German forces.

Another indication of the success of the subtle methods used by Kendrick's teams was the way that some prisoners were 'turned' to work for the British.

They might be sent to Milton Bryan in Bedfordshire, not far from the code-breaking site of Bletchley Park. The modest complex at Milton Bryan was occupied by a section of the Political Warfare Executive, under the direction of Denis Sefton Delmer, a former journalist. It masqueraded as a German radio station, broadcasting news items that became popular with the German armed forces. It often used material that had come from the M Rooms and had an air of authenticity about it.[15]

'A gentlemen's club'

Kendrick's unit may have generated vast amounts of paperwork from interrogations and recorded conversations, but one of his most important jobs at this time involved something that he was exceedingly good at – hosting lunches and dinners. In the panelled library and dining room on the ground floor of the house, he frequently wined and dined the intelligence chiefs and other important visitors. These included guests from the Air Ministry, Admiralty, Bomber Command, MI5, the Political Warfare Executive and other departments. He continued to foster the close working relationship with Bletchley Park and held regular meetings with its liaison officer, thought to have been Hanns Vischer.[16] Over luncheon where the wine and port flowed, Kendrick would discuss the progress of the war and the latest intelligence from the prisoners. His visitors primed him on the information they needed from POWs, especially new German technology. It was an extension of a gentlemen's club, where the nation's secret operations could be discussed in total privacy.

One visitor was General James Marshall-Cornwall, who afterwards wrote Crockatt a letter of appreciation, in which he described Kendrick as 'an old-stager on our side of the house'.[17] Kendrick was completely at home in this setting – doing what he loved most, harking back to his days as a master of espionage in Vienna. This was as much a vital part of HUMINT as the intelligence reports being generated on an industrial scale in the M Room at the top end of the site.

Those figures with top-level security clearance were sometimes taken on a tour of the site, so that they could understand the practical daily workings of the operation and appreciate its importance to the war effort. In April 1943, Vice Admiral Rushbrooke (the new director of naval intelligence) was escorted around the operation, afterwards writing to Kendrick:

I was very much impressed with all I saw. You obviously have a most efficient organisation, and the inter-team work is of the highest order. I only hope my visit did not throw your busy machine out of order for half a day.[18]

Importantly, Rushbrooke promised to support Kendrick in any way necessary for the naval intelligence aspect on site.

Kendrick was mindful of the constant need to keep the different heads of departments and services in Britain on side, and he deployed his hospitality and charm to ensure smooth cooperation from figures who could be apt to be difficult or to allow inter-services rivalries to overtake the priority of the work itself.

Small glimpses of Latimer's secrecy would only emerge decades later. As, for instance, when it came to light that the US ambassador, John Winant, moved out of central London to a farmhouse on the estate in order to avoid the Blitz.[19] He enjoyed a special friendship with Prime Minister Winston Churchill, who often spent weekends there with Winant. Now demolished, the farmhouse is shown as a modest building on older Ordnance Survey maps. As a former RAF officer, Cyril Marsh, recalled:

It was a plain or even ugly looking farmhouse, two storeys high. It would have been inside the perimeter fence, on the opposite side of the road four or five hundred yards from Latimer House and about one hundred yards before the M.T. [motor transport] depot.[20]

It is perhaps not surprising that the Latimer estate should have been chosen: the security surrounding it afforded the US ambassador complete privacy.

A VERY SECRET PLACE

Hess and Latimer House

There are persistent rumours that Hess was held at Latimer House during the war. It is interesting that the official MI9 war diary noted that during construction work in 1941, 'the premises at Latimer were to be made available by 19 May 1941'.[21] This particular date is intriguing, as the estate was not operational as a CSDIC site until the following year. Hess was transferred to Mytchett Place, near Aldershot, on 20 May 1941, and it is possible that he was held overnight at Latimer House on 19 May, during his transfer from the Tower. Although Mytchett Place is less than two hours' drive from the Tower of London, Hess could have been held at Latimer for some other purpose. The files on Hess's stay in the Tower have not been declassified.

Since the late 1980s, Latimer House has operated as a luxury hotel and conference centre, under ownership of the hospitality company De Vere. Over the decades, some of the staff have heard stories that Hess was indeed held there. On various visits to the house – both for research purposes and to give talks – mention was made of Hess having been there. I was dismissive of the claims, until one day a member of staff asked, 'Do you want to see his room?'

If the bedroom had 'provenance' in this oral tradition, then perhaps there was some truth in it. . . . I was shown 'Hess's room' on the first floor. In the 1980s, the room was divided into two smaller conference rooms. But in the 1940s it looked across the Chess Valley, secluded and tranquil, and Hess would have had no idea of his location.

I turned to the member of staff and asked: 'How do you know Hess was in here?'

He replied: 'Because over the years, former interrogation officers have come back to visit us and told us. We had an American interrogator a few years ago who said this was Hess's room.' What gives some credence to this story is that 'Hess's room' was right next to Kendrick's office. Was this why John Whitten had described Latimer as 'a very secret place'?

Just a week later, I delivered a talk at the house with former secret listener Fritz Lustig. A question was raised by the audience about Hess and Latimer

House. This was reinforced by two other attendees, who were positive about the Hess/Latimer connection. Indeed, there had been sightings in the area during the war. Patrick Filsell was 10 years old when he saw Hess at Piper's Wood, near Hyde Heath, just a few miles from Latimer. He was with his grandfather, Dr Humphrey England, at the time: Patrick had just had an operation for appendicitis and was spending a few days with him.[22] Dr England had been brought out of retirement as medical officer for the Buckinghamshire area. 'In this capacity as a doctor, he visited all kinds of odd places, including the wartime POW transit camp at Piper's Wood,' recalled Filsell. 'I don't remember the transit camp being particularly well guarded.'[23]

The camp was well hidden among the dense trees, so that the Luftwaffe would not have seen it from the air. A main public road ran through the camp and the woods, with buildings on either side of it. There is still evidence of the derelict base of the camp in the undergrowth today. Filsell vividly remembered the day he saw Hess:

My grandfather pulled in and parked the car. At that moment, he pointed to a man being escorted across the road and said to me, 'That's Hess.' I knew who Hess was because of the newspaper reports after his capture. I stayed in the car while my grandfather quickly popped into the camp for something. He never discussed his work and I didn't ask any questions.

On 23 March 2014, Filsell took me back to the exact location in the woods where he had seen Hess crossing the road in front of him. He stood looking out across the woodland as he commented: 'Of course I don't know if it was the real Hess or a double. Hush-hush things went on in the Buckinghamshire countryside during the wartime that may be impossible to verify now.'

The story leaves many fascinating, unanswered questions about why Hess could have been in the area. Was he being taken for a walk that day for exercise? Was it the real Hess?

The oral traditions linking Hess to Latimer House began to seem so strong that I looked again at the files. Re-examination of the Hess files revealed a gap around June 1942, when Hess was moved from Mytchett Place to variou̱ unknown locations.[24] Could this be when he was accommodated at Latimer House? June 1942 correlates with the time when Filsell was recovering from his operation. Finally, on 26 June 1942, Hess was moved to Maindiff Court Hospital in Abergavenny, South Wales, for the duration of the war.[25]

Wartime personnel from Latimer often frequented the Green Dragon pub at Flaunden, about a mile away, where the landlady overheard talk about Hess being at the house, including from the driver who moved Hess around.

I also had a brief exchange with a Buckinghamshire resident, who had met a lady whose father's job during the war had been to interview defectors at Latimer and listen in to prisoners of war. He had confirmed that Hess had definitely been at Latimer. Another person commented: 'Hess was definitely at Latimer. My grandfather told me.' A number of other independent oral traditions place Hess for a short time at Bois Mill at Chesham Bois, about a mile away. A photograph of the mill, taken by a secret listener, John Gay, in 1944, exists in the archives of English Heritage and shows bars on one of the side windows of the property.[26]

Questions have sometimes been raised about whether Churchill ever secretly met Hess. This is unlikely, because Hess believed Churchill to be a warmonger and not open to any peace mission. But possibly Churchill could have watched from one of the windows of Latimer House while Hess walked in the gardens. A local resident (who wishes to remain anonymous), wrote to me:

> The rumour about Churchill [at Latimer] is just that, a rumour, almost certainly off record and deniable. But there are some facts that lend some credibility. Latimer is a short detour off the route between Downing Street and Chequers. Hess made repeated requests to see the King and did not understand the British constitution. Churchill was known to visit Latimer as a guest of American ambassador John Winant. Presumably his visits to Winant were informal or even a secret means of communicating with Roosevelt.

written documentary evidence has come to light that firmly
atimer House, the existence of so many variant and strong oral
it a possibility. As far as is known, Kendrick had no dealings
.... after 1942.

During that year, Kendrick's career took another extraordinary turn as he was tasked with taking care of Hitler's top commanders captured on the battlefields of North Africa and gaining vital intelligence from them. Now the spymaster really came into his own: with the intelligence chiefs, he had to devise ways of getting the German commanders to spill the most closely guarded secrets of the Nazi regime. He and his intelligence officers created 'a dramatic stage set' that would provide the backdrop for an extraordinary daily life in the mansion house at Trent Park. In May 1942, infantry general Ludwig Crüwell became the first German general to be taken prisoner by the British, when his plane was shot down over British lines in North Africa.[27] Then General Ritter von Thoma, commander of a Panzer tank division, was captured on 4 November 1942 at Tel-el-Mapsra, west of El Alamein.[28] Crüwell and von Thoma were brought to England, where Kendrick was ready to receive some of the most valuable prisoners to be captured in the war. Trent Park was reserved for them.

Hitler's senior commanders

General Crüwell was brought to Trent Park on 22 August 1942.[29] Ten days earlier, Kendrick had hosted a meeting at Latimer House to discuss the handling of high-ranking German officers who would be captured in the North Africa campaign in the coming months.[30] Between Crüwell's capture in May 1942 and his arrival at Trent Park in August, Kendrick arranged for engineers from Dollis Hill Research Station to return to the mansion house to wire it further. This second wiring was done in much greater haste, with cables running under floorboards to microphones hidden not only in light fittings and the fireplaces, but also in plant pots, the billiards table, behind paintings and mirrors, and even in the trees in the garden. There were now three M

Rooms in the basement, wired to the living rooms on the ground floor and to the bedrooms on the first.[31] No opportunity would be wasted to gain intelligence from Hitler's senior commanders.

In November 1942, Crüwell was joined at Trent Park by General von Thoma.[32] By the end of the war, the special quarters at Trent Park housed 59 German generals, 40 senior officers and at least 2 field marshals. The men were given the freedom to roam the communal rooms on the ground floor and were allocated bedrooms on the first floor. This was a deliberate ploy on the part of British intelligence, to enable the generals to relax and to facilitate unguarded conversations.

After the Afrika Korps collapsed and surrendered on 12 May 1943, 11 more generals joined Crüwell and von Thoma at Trent Park, including the Afrika Korps commander, General Hans-Jürgen von Arnim. They were brought by military vehicles through the double barbed-wire enclosure at Trent Park and alighted in front of the house. Dressed in full German uniform, complete with medals, the commanders were saluted by General Sir Ernest Gepp, director of prisoners of war (administration). They were then taken to their new quarters, along with their batmen. In the coming months, they were the key characters in the disputes and personal rivalries in the house, and yielded first-rate intelligence.[33] The prisoners spent their time painting and drawing, playing cards or chess, learning languages, reading books and newspapers and listening to radio broadcasts. Some of the newspaper reports were faked, in an attempt to encourage leaks of information from the generals.[34] The batmen dined separately and were assigned duties that included making the generals' beds and polishing their boots. On one occasion, Luftwaffe General Bassenge was overheard complaining to Panzer General von Broich that the batmen even had pictures of Hitler on their bedroom walls at Trent Park.[35]

Highly skilled as he was in HUMINT techniques, within the house Kendrick – ably assisted by Major Arthur Rawlinson (a scriptwriter in civilian life) – created a façade where nothing was as it seemed. By bringing the generals to a country house, he played to their egos and sense of self-importance. They felt they deserved to be treated as befitted their rank, and mistakenly assumed that their war was over. But British intelligence would reap the benefits of Kendrick's deception plan. Little did the generals realize that the majority of the minders were actually members of the Intelligence Corps. It was Kendrick's belief that by enabling the generals to feel relaxed in the house, surrounded by beautiful parkland and with a view over a large lake, he could achieve results far beyond anything that could be gained from interrogation. The Germans very quickly forgot the warnings they had received before they left Germany that, if they were captured, their conversations would be bugged by the British.

When a senior German commander was brought to Trent Park, he would first be welcomed by General Sir Ernest Gepp,[36] British intelligence officer Major Charles Corner, Colonel Spencer of the United States Army Air Force – and a fake aristocrat, 'Lord Aberfeldy', who was introduced to them as their welfare officer. Lord Aberfeldy was, in fact, a senior intelligence officer named Ian Munro.[37] Kendrick had discussed with intelligence chiefs that it would be a good idea for the generals to have such an officer to befriend them. When the rank was discussed – should it be a major or a colonel? – Kendrick had interjected: 'No, no, the generals love an aristocrat.' Was it perhaps Kendrick's old-fashioned sense of humour that caused him to title the 'lord' after a whisky distillery?

Lord Aberfeldy would go into central London once a fortnight to pick up odd items for the high-ranking prisoners – cigarettes, boot polish and a plentiful supply of wine and whisky. He was

> a delightfully outgoing and intelligent Scot . . . the prototype of the officer and gentleman and his contribution to the war was to act this out in full. He took his guests on walks, to restaurants, galleries and shops in London, disarming not a few with the snob appeal of his assumed title.[38]

The relative luxury that these senior German officers enjoyed did not always prevent them from trying to improve their conditions even further. The first priority for Colonel Egersdorff on his arrival was to seek out Lord Aberfeldy and ask whether they could have 'parole for pheasant shooting and a plentiful supply of whisky'.[39] Not unsurprisingly, this request was denied.

Life inside the 'special quarters'

A vivid picture of life emerges from the intelligence reports for this period. One can well imagine Kendrick chuckling behind the scenes at the daily antics unfolding at Trent Park.

The generals would sometimes be taken into central London for lunch at Simpsons on the Strand or for a shopping trip at Harrods.[40] Eric Mark, a secret listener, would accompany them:

> They [the generals] thought we were being so nice to them because, they believed, we were trying to seek favours with them, so that when they won the war, we would be well treated, too. It did not occur to them that it was all part of the bugging deception plan.[41]

The generals looked forward eagerly to these lunches. But one day Churchill entered the restaurant. So furious was he at what he witnessed that he summoned Kendrick to a private meeting and forbade him to 'pamper the generals'. Churchill's orders were ignored, however. Kendrick and his officers were already gaining vital secrets from the recorded conversations at Trent Park and so the pampering had to continue. That way the generals remained relaxed and suspected nothing. In typical style, Kendrick merely relocated the lunches to the Ritz. Churchill never found out.

Dudley Bennett recalled that his father was always reluctant to speak about his time as an intelligence officer at Trent Park:

> They were given sugar, a luxury in wartime, and taken to smart restaurants. My father also mentioned the thousands of faces that passed before him as an interrogator. He spent time sifting scraps of information about troop movements and the V-2 building sites. That was about as much as he would reveal of his secret past.[42]

On other occasions, the generals were taken to Kendrick's own home of Woodton in Oxshott, Surrey, where his wife prepared cucumber sandwiches, cake and tea. Norah never asked questions or raised an eyebrow at the arrival of top-level guests in German uniform. In the living room, Kendrick played the piano and his grandchildren entertained them with First World War songs. The generals never questioned their fine treatment, believing that Kendrick had arranged all this so that, when Germany won the war, he would receive preferential treatment from the new German leadership. At no point did they recognize him as the spymaster who had been expelled from Austria, and nor did they suspect him of working for the British secret service. To them, he was a military man of honour who understood their situation, even though they were on opposite sides in the war. He laughed and joked with them and treated them fairly. In return, they accorded him an unprecedented level of trust.

The senior commanders fell into two distinct and opposing groups: pro-Nazi and anti-Nazi. From the M Rooms in the basement, the secret listeners recorded their intense political discussions and arguments. Crüwell led the vehemently pro-Nazi clique;[43] von Thoma headed the anti-Nazis.[44] Crüwell and von Arnim were horrified by the defeatist attitude of the anti-Nazis and suggested that the disloyal generals would be shot once they were repatriated to Germany at the end of the war. Divisions were so deep between the two factions that, when Kendrick arranged for photographs to be taken and sent home as Christmas cards for their families, the pro-Nazis refused to sit with the anti-Nazis. In consequence, the groups were photographed separately. These photographs survive to this day. One general wrote on the back of the card to his wife: 'Wish you were here, but without the barbed wire!'

In an interesting development, some of the anti-Nazis expressed their readiness to unite with Lord Aberfeldy against Hitler. General Hans Cramer asked a British army officer whether Britain would make peace if the Nazi leadership were to go – although he admitted that he did not know who could lead such a revolt.[45] The British officer replied that it was not only a matter of removing the Nazi leaders: the whole system would have to be replaced. Cramer responded that there were still many communists in Germany and there was a danger that they could seize power when the Nazi Party eventually had to go.

One Friday night, over dinner in the dining room, von Arnim berated the pro-Nazis for complaining about his alleged sympathy for the anti-Nazis. They jeered him from across the table, and he responded that he was trying to 'save the defeatists [anti-Nazis] from court-martial when they finally returned to the glorious Fatherland'. Others seated at the table suspected him of suffering from psychosis. The microphones picked up every single word.[46]

The daily rhetoric and intense arguments provided important insight into cracks in the leadership of the military commanders. These scenes were tolerated by the British minders, because the melodramatic scenes inside the house gave the spymaster the intelligence that Britain needed to keep ahead. But the transcripts yielded an unexpectedly dark side, as the secret listeners overheard graphic details of war crimes and the mass murder of Jews, Poles, Russians, the elderly and Allied personnel.[47] At Trent Park, General Dietrich von Choltitz admitted to von Thoma: 'The worst job I ever carried out – which however I carried out with great consistency – was the liquidation of the Jews.'[48]

Mention of mass murder and the annihilation of European Jews cropped up in the conversations of prisoners of all ranks. As early as 1940, Kendrick referred in a report to massacres committed by the SS in Poland, overheard in conversations recorded in the M Room.[49] He specifically instructed the secret listeners to keep the acetate disc recordings of atrocities; while these appear not to have survived, the typed transcripts do. They show that his unit amassed a substantial quantity of evidence covering most of what is known today about the Holocaust.[50] Kendrick instructed interrogators to ask prisoners who had spent time at a particular concentration camp to draw the layout of it. Thus, detailed sketches of Dachau and Auschwitz survive in the CSDIC files, including a crude sketch of a camp crematorium. All of them – remarkable for their accuracy – were drawn in 1944, in some cases at least four to six months before the liberation of the camps.[51]

Today, the transcripts provide incontrovertible evidence that the German army was complicit in war crimes and had knowledge of the concentration camps and the Final Solution.

Anglo-American intelligence cooperation

The bombing by Japan of the US naval base at Pearl Harbor in the South Pacific on 7 December 1941 had brought the United States into the war. Within a fortnight of the attack, a contingent of US personnel arrived at Latimer House. This marked the beginning of a new joint Anglo-American intelligence cooperation, complementing the close relationship between the Americans and Bletchley Park. And Kendrick was at the heart of it. Under his direction, the US officers received training in British methods of intelligence work and interrogation before they were integrated into CSDIC operations.[52] This was a contribution for which Kendrick would later receive a Legion of Merit award from the White House. All copies of transcripts from the M Room could now be shared with the Americans and copies could be sent to Washington.

Kendrick was the pivotal figure at the centre of this new relationship. To date, this has not been fully appreciated in studies of the historic Anglo-American intelligence cooperation. Ever charming and relaxed, he welcomed senior officers of the Office of Strategic Services (OSS, forerunner of the CIA) to his headquarters at Latimer after the formation of the OSS in June 1942. In mid-August 1942, OSS officers Witney Shepardson and Mr Maddox travelled from the US to meet Kendrick. The following month, Mr H. Kimball of the FBI came to view the work on site and was impressed by the efficiency. Afterwards, J. Edgar Hoover (head of the FBI) sent a letter of thanks to Kendrick:

> My dear Colonel, I am writing to express to you my deep appreciation for the assistance which you rendered to Mr H.M. Kimball of this Bureau during his recent visit to London. It was very good of you to be so helpful, and you may be sure that your kindness is sincerely appreciated by me.[53]

From 1942 until the end of the war, Kendrick hosted numerous visits from US military chiefs, including Brigadier General Kroner, chief of the US military intelligence section.[54] It was due to Kendrick that Latimer House became one of the most important centres for Anglo-American intelligence cooperation in the war. He never talked about this collaboration outside his inner circle, not even to his own family. On 2 December 1942, as a key adviser and mentor to the OSS from the British side, he boarded a passenger liner for a special trans-Atlantic mission to Washington and New York on behalf of MI6. He was to liaise with the Americans over matters of intelligence and the training of their new officers. It is not clear whether he visited the White House while in Washington, but it is known that he met key advisers in the FBI. While in New York, he visited the British Security Co-ordination (BSC), a covert organization set up by MI6 to protect British interests in the United States, cover all clandestine operations in that area and liaise with US intelligence. Based in Room 3603 of the Rockefeller Center, the BSC was headed by William Stephenson, a wealthy Canadian businessman, who was on the payroll of SIS. Stephenson carried out operations in conjunction with Allen Welsh Dulles, the first director of the OSS. Also in New York, Kendrick met up with his former agent and friend Charles 'Dick' Ellis, who was working for SIS and Stephenson. As with so many aspects of Kendrick's life, a degree of mystery continues to surround the trip and this part of his life.

Secret listeners

In January 1943, Kendrick returned from the United States to be honoured with an OBE in the New Year's honours list. This came in recognition of his success in setting up and running the listening stations, but most especially uncovering the X-Gerät and Knickebein being used by the Luftwaffe. In a letter which survives among the Kendrick papers, Norman Crockatt, head of MI9, wrote to congratulate him on 'the best merited OBE of the war'. The unit's work, he wrote, was of vital importance. As well as 'being a personal triumph for you as their leader', the OBE was a tribute to the efforts of the staff, who 'have worked hard and loyally'.[55]

A pressing concern now faced Kendrick. The volume of work necessitated an increase in M Room personnel; but, as former secret listener Peter Hart has written: 'Not only was it necessary to have a complete mastery of the German language, but often prisoners coming from regions where dialects were spoken, were extremely difficult to understand, unless one knew the dialect well.'[56] Until 1943, the secret listeners were primarily British-born men who had some fluency in German because they had a degree in German or had been raised in Germany. Now Kendrick needed native German speakers to monitor the 30 bugged rooms at Latimer House and Wilton Park, as well as to support ongoing operations at Trent Park.[57] In a memo to intelligence chiefs, he wrote:

> The difficulty of finding suitable M Room personnel cannot be over stressed. Very frequently it was found that Englishmen with a perfect academic knowledge of German were quite unsuited for M Room work . . . [An operator] must acquire an extensive knowledge of service slang, conditions and technical gadgets. This of course takes time, and experience has shown that at least three months are required to train an operator.[58]

Several thousand German-speaking refugees, over 90 per cent of them Jewish, were serving in the British army's Pioneer Corps. They had fled Nazi Germany and Austria and proved ideal recruitment material. Kendrick began a drive to enlist 103 German-speaking refugees into CSDIC sites in the UK, interviewing candidates at the War Office in London. The selection process comprised a day of interviews, conducted by Kendrick himself, along with a female intelligence officer, 21-year-old Catherine Townshend. She later wrote:

> I attended the interviews, sought security clearances through MI5 afterwards, and in the weeks that followed, sent successful candidates their instructions to report to Beaconsfield or Latimer. The long and careful questioning by Kendrick prepared me for the role of interviewer, a task that I had to assume in the year ahead.[59]

If successful, then a few weeks later an interviewee would receive a railway ticket to Chalfont & Latimer station on the Metropolitan line, where an army driver would pick them up. None knew the real nature of the work until they came before Kendrick on the following day. The morning after arriving at Latimer, secret listener Fritz Lustig was called into Kendrick's office:

He explained to me the nature of my work – that I would be listening into the prisoners' cells in a specially equipped room. He impressed upon me the importance of not telling anyone about it, not even my immediate family. He then passed me the Official Secrets Act to sign.

Kendrick then said something which Lustig never forgot: 'Your work here is more important than firing a gun in action or joining a fighting unit.'[60]

Kendrick developed a strong and special relationship with the secret listeners and commanded respect from them. Former listener Paul Douglas remembered him as 'a fair man, discreet and the right man for the job. He understood our situation – the situation of the refugees who worked for him.'[61] It is interesting how so many aspects of Kendrick's life would come full circle. He had been inextricably linked to the lives of Europe's Jews in the 1920s and 1930s – those who worked for him as agents or contacts, and then some in Austria whom he had helped save from the Holocaust in 1938. George Pulay, grandson of the eminent skin specialist Dr Erwin Pulay and friend of Sigmund Freud, was one of those saved in Vienna who went on to become a secret listener.

All were required to sign the Official Secrets Act and were bound by an oath of silence. For the next three years, day in and day out they worked long shifts in the M Room, bugging prisoners' conversations. They were organized into squads of up to 12 operators, each squad divided into two shifts. As Lustig recalled:

We sat at tables fitted with record-cutting equipment. Each operator usually had to monitor two or three cells, switching from one to the other to see whether something interesting was being discussed. As soon as we heard something that was valuable, we began recording onto acetate discs.[62]

The policy of recruiting listeners from the army (rather than the air force or Royal Navy) was not without its critics. Kendrick's colleague Felkin submitted a report at the end of the war in which he argued that recruitment exclusively from the army meant that the listeners had only a superficial understanding of air intelligence.[63] He suggested that it would have been of enormous value to the secret listeners to have spent time at an air base. However, this was impractical in wartime when the listeners were required for immediate duties in the M Room: there was no time to train them or provide extra experience outside their base. Felkin also overlooked the primary qualification that Kendrick was seeking – that the recruits be *native* German speakers. Such people were only to be found in the army's Pioneer Corps at that time.[64]

With just a few exceptions, the secret listeners went to their graves without breathing a word about their wartime work. The unit's existence had to be kept secret at all costs. If it were betrayed, its methods could no longer be used – and the outcome of the war (indeed Britain's survival) was at stake.

Personal tragedy

The summer of 1943 brought personal tragedy, when Kendrick's nephew George Pearson (Rex Pearson's son), a fighter pilot in the RAF, was shot down over Belgium on 11 August. He is buried in the cemetery at Aarsele. Following his death, Kendrick returned home to Oxshott for a few days of compassionate leave. Rex Pearson and his wife, Olga, were living there, too, during the war. In Kendrick's absence from Latimer House, Lieutenant Colonel Huband deputized. On the evening of 12 August, Huband continued with a pre-arranged cricket match between officers from MI9 and MI19. It was a fierce competition between these two intelligence services, but light relief for the staff after long hours of interrogation work. The event was attended by Crockatt, head of MI9, who sent Kendrick a letter to thank him for the hospitality shown in his absence: 'After the match a magnificent supper was served at a late hour, followed by games of snooker and ping-pong well into the early hours of the morning.'[65] The 'old boys' club' of the secret service carried on as it always had, but it also gave a backbone of military and moral support to its personnel.

Kendrick spent long periods away from home. Norah kept busy with activities to support the war effort with the Women's Voluntary Service. Grandson Ken recalled:

> She was not afraid to roll up her sleeves and work hard. She could be seen in the garage, putting fruit into cans and sealing them with a cloud of wasps around her. She would pick up a wasp that was annoying her and pinch its head! She was always happy and affectionate and a good cook herself.[66]

Kendrick and Norah supported refugees in Britain by employing an ex-refugee Jewish cook and maid. Kendrick himself provided references of support for a number of German-Jewish refugees appearing before British tribunals as 'enemy aliens' at the outbreak of war.

The grandchildren went to stay at Oxshott during the school holidays and they have happy memories of Kendrick arriving from time to time in an army vehicle driven by his chauffeur, Buffrey. The family was exceptionally close. As Barbara Lloyd recalled: 'Grandpa was such fun. He was always bringing a laugh and prank to us.'[67]

The family had no idea, of course, about his true role. For Kendrick could switch smoothly between his double life as loving grandfather and spymaster.

13

SPECIAL INTELLIGENCE

From its embryonic beginnings in 1939 to its scaled-up operations from 1940 and through to the end of 1942, Kendrick's unit amassed volumes of information and thousands of recorded conversations from German POWs, covering all aspects of the war. It made a material difference to the intelligence picture being filtered through to the commanders of all fighting forces. At the beginning of 1942, Admiral Godfrey (head of naval intelligence) submitted a report on the state of intelligence and on the ineffectiveness of SIS ever since the Venlo incident of November 1939. He commented that SIS 'leaves a great deal to be desired both in the quality of its agents and in the quality of information it produces'; he made no judgement on whether that was due to lack of funding in the period prior to 1939 or incompetence after the summer of 1939. He contended that, with the fall of France and the Low Countries in 1940, SIS struggled and lost a proper presence in Europe. Only by 1942 was it flourishing, with new organizations (which he does not name) set up 'under the eyes of the enemy' and doing well in Norway, Belgium, Holland and France. He added that 'we are badly placed for intelligence from Germany'. This was due to strict security there and implementation of the death penalty, which made it hard to infiltrate any agents. Godfrey then argued that it was 'special intelligence' – i.e. intelligence coming from Kendrick's sites and Bletchley Park – that had saved the situation until 1942.[1]

The hard-fought Battle of the Atlantic was one example: supremacy of the seas depended on good and early intelligence from 'special intelligence' sites. Britain faced a constant threat from U-boats and the risk of a German blockade to starve her into submission. The M Rooms brought details of a change in U-boat tactics and descriptions of the U-boat shelters at St Nazaire, which were simply not visible from RAF reconnaissance missions, as they were cut deep into the coast and could not be seen from above.[2]

The period between November 1943 and February 1944 was a busy time for the interrogators as the 36 survivors of the German battleship *Scharnhorst*, sunk on 26 December 1943, were brought to Latimer House, as were the survivors of nine sunken U-boats.[3] Prisoners soon revealed the latest location of displaced German war industries, a large synthetic oil plant at Auschwitz and underground sites that could not be identified from aerial reconnaissance missions.[4] Of particular value was information from prisoners on new underground factories in Germany and Czechoslovakia: for example, Mittelwerk Niedersachswerfen, near Nordhausen, which was manufacturing V-2 rockets, Junkers aero engines and jet propulsion units.[5]

Prisoners at Latimer House and Wilton Park carelessly gave up information on the Abwehr. Though the fact has never before been revealed, it is clear that, by the end of 1942, Kendrick had overseen the compilation of a comprehensive report that gave details of Abwehr headquarters, its sub-divisions and the structure of its base in Berlin, and an index of Abwehr personalities.[6] A list assembled in April 1942 named 36 Abwehr individuals – including agents and their handlers – while another provided the names of a further 44 Abwehr operatives gleaned from interrogations.[7] The reports contain physical descriptions of the agents, where they were based, who they were working with and in which country. Under Kendrick's direction, the unit was able to reconstruct the structure of Abwehr I (Intelligence), Abwehr II (Sabotage, with a section on propaganda) and Abwehr III (Counter-espionage, with connections to the Gestapo). The information was analysed and indexed, with copies of reports kept in the reference library at Latimer House.

This is an example where CSDIC not only gathered information of direct relevance to the war, but intelligence on every aspect of Nazi Germany, including its secret service. Under Kendrick's jurisdiction, his teams successfully mapped the structure and operations of the Abwehr – something that had perhaps eluded him in the 1930s. Without further declassified files for the 1930s, it is not possible to make a complete judgement on that.

Today, it is not a straightforward task to trace the impact of certain pieces of intelligence and their outcome for aspects of the war. This is primarily because much of the intelligence from CSDIC was disguised when it was sent to other departments, in order to prevent its true source from being revealed. In this respect, it paralleled Bletchley Park, where intelligence from decrypts had to be obscured to stop the Germans ever discovering that Enigma had been broken. However, it is possible to gain some understanding of how Kendrick's operations played a crucial part in the Allied victory.

Rocket technology

In a previous book, *The Walls Have Ears*, I traced a direct link between the recorded conversations at Latimer House and Trent Park in the spring of 1943 and the Allied bombing of the weapon development site at Peenemünde.[8] Those conversations were used to provide a detailed analysis of Hitler's secret weapon programme. However, new evidence has emerged in recent research to support my earlier claims.

During 1942, two secret agents working behind enemy lines had sent back information about a German programme to develop long-range rockets.[9] However, this had come from an untried source and British intelligence required further independent corroboration. In late 1942, the interrogating teams at Latimer House and Wilton Park were briefed about a possible German rocket programme and asked to gain information from prisoners of war. The break-through came at Latimer House on 11 March 1943, when two lower-ranking prisoners started speaking about rocket technology in their cell, following an interrogation.[10] Kendrick and Felkin pored over the transcript. Kendrick then telephoned the Air Ministry on a secure line, while Felkin returned to the 'Spider' to brief the interrogators in the hope of gaining more information.

The intelligence coup came 10 days later at Trent Park. Events had taken a dramatic turn on the Russian Front: German Field Marshal von Paulus, in charge of the German 6th Army, which had been trying to take Stalingrad, surrendered to the Soviets on 2 February 1943.[11] The German generals and senior officers at Trent Park listened in to radio broadcasts detailing the German military losses and became extremely pessimistic. Some believed that the war was now all but lost. On 22 March 1943, sitting by the fireplace in one of the drawing rooms, von Thoma whispered:

> . . . but no progress whatsoever can have been made in this rocket business. I saw it once with Feldmarschall [Field Marshal] Brauchitsch, there is a special ground near Kunersdorf (?) [i.e. Kummersdorf] . . . They've got these huge things which they've brought up here . . . They've always said they would go 15kms into the stratosphere and then . . . You only aim at an area . . . If one was to . . . every few days . . . frightful . . . The Major there was full of hope – he said 'Wait until next year and then the fun will start!' . . . There's no limit to the range.[12]

The chiefs of staff were immediately briefed.[13] Von Thoma's rocket statement was slender evidence, but 'it represented a crucial point in the intelligence picture at that date'.[14] The result of the dialogue, recorded in the M Room, was that any prisoner, of any rank, with knowledge of specially propelled aircraft was sent to CSDIC for interrogation and his conversations recorded.[15]

In the coming weeks, prisoners across all three of Kendrick's sites talked about rocket technology, the V-1 and V-2.[16] Evidence being gathered by British intelligence pointed to experiments with rockets on the Baltic coast. There was also some suggestion that, because their construction involved certain specific engineering challenges and they required special propellant fuels, experts would have to be employed. A request went out that any POW with general information on Peenemünde, or who had worked there, should be transferred to one of Kendrick's sites for special interrogation. That included personnel engaged in the transport network who may have had knowledge of specialist equipment and parts being taken by rail and road, or knowledge of fuels or of any companies engaged in manufacturing the special parts.[17] Prisoners captured in the Middle East or Mediterranean theatres of war who had knowledge of specially propelled aircraft were dispatched to the UK for interrogation.

Reports were still coming into MI6 from agents behind enemy lines, bringing information on solid emplacements on the coast of France, Belgium and Holland for guns with a range of 230 miles.[18] Such importance was attached to V-weapon intelligence that a special committee had been formed in London, and the efforts to find out more information had assumed a status of 'great urgency and importance'.[19] The RAF was sent to reconnoitre the areas, and the results were to be delivered to MI6 and MI9 within a matter of days. Intelligence was required on four key areas of German technological development: very high-altitude aircraft; jet-propelled aircraft; turbine-driven aircraft; and pilotless aircraft.[20] Photographs from new air reconnaissance flights over Peenemünde were analysed at RAF Medmenham, at Danesfield House in Buckinghamshire. The analysis confirmed the secret experimental site for the V-weapons, and it is possible to trace a direct link between the intelligence garnered from Kendrick's sites and the bombing of Peenemünde on 17/18 August 1943.[21]

In the month before that night attack, intelligence was still emerging from German POWs at Kendrick's special sites which demonstrated just how serious Hitler's rocket programme was. It was deemed so urgent that information contained in two bugged conversations from survivors of U-607 was sent, by scrambler, by one of Kendrick's officers, Major Rittner, across a secure telephone line to MI19.[22] One of the prisoners – Jeschonnek by name – was the brother of General Jeschonnek (chief of air staff in Germany). He was in discussion with a certain naval POW named Gassauer.[23] Rittner's handwritten report, which has never been quoted before, is worth citing here because of its importance:

> Gassauer suggests that the time for the invasion will be September. They are expecting a lot from the rockets. They have 200 kilos of explosives in them, and experiments are taking place on the Baltic, NE of Berlin. Jeschonnek has said that as soon as this new apparatus begins to be used, the war will be over. These are rockets with tremendous range and effect.[24]

This intelligence highlighted for the first time that, as soon as the V-1 was ready, Hitler intended to use it to support an invasion of Britain, in September 1943. The two prisoners confirmed that Hitler had not actually abandoned his plan to invade Britain, and he was close to making the V-1 fully operational in July/August 1943. It could have proved costly to ignore such intelligence, and its importance cannot be underestimated. Nothing could be left to chance by British intelligence in the fight against this enemy. The bugged conversations provided the final confirmation that Peenemünde had to be rendered non-operational by means of an intense night attack. The intelligence from Jeschonnek was considered to be insider information from the brother of the chief of air staff in Germany, and therefore reliable.

A few days before the RAF raid on Peenemünde, a special copy of the *Daily Herald* was mocked up, carrying a bogus article. In it, a 'Swedish correspondent' referred to the rocket weapon. The newspaper was casually left on a table in the house so that the generals would find it. This had the desired effect and was the subject of conversation between von Arnim and Colonel Wolters.[25] The latter spoke of huge rockets that could be fired from Brussels or from the coast and that would fall on London, Dover, Plymouth and Portsmouth. Von Arnim added that a rocket projector barrel was 'quite a simple thing . . . and similar to that used with the Nebelwefer (Do. Gerät) [Doodlebug]'.[26]

On 17–18 August 1943, pilots from Bomber Command carried out a first attack on Peenemünde. Codenamed Operation Hydra, this was the start of a much larger Anglo-American offensive against V-weapons, codenamed Operation Crossbow. It rendered the site non-operational and meant that the first V-1 did not fall on London until 13 June 1944, approximately a week after D-Day.[27]

References to the V-1 and V-2 continued to emerge in conversations at Trent Park from 1943 until the end of the war. The RAF periodically carried out bombing raids on Peenemünde and the mobile launch sites, whenever the locations of the latter were leaked by prisoners.

During 1944, the interrogation of prisoner Lauterjung was described by Lieutenant Colonel Pryor of the Air Ministry in a comment to Major

Rawlinson (head of MI19) as 'the corner stone in the whole structure which we have now built up concerning the mobile operation of the big rocket, and was therefore as near to being a war-winner as any single report I have met'.[28] This comment supports a long-held belief, founded on my own research, that the intelligence on V-weapons gleaned from prisoners' conversations could indeed be described as 'war-winning'. Fleeting inter-service jealousy surfaced over this intelligence in a comment made by Major Le Bosquet of CSDIC to Rawlinson, after Pryor had admitted to owing his promotion entirely to this intelligence – intelligence that had come solely from CSDIC. As Le Bosquet wrote to Rawlinson: 'the best way to win the war is to promote Colonel Pryor on the basis of other people's reports!'[29]

Just how close the Allies may have come to losing the war, had the V-weapons not been discovered in time, is confirmed in the recent discovery of a report on the interrogation of a Dutch student and a party of Dutch escapists who entered Britain. They were interrogated at the Royal Patriotic School (MI19's interrogation centre for civilians entering Britain during the war), where they disclosed that they had been told by a friend that Germany had a new weapon due to be used in August or September 1943. This weapon would surprise and defeat the Allies, and experiments using it had been conducted near Vienna.[30]

The attack on Peenemünde in mid-August 1943 was fundamental in halting Hitler's deadly weapons programme. The direct consequence of the V-weapon intelligence from prisoners at Kendrick's sites was twofold: it prevented a German invasion of Britain in September 1943; and it delayed Hitler's rocket test launches, so that the secret weapon programme was not operational for a further nine months. Without this intelligence, it is doubtful that the Allies could have successfully mounted the D-Day landings. Indeed, failure to delay Hitler's rocket programme in August 1943 could have cost the Allies the war, as Hitler could have invaded Britain and also used his V-weapons on any Allied forces in Europe (including in Sicily and Italy). He could have won the war via technology. That is the stark reality. It is no exaggeration to say that this intelligence coup thwarted Germany's quest for weapons superiority.

The case of Cleff

In terms of technological and military intelligence, one of the most valuable prisoners to be 'turned' was Herbert Cleff, of the German army's scientific civil service. The difficulty faced by Kendrick's team when prisoners such as Cleff gave up details of new German technology was that certain government departments in Britain did not believe it was scientifically feasible and were inclined to reject the intelligence. As an experienced spymaster, Kendrick was persistent and encouraged his officers not to dismiss any information from prisoners. His instinct was to prove correct on many occasions – but especially in the case of Cleff.

Cleff was brought to Latimer House for detailed interrogation after his capture at the end of 1942. The interrogators called him 'Peter'. Naval interrogator Donald Welbourn described him as 'probably the most brilliant all-round engineer I have ever known, being skilled with his hands at anything from watch-making to general fitting, and being certainly the most original kinematician of his generation'.[31] Because of his knowledge of tanks, Cleff was first processed by army interrogators. Then he was partnered in a cell with a stool pigeon masquerading as a Luftwaffe officer. Their conversations revealed that Cleff knew a lot about new planes and U-boats. What was recorded from their conversations was so startling that Cleff was interviewed by camp psychologist Lieutenant Colonel Henry Dicks to ascertain how he could be persuaded to cooperate further. Cleff's brilliance and quick thinking meant that he managed to fool Dicks; but he soon found himself walking the fields around Latimer with Welbourn for the befriending treatment.[32]

Cleff was an interesting case because, in the end, it was personal tragedy that convinced him to work for the Allies. While at Latimer House, he received the news that his brother, whom he idolized, had been killed fighting in Russia. This news was a turning point for Cleff, who was prepared to help bring about the defeat of Hitler in whatever way he could. He opened up and explained how Germany could win the war: he knew the exact capability of the German war machine and what was being developed. He went on to give specific, if inexact, information to Felkin about U-boats that had high-speed turbines built by Brückner, Kanis KG in Dresden, and about a novel form of propellant that produced nothing but steam on combustion. He said that the same propellant was to be used in a new type of jet fighter. He admitted to Felkin that he knew of a new type of aircraft engine working on the ramjet principle. Within a few months, this was identified as the V-1.[33]

A few details of the V-2 were known to Cleff, but not yet enough to put British intelligence on full alert. He had knowledge of small, remote-controlled tanks and tanks with steam propulsion built by Henschel, as well as information on German gas turbines. Welbourn took him for lunch at the Maison Basque in Dover Street, Mayfair, to meet Sir Harry Ricardo, the designer of British tank engines in the First World War, who had also developed the sleeve-valve aero engines for the Second World War. Cleff and Ricardo discussed the German designs of diesel engines and new developments with German tanks. Cleff went on to provide a long list of new technology being used or in development by the Nazi regime. The information which he revealed about German gas turbines led Felkin and Welbourn to visit jet-engine scientist Frank Whittle at Brownsover Hall near Rugby. It was Whittle's ingenuity and energy that drove forward the first gas turbines in Britain. Whittle took in all the information that had been gathered from Cleff and, most importantly, believed the intelligence to be possible. Welbourn recalled:

He [Whittle] was particularly fascinated by what we had to tell him about the ram jets, *Düsen* in German, for which we had no translation. He kept refer-ring to them as aero-thermodynamic ducts, and in the car on the way back, faced with a lot of translation to be done, we shortened this to *athodyd*, the word remained current in the English literature until about 1950.[34]

A short time later, Kendrick hosted a luncheon for Whittle at Latimer House, at which Felkin, Commander Cope (head of the naval intelligence section) and Welbourn were present. Relaxing in wing-back chairs in the library afterwards, with cigarettes and a glass of wine, the men discussed the latest German technological developments. Welbourn explained to Whittle about the naval information that Cleff had given them and how the director of naval intelligence and torpedoes had already dismissed the possibility of high-speed U-boats. But Whittle understood the technology and believed that it could work. Later that day, he returned to his base and set his staff to work on the mathematics. Subsequently, he wrote a technical paper, in which he outlined how a submarine could be designed to do 20 knots submerged.[35]

A technical paper from a section of the Air Ministry that, in effect, told the Admiralty how to do its job was dynamite. It was important for this intelligence to be taken seriously and not be drowned in inter-departmental rivalry (something that had happened during the First World War, in a spat between London and a section of military intelligence at Folkestone). The cooperation between Cleff and Whittle offers a concrete example of a situation where Kendrick was instrumental in keeping matters on track and avoiding any escalation of inter-service rivalry. His ability in this respect would later be acknowledged in a letter to him from Crockatt, the head of MI9. Departmental rivalries had to be set aside, because the intelligence coming from Kendrick's efficient operation demonstrated, without a shred of doubt, that the Germans were far advanced in the development of jet aircraft.

In the case of Cleff, his 'turning' to work for Kendrick's officers, and the intelligence which he divulged, resulted in the Ministry of Aircraft Production authorizing Whittle to proceed with the development of the British jet projects. Without that, the Allies could not have developed sufficient countermeasures in time and Germany would have inched still closer to winning the technological war.

Cleff could not be held indefinitely at Latimer House. To transfer him to another POW camp was considered a waste of valuable talent. And so, in January 1944, he was assigned to Sir Claude Gibb (director general of armoured fighting vehicles) and worked on solving the design fault of suspension in the Morris tanks.[36]

Intelligence on Russia

There is a further – perhaps even less well appreciated – dimension to Kendrick's role as spymaster: that of Russia. In 1943, British intelligence had precious little information on Russia; this was because Britain had not been conducting surveillance on its ally. That said, though an ally, Josef Stalin was not totally trusted by the West. It is not easy to pinpoint an exact moment when the Allies again become significantly concerned about future Russian intentions. Rather, the unease was one that developed gradually. The hard-fought Russian victory over the German forces at Stalingrad marked a turning point, signalling that Germany was not going to succeed in its designs on Russia. To assess the potential threat to the West from Russia, British intelligence needed crucial information on the Soviet Union's fighting capability, frontline operations and technological advances.

The challenge for British intelligence was where to gain this information. And the answer came from Kendrick's eavesdropping programme on Axis POWs of all ranks, but in particular the German generals at Trent Park. The bugged conversations took on fresh significance, as Kendrick briefed the interrogators on the need for intelligence about Russia: they had to ensure that the secret listeners recorded all prisoner conversations that mentioned Russia. Now it was a matter of amassing intelligence on Germany and Russia. This is an aspect of Kendrick's work that has previously been overlooked.

The majority of the German generals being held at Trent Park had served on the Eastern Front and had been eyewitnesses to the fighting. They would supply the clues to building up a broad picture of Russia. They spoke freely among themselves about Russian forces, equipment and the battlefields, and were concerned that Russia was the real threat that Germany and Western Europe would face after the war. The first generals to arrive at Trent Park in May and June 1943 frequently discussed the effectiveness of the Russian T-34 battle tanks. The T-34 was admired for its speed, manoeuvrability, weaponry and armour. They chatted to each other about how the Russians were concentrating on the production of this one type of tank, and estimated that Soviet Union was turning out a thousand T-34s a month, compared to Germany, which was producing only around 300 to 400 tanks a month. They revealed how Germany had developed an effective weapon against the T-34, but would be unable to produce it in sufficient quantities to 'mount a successful offensive against Russia that summer [1943]'.[37]

In response to the production of the new T-34, Germany was developing its Tiger tank; by the summer of 1943, it would be tested in the latest fighting against Russia.[38] Although the Tiger tank had been used in North Africa, it had not been a success there because of the terrain. For that region, Cramer told his fellow generals, a quicker, smaller tank was needed. The Russians had now switched to heavy use of artillery and mines as the best defence against the Tiger tanks.[39] The generals discussed the likelihood of an Allied invasion of Europe and how there was a lack of German tanks in western divisions, because they had been sent to fight in Russia.[40] Personnel had been dispatched to France to recuperate and had been promised by the German High Command that tanks would follow for fighting there; but even after three months the tanks had not arrived.[41] This, said the generals, had affected the German fighting capability in France.[42]

In terms of the state of Russian fighting forces, Cramer confirmed in conversation with General Georg Neuffer that, in spite of the filth and squalor in Russia, its troops were physically 'of a very high standard and very brave indeed'.[43] He also commented to the other generals that the Hungarian and Romanian troops fighting the Russians were ineffective, due to their poor equipment and the fact that they had saved their best troops to guard their own borders. Nor did the Hungarians and Romanians have a sufficiently developed munitions industry to manufacture weapons.[44] Bassenge concurred with the view that the Russians were brave fighters and superior in manpower and materiel.[45] He reckoned that the real danger for both Britain and Germany came from Russia and Japan.

Important insights came from von Arnim, who had served for two years on the Russian Front. He expressed the belief that if Germany had not attacked Russia in June 1941, Russia would have invaded Germany: 'The Russian Front must hold or the whole of Europe will be overrun with Communism.' He bragged to fellow generals that he had had access to German intelligence reports on Russia.[46] The last report he had seen stated that the bread ration of

Russian troops had been cut by a fifth, and millions of the population were starving. In these circumstances, a German blockade of Russia, he argued, would be more effective than an offensive. He knew that the Russians were sending boys as young as 16 to the front; though trained to fight, they were less tough.[47] Russia had a shortage of infantry weapons and was relying on taking guns from the dead. Von Arnim revealed a complex picture of the fighting, because Soviet partisans near Bryansk, who had been fighting the Bolsheviks ever since the 1917 Revolution, were helping German troops against the Russian communists. His bugged conversations proved significant in gaining a reliable overview of the Russian situation because of both his first-hand experiences and his access to German intelligence reports.

Lieutenant General Gotthard Frantz (who had taken three weeks to learn that it was not Lord Aberfeldy's duty to scour London shops for red-brown polish for his boots) proved useful in intelligence terms. Frantz told fellow officers that, while in Tunisia, he had received reports that vast concentrations of troops were being observed behind Russian lines on the Kursk–Belgorod sector.[48] His interpretation was that Russian troops were preparing for the second front into southern France with Anglo-American forces. Von Arnim piped up that a plane had been sent to evacuate him from Tunisia to defend Italy, but he had said his duty was to stay with his men. Interestingly, the conversation shows that he may have disobeyed Hitler's orders to help defend Italy from Allied invasion.

The Russian threat

Conversations at Trent Park in the autumn and winter of 1943 were taken up with the Russians, the state of German forces and whether Britain would be overtaken by Bolshevism.[49] Whether they were in the pro-Nazi or the anti-Nazi camp, the generals were united in their belief that the real threat to Europe was Russia. Lieutenant General Theodor von Sponeck expressed his fear that Germany might make an alliance with Russia, which would mean Germany turning Bolshevik. Fear of Russia was a persistent theme in the conversations. The generals were unanimous in their belief that the next world struggle was likely to be between communist Russia and western capitalism. They argued that their only hope was to support western capitalism against eastern communism.[50] This anxiety would seem all too familiar to Kendrick and his SIS colleagues, who had been monitoring the same threat in the 1920s and 1930s. Von Arnim argued that the only hope was for Germany to make peace with Britain and 'form a bloc against the danger from the East'.[51]

The generals blamed Germany's troubles entirely on Hitler and the Nazi regime. The decision to fight Russia, they said, was costing them the war; and Hitler had taken this action against the advice of his generals. They discussed whether they themselves could stage a coup; but it was agreed that such action would be difficult before the Allies had mounted an invasion. Any chance of success in this respect would only come in the final stages of the war, during the collapse of Nazi Germany.[52]

The conversations between the generals revealed that they still harboured the idea of world domination; they were planning for the next war, in the belief that Germany would recover to become a world power. The anti-Nazis thought, somewhat naively, that they could still hold on to power in post-war Germany. At no point before 1945 did any of the generals at Trent Park consider that they might face charges as war criminals. Their discussions led to an interesting final conclusion in an intelligence report:

> The question of how to handle these men [the German generals] in such a way as to prevent them from leading yet another attempt at world domination, is one of the most important of those to be faced [by the Allies] after the war.[53]

By spring 1944, the generals were discussing the Russian advance towards Germany and the overwhelming power of Russia as the greatest danger facing Europe.[54] They were frustrated that the United States was sending supplies to Stalin that enabled Russia to fight on and avoid being beaten by Germany. Von Thoma believed that the Russian strategy was to advance down the Romanian coast, take the oilfields and occupy Bulgaria; then make peace with Germany against the western democracies. Von Broich considered the danger from Russia to be very great: he feared Russia would rout Germany and turn the country communist.[55] The answer, said Neuffer to Bassenge, was for German forces to withdraw from the Balkans, because Germany no longer had the strength to mount further attacks on the Russians there.[56]

Kendrick's career had come full circle. The spymaster was once again monitoring the communist threat to western democracy, but this time from British shores.

14

D-DAY AND ITS AFTERMATH

As 1944 dawned, Allied commanders were preparing for the largest invasion in history – D-Day. The mammoth task of collecting intelligence ahead of 6 June continued in the M Rooms. German prisoners had been escorted from the battlefields of North Africa, Sicily and Italy for processing at CSDIC sites during 1942 and 1943. Several other POW centres – known as 'cages' – were situated at various locations in the south of England.[1] Ahead of D-Day, intelligence was being amassed from interrogations and recorded conversations: intelligence concerning fortifications along the French coast, German patrol routes and the construction of German concrete bunkers along the coast. The Dieppe raid two years previously, in August 1942, had failed in its prime objective of capturing the four-rotor Enigma machine, which would have aided the work at Bletchley Park.[2] But four prisoners had been brought back to Latimer House. Kendrick noted that from those four prisoners it was possible to produce a very thorough and detailed report on static defence batteries; this thereafter served as a template for all investigations and interrogations on that subject.

One of the major benefits of this raid (from a CSDIC point of view) was that it provided 'valuable experience which was later turned to account in the pre D-Day investigations of the Atlantik Wall [sic]'.[3] As former interrogator Derrick Simon wrote: 'Every small detail which could be of use to an invading army was obtained from persons who had been in the appropriate areas of the coastal strip.'[4]

There could be no complacency, because Germany was racing to gain superiority of the air and sea: its huge technological leaps seemed almost like science fiction to the British Admiralty and Air Ministry. It remained a difficult war – and one that would have been lost without the continuous stream of intelligence from Kendrick's unit and codebreaking at Bletchley Park.

That year, 1944, would see the liberation of Belgium and Holland, and the invasion of Germany. It was also a significant year for Kendrick as he witnessed the largest influx to his sites of captured senior officers, German generals and at least two field marshals. His highly efficient establishment was ready for them. Extraordinary scenes are reported in the intelligence reports about the generals and the 'Mad Hatter's tea-party' of daily life at Trent Park. On 11 January 1944, M Room operators overheard the anti-Nazi clique debating whether they should set up their own official political council in captivity.[5] The rancour between the pro-Nazis and the anti-Nazis was as bitter as ever. Crüwell realized that he had become the most unpopular general: the others avoided sitting with him at mealtimes. He started to spend more time in his room. The others also occasionally preferred to spend time in their bedrooms; this was fine, as the fireplaces there had hidden microphones and could pick up any conversations the generals had over cards or chess.

Just before Hitler's birthday on 20 April, the generals discussed how they would mark the occasion. The discussion became quite heated, with the pro-Nazi clique concerned that the anti-Nazis might not raise their glasses in a toast to Hitler at supper. Crüwell concluded that if Bassenge messed up preparations for the Führer's birthday and von Thoma refused to toast him, they would be expelled from the corps of officers and prohibited from eating in the officers' mess at Trent Park. On the morning of 20 April, it was obvious that it was no ordinary day:

The German batmen were dressed in their Sunday best – the officers were not! At 12.30 hrs, General von Arnim, supported by Captain Meixner, visited the batmen's dining room and a toast was drunk to Hitler, and von Arnim made a speech.[6]

These scenes were quite extraordinary; but as far as Kendrick was concerned there was one overriding goal: to harvest intelligence that would secure the outcome of the war for the Allies.

Kendrick and the generals

Outrageous as the frivolous life of the generals may seem, actionable intelligence was being received by Kendrick's teams. And it was contributing to the military might of Nazi Germany being gradually dismantled and defeated. Without exception, the generals – whether pro- or anti-Nazi – had respect for Kendrick, whom they saw as a decent and honourable military man, who, in turn, respected their ranks as military commanders. The deception was working: Kendrick's interpersonal skills could dupe even Hitler's top generals. They were no fools, but their egos and self-importance clouded their judgement of Kendrick, so that they failed to appreciate the covert operation that he had masterminded to gain Nazi secrets.

Major General Heinrich Kreipe came to have a particularly close rapport with Kendrick. Kreipe was the subject of a daring kidnap in Crete by SOE on 25 May 1944.[7] The abduction was thought to have been undertaken to undermine morale in the German High Command – the sub-text being that SOE could take out any German military leader. Kreipe was taken first to Wilton Park, and then to Trent Park. Summaries of his interrogation and of a number of conversations with British army officers have survived.[8] During his time there, Kreipe discussed the putative 'secret weapon' with the other senior German officers, expressing his belief that it really did exist.[9] He was entertained at Kendrick's home in Oxshott, as grandson Ken Walsh recalled:

I have vivid memories of Kreipe being entertained at my grandfather's house where I lived with my mother and sister for over a year and where we also spent our school holidays. General Kreipe took a liking to me and made little cranes complete with a cab, a jib and a bucket. One of the cranes had an operator's revolving cabin on a strip used to seal fish paste jars.[10]

What Kendrick thought of Kreipe is not known; nor is it clear whether he secured any information from him in private conversation.

D-Day: 6 June 1944

D-Day, 6 June 1944, and the subsequent Allied military success led to the surrender of several German military commanders and thousand of soldiers. All POWs needed to be assessed at one of MI19's 'cages', in order to ascertain whether they should be transferred to one of Kendrick's sites for detailed interrogation.[11] It was a massive logistical challenge for CSDIC, but Kendrick was prepared. From D-Day until 31 August 1944, just over 1,600 POWs passed through Wilton Park and Latimer House, 523 of them officers.[12]

In total, 98 senior German officers would be held at Trent Park, 59 of them generals.[13] Among those captured after D-Day were Admiral Walter Hennecke, commander of all German sea defences in Normandy; Lieutenant General Karl von Schlieben, the commander at Cherbourg; Lieutenant General Ferdinand Heim, the commander of Boulogne; Colonel Andreas von Aulock, commandant of the fortress of St Malo; and Colonel Eberhard Wildermuth, commandant of Le Havre. They came with eyewitness accounts of D-Day that are particularly revealing.[14] Admiral Hennecke confirmed that, as soon as he saw the vast resources of the Allies hoving into view on the horizon, he knew it was all over for the German forces. He and his colleagues were overwhelmed and dispirited by the size of the Allied air superiority. They had not expected the invasion to begin before August, and the sea defences and gun emplacements near Cherbourg had not yet been completed. He confessed that he had been ill supplied with intelligence, chiefly because of the inability of Germany to conduct air reconnaissance after the defeat of the Luftwaffe.[15]

August 1944 saw the arrival at Trent Park of General Dietrich von Choltitz, the commander of Paris, who was finally arrested on 25 August.[16] He figures prominently in transcripts from Trent Park at this time. Hitler's commanders continued to be brought from the battlefields of France between D-Day and the end of the war in Europe, in May 1945. They had vital information about the state of the German war machine and fighting on the Western Front.[17] Major General Carl Wahle, who had commanded 42 Infantry Division, confirmed in conversations at Trent Park that German forces had suffered heavy losses and their communications had completely broken down. He admitted that the men in his division had severe frostbite, sustained earlier in the harsh Russian winter, and were in no fit state to continue fighting.[18] Other noteworthy information came from General Heinrich Eberbach, who revealed that the total German tank strength in Normandy had been 800, half of which had been destroyed by the Allies.[19] Information like this was important as it enabled Allied intelligence to assess the military threat that could still come from Axis forces, as well as the impact of Germany's losses on its fighting capability.

Again, the generals expressed dismay that they were losing the war, and this led to further discussions about the secret weapon. It became clear that they were pinning their hopes on this, if Germany was to win the war. Just four days after D-Day, Kreipe expressed to Bassenge his disappointment that Germany had not yet started using the weapon in retaliation.[20] To this Bassenge replied:

I am interested in the rocket business. I know all about this great problem of the rockets with liquid propellant. I knew about them years ago in peace time. I was constantly at the experimental establishment at Kumersdorf (?) [i.e. Kummersdorf].

MI6's leading scientist, Professor R.V. Jones, wrote that the information gleaned from prisoners enabled British intelligence to gain a complete under-standing of the German V-2 programme and vital intelligence on the mobile launch sites of the V-1 and V-2.[21]

An even greater revelation was about to break. It came in a conversation between Heinrich Eberbach and Major General Alfred Gutknecht. Eberbach had served in several key campaigns, including on the Russian Front, and by July 1944 had been appointed commander of Panzer Gruppe West.[22] On 31 August 1944, he surrendered at Amiens and was taken to Wilton Park.

It was on 1 September – his first day at Wilton Park – that he said, within earshot of the microphones: 'Above all they are counting on the V-3.'

Gutknecht corrected him: 'The V-2.'

'No, the V-3,' persisted Eberbach.

Gutknecht did not know about the V-3 and asked what it was. Eberbach replied: 'V-3 is that large rocket which flies through the stratosphere, and which is said to have several times the effect of the V-1.' He went on to speak of the development of the weapon (otherwise known as the 'London super-gun') and how it would be propelled up a ramp from 100 feet under the ground.[23]

This offers a clear example of why these military commanders had to be brought swiftly from the battlefield to one of Kendrick's sites: they brought with them fresh intelligence that was given up to the microphones. They could also be used to stimulate conversation with the other generals who had been in captivity for longer and who were eager for information.

Three days later, Eberbach found himself in discussion with a British army officer who openly asked him about the V-3.[24] Eberbach told him that it was a long-range radio-controlled 'rocket'; it had a longer range than the V-1 and could be fired at England from western Germany. In his view, there were still challenges to be overcome, specifically on the construction of the firing ramps; but, with uninterrupted and undetected work day and night, it would be possible to complete such a ramp in eight days.[25]

These conversations were essential to British intelligence as it was not possible to identify the underground sites solely from RAF aerial photography. The end result of the conversations mirrored that of the Peenemünde intelligence: Allied aircrews flew reconnaissance missions over the V-3 sites and bombed them. Although the Germans did not manage to make the V-3 fully operational, they did launch a test weapon into Holland in 1944. Had the M Rooms at Wilton Park not provided the valuable information, Hitler could have succeeded in firing this deadly new super-gun at England from inside Germany. And there would have been little hope of the Allies finding the launch sites until the invasion of Germany.

Thus, had this new technology and its whereabouts not been discovered, the tide could have turned in favour of Germany and the Allies could have lost the war.

D-DAY AND ITS AFTERMATH

Valkyrie: 20 July 1944

Few generals at Trent Park now believed a German victory to be possible, and discussion turned to how a complete collapse of Germany could be avoided. Cramer admitted: 'I am in favour of fighting to the last ditch, but I don't want to find Goebbels sitting in the last ditch.'[26] The generals believed they themselves were the only ones who could bring about political change in Germany. Such conversations were as important to the British as operational intelligence. Kendrick realized how useful it was to gain an insight into the military mindset of the commanders – not only to understand how they might conduct their battle plans, but also to detect any cracks in the Nazi leadership that could be exploited by the Allies. Fear of the Russians became one of the most persistent themes in the chats: the desperate hope was that the British and the Americans would reach Berlin before the Russians. The senior German officers believed that Britain would soon unite with Germany against Russia.[27]

The news of an attempt on Hitler's life came in at 6 p.m. on 20 July 1944. A British army intelligence officer sent for General Sponeck and gave him the news that Hitler had survived the plot by Claus von Stauffenberg. This information was to be passed on to the generals. Sponeck duly did so. Kendrick immediately instructed his intelligence officers to alert the secret listeners to record the generals' reactions.[28] Their responses varied, but Admiral Hennecke, Hitler's commander of all the sea defences of Normandy, was realistic, declaring: 'This is the beginning of the end.'[29]

How did Kendrick react to the attempt on Hitler's life? He shared the belief common within MI6 that, had Hitler been successfully assassinated, the Allies may have been forced to make peace with a more moderate German leader, but that this would not necessarily have led to democracy. Furthermore, it was believed that Hitler was making so many bad military decisions that it was better to have him in power than for a new leader to take over who might win the war.[30] Kendrick knew that Germany had to suffer total defeat and unconditional surrender in order to ensure that there was no repetition of the mistakes at the end of the First World War, the consequences of which he had lived through. The full restoration of democracy in Germany had to be assured, and that would not happen if any of the top Nazi leadership remained in power.

While the generals discussed Hitler's security and the attempt on his life, senior commanders continued to be brought from the battlefields of Europe to Kendrick's three sites: during the autumn and winter of 1944, 22 German generals arrived.[31] But some of Hitler's elite troops also arrived after their capture.

Elite German paratroopers

Kendrick took the decision that captured German paratroopers and POWs from anti-aircraft units were to be interrogated mainly by army interrogation officers, rather than RAF interrogators, even though the POWs were part of the German air force.[32] This decision appears to have been based on the kind of information that these particular prisoners would hold. It demonstrates his foresight in adapting to the needs of intelligence at different stages in the war and his understanding of how best to secure intelligence from high-value POWs.

Paratroopers captured in Sicily and Italy were being brought to Kendrick's sites for detailed interrogation from as early as 1943. But after D-Day, there was an increase in the number of such prisoners. The CSDIC reports reveal that the majority were anti-Nazi, as noted on their interrogation reports.[33] This is rather a surprising discovery, since the elite forces might be assumed to have been die-hard Nazis. In interrogation, they gave up a huge volume of intelligence on the different para regiments and battalions of Hitler's airborne forces, including information about German operations at Nettuno, Anzio and Catania, and about discussions of Allied tactics in the region.[34] The extraordinary level of detail extended to particulars of their training and the locations of schools for airborne forces; the equipment used in airborne operations; the history and foundation of each regiment and battalion; offensive tactics; and eyewitness accounts of various campaigns.[35]

Interrogations provided a picture of the scale of Germany's continued build-up of specialist fighting troops that could be deployed to support advancing ground troops. CSDIC interrogators even managed to gain information about a para regiment called 'Legion Turkestan', which had its own insignia and comprised 90 per cent Russians (Cossacks and Mongolians).[36] In 1941, they had jumped at Minsk, but details of that top-secret mission remained sketchy until they were revealed during an interrogation by an American, Heimwarth Jestin, at Wilton Park. There was confirmation, too, that German para divisions in Crimea and Odessa had sustained heavy losses.[37] There was talk among prisoners of the 6th Para Division, which had jumped at Vilna and fought on the Eastern Front, again with heavy casualties.[38]

After D-Day, paratroopers passing through Kendrick's sites enabled Allied intelligence to chart the complete chain of command and structure of the Parachute Army under Luftwaffe General Kurt Student, who would himself be brought to Trent Park in June 1945.[39] Within a fortnight of D-Day, Lieutenant Hoffmann, a paratrooper, was arrested near Cherbourg and taken to Wilton Park, where he was interrogated by the 24-year-old Jestin, who was attached to CSDIC. Hoffmann, who only knew Jestin by his cover name of 'Lieutenant Colonel Jenkins', had guarded the secret installations for flying bombs in northern France and gave up intelligence on these.[40] Paratrooper Deiser, captured at Nancy on 14 September 1944, spoke of how the 4th, 5th and 6th Para Divisions had been wiped out in Normandy and were reforming in Germany.[41] Other paratroopers painted a comprehensive picture of the operational deployment and movements of the 2nd Parachute Corps and information on its reconnaissance battalion.[42]

Hermann Ramcke, a paratrooper general who had served in North Africa, the Soviet Union and Italy, was finally captured by US forces in his bunker at Brest, in northern France, on 19 September 1944. With him were found a large quantity of French brandy and liqueurs, a French mistress, an Irish setter dog, at least 20 high-quality uniforms and a complete dinner service. He was brought to Wilton Park just two days after his capture and housed in a cottage on the site together with Lieutenant Generals Heyking and Heim and Vice

Admiral Weber.[43] Ramcke was particularly tight-lipped and gave nothing away in his conversations. Jestin, an expert on German paratroops, was sent to interrogate him. He knocked on the door of the cottage, a bottle of cognac in his hand.[44]

Ramcke was dismissive of Jestin, but the American persisted and said he had come to celebrate: Hitler had awarded Ramcke the highest level of the Iron Cross, the Knight's Cross with diamonds, for valour. Jestin handed him a newspaper with the announcement.[45] Ramcke reluctantly conceded, let Jestin in and agreed to celebrate. The drinking continued all evening. By 11 p.m., Jestin was feeling rather drunk and had to be helped back to his billet by a guard. At just before midnight, Ramcke gave up to his comrades the vital intelligence that the M Room operators were waiting for and that Jestin had failed to gain in interrogation – military strategy, details of glider installations and troop information.[46] The irony is that Ramcke died in 1968 without ever finding out that the medal from the Führer had been fake: it had been a masterful piece of deception on the part of Jestin to secure the intelligence. And fully in keeping with Kendrick's views on how to secure Nazi secrets from unwitting Axis commanders.

Another significant paratroop commander to be captured was 37-year-old Friedrich von der Heydte, taken at Monschau, near Aachen, on 23 December 1944. He had commanded a German airborne group that was dropped behind the American lines in the Ardennes offensive and the Battle of the Bulge in December 1944. He gave his CSDIC interrogators detailed information about the history, active service and formations of the majority of the regiments and divisions of the airborne troops, as well as types of weapons carried, signals equipment and battle plans of the Ardennes operation.[47] As an expert on gliders and glider techniques, he provided valuable details, but was also an eyewitness to the Ardennes offensive.[48] The Germans intended this offensive to be the last great push to hold back advancing Allied forces, and von der Heydte described one of the night-time drops:

There was no moonlight. The men jumped in sticks of 13 men each; the orders were to drop from a height of 125m, but in point of fact it varied from 60 to 300m . . . the Bonn-Hangelar airfield illuminated, flares shot up in a stream . . . From the front line to the DZ [drop zone] the way was indicated by parachute flares dropped by a pathfinder aircraft. They flew at a height of 600–800m.[49]

He confirmed that if all the supplies and men had been dropped with him, they could have survived for 8–10 days without fresh supplies. He spoke, too, about another secret offensive mission in December 1944, which used two parachute parties: one landed on the right flank of the German attack near Eupen, and the other west of Malmedy. He recounted the mission in detail, day by day, from 8 to 23 December 1944, and revealed that they had sustained 50 per cent casualties during the descent by the airborne forces.[50]

During another interrogation, von der Heydte gave details of a number of other airborne operations that he had helped with at the planning stage, but that had never been carried out. These included the invasion of Britain in 1940, codenamed Seelöwe (Operation Sealion); also information on a planned attack on Gibraltar in autumn 1940; a jump into the region near Kholm in Russia in 1942; and a four-phased attack on Malta for 1942 and 1943.[51] The intelligence was so significant that von der Heydte was held at Wilton Park for several weeks, during which time he underwent several interrogations. He complained to Jestin that he did not have any useful information and that he should be transferred. He was eventually escorted to Trent Park.

A paratrooper captured in spring 1945 gave details of textile mills at Vorarlberg that had been converted into a factory complex for the production of parts for the V-weapons.[52]

The sheer detail of the information about Hitler's airborne troops offers yet another example of how Kendrick's operation was able to build up a complete picture of the enemy. Under his command and direction, Allied intelligence secured the most comprehensive intelligence on the German paratroops. The volume of the special intelligence that continued to come from Kendrick's sites until the end of the war (and its detail) is astonishing. It was a huge achievement by the commander himself to establish and oversee such a large-scale intelligence operation, and its success underscored just how correct Hugh Sinclair had been, back in the autumn of 1938, when he decided that Kendrick was the right man. Sadly, Sinclair did not live to see either the Allied victory or Kendrick's success, as he died in November 1939.

Towards surrender

As the war entered what would be its final year, there was no let-up at Kendrick's sites; indeed, the pressure intensified. From March 1945, a special aircraft flew into Britain at least twice a week for the sole purpose of bringing special prisoners to Latimer House, along with documents impounded in the various parts of Germany that had been overrun by Allied forces. The documents were brought in so many sacks, crates and boxes that the teams at Kendrick's headquarters could not cope with the volume of translation work and assessment for intelligence purposes. Felkin, head of ADI(K), engaged an extra 36 German-speaking refugees to help with microfilming the material and distributing it to the relevant services.[53]

In March 1945, Hitler retreated to his bunker in Berlin for the final battle. On 30 April, rather than surrender in the besieged city, he and his new wife, Eva Braun, committed suicide there. Whether wartime commanders such as Kendrick and Edward Travis (who had taken over from Alastair Denniston at Bletchley Park) ever foresaw that Hitler would take his own life is not clear. The German generals certainly reacted to the news in their 'special quarters'. Rather than mourning the loss of their leader, as might have been expected, they discussed whether Admiral Dönitz was a suitable successor, and how they could avoid being prosecuted for war crimes.

By the end of April 1945, just weeks before Germany's unconditional surrender, Kendrick's three sites were full of the top echelons of the surrendering German forces. Fifty senior German officers were captured in April 1945 alone.[54] On 7 May, Germany signed the unconditional surrender. The war was over. There was a huge sense of relief across Europe and great celebrations on the streets of cities and towns across Britain. For Kendrick and his personnel, the war might have been over, but their work was far from complete: Hitler's commanders continued to arrive from the battlefields. In May 1945, Kendrick's sites took in 106 senior German officers and lower-ranking POWs. All had to be interrogated and assessed for intelligence purposes. By July, they had been joined by two field marshals: Erhard Milch (Luftwaffe) and Gerd von Rundstedt (commander-in-chief in the west).[55] The latter was the most senior German commander to be held at Trent Park and, in an extraordinary gesture on Victory over Japan Day (15 August 1945), he sought out the British army officers to offer his 'congratulations on a great victory'.[56]

Post-war Germany became a hunting ground for the top leadership of Hitler's government. Many of them, if they had not committed suicide already, had gone into hiding. Among Kendrick's private papers was a letter dated 8 May 1945, signed by Heinrich Himmler and originally intended for Field Marshal Bernard Montgomery. Himmler, head of the SS and the main architect of the Holocaust, was high on the list of men wanted by the Allies. On 23 May 1945, two days after his capture, he was brought to the British interrogation camp at Fallingbostel, in the British zone of occupation, where the guards did not immediately recognize him. He died there after crushing a cyanide pill with his teeth. The letter that he had written to Montgomery reads in translation:

Field-Marshal!

Sir,

I know that I have a prominent place on the list of so-called war Criminals. I am also aware of the heavy accusations against me. In spite of that I beg you grant me, the Commander-in-Chief of the Waffen-SS in this war, a personal meeting or authorize a senior member to this task. I am certainly prepared to discuss the accusations against me. Above that I am hopeful and convinced that a discussion with you, the victorious Field Marshal and me, a soldier and politician of the defeated people, would be of great value.

Signed: H. Himmler

It is not known how Kendrick came to be in possession of the letter, but Himmler had been in contact with British intelligence in the spring of 1945, when he tried to negotiate the release of Jewish inmates from concentration camps, in exchange for not being prosecuted as a Nazi war criminal. There are uncorroborated rumours that Himmler was brought briefly to Latimer House for interrogation by Kendrick's intelligence officers. The original was missing from Kendrick's private papers on their transfer to England from South Africa a few years ago and so the mystery surrounding it continues.[57]

All that was achieved by the unit under Kendrick's command – including the enormous volume of valuable intelligence – was achieved without any 'third degree methods' (rough treatment or torture) at his sites.[58] Norman Crockatt (head of MI9) wrote to Kendrick in praise:

> You have done a Herculean task, and I doubt if anyone else could have carried it through. It would be an impertinence were I to thank you for your contribution to the war effort up to-date: a grateful country ought to do that, but I don't suppose they will.[59]

And sure enough, the nation did not honour Kendrick. It could not, because the existence of MI5 and MI6 was not publicly acknowledged.

15

STILL LISTENING

What did Prime Minister Winston Churchill make of the wartime bugging operation?

For him, the transcripts of bugged conversations were regular bedtime reading.[1] Although he had been outraged by the pampering of Hitler's generals, he had admiration for the achievements at Kendrick's sites and wrote to the chief of staff, General Ismay that

> the records of conversations between enemy prisoners of war afford an excellent insight into the German character and the results of the Nazi regime. I am informed that special files have been kept of the more remarkable conversations under subject headings and that these contain accounts of atrocities that have been committed by the enemy . . . If a summary of these conversations were prepared by a skilful writer, with a number of the conversations in original as annexes, this might prove a most educative book for the public after the close of hostilities.[2]

In spite of Churchill's aspirations, nothing official could be published on the subject. European hostilities may have ended, but the intelligence work was far from over, and the same methods of gathering intelligence were needed. For the new threat facing Europe was one that Kendrick was familiar with – Russia and communism. Europe had entered the Cold War, and Russia was no longer an ally of Britain and America.

The spymaster's work went on after the unconditional surrender of Germany: Kendrick's sites did not close until November or December 1945 and their existence remained a closely guarded secret. What histories of intelligence or of the Second World War have thus far failed to appreciate is the level of intelligence gathering on Germany, even after the surrender was accepted. Kendrick commissioned his officers to write comprehensive reports on every aspect of Germany using intelligence gained from prisoners of war via both direct interrogation and transcripts of conversations. These full reports, which survive in the CSDIC files, often run to 20 or 30 pages each, and are staggering in the level of detail and in their specialisms. They provide a complete intelligence picture of Germany.[3] They cover subjects such as the German war machine and its resources; the history of German units and operations; the German cryptographic service with the German army; an overview of the German secret service; the history of anti-aircraft and infantry divisions, as well as of the armoured division; and German intelligence on Japan.[4] These offered an overview to help understand the German capability, new technology and the condition of its three services – the army, air force and navy. These specialist reports were still being compiled by Kendrick's unit in the autumn of 1945.[5] One report outlined intelligence gained on the war in East Prussia and Russian plans, as well as German counter-espionage targeting Russian intelligence and agents, and was based largely on information carelessly given up to the microphones by General von Manteuffel (commander of a Panzer division).[6] Another report studied tactics and logistics on the Eastern Front and Russian battle strategy.[7] As has already been mentioned, intelligence on Russia was particularly hard to acquire, as Britain had not spied on its ally during the war. It was essential now to understand what Russia might acquire in those areas of Germany that the Russians had overrun and occupied. The new stand-off (soon to be known as the Cold War) was as dangerous as the 'hot' war from which Europe had just emerged. The most urgent priority for Britain and the United States was to gain knowledge of Germany's atomic programme. How close had it been to succeeding with a nuclear bomb? Having such a weapon would give any country the upper hand in the new and dangerous times. Thus, the hunt for Germany's scientists amidst the post-war chaos became the highest priority. Many had gone into hiding.

Once again, a glittering prize of intelligence – this time concerning Germany's atomic programme and whether the Russians had made much progress – would come the way of one of Kendrick's sites.

Interrogation of Dornberger

Lieutenant General Walter Dornberger was one of those being held at Trent Park. To date, historians have not considered him to have been an intelligence asset and yet his interrogation is said (by an unnamed source) to have been the most important ahead of the Cold War.[8] His case provides yet another example of the achievements of the unit under Kendrick's command.

Dornberger's interrogation is worth examining here, because it helps us understand the enormity of what Kendrick achieved and why his unit's work should be considered on a par with the codebreaking at Bletchley Park. Ultimately, it enabled MI6/SIS to survive.

The 49-year-old Dornberger was captured on 2 May 1945 at the ski resort of Garmisch-Partenkirchen, in Bavaria. He had served as the site commandant of Peenemünde and was 'inspector of the long-range rocket arm' (*Inspekteur der Fernraketentruppe*).[9] His vast experience of Germany's V-weapon development programme made him one of the most valuable prisoners of war ever captured, and his knowledge of V-weapons was virtually unparalleled in the Nazi regime. In the 1930s, he had been in charge of the site at Kummersdorf, which was set up for the purposes of rocket experiments. By 1933, he had become chief adviser to the Department for Development and Testing of Weapons. His ideas for powder-fuel propulsion in 1935 and 1936 were adopted, and the Do-Geräte (Doodlebugs) took their name from the first two letters of his name. As leader of Group D, he persuaded the Army Ordnance Branch to take up liquid-fuel rocket propulsion. As a result, the Peenemünde experimental site was established, which he headed in 1937.[10] From then until his capture in May 1945, he exercised complete oversight of Hitler's V-weapon programme.

Dornberger was so valuable, because he provided Kendrick's officers with a complete history of the German rocket programme.[11] In an unguarded moment, he told Lieutenant Generals Ferdinand Heim and Maximilian von Herff:

Our people tried to split the atom by means of higher tension current. About 50 million volts are needed to get the pitchblende, mixed with heavy water, to disintegrate. But the amount of energy released was only as much as that put in. We haven't yet got it to the stage where the process will continue independently.[12]

Dornberger believed that the results of this work could have materially influenced the development of V-weapons.[13] He explained further about the disintegration of the atom in the presence of certain chemicals: this effect could be harnessed and would use considerably less energy. In an interesting admission, he told Heim that Hitler had not originally believed in the V-2 rocket, and consequently had not authorized its development. He spoke of how, during the 1930s, Hitler had received regular updates on the experimentation progress at Peenemünde via the minister for armaments, Albert Speer. Then, for a while, Hitler's contact with the project dissipated, and Dornberger and the scientists were left largely alone to carry on their experiments. Contact with Hitler's headquarters only resumed again when Dornberger had a brief five-minute conversation with Hitler in 1942. He told the Führer that the programme for the long-range weapon was complete and the rocket should be able to fly. Hitler showed no interest and said nothing. Field Marshal Keitel followed Dornberger out of the headquarters. Dornberger turned to him: 'Sir, what now? I need a certificate of priority, otherwise we cannot go on.'

Keitel replied: 'I can't help you. You'll have to fend for yourself.'

By May 1943, Dornberger and Field Marshal Brauchitsch took the decision to continue the V-weapon programme. The matter was passed to General Friedrich Fromm (head of the reserve army), who turned it down on the basis that he did not believe the technology could work. Dornberger responded:

'What are we to do, if we do not get any support? I get no aluminium or electric power, no raw materials, no cement. I can't work if I do not get the support.'

Fromm replied: 'Get on as best you can. Everything will be much easier once you have fired projectiles.'[14] It is extraordinary to think that if the Nazi elite and Hitler himself had fully supported the rocket programme in the earliest days of its development, the outcome of the war could have been very different.

The situation for Dornberger and the scientists changed when Hitler visited Peenemünde in May 1943 and was escorted around the site personally by Dornberger. The Führer was impressed by what he saw, and commented, 'If only I'd believed in it!' He then turned to Dornberger and said:

There are two people in my life whose pardon I must ask. One is Field Marshal Brauchitsch who said at the end of each report he made to me: 'My Führer, think of Peenemünde!' and the other is you, General, for not having believed in you.[15]

Dornberger became so valuable to Hitler that, as Allied troops advanced across Western Europe, he issued an order that Dornberger, Wernher von Braun and 450 scientists and technicians at Peenemünde were not to be captured under any circumstances. He issued an instruction that Dornberger was 'to liquidate them all beforehand' and commit suicide himself.[16] This did not happen, because Braun and Dornberger had already realized that the situation was bad for Germany. By the end of 1944, they had contacted the General Electric Company, through the German embassy in Portugal, to try to come to an arrangement with the Allies.[17] In recorded conversations at Trent Park, Dornberger did not elaborate further on this.

During his interrogation – more like a friendly, casual chat with a British army officer – Dornberger confirmed that development had started at Peenemünde in 1936.[18] There were initially 3 testing areas on site, and eventually 11. He confirmed that building work on the site never really concluded and it was always being expanded. In the spring of 1937, the personnel from a smaller site at Kummersdorf were all transferred to Peenemünde, with the exception of those in the propulsion unit, which stayed at Kummersdorf. He then spoke about the V-weapon 'bunkers' at Cherbourg and Watten: they both had a concrete bunker, a firing bunker, a store bunker and a fuel bunker. Construction on these had begun in October 1943, and he estimated that in 1945 they were around 8–12 months from completion. The plants for producing oxygen for the experimental firing of V-weapons were at Peenemünde, Schmiedebach and Friedrichshafen. For operational use, oxygen was produced at a large plant at Wittlingen, but it could not manufacture enough. Hitler's aim was for 2,000 projectiles a month, but there was only oxygen enough for 900 a month. There was also a great shortage of alcohol to mix with petrol for the fuel for vehicles and aircraft, and Germany did not have its own alcohol plants. The Germans instead turned to synthetic fuel production through the Reich Monopoly Administration for Spirits and Alcohol.[19]

British intelligence now had a detailed history and picture of the most secret parts of Germany's rocket programme. But it had no information on Russian advances in rocket technology. Again, it was Dornberger who provided this – via unguarded discussions with fellow generals at Trent Park. From a conversation he had with Bassenge on the V-2, British intelligence learned that the Russians had secretly contacted the German scientists and offered to double any American bids for it.[20] It is not clear when this offer was made, but the Russians wished to rebuild Peenemünde and construct a parallel factory in Russia. Of the offer, Dornberger commented: 'We turned it down flat.' He went on to say how the Russians had tried to kidnap Professor von Braun at Witzenhausen: 'They appeared at night in English uniform; they didn't realise it was in the American zone . . . Real kidnapping, they don't stick to the boundaries at all.' Fortunately, the quick-thinking guards realized the ruse and did not allow them through the checkpoint, even though those Russians in British uniform had acquired the proper passes.

There was another conversation with General Kurt Dittmar, in which Dornberger expressed his belief that Russia would soon be in a position to produce the bomb. The Russians would acquire the knowledge from Jewish scientists living in Russia:

just in the same way as the Russians stole all the secrets of armaments production from Great Britain and from Germany through their Communist Party, for the Communist Party is everywhere . . . the Russians will plant their agents systematically in all the countries concerned.

Dornberger's presence in the house sparked a number of separate discussions among the generals about the atom bomb. Von Thoma said to him: 'Don't forget the number of our scientists whom the Russians have got.'

Another conversation of relevance was one in which General Pfuhlstein confirmed to Dornberger and Dittmar that the Russians already had access to scientific data on splitting the atom. This intelligence had been gleaned by German commanders, as German forces advanced into Russia in 1941. Pfuhlstein commented: 'When we got to Dnipropetrovsk, we found that the Russians had similar apparatus, also for splitting the atom, and were just one step further than the people in Heidelberg.' At that time, the Russians were keeping quiet about their progress on this. Dornberger understood the seriousness of the atomic technology in development and replied: 'weapons of such a nature in the hands of irresponsible elements will bring about the utter disappearance of nations who are not members of some bloc of powers'.[21]

The significance of all this is vividly brought home by the words of Kendrick's colleague Leo St Clare Grondona, who wrote after the war: 'Had it not been for the information obtained at these centres [Trent Park, Latimer House and Wilton Park], it could have been London and not Hiroshima which was devastated by the first atomic bomb.'[22]

Atomic secrets and Farm Hall

While Dornberger was being held by Kendrick's unit, Kendrick himself was planning the next stage of operations that would seek to gain intelligence surreptitiously from Hitler's top scientists. The race was on for the British and the Americans to find Hitler's atomic scientists (wherever they were hiding in

Germany) and bring them to Britain and the US, before the Russians could capture them and tap into their scientific knowledge.[23] Special British task forces searched for them across Germany, as Kendrick prepared Farm Hall, at Godmanchester, near Cambridge. This was a site that had already been used by MI6 for agents preparing for missions abroad during the war.

Twelve senior German atomic scientists were picked up in various locations in Germany, with the help of counter-intelligence sections, field security units and Ian Fleming's 30 Assault Unit. They were held at a site known as 'Dustbin', a detention centre set up at Château du Chesnay (France), later moving to Château le Facqueval (Belgium),[24] before transfer by special flight to Tempsford airfield in Bedfordshire.[25] On arrival in Britain, they were taken to Farm Hall, where they were interned for six months – from 3 July until December 1945 – in a highly classified operation codenamed Operation Epsilon. By the time of their arrival, Kendrick had already arranged for the house to be wired for sound, with microphones again hidden in the lights and fireplaces.[26]

The scientists were not POWs, but civilians, and no reasons were given for their internment. The purpose of holding them, before their eventual transfer to the United States, was to gain scientific intelligence and ascertain their reactions to the bombing of Hiroshima and Nagasaki in August 1945.[27] Discussions covered the topics of uranium production, isotopes, radium and heavy water. They admitted that they had not had enough uranium to succeed with an atomic bomb.[28] These were important insights for British and US intelligence, as it sought to piece together how far Hitler's atomic bomb programme had progressed.

From the M Room at Farm Hall, the secret listeners overheard Professor Heisenberg saying: 'Microphones installed? (laughing). Oh no, they're not as cute as all that. I don't think they know the real Gestapo methods; they're a bit old fashioned in that respect.'[29] Ironically, nothing had changed in the attitudes of German personnel since Kendrick's teams first listened to the conversations of prisoners of war in 1939.

STILL LISTENING

Dear Tommy . . .

From May 1945 and over the summer, personnel began to leave their posts at Kendrick's sites, some for demobilization and civilian life. Memories of their war under his command were strong, and the impact he had had on them as a commander is reflected in letters written to him at this time. Senior intelligence officers always began their letters 'Dear Tommy'.

Kendrick had been a fair, honest man, who was clearly supportive of his staff. Dr W. Stark, who became a lecturer at the University of Edinburgh, wrote: 'I beg to assure you that I was always happy in the work which I had the privilege to do under your command.'[30]

Army psychiatrist Henry Dicks wrote to express his sense of gratitude

for all the kindness and hospitality shown me by you personally, and all the people under you during my attachment to the centre. Your toleration and forbearance of this queer 'foreign body' within the organisation of your unit, has enabled me to be of some help to my various departments. As is usual, the job developed far beyond the original brief on which I was sent to No. 1 [Latimer House].[31]

In November 1945, the musician Aylmer Buesst told Kendrick:

On my return to civilian life, I would like to express my appreciation of your kindness during the time I served under you. I shall always consider myself lucky to have come under your notice. It could so easily have been otherwise and many people were inclined to be – well, unenthusiastic, in regard to a man of my age, and preferred to pass them over to someone else.[32]

In another letter, signature indecipherable, an officer wrote:

On July 2nd 1940, in a grey suit, I joined. Five years later, I have had a very great deal to thank you for. I always felt, and still feel, that I was the worst linguist in your command, so I am particularly grateful for the fact that you took me on at all, and that having done so, you helped me along so kindly.[33]

There was praise from female officers. Betty Cole (Women's Royal Naval Service) wrote: 'I have had a very happy time at 1 DC, and I shall look back on it as one of the pleasantest periods of the war. May I wish you, Sir, all prosperity in the future.'[34]

Secret listener Albert Hollander assured him that 'it was always an honour and pleasure to me to serve under your command and that I was really happy at both No. 1 and No. 2 DC . . . accept my grateful thanks and respects for all you have been to me'.[35] In July 1945, when secret listener Fritz Lustig wished to marry Susan Cohn (ATS), also a Jewish émigré from Germany, it was army protocol to ask permission for marriage from the commanding officer. Kendrick readily gave it.[36]

The distant days of the spymaster's life in Vienna could not be forgotten. Kendrick wanted to establish the safety of friends in occupied Austria. When he discovered that a British officer (unnamed) was being posted to Vienna, Kendrick asked him to make contact with his friends and to call on Count Wilczek, to check whether he had survived the war.[37] Wilczek had survived, although in very poor health. He had used all his finances to support Austrian Jews in hiding from the Nazis and, by the end of the war, was struggling to find food for himself.

Again, on Kendrick's instructions, the British officer travelled to Prague to visit Count and Countess Sternberg, where they had lived with their daughter throughout the war. The Sternbergs had refused to bow to Nazi ideology and, as a consequence, had been forced to lead a very restrictive life. They were permitted to return to their estate at Častolovice in Czechoslovakia, where they carried on entertaining as in the olden days. They were keen to learn from the British officer about his visit to Wilczek. Over a cup of tea, the countess asked him: 'Who sent you to him?'

'I'm afraid I can't tell you that,' he replied, 'except that it was someone pretty high up at home.' As the Russians tightened their grip on Eastern

Europe, the Sternbergs emigrated in 1948 to the United States, where they struggled financially until the countess's talent as an artist again brought a decent standard of living.

It was in the post-war period that Kendrick heard word about the Italian naval officer from whom Kendrick's SIS secretary Clara Holmes had tried to gain intelligence in Italy via 'pillow talk'. He is also unnamed, but it was known that he had betrayed his friends to the Nazis. Over dinner one evening after the war, mutual friends of Holmes and Kendrick in Vienna reassured her that the man 'had been dealt with'. Daughter Prudence Hopkinson commented: 'We understood perfectly well the implication of that. During a meal he was poisoned for betraying those friends.'[38]

CSDIC at Bad Nenndorf

Kendrick's operation throughout the war had proved so successful that Field Marshal Montgomery requested the establishment of such a unit for 21 Army Group in post-war Germany. This became known as No. 74 CSDIC or CSDIC (Western Europe Area) and was located at Bad Nenndorf, in the British occupied sector of Germany. It opened in September 1945 with a skeleton staff, including secret listeners dispatched from Kendrick's wartime sites. Kendrick did not command this CSDIC unit himself, since he was considered by MI6 and the director of military intelligence to be too valuable to be sent to Germany, although the precise reasons were not outlined by them.[39] Instead, No. 74 CSDIC was run by a wartime colleague of his, Colonel Robin ('Tin-Eye') Stephens of MI5, who had commanded the MI5 interrogation centre at Latchmere House, near Richmond. Kendrick's success during the war in methods of intelligence gathering had again provided the template for No. 74 CSDIC, where Stephens' intelligence personnel secretly recorded the interrogations and conversations of German political prisoners, technologists and suspected Nazi war criminals.

In an interesting twist of fate, it was at CSDIC Bad Nenndorf in October 1945 that Abwehr officer Captain Sokolowski was interrogated, during which he referred to Kendrick's arrest in Vienna in 1938. Sokolowski admitted to having worked for the Abwehr branch Amt. III (F), counter-espionage, in Wilhelmshaven, although he had not been engaged on deception work. He was able to recall the case of an Austrian, Tucek, whose first name he never knew (see chapter 4). Tucek had been sent out from the Abwehr station in Vienna (known as Ast. Vienna) to Ast. Wilhelmshaven. Sokolowski passed him on to Captain Stobbe, the Abwehr naval officer based undercover in the dockyard. The summary interrogation report then reads:

> Tucek was in contact with a British intelligence officer in Vienna, whose name Prisoner [Sokolowski] believes was Candrick or Kendrick. Candrick wished Tucek to obtain drawings of U-boats. Tucek informed Ast. Vienna, and with the agreement of Stobbe he was employed in the drawing office in the naval dockyard. Prisoner believes that on two or three occasions *Irreführungsmaterial* [chicken feed] was passed through Tucek to Candrick, but the nature of this material is not known to him. Tucek was also sent to Switzerland in order, Prisoner thinks, to find Candrick's contacts there. At a subsequent meeting between Tucek and Candrick, the latter was arrested, but after a few days was allowed to proceed to England.[40]

This provides a rare eyewitness account of the Abwehr's deception operation against Kendrick, and confirms what has been discovered elsewhere about Kendrick's betrayal – that his real name and identity had eluded the Abwehr until his arrest. He had remained the 'elusive Englishman'.

The fate of Kendrick's sites

Valuable prisoners were still being brought to Latimer House in autumn 1945. From 1 September, all the members of the German air force staff who had been captured by British and US forces in Germany were brought to Latimer House, under the jurisdiction of ADI(K).[41] The site changed its name from No. 1 Distribution Centre to No. 2 Personnel Holding Unit. It was capable of holding up to 300 German air force personnel.[42]

Among the Luftwaffe commanders to arrive at nearby Bovingdon aerodrome were Field Marshal Hugo Sperrle, General Karl Koller (chief of the general staff of Luftwaffe) and General Adolf Galland, together with many significant civilian technicians.[43] German air force personnel continued to arrive on a daily basis throughout September. They were interrogated chiefly about technology and weaponry, and from them British intelligence was able to compile a comprehensive report on German policy, as well as map the technical developments of German research and technology.[44] They remained at Latimer until December 1945, when they were repatriated to Germany.

Hermann Goering was interrogated at length by Felkin, who flew to Luxembourg, where Goering was being held in a special detention centre. The three services had prepared over 500 questions for him. It is understood that Goering may have been brought – very briefly – to Latimer for interrogation, but this has not been verified.[45]

The CSDIC side of Latimer House under Kendrick formally closed on 7 November 1945. It had been an extraordinary war, as John Whitten, an interrogator who specialized in fighter pilots, recalled: 'Latimer was the most exciting year of my career.'[46] Lord Chesham never occupied the Latimer estate again. It was the subject of a compulsory purchase order, and from 1947 became a site for the Joint Services Staff College, then the National Defence College. Today, it is a hotel and conference centre.

Wilton Park became No. 300 POW Camp, where thousands of German POWs underwent a re-education and denazification programme, in readiness for their repatriation to Germany. Afterwards, Wilton Park continued to have military links, and by the 1980s had become an army languages centre. It has since been sold for development.

In December 1945, Trent Park finally closed as 'special quarters', but the full extent of its clandestine wartime operations did not come to light until files were declassified between 1999 and 2004. By 1948, the generals had been repatriated to Germany. With operations concluded, Kendrick authorized the clearing of the three sites to remove all evidence of the bugging operation.[47] Between January and summer 1946, a team of engineers from Dollis Hill quietly dismantled the microphones at Trent Park, although the original wiring, which was deeply embedded in the fabric of the house, remained: it was discovered in 2017.[48]

For over 65 years, a shroud of secrecy descended over the whole wartime work that had been carried out behind the barbed-wire fences of Kendrick's three sites.

Kendrick returns to MI6

On 7 November 1945, Kendrick was posted back to MI6 for 'special duties'.[49] The discussion about his future had already begun the previous year, when John Sinclair ('Sinbad'), director of military intelligence, wrote to Menzies (head of MI6): 'We are all grateful to you for the loan of his services . . . He has such wide experience that I feel that care should be taken to see that he is used to the best advantage.'[50]

Menzies replied:

So long as he is capable of work, I feel strongly that his vast knowledge of Germans should not be lost to the war effort, and I would be prepared to retain him with a view to taking a later decision as to where he could best be employed. I am not particularly anxious to offer him to the Control Commission until you and I have made up our mind that there is not a more important role for him.[51]

In September 1946, rather than a posting to the Control Commission in Germany, Kendrick was sent to the Intelligence Corps depot, Oudenarde Barracks at Aldershot, for unspecified duties.[52] His personal army record states that he returned to MI6, but the nature of that posting has never been divulged.[53] He had, in fact, always been part of SIS, even though he had been attached to the Intelligence Corps from 1939 to 1945. It was a proud moment when, in 1946, he was given the Legion of Merit award for his services to US intelligence. The citation, signed personally by President Truman, noted that he had rendered exceptionally valuable services as commanding officer of a special center for interrogation of enemy prisoners of war . . . He willingly made available to the United States intelligence units all facilities at his command, and contributed greatly through his earnest cooperation to the effective training of American intelligence personnel.[54]

From the British side, there was no further recognition beyond his OBE of 1943. Today, when people hear about the achievements of Kendrick, they question why he was not given greater recognition.

Although nothing official could be written about the wartime operation (because it remained classified for over 60 years), it was fictionalized in 1965 in a three-part BBC radio play entitled *Lord Glenaldy* – a take on Lord Aberfeldy, the fake aristocrat at Trent Park.[55] The script was by the former head of MI19, Arthur Rawlinson, and he changed the names of intelligence officers to hide their true identities. Kendrick was rather disconcerted by the main character's name – 'Tommy Kaye' – because he thought 'Tommy' as a first name might give him away.[56] Rawlinson reassured him that Tommy Kaye was only loosely based on him; but he did tell Kendrick that the chief characteristics of Tommy Kaye, as 'a wise, efficient and sympathetic personality', accurately reflected Kendrick's own disposition.[57]

The play was humorous and accurately reflected the ingenious deceptions and tricks that Kendrick and his colleagues used to charm Hitler's generals. Billed as 'faction', it enabled the public to enjoy the amusing anecdotes of a wartime operation – though based on facts, they were still officially classified and not definitely confirmed as having taken place.[58] In the piece, Rawlinson provided a rare insight into the qualities of Kendrick, the spymaster – a man about whose personality nothing is written elsewhere.

In retirement

In 1948, Kendrick retired from SIS after four decades of distinguished service to British intelligence.[59] In retirement, he enjoyed membership of the Royal Automobile

Club in Pall Mall and matches at Lord's Cricket Ground, where he joined his MI6 colleagues in the gentlemen's box. Here the old boys' network was in full swing: smoking cigars or cigarettes on the terrace, they would rag one another, with jokes and veiled references to their clandestine life. Perhaps, even then, he had not retired.

Fact can certainly be stranger than fiction. Not for the first time, Kendrick's past resurfaced after he and Norah moved from Woodton to Briarholme, still in the village of Oxshott. Living next door was his colleague and one-time agent Charles 'Dick' Ellis. Ellis had risen high in SIS, and had later became an instructor for the Office of Strategic Services in the United States, and then a founder member of the Australian Secret Intelligence Service. A question mark has always remained in Kendrick's family over whether it was Ellis who betrayed Kendrick in Vienna. Ellis came under suspicion after the defection to Moscow of Guy Burgess and Donald Maclean in 1951, and of Kim Philby in 1963, when the intelligence services began a molehunt for other traitors. But, as this biography has shown, it was actually Karl Tucek, not Ellis, who betrayed Kendrick to the Abwehr in 1938.

In Kendrick's twilight years, life became something of a struggle, as he and Norah tried to survive on a small army pension. Barbara Lloyd has fond memories of regularly cooking Kendrick's favourite dish of tripe and onions for him when he was old. His life was simple and yet he never complained. It was a far cry from the clandestine world and high-society circles that he had penetrated during his days as the spymaster.

Death of the spymaster

Kendrick died in Weybridge Hospital, in Surrey, on 3 March 1972 at the age of 91. A few days later, family and friends gathered at the Church of the Sacred Heart in Cobham for the funeral service. Standing aloof from other mourners were several men in black suits, raincoats and trilby hats.

Grandson Ken Walsh turned to his mother to ask: 'Who are they?'

'Oh, they're from the secret service,' she whispered.

This was the world that Kendrick had inhabited: not the fast cars and ostentatious gadgets of Ian Fleming's James Bond novels, but the grey, gritty world of Graham Greene's *The Third Man* or John le Carré's *Tinker, Tailor, Soldier, Spy*.

After the church service, a small group of mourners drove to the municipal cemetery in the leafy middle-class suburban town of Weybridge. Sheltered from the noise of the local traffic, time seemed to stand still in this burial ground. Pockets of crocuses defied the crisp, cold March day to demonstrate that spring had arrived. Daffodils were beginning to make a show. Family and friends fell silent as the cortege came into view and pulled up at the main gates. They watched as the coffin was gently lifted out. The four pallbearers began the slow walk down the main path, past the tiny Jewish burial section and row upon row of Christian headstones. At a junction in the path, they turned left and the coffin was brought to rest on the wooden supports across the grave. Prayers were said for 91-year-old Thomas Joseph Kendrick, who was being buried that day, and the mourners remembered him in their thoughts.

Norah lived on for five years after his death, passing away in 1977, but not before traces of her husband's secret life had started to emerge. Grandson Ken recalled seeing a suitcase in the attic:

It had gadgets in it, like hairbrushes with secret compartments, fountain pens with compasses hidden in them, and silk maps of Europe carried by spies. As children, we picked up vibes that prevented us asking questions about Grandpa's goings on.

With a keen interest in cricket and rugby, Kendrick had been loved and respected in many circles, even by Hitler's generals in the Second World War, who had no idea that he was actually working for the British secret service. Kendrick never spoke about that life, except to make an occasional, veiled reference or fleeting comment. He left behind no paper trail, diary or footprint that could compromise the organization headquartered then at Broadway Buildings. There was no obituary or any tributes in the national press – in contrast to 1938, when his unceremonious expulsion from Vienna on allegations of spying made headlines around the world.

Behind the jovial mask of culture and old-fashioned humour, this gregarious military man hid an epoch of state secrets even from his own family. In the end, they did have a notion that he had worked for SIS; but that was the extent of their awareness. To them, he was a husband, father or grandfather, who frequently came home in army uniform and who taught his grandchildren songs from the First World War: 'It's a Long Way to Tipperary', 'Hello, Hello, Who's your Lady Friend' and 'Keep the Home Fires Burning'. Barbara recalls: 'When entertaining at home, Grandpa often asked myself and Ken to perform these songs to his guests and made many recordings of their singing onto wax records with his old cumbersome recording machine.'[60]

And, even though Barbara went on to work for 'the Office' for a short period in the 1950s, Kendrick never disclosed to her what he had done in the same world. She knew better than to ask.

Neither Barbara nor her brothers had any inkling that he was one of the greatest spymasters of the twentieth century. Only a couple of paragraphs about him appeared in the official history of MI6 in 2010, obscuring his true significance in the organization. In fact, Kendrick's life provides a window onto that intimate and mysterious world of MI6, played out against the backdrop of the macro-events of Europe in the twentieth century. But most of all, Kendrick could be trusted in an era of double agents and defectors. That is a shadowy world that continues to fascinate, and Kendrick's story is no exception. He served five British monarchs and gained huge respect and legendary status within MI6. His long and rewarding life as a spy spanned over 40 years in the top echelons of British intelligence. He had achieved more than most in the service, and yet only the men in trench coats at his funeral knew or understood his enormous legacy. No one could speak about it in the eulogy: MI6 did not officially exist. Kendrick took to his grave some of the most sensitive and closely guarded secrets of a nation and its secret service.

Vienna's 'Oskar Schindler'

As of this book's publication, Kendrick has not yet been recognized as a 'righteous gentile' at Yad Vashem in Jerusalem, although efforts are under way to rectify this. One reason is that those people whom he rescued have long since passed away, and Yad Vashem has traditionally required eyewitness testimonies. It is hoped that the material in this biography – alongside the accounts in Lord Weidenfeld's autobiography and in the autobiography of Eric Sanders, whom Kendrick saved in Vienna – will enable him to be officially recognized.

On 20 November 2008, the Foreign Office in London unveiled a plaque to acknowledge the British diplomats and consular staff who saved Jews from the Holocaust in various cities across Europe. Many of those listed were prominent members of the British secret service who had been on active service abroad and among the names was that of Kendrick. Eleven years later, in November 2019, a plaque to Kendrick was unveiled on a special memorial wall in the Jewish cemetery at Hoop Lane, Golders Green. The other plaques on this wall recognize the humanitarian efforts to rescue Jews made by a number of gentiles, including Kendrick's SIS colleague Frank Foley. This is currently the only plaque dedicated to Kendrick as a righteous gentile for his part in saving thousands of Austrian Jews in 1938.

As far as possible, I have always believed it important to see the places and sites relevant to my research: it provides a sense of place and history, and offers a chance to understand the surroundings and to make observations. Accordingly, one autumn day in 2010, I drove to the cemetery at Weybridge. As I stood at Kendrick's grave, nearly 40 years after his passing, I felt the presence of that lost world of espionage; and I sensed that something of the secret service had died with him. I picked up a small pebble and placed it on the polished granite gravestone (something that is customary in the Jewish tradition). That pebble was for the thousands of Jews whom Tommy Kendrick had rescued from certain death in the Holocaust; for their descendants who would not have been born; and for freedom, which he had spent a lifetime defending.

EPILOGUE
A LIFE OF SECRETS

Kendrick understood the long-standing principle in espionage that no war or enemy threat can be successfully fought without good and early intelligence. This belief underpinned the whole of his career in military intelligence and in SIS. All his life, he had successfully 'hidden' in plain sight of everyone, even his own family. It is perhaps inappropriate to describe that life as 'ordinary', since he had been at the heart of the most extraordinary and defining moments of twentieth-century espionage.

That mysterious world of espionage inhabited by Kendrick leaves a trail of unanswered questions. Two key figures whose paths crossed with his remain an enigma: Rudolf Hess and Kim Philby. Regarding Hess, there is little to add until – or unless – further files are declassified. The rumours of Hess having been at Latimer House and nearby Chesham Bois will continue to surface periodically.

As for Philby, the key to understanding his early career seems to lie in the Vienna period of his life, in 1933 and 1934 – a period that often is not covered in detail in biographies about him. I suggest it was no coincidence that Philby should have gone to Vienna in 1933, one of the most turbulent periods in Austria prior to the Anschluss, and one in which Kendrick and SIS needed intelligence. Philby's cover in the city (that he wanted to learn German) was just that – a cover: according to his closest friend and colleague, Nicholas Elliott, it was a language Philby already spoke fluently.[1] Philby was there as a student to get to the heart of the communist underground resistance movement, possibly working ad hoc for Kendrick, but certainly mixing in the same circles as Kendrick's agents. Elliott himself visited Vienna in the summer of 1934, after Philby had left, and commented that the political situation was calm again.[2] He had been given a list of friends and contacts to visit by Philby, including Eric Gedye, but Gedye was out of the country at the time. Researching this period of Kendrick's life has led, unexpectedly, to a fresh understanding of Philby's time and status in Vienna in 1933–34. If it is correct – that Philby was sent there informally by SIS, under the guidance of Kendrick – it still does not change the traditional narrative and timeline of precisely when Philby was recruited by Russian intelligence, namely after his return to London in 1934. Nor does it alter the facts surrounding Philby's later defection to Moscow.

Previous interpretations have suggested that Litzi Friedmann and Edith Suschitzky/Tudor-Hart – two key communists in Vienna in the 1930s, both of whom married English communists – were missed in SIS surveillance of senior communist figures in Vienna. Documentary evidence presented in this book shows that Kendrick was in fact tracking them. He was too shrewd a spymaster to forget names and this may still raise questions about why Philby was officially taken into SIS around 1939. Historians can make up their own minds about the significance of this new material.

Why did they betray secrets to the Russians? Tudor-Hart's brother, Wolf Suschitzky, answered this question in relation to his sister, commenting that she passed atomic secrets from scientists at Cambridge to the Russians in the 1940s because she believed that it was wrong for Britain and America to withhold the information from their (then) ally.[3] It did, of course, enable Russia to build the atomic bomb. As for Philby, the KGB never fully trusted him after his defection, and he died in Moscow in poverty, for an ideology that was already crumbling. Many mysteries continue to surround these figures. Kendrick probably knew the answers.

So what of Kendrick's legacy?

Across more than four decades of his career in military intelligence, Kendrick made a material difference to the direction and methodology of intelligence gathering by the British secret service. From his early days of cycling behind enemy lines in the Boer War to his interrogation of prisoners of war in France during the First World War to Vienna in the 1920s and 1930s, Kendrick had become one of SIS's most important and experienced spymasters by the time another war broke out in 1939. During the 1920s and 1930s, when the threat to democracy came from Russia and communism, he successfully mapped and tracked Soviet and communist agents working in Vienna and across Europe, primarily into Hungary and Czechoslovakia. No appreciation of his achievements in this respect has previously been recorded in histories of the British secret service or espionage. Kendrick operated so totally in the shadows that history has essentially forgotten him. SIS had little success in infiltrating agents into Russia in the 1920s and 1930s, but that was not part of Kendrick's brief. His focus was largely on Eastern Europe and Germany.

Pitched against his successes in this era, SIS entered a period of mortal danger when the SIS network in Europe was severely compromised by Kendrick's arrest in Vienna in August 1938. SIS recalled its officers working undercover in passport offices across Europe, although they were able to return to their posts shortly afterwards (albeit for only a year, until the outbreak of war in 1939). Due to lack of funds, SIS was, arguably, ill equipped by the autumn of 1938 to deal with the very real threat of war from Adolf Hitler. Kendrick was one of the leading intelligence figures tasked with preparing SIS for that war. With no blueprint to follow, he set up a new unit to gather intelligence from prisoners of war (HUMINT) that would work alongside and cooperate with Bletchley Park. The codebreakers at the latter site would go on to break the German Enigma codes and intercept Hitler's communications (SIGINT).

Surviving Venlo

The Venlo incident, in autumn 1939, was the most disastrous thing to befall the British secret service in its 30-year existence. Claude Dansey had already relocated the headquarters of his parallel Z Organisation from London to Switzerland, but by October 1939 even that was compromised following the arrest of an SIS agent in Switzerland.[4] Behind the scenes, German intelligence was already instigating its covert operation to snare SIS at Venlo. In the wake of Venlo, the Z Organisation did not survive beyond 1940, and SIS continued to struggle to establish robust networks to penetrate Germany and Italy for intelligence. All this came against a background of operational constraints, with SIS starved of money and (arguably) lacking any strategy. Ironically, the war breathed new life into the secret service, as it led to the creation of a new tri-service unit by Kendrick. CSDIC was, arguably, his finest achievement, and it is no exaggeration to say that it enabled SIS to survive the Venlo affair.

From 1939 until 1945, Kendrick masterminded and commanded the new tri-service cooperation in intelligence that would continue beyond the Second World War. CSDIC gathered information on an industrial scale and secured intelligence that made a material difference to the outcome of the war. In terms of its scale and logistics, nothing like CSDIC had ever before been created in the history of SIS or British intelligence. Thanks to the stunning success of CSDIC, Kendrick was able to overcome the tragedy of Venlo and tackle the serious challenges of the new war.

Kendrick was not in the traditional mould of SIS officers. First, there was his colonial South African background (though still as a British national); secondly, he had not attended any of the select band of public schools that traditionally fed SIS/MI6; and third, his American heritage enabled him to be more international and less hidebound in his thinking. Having an American parent was something he had in common with Winston Churchill (Kendrick's father was American, and so was Churchill's mother), and this enabled both men to think as outsiders and to understand different points of view so as to bring a new perspective to the intelligence arena.

Britain survived and gained the edge over Germany in the early years of the war (between autumn 1939 and 1942) because of two primary intelligence operations: Bletchley Park and Kendrick's bugging unit. Bletchley Park was essentially a gift from the Poles: without the replica German Enigma machines developed by Polish cryptographers, the site could not have succeeded. Kendrick's operation, by contrast, was 'homegrown' and was one of the finest British contributions to the war.

Its success was down to our man Kendrick. His was an enormous achievement that deserves to be fully recognized today in narratives of the Second World War. In the end, the impact of both Bletchley Park and Kendrick's operation was felt beyond just the early years of the war: both operations remained relevant and essential throughout the war. It is said in intelligence circles that, without the two operations, even as late as February 1945 the Allies could have lost the war had Germany succeeded in gaining the technological upper hand. In spite of the Allied military advances, if Germany had fully unleased its rocket or atomic technology, the course of the war could have been altered – and the Allies may ultimately have lost. These intelligence operations also required an extremely efficient administrative framework to enable the information to be processed, analysed and passed expeditiously to the correct commanders and departments.

As an official report once noted: 'Secret Service is not a matter which can be organised or controlled entirely by correspondence; in this work above all other the personal touch and inspiration are what are most required.'[5] Aside from Kendrick's vision and administrative skills, a large part of the unit's success can be attributed to his ability to bring together the different heads of the services and to control the rivalry that existed between the army, the navy and the air force. Aside from his genius as a spymaster, his personality, his understanding of human psychology and his interpersonal skills all enabled him to navigate the minefield of egos and conflicting agendas. Sinclair (head of MI5) wrote to Menzies (head of MI6) that Kendrick had achieved incredible results in running 'an Inter-Service organisation for five years without a single Inter-Service fracas!'[6]

It has been shown that, by spring 1940, Kendrick's unit was gaining intelligence that either could not be secured elsewhere or that could be used to corroborate information from other sources, such as agents behind enemy lines or aerial intelligence. Consequently, in 1941, Winston Churchill authorized an unlimited budget for Kendrick to expand the wartime listening stations. This in itself was an indication of just how essential the intelligence coming out of CSDIC was for the outcome of the war. Failure to handle Axis prisoners of war decorously – especially Hitler's top commanders and generals at Trent Park – could have led to a very different outcome. Indeed, the Allies might well have lost the tech war against Nazi Germany – and consequently the war itself. The stakes were extremely high.

Kendrick's accomplishments extended further, to include the forging of a new intelligence relationship with the United States from as early as the beginning of 1942. He became a central figure at the British end, responsible for training and shaping the nascent US intelligence organization, the OSS (later CIA), at his sites, after US intelligence officers began to arrive in Britain at the end of 1941. Two of his colleagues at various times – Dick Ellis and St Clare Grondona – went on to found the Australian Secret Intelligence Service, using the same methods that had been developed under Kendrick.

As one works through the tens of thousands of transcripts for this unit at the National Archives, one gains a huge sense of awe at the skill behind the whole deception operation. It was an organizational and psychological masterpiece. The success of this loyal, efficient, inter-service organization that Kendrick built up from scratch can be judged from the intelligence it generated. From September 1939 until May 1945, the unit produced around 75,000 intelligence reports and transcripts of prisoner conversations and interrogations. Kendrick's wartime centres gathered intelligence on every conceivable subject, and in many cases the first indication of a new enemy weapon or device came via the conversations recorded there: they alerted British intelligence to the reality of the deadly V-weapon programme – recognized at the time as 'war-winning intelligence'. Furthermore, it was estimated that reports from the air intelligence section covered '95% of the whole developed and developing field of German radar and anti-radar devices with accuracy little short of 100%'. This alone made 'an enormous contribution to minimising Allied losses in night attacks over Germany'.[7]

Crucial information was gained on the Battle of Britain, night fighter tactics, navigational methods and new kinds of aircraft; on bombs, guns and night radar appliances; and there was advance information on the bombing of Coventry and Glasgow.[8]

On naval aspects, the centres provided lists of U-boat types and personnel; information on U-boat tactics; the names of commanders; details of methods of attack; intelligence on torpedoes and mines (magnetic and acoustic); information on codes and naval Enigma, cyphers, gunnery and human torpedoes; and details of the major units of the German navy, as well as information on the sinking of the *Bismarck*, *Scharnhorst* and *Tirpitz* – the survivors of all three coming through Kendrick's sites. The importance of this work was underlined by the director of naval intelligence: 'During five years of war, the interrogation of prisoners of war has been developed from an incidental source of intelligence to one of unique value. The Royal Navy and other services have become reliant on it.'[9]

On military matters, the unit provided a detailed picture of German tanks (new models and production) and rockets; very detailed information on the Gestapo; character profiles of senior German commanders and their relationship with Hitler; orders of battle; and intelligence on the state of the German fighting forces.

It was reported that Kendrick's unit was 'one of the most valuable sources of intelligence on [German] rockets, flying bombs, jet propelled aircraft and submarines'.[10] The air intelligence unit working as part of CSDIC was able to report throughout the war on Germany's weapons research – chiefly anti-aircraft rockets and guided projectiles, but also radio, radar and high-frequency communications (often in full even before they came into use). Civilian technicians who were interrogated described the weapons and equipment that Germany had intended to employ, the purposes for which it was to have been used and the firms and personalities undertaking the work. This meant that 'the Allied investigating formations in Germany and in England had a clear picture on which they could base their own technical studies'.[11]

An old enemy

Even after Victory in Europe Day, important prisoners and civilian scientists continued to pass through Kendrick's sites. From May 1945 until the end of that year, his unit interrogated German atomic scientists and secured vital information from one of the most senior V-weapons commanders, Dornberger. His interrogation was the most important ahead of the Cold War and provided a complete understanding of the history, development and current state of Germany's V-weapon and atomic bomb programmes.

Kendrick's officers succeeded in compiling comprehensive reports on every aspect of Germany's war machine, its three combat services (including their history, capabilities and new technology) and its secret service. This allowed British intelligence to build a complete picture of Germany at the end of the war. The spymaster thus continued to do the job he had always done – provide a full picture of any threat facing Britain and its allies. Reading the declassified files today, it is staggering how much intelligence he secured.

By 1945, an old adversary was emerging as the most serious threat – one with which Kendrick was very familiar: the Soviet Union. Through CSDIC, Kendrick was able to gain from POWs an important idea of the Russian situation, albeit more limited than he would have liked.

If we look back on his long career, we can see that Kendrick was not immune from errors as a human being. It is clear that he made a serious mistake in 1938 by agreeing to meet Tucek: this led directly to his arrest a few months later and his expulsion from Austria. But was this a lack of judgement on Kendrick's part? He had been waiting for London to give him authorization to meet Tucek face to face. Was it London or Kendrick himself who made the final decision to meet the double agent? The incident demonstrates Kendrick's vulnerability and how judgements and decisions taken in the field can have dire consequences.

As one military intelligence report underlined: 'Actual experience of Secret Service work is the only real guide to the attainment of the ideal system to be adopted.'[12] Kendrick could only succeed in the Second World War because of his experience in intelligence from 1901 until 1939. His life as a spymaster in Europe had given him the grounding and understanding to enable him to define and shape the way in which intelligence would be conducted from 1939 to the present day. He would have shied away from any public accolades and laughed off any suggestion that he had changed the fortunes of SIS. He spent a lifetime doing a job that he loved, during the most turbulent periods of the twentieth century. And he was one of only a very few officers to have served British intelligence in three wars – the Boer War, the First World War and the Second World War.

It can now be stated with certainty that Kendrick was part of the higher echelons of the British Secret Intelligence Service. His significance has hitherto gone unnoticed and unremarked in any history of the service. But one might go so far as to conclude that Kendrick was the man who saved MI6. This was surely his greatest legacy.

AFTERWORD
SECRETS TO THE GRAVE

Kendrick took a lifetime of secrets to the grave. It is not possible or desirable to compile a complete picture of his agents and networks, given the – justifiable – continued secrecy surrounding MI6. Even so, one female figure from Kendrick's network has come to light during the writing of this book. A source who cannot be named has affirmed that Countess Marianne Szápáry – the mother of Her Royal Highness Marie-Christine, Princess Michael of Kent – worked for Kendrick and SIS in the 1930s, probably also for Claude Dansey. Over the decades Princess Michael and her brother have weathered intense scandal and rumours about their father, Baron Günther von Reibnitz, on the basis that he was a member of the SS.[1] The media focus on him has meant that no attention was given to their mother.

Countess Marianne's work on behalf of Kendrick and SIS has been verified, though it is not yet possible to be precise about her activities. Yet it places on record that she was actively on the side of the Allies, even if in ways that cannot be totally understood currently. However, reviewing her life story, associations and movements before and during the war enables us to contextualize this new information and to piece together how it slots into Kendrick's sphere of operations.

Countess Marianne Szápáry was the daughter of Count Frederick Szápáry, the last Austro-Hungarian ambassador to the Court of the Tsar in St Petersburg before the outbreak of war in 1914. The family ancestry was like 'a roll call of the outstanding families of the Austro-Hungarian Empire',[2] and its estates fell within the regions of Czechoslovakia and Hungary that were covered by

Kendrick. Countess Marianne, christened Maria Anna but known as Marianne, was educated in Hungary and read history at the University of Vienna. During her time at the university, she met Wright Morris, an American author, who was studying there in 1933 and 1934, a politically turbulent period under the Dollfuss regime and one being monitored by Kendrick, who had connections to students at the university. The countess, who may have been in Kendrick's circles in this era, had met Wright Morris socially through mutual friends, both attended the university Foreign Language Club, and he helped her to improve her command of English.[3] He later described her as a powerful young woman with eyes that sparkled, something which he thought a special feature about Hungarians.[4] He taught her to dance, and she took him to her tennis club. She loved American jazz as well as songs by Bing Crosby.

An international skier, Countess Marianne won the Hungarian champion-ship in the winter of 1936 and represented Hungary in the Winter Olympics in Garmisch-Partenkirchen (Bavaria) that same year, but having broken her leg in a training run she could not race. She shared a number of inherited proper-ties with her siblings in Austria, Czechoslovakia and Hungary, and after her father's death in 1935 she lived in Heiligen (now Světce, formerly in Bohemia), from where she managed the nearby family estate based in Tachau (now Tachov), on the Bavarian frontier. After the 1919 Treaty of Versailles, Bohemia had come within the borders of the newly established Czechoslovakia; she had Hungarian nationality (from her father), and although she was living and working in Czechoslovakia she did not take Czech nationality.

Countess Marianne was determinedly anti-Nazi. After the Germans overran Czechoslovakia, she was observed refusing to rise to 'Heil Hitler' in Tachau, had been caught listening to the BBC, and was viewed by the Nazis as totally unsupportive of the Führer.[5] Even before the war, one source has claimed that Countess Marianne participated in anti-Nazi demonstrations in the 1930s.[6] Although not illegal prior to Czechoslovakia's annexation in March 1939, it pointed to her strength of character in being prepared to undertake such activi-ties. It was not uncommon for discreet women like Countess Marianne to attend anti-Nazi rallies to observe what was going on and possibly report back to the British. Further, as part of managing the timber company, she often travelled on family business from Czechoslovakia to Austria and Hungary. Her observations during any German troop movements could have been useful to Kendrick, especially in 1938 when Hitler threatened both Austria and the Sudetenland. Later, her activities were to become the subject of interrogations by the Gestapo who had collected a thick file of evidence on her.[7]

Shortly before the outbreak of war Countess Marianne made a visit to England. Whether she met with Kendrick then is not known, although by now he was handling agents for SIS from London, having been expelled from Austria the previous summer on suspicion of espionage. During that visit, Countess Marianne invited two Englishmen to stay at her home in Heiligen before their upcoming visit to Berlin. They were William Douglas Home and clergyman Peter de la Poer Beresford-Peirse, British secret service agents who were part of Kendrick's small world of SIS. Home was already acquainted with the countess from before that visit to England, having skied together sometime in the 1930s.[8] A playwright and brother to future British prime minister Alec Douglas Home, William Douglas Home was educated at Ludgrove (New Barnet, north London),[9] then Eton College and New College, Oxford. In the 1930s he studied at the Royal Academy of Dramatic Art (RADA), during which time he took at least one trip touring Germany, Italy and Spain.[10] Peter de la Poer Beresford-Peirse was educated at Eton College and graduated from the University of Oxford in 1929. There is no information on his whereabouts in the 1930s, but he served in the British army during the Second World War, then in post-war civilian life as a vicar of a number of parishes.[11]

Home and Beresford-Peirse stayed with Countess Marianne for about a week in Heiligen in August 1939. On the 13th she took them to see the Graf Zeppelin flight from Eger over the Sudetenland, which may have aroused some suspicions, as she herself commented later. Thousands of spectators flocked to these propaganda flights, though Home and Beresford-Peirse might well have been specifically observing whether the Zeppelin had any new features or aerial equipment. Only a fortnight earlier, between 2–4 August, a Zeppelin had taken a 48-hour flight, known as the 'espionage trip', to secretly collect information on the British radar system, and had flown along the coast of Britain as far as the Shetland Isles. This flight was believed to have photographed the new Supermarine Spitfire from a 'spy basket'.[12] The Zeppelin journeys were a combination of espionage and propaganda for Germany, but they were not to last; the Sudetenland flight on 13 August was in fact the penultimate flight of any Zeppelin, the final one taking place on 20 August 1939.

Home and Beresford-Peirse then travelled on to Berlin to try to persuade Unity Mitford, one of the famous Mitford sisters and a Nazi sympathizer, to return to England. They failed in their mission with Mitford; but afterwards they sent an open postcard to Countess Marianne on which they wrote something along the lines, 'Silly Unity still isn't coming, she wants to stay at the feet of her lover boy' – meaning Adolf Hitler.[13] The postcard was intercepted and read by the Germans.

The Gestapo believed that Home and Beresford-Peirse were SIS and knew that they had stayed with Countess Marianne. It deepened the German authorities' mistrust of her and she continued to fall under their suspicion until May 1945; indeed, towards the end of the war, Countess Marianne endured a permanent presence of an SS officer at the family estate.[14] An important factor in all of this is that the Germans certainly believed she had been a source of information to the British and they claimed to have reliable evidence for it.

Countess Marianne's contacts with the British were good and she enjoyed a wide circle of friends. It included the British alpine skier and world downhill champion Evelyn 'Evie' Pinching who became a lifelong close friend. From trips to the European ski resorts in the 1930s, Pinching introduced Countess Marianne to a group of Australians who became equally close to her. Another in this skiing circle was Audrey Durell Drummond Sale-Barker, known to friends and family as Wendy. Sale-Barker was captain of the British women's skiing team at the 1936 Winter Olympics and, in 1947, married George Nigel Douglas-Hamilton, tenth earl of Selkirk. Selkirk already had a link to Vienna because he had studied at its university in the 1930s. Kendrick and his wife frequently entertained British university students in their Viennese apartment, and it is possible that their paths crossed. During the Second World War,

Selkirk went on to serve as an intelligence officer in the RAF, and later received the Order of St Michael and St George, an honour awarded to men and women who held high office or rendered extraordinary or important non-military service in a foreign country. It is not unusual for it to be bestowed upon senior intelligence officers, and as such provides yet another connection to intelligence circles in Countess Marianne's orbit.

In June 1941, Countess Marianne visited an uncle (an orthopaedic surgeon) in Carlsbad who treated her for ongoing problems from a ski fracture sustained the previous winter. It was there that she met Baron Günther von Reibnitz, a 46-year-old cavalry officer of the First World War, on medical leave from his Wehrmacht regiment to take the waters in the spa town to alleviate his heart complaint. He had served as a captain in the Wehrmacht and in 1933 was appointed an honorary officer of the SS Cavalry Brigade (SS-Kavallerie-Brigade). An umbrella organization for the old German horse clubs, the SS Cavalry was the only Nazi unit cleared of wholesale guilt at the Nuremberg trials after the war.[15] To Countess Marianne it was obvious that Reibnitz was disillusioned with Nazism and openly against the Hitler regime.[16] She explained to him about her ongoing difficulties with the German authorities: her passport was stamped 'undesirable',[17] and her authority to travel from Czechoslovakia to Austria and Hungary on family business had been revoked. When she was summoned to appear before the Gestapo, Reibnitz offered to help by accompanying her to Berlin to confront the Gestapo himself in an attempt to resolve the situation in her favour. After a lengthy interrogation, Reibnitz agreed to be responsible for her, and Countess Marianne was released into his care. Her rights to travel were restored. There is no doubt that Reibnitz's position and reputation within the Nazi Party had protected her.

In December 1941 the couple married and settled in Breslau, Silesia. Reibnitz returned to his pre-war role as provincial director of hunting, an honorary (unpaid) post to which he had been appointed in 1933 by Hermann Goering, head of the German Hunting Society. But a cloud of suspicion hung over the couple. Reibnitz, who had responsibility for all aspects of hunting in the province of Silesia, including the granting of hunting licences, was accused by the German authorities of issuing hunting licences to Jews, something which was forbidden in the Third Reich. He refused a hunting licence to the Gauleiter of Silesia, the highest-ranking Nazi in the province, on the very reasonable basis that he could not shoot straight; nevertheless, Reibnitz's decision made him unpopular.

By 1943, Countess Marianne was back on the family estates, still under surveillance by the authorities, while Reibnitz remained in Breslau in the insurance business, and the couple saw each other now and again. Things came to a head in early 1944 after Reibnitz referred to the SS leader Heinrich Himmler as 'the chicken farmer'. He was called to face an SS trial for disloyalty – a charge compounded by the fact that he had not informed the authorities that he sought to marry Countess Marianne in a Roman Catholic ceremony, that he had agreed to raise the children in the Catholic faith (into which their son was baptized), and that he and his wife practised their faith openly. He was expelled from the SS Cavalry, and then in mid-1944 from his honorary position as director of hunting. At a trial *in absentia* in November 1944, Reibnitz was thrown out of the Nazi Party. Countess Marianne, by now seven months pregnant, had been called in for questioning in what were extremely frightening circumstances and it was clear that she was still under suspicion. Reibnitz had been ordered to serve in a special 'punishment' unit in a region of fighting where he would not be expected to survive. But, with the help of an old friend, his orders were 'lost', and he re-joined his old Wehrmacht regiment.

Countess Marianne did not see her husband until after the end of the war. Russian forces were advancing, and, fearing the fate of old European aristocratic families under the Communists, in May 1945 she fled with her two children into US-controlled Bavaria to escape them. Reibnitz was taken prisoner by the Russians in the final days of the war and only managed to escape on 8 May 1945, Victory in Europe Day, while the camp guards were celebrating. He journeyed via Poland to Bavaria where his wife was then living with the children and was reunited with them. The marriage had become an unhappy one and the couple decided to divorce in 1946.

Reibnitz settled in South Africa in 1950, having followed his then-partner Esther Schütte to Johannesburg, where she became his third wife. In the same year Countess Marianne immigrated to Australia with the children. This is believed to have been on the sponsorship of the Australian friends she had met skiing in the early 1930s. But a source, who wishes to remain unnamed, asserts that they were, in fact, sponsored to settle in Australia by her SIS handlers, on the instructions of the British.

On 30 June 1978, Reibnitz attended the wedding of his daughter Marie-Christine to Prince Michael of Kent in the town hall in Vienna. Hereafter, she took the title Her Royal Highness Princess Michael of Kent. Over the decades, controversy continued to surface about her 'Nazi father'. According to one suggestion, Reibnitz had been planted in the SS by Goering to keep an eye on Himmler and the wider organization; currently no documentary proof has been found to support this.[18] A denazification court tried Reibnitz in Bavaria on 14 May 1948 and concluded that he was a follower, not a supporter, of the Nazi regime, and that there was no evidence to link him to Nazi atrocities and the Holocaust.[19] Evidence was produced in his defence that included affidavits from Jews whom he had helped to obtain hunting licences and employment.

Of Countess Marianne, her clandestine operations for SIS – as part of Kendrick's network in the 1930s and then for MI6 during the Second World War – have been asserted by a reliable source. Although the precise nature of her activities has not yet been officially disclosed, the Germans certainly had their suspicions, which if proven would have had dire consequences for her. Her location and movements within Czechoslovakia and Hungary, as well as to Vienna and London, at one of the most pivotal moments in the twentieth century, would have made her a valuable source of intelligence for Kendrick.

Of course, it was something which neither Kendrick nor Countess Marianne could ever tell their respective families.

ENDNOTES

Abbreviations used in the endnotes

GR   General Report
GRGG   General Report, German General
KV   Prefix for MI5 files in The National Archives
NID   Naval Intelligence Division
SIR   Subject Interrogation Report
SR   Special Report
SRA   Special Report, Air Force POWs
SRGG   Special Report, German Generals and Senior Officers
SRM   Special Report, Army POWs
SRN   Special Report, Naval POWs
SRX   Special Report, POWs of Different Services

Author's note

1. Keith Jeffery, *MI6: The history of the SIS, 1909–1949*, Bloomsbury, 2010.
2. See the SIS official website, www.sis.gov.uk
3. Correspondence between the author and the Foreign Office over a Freedom of Information Request to release the Hess files for his four days in the Tower of London in May 1941. These files cannot be released in the interests of international security.
4. Letter from Arnold Bax addressed to Harriet Cohen at the embassy in Vienna, 16 March 1933, British Library, ref: 1999/10. See also Helen Fry, *Music and Men: The life and loves of Harriet Cohen*, The History Press, 2008, pp. 211–12.
5. Michael Smith, *Six: A history of Britain's Secret Intelligence Service*, Dialogue, 2010, p. 331.
6. Harriet Cohen, *A Bundle of Time*, Faber & Faber, 1969; Harriet Cohen archive at the British Library, consisting of over 3,000 letters between Bax and Cohen, ref: 1999/10.
7. Letter from Cohen to the BBC in her personal file at the BBC Written Archives, Caversham.
8. Fry, *Music and Men*, p. 212.

Introduction

1. Some of Kendrick's siblings were born to his father's second wife, Winifred. The fate of his natural mother is unclear, and extensive research has found nothing. She may have died after childbirth. Kendrick never spoke about his mother to his family.
2. Copy of the Oath of Allegiance to Queen Victoria in Kendrick's personal military record.
3. See D.R. Maree, 'Bicycles in the Anglo-Boer War of 1899–1902', *Military History Journal*, 4:1 (1977) (South African Military History Society); Brian Parritt, *The Intelligencers: British military intelligence from the Middle Ages to 1929*, Pen and Sword, 2011, pp. 210–11.
4. Anthony Clayton, *Forearmed: A history of the Intelligence Corps*, Brassey's, 1993, pp. 10–11; also Maree, 'Bicycles'.

5. 'Field Intelligence from 29 November 1900 until the Cessation of Hostilities', report by Lieutenant Colonel Henderson (Director of Military Intelligence, South Africa) in WO 32/8112.

6. Parritt, *The Intelligencers*, pp. 159–84.

7. Clayton, *Forearmed*, p. 13.

8. Author's interviews with Barbara Lloyd and Kendrick's personal army record.

9. Sarah Helm, *A Life in Secrets: The story of Vera Atkins and the lost agents of SOE*, Little, Brown, 2005, pp. 172–73.

10. References in Vera Atkins' personal naturalization file, HO 405/45567. Another reference was given by Rex Pearson, Kendrick's brother-in-law and also SIS. Pearson's reference stated that he had known Vera's parents and grandparents for many years in South Africa. Kendrick wrote that he had known Vera for 15 years, but did not provide details on how or where.

11. Anthony Read and David Fisher, *Colonel Z: The life and times of a master of spies*, Hodder & Stoughton, 1984, pp.173, 182.

12. While in India at the end of the eighteenth century, Francis Baring-Gould had seen an advertisement for the Kimberley Mine and decided to travel to South Africa. His elder brother Sabine soon joined him. Barney Barnato, one of the richest Jewish diamond magnates, was the largest shareholder of the Kimberley Mine. In 1885, Barnato merged his original company with Baring-Gould's Kimberley Central Mining Company. Francis Baring-Gould became the chairman. Another wealthy diamond trader, Cecil Rhodes, persuaded Barnato to merge the Kimberley Mine and de Beers. Barnato's life became shrouded in secrecy after he died in mysterious circumstances on 14 June 1897, having fallen overboard from his yacht near Madeira on his way back to England.

13. Vera Atkins sent agents into Nazi-occupied France for Special Operations Executive.

14. Staff Officer Caryl Baring-Gould worked in the air intelligence branch called ADI(K) in the Second World War, attached to Kendrick's unit at Trent Park and Latimer House.

15. Ted Baring-Gould was sent into Riga in the 1920s as an intelligence officer, running agents such as Sidney Reilly into Russia.

16. Dansey had arrived in South Africa from England to serve with the British South African Police during the Matabele Rebellion in Rhodesia (now Zimbabwe). From 1899 to 1900, he fought bandits in Borneo; after the Boer War, from 1902, he was engaged in similar reconnaissance missions for Kendrick in South West Africa. From 1904 to 1909, Dansey served as colonial political officer in Somaliland. See Dansey's personal army record, WO 339/10993.

17. Read and Fisher, *Colonel Z*.

18. M.R.D. Foot and Jimmy Langley, *MI9: Escape and evasion 1939–1945*, BCA, 1979, p. 36.

19. Christopher Andrew, *Secret Service: The making of the British intelligence community*, Book Club Associates, 1985, p. 358.

20. Pearson arrived in South Africa aboard the *Tintagel Castle*. Information from family member, John Vignoles.

21. For the first year, Pearson was engaged as a consultant engineer in Durban (Natal) and then worked for a number of other mining companies as chief engineer.

22. Rex Pearson worked in the region for G.A. Troyes of Johannesburg. Information from John Vignoles.

23. Norah Wecke was born in May 1891 in East London, Eastern Cape (South Africa). Her father, Frederick Wecke, was German, her mother Irish.

24. Western Cape Archives, Cape Town, South Africa. Details provided by John Vignoles.

25. Wecke & Voigts was founded in 1892 by Fritz Wecke and the brothers Albert and Gustav Voigts. It exchanged goods for cattle, often trekking with cattle between South Africa and Namibia. Albert Voigts had arrived in South Africa from Germany in 1890 and became Wecke's assistant at a trading station at Schweizer-Reneke, between Kimberley and Johannesburg. A third brother, Richard Voigts, joined the firm in 1893. Today Wecke & Voigts Retail is the oldest department store in Windhoek. Correspondence with John Vignoles.

26. Unpublished private family memoir by Phyllis Pearson.
27. Information provided by John Vignoles. Schists Syndicate Ltd traded until August 1912.
28. Jeffery, *MI6*, p. 4.
29. This period of Alexander Scotland's life is covered in more detail in his unpublished memoirs, WO 208/5381, pp. 17–23. He soon became fluent in German and Cape Dutch.
30. Confirmed by his personal army service record. Alexander Scotland was close to British intelligence for decades, and many of his closest colleagues and friends became members of SIS after 1909. For Scotland's own experience in intelligence, security and MI5, see Helen Fry, *The London Cage: The secret history of Britain's WWII interrogation centre*, Yale University Press, 2017, pp. 187–89. He officially worked for MI9 and MI19 in the Second World War.
31. Andrew, *Secret Service*, p. 73.
32. Jeffery, *MI6*, p. 8.
33. ibid., pp. 50, 162. See also Smith, *Six*, pp. 274–75; and the history section of the SIS official website, www.sis.gov.uk Information on the history has also been provided by Fred Judge, Intelligence Corps historian.
34. Andrew, *Secret Service*, p. 240.
35. Kendrick's personal army record, copy in the author's possession. For background on this work, see Parrit, *The Intelligencers*, pp. 228–33.
36. Kendrick's personal army record.
37. Information provided by John Vignoles from the *Journal of the Institution of Mining Engineers* (1915).
38. The Intelligence Corps existed as a distinct unit in the First World War, formed on 12 August 1914, then disbanded in 1929. It was formed by Army Order 112 on 19 July 1940 and is still in existence today. See Clayton, *Forearmed* and Nick van der Bijl, *Sharing the Secret: The history of the Intelligence Corps, 1940–2010*, Pen and Sword, 2020.
39. Pearson is mentioned several times in General Sir Walter Kirke's pencilled war diaries in the Imperial War Museum. Details of Pearson's work with pigeons and gadgets is contained in WO 106/45. See also Gordon Corera, *Operation Columba – The Secret Pigeon Service: The untold story of World War II resistance in Europe*, William Morrow, 2018.
40. Pearson went on to develop various inventions and gadgets involving clocks and timers, all for secret operations with pigeons. One was a special timer to trigger a basket of pigeons to drop behind enemy lines at a set time. Local civilians sent the homing pigeons back with messages attached. Author's interview with John Vignoles. Towards the end of the war, Pearson was sending pigeons over enemy lines with propaganda leaflets and material for the civilian population.
41. Letter dated 2 November 1917 from Government House (Windhoek) to Kendrick, copy given to the author.
42. Letter dated 21 April 1918 from General Headquarters to Commandant Intelligence Corps, copy in Kendrick's personal army record.
43. Letter dated October 1917, copy in Kendrick's personal army record.
44. Names of the referees in Kendrick's personal army record.
45. Information from Fred Judge, official Intelligence Corps historian, Chicksands.

Chapter 1: The slow war

1. Copy of the training programme in the papers of Eric Gedye, Imperial War Museum.
2. George Eric Rowe Gedye was born in 1890 in Clevedon, Somerset.
3. 'History of Intelligence, British Expeditionary Force, France from January 1917 to April 1919: The Secret Service', WO 106/45. See also Kirke's war diaries for the period, contained in General Sir Walter Kirke's papers, IWM.
4. A.F Judge, 'History of the Intelligence Corps, 1914–1929', unpublished, copy at Military Intelligence Museum, Chicksands, pp. 27–34.

5. Frank Foley had been trained to recruit agents, but his work consisted primarily of debriefing several thousand, mainly Jewish, Belgian refugees who had to flee to France because of anti-Semitism in Belgium. The majority were Jews from Antwerp who had been in the diamond trade there, were blamed for the war and made scapegoats. See Michael Smith, *Foley: The spy who saved 10,000 Jews*, Politico's Publishing, 2004, p. 13.

6. It is known that Burnell was not only attached to the Intelligence Corps, but was also SIS. In the Second World War, he headed MI9/MI19's Royal Patriotic School for the interrogation of civilians entering Britain. Bertie Acton Burnell's personal army record, courtesy of the family.

7. Jeffery, *MI6*, p. 162. Dansey divided the General Headquarters (GHQ) into six sections: Section I: Economics, Section II: Aviation, Section III: Naval, Section IV: Military, Section V: Political and Section VI: Organisation and Administration. As head of Section IV, Dansey prepared military reports on counter-intelligence for MI5 and counter-espionage for MI1(c), as well as liaising with Scotland Yard and MI5 on matters of security.

8. Smith, *Foley*, pp. 13–14.

9. Read and Fisher, *Colonel Z*, p. 154.

10. Madame Rischard happened to have been trapped in France with inadequate papers to return home during the war. Her country was under occupation and Bruce provided her with false papers to return to Luxembourg, where she enlisted the aid of her husband (a doctor to the Luxembourg state railways) to successfully build up watch posts for Bruce behind enemy lines. For further details, see Janet Morgan, *The Secrets of Rue St Roch*, Penguin, 2005, and 'History of Intelligence, pp. 19–21, WO 106/45.

11. Henry Landau, *The Spy Net: The greatest intelligence operations of the First World War*, Biteback, 2015 edition.

12. 'History of Intelligence, British Expeditionary Force, France from January 1917 to April 1919: The Secret Service', p. 72, WO 106/45.

13. ibid., pp. 22–28. See also the diaries and papers of General Sir Walter Kirke, IWM.

14. 'History of Intelligence, in WO 106/45. See also Edwin Ruis, *Spynest: British and German espionage from neutral Holland 1914–1918*, The History Press, 2012.

15. Jim Beach, *Haig's Intelligence: GHQ and the German army, 1916–1918*, Cambridge University Press, 2013, p. 307.

16. As outlined in a post-war lecture: Major General Sir William Thwaites, 'The role of forward troops in the collection of intelligence in the field', lecture to the Royal Artillery Institution, Woolwich, 9 December 1924, Military Intelligence Museum, Chicksands, p. 244. See also Alexander P. Scotland, *The London Cage*, Evans Brothers Ltd, 1957, pp. 38–39.

17. Smith, *Six*, pp. 78–83.

18. Clayton, *Forearmed*, p. 35.

19. ibid., p. 56. Lieutenant Colonel R.W. Oldfield, 'Memorandum on the Work of the Section of Civic Affairs and Security, General Staff, British Army of the Rhine', Military Intelligence Museum, Chicksands.

20. Clayton, *Forearmed*, p. 56.

21. 'History of Intelligence, pp. 19–21, WO 106/45. See also Clayton, *Forearmed*, p. 56.

22. Unpublished family memoir, copy given to the author.

23. Clayton, *Forearmed*, p. 56.

24. Smith, *Foley*, p. 17.

25. Vischer had served as a Christian missionary in Nigeria immediately after the Boer War. In 1915, he had been recruited by military intelligence for secret operations in Europe.

26. At the school in Kitzbühel during the 1930s, they received their most famous recruit, Ian Fleming, who went on to work as personal assistant to the director of naval intelligence in the Second World War, as well as carrying out activities for SIS.

27. Jeffery, *MI6*, p. 202.

Chapter 2: Red Vienna

1. Andrew, *Secret Service*, p. 347.
2. Jeffery, *MI6*, p. 301.
3. Author's interview with Prudence Hopkinson.
4. Scotland, *The London Cage*, p. 15.
5. Jeffery, *MI6*, p. 202.
6. Author's interviews with Barbara Lloyd.
7. Kenneth Benton, 'The ISOS years': Madrid 1941–3', *Journal of Contemporary History*, 30:3 (1995), pp. 362–63.
8. Hodgson received an OBE for intelligence work during the Second World War.
9. Author's interviews with Prudence Hopkinson. Clara was the daughter of the rector, Revd Guy Bates.
10. Author's interview with Prudence Hopkinson.
11. Hanns Vischer transferred to Vienna for a short time; then, during the 1920s, he returned to Africa. He was called up by military intelligence in the Second World War and worked at Bletchley Park. See also Jeffery, *MI6*, p. 201–02.
12. ibid.
13. ibid., pp. 194–95.
14. Phillip Knightley, *The Second Oldest Profession*, Pan Books, 1987 edition, pp. 83–84.
15. Author's interviews with Robin Gedye.
16. Copies of all his newspaper articles from this period survive at the Imperial War Museum.
17. Eric Gedye, *Fallen Bastions*, Victor Gollancz, 1939, p. 11.
18. Eric Gedye, unpublished memoirs, pp. 2–3.
19. May Atkins was the aunt of Vera Atkins.
20. Charles Mendl had served in British intelligence in the First World War, been knighted for his services and in the 1920s was appointed press attaché at the Paris embassy. From there he continued his intelligence work for SIS and organized lavish parties for high society. Many British spies later moved in his circle in Paris, including Kim Philby.
21. Kendrick's work is known (albeit with an incomplete picture), because of SIS reports that have survived in declassified MI5 files at the National Archives. This is because SIS shared information with MI5 for the purposes of home security and counter-espionage, in many cases where MI5 requested details on particular personalities who might infiltrate Britain from abroad for espionage or subversive purposes.
22. Extensive details of Kendrick's successful penetration of Soviet intelligence have survived in KV 3/230 and KV 2/593.
23. 'Details of the Personnel of the Vienna Centre', report dated 29 April 1925, KV 3/230.
24. CX/1178, 'The Vienna Centre of the Communist International', 17 May 1926, KV 3/230.
25. 'Details of the Personnel of the Vienna Centre', report dated 29 April 1925, KV 3/230.
26. ibid., pp. 2–5.
27. They are named as Gabriel Kunzitine, Vrublevski and Viederbach.
28. CX/1178, 'The Vienna Centre of the Communist International', 17 May 1926, KV 3/230.
29. ibid., p. 3.
30. The heads of propaganda sections were Mayer for Germany, Tikhonov for Hungary, Kotzubinski for Poland and Dimitrov for the Balkans.
31. SIS ref: CX/1178, 'The Vienna Centre of the Communist International', p. 3, 17 May 1926, KV 3/230.
32. SIS ref: CX/1086, 'Czechoslovakia', no date, KV 3/230.
33. ibid.
34. Béla Kun's personal MI5 security file is KV 2/578.
35. Kun's letters in KV 2/578.
36. Kun's personal MI5 security file KV 2/578.
37. CX/737, 'Arrest of Béla Kun and his Associates', 4 June 1928, and supplementary report to CX/737, dated 15 May 1928, in KV 2/578.

38. CX 6561, 'Bolshevik Activities Abroad', 21 October 1927, KV 3/230.
39. Continuation of CX 6561, 4 November 1927, KV 3/230.
40. CX 6561, 'Bolshevik Activities Abroad', 21 October 1927, KV 3/230.
41. Stephen Dorril, *MI6: Fifty years of special operations*, Fourth Estate, 2001, pp. 198–99.
42. Continuation of CX 6561, 4 November 1927, KV 3/230.
43. CX 4764, report entitled 'Yugoslav Espionage', 4 June 1928, KV 3/230.
44. CX 10996, 'Soviet S.S. Activities in Vienna', 22 June 1928, KV 3/230.
45. CX 1387, 'Activities of Austrian Front-Kämpfer', 16 July 1928, KV 3/230.
46. They were Andreiev, Blukis and Kork.
47. CX 1387, 'Activities of Austrian Front-Kämpfer', 16 July 1928, KV 3/230. Kork had served as a major in the Russian forces on the Western Front during the First World War, had become chief of staff of the Estonian army after the Russian Revolution, and was then serving in the Red Army.
48. CX 1251, 'Soviet Military Intelligence', 26 August 1929, KV 3/230.
49. CX/12999, 'Hungary: Gas Warfare', 27 November 1929, WO 188/796.
50. CX 12808, 'Czechoslovakia: Bombs', 15 August 1928, WO 188/796.
51. CX 12808, 'Czechoslovakia: Chemical War Industry', 21 August 1928, WO 188/796.
52. CX/12808, 'Summary of the Position of Gas Warfare in Czechoslovakia up to 5 March 1929, compiled from Secret Information only', 5 March 1929, WO 188/754.
53. CX/12999, 'Hungary: Gas Warfare', 31 May 1927, WO 188/796.
54. CX/12999, 'Hungary: Gas Masks', 13 March 1929, WO 188/796.
55. CX/12999, 'Hungary: New Hand Grenades', 24 March 1929, WO 188/796.
56. CX/12999, 'Hungary: Gas Warfare', 27 November 1929, WO 188/796.
57. 'Secret police arrest British passport chief', *News Chronicle*, 19 August 1938.
58. Vera Atkins went on to head F Section of SOE in the Second World War.
59. The guests included Baron and Baroness von Lichtenberg, Baron von Löwenkreuz, Baron Reichlin, Baroness Daisy Weigelsperg (later Daisy Carol), Lady Phipps and Sir Eric Phipps, Admiral Yannopoulos, His Excellency von Wavrik, Dr and Mrs Landegger, General von Lerch and his wife, Miss von Wolitzky and Dr Adam Bauer (the family doctor). For a full list, see 'British Wedding in Vienna', *Vienna Herald*, 4 April 1931.
60. For example, see Edmund de Waal's family memoir *The Hare with the Amber Eyes*.
61. Phyllis Pearson, unpublished memoir, copy given to the author by John Vignoles.
62. In February 1932, the first child, Barbara, was born; a son, Ken, was born two years later, in October 1934.
63. *The Times*, 28 July 1931. See details also in KV 2/2349.
64. *Daily Telegraph*, 15 August 1931.
65. Engelbert Broda was still subject to surveillance by MI5 after he entered Britain in 1938. See KV 2/2349 to KV 2/2354.
66. CX/1387, 'Police Raid on Vienna Communists', 28 August 1931, KV 2/2349.
67. The original document survives in the Bavarian State Archives in Munich, in a box of Hitler's personal possessions that came out of the bunker in Berlin after his suicide on 30 April 1945. The author has seen these original possessions while filming for a Channel 5 documentary, *The Hunt for Hitler's Missing Millions*.
68. Robert Wistrich, *Anti-Semitism: The longest hatred*, Methuen, 1991; Martin Gilbert, *The Holocaust: The Jewish tragedy*, Harper Collins, 1989.

Chapter 3: Tangled web

1. Knightley, *The Second Oldest Profession*, pp. 82–83.
2. Author's interviews with Robin Gedye. Back in Britain, Winston Churchill awaited Gedye's newspaper reports as reflecting the real situation in Europe. Reading Gedye's articles enabled Churchill to issue his own warnings to the British parliament of the dangers of Germany's rearmament programme.
3. Felkin obituary, *Jersey Evening Post*, 15 January 1973.

4. Author's interview with Anne Walton.
5. Among the guests at Felkin's parties were military attachés and staff from various diplomatic missions; also Princess Erbach Schoenberg, Prince Emanuel von Liechtenstein, Baron and Baroness von Riedl-Riedenstein, Baron Wolfgang von Seybel, Count Erich Attems, Baron and Baroness von Buttlar-Elberberg, Baroness von Flotow and many others.
6. Peter Kurth, *American Cassandra: The life of Dorothy Thompson*, Little, Brown, 1990, p. 63. It was in March 1933 that Dorothy Thompson first met concert pianist Harriet Cohen during Cohen's visit to Vienna. Both women were dynamic and forceful and fought to bring the fate of Jewish refugees to the attention of their respective governments. See Fry, *Music and Men*, p. 212. Also a letter from Dorothy Thompson to Harriet Cohen, 18 March 1933, British Library, ref: 1999/10. Cohen was a close friend and briefly the mistress of British Prime Minister Ramsay Macdonald, which meant she could discuss the Jewish problem with him directly. See correspondence between Harriet Cohen and Ramsay Macdonald, British Library, ref: 1999/10.
7. Read and Fisher, *Colonel Z*, p. 184.
8. Genrikh Borovik, *The Philby Files*, Sphere, 1995, p. 17.
9. Edward Harrison, *The Young Kim Philby*, Liverpool University Press, 2012, p. 30.
10. E.H. Cookridge, *The Third Man: The full story of Kim Philby*, Putnam, 1968, p. 29. Edward Spiro was born in Vienna in 1908 and became foreign correspondent for a number of British and American newspapers.
11. ibid., p. 30.
12. Harrison, *The Young Kim Philby*, p. 30.
13. Author's interview with Robin Gedye.
14. Author's interview with Prudence Hopkinson.
15. Brian Brivati, *Hugh Gaitskell*, Richard Cohen Books, 1996, p. 36.
16. Author's interview with George Weidenfeld.
17. W.T. Rodgers, *Hugh Gaitskell 1906–1963*, Thames and Hudson, 1964, p. 47. Rodgers worked with Gaitskell and Hugh Dalton in the Ministry of Economic Warfare during the Second World War.
18. Brivati, *Hugh Gaitskell*, p. 37.
19. Naomi Mitchison, *Vienna Diary 1934*, Kennedy & Boyd, 2009, p. 287.
20. Brivati, *Hugh Gaitskell*, p. 47.
21. Mitchison, *Vienna Diary*, entry for 1 March 1934, p. 72.
22. Brivati, *Hugh Gaitskell*, p. 36.
23. ibid., p. 37.
24. Mitchison, *Vienna Diary*, pp. 82–83.
25. ibid., entry for 9 March 1934, p. 172.
26. ibid., entry for 1 March 1934, pp. 78–79.
27. Harrison, *The Young Kim Philby*, pp. 30–31.
28. Ian Kershaw, *Hitler 1889–1936: Hubris*, Allen Lane, 1988, pp. 456–58, 731–32.
29. Cookridge, *The Third Man*, p. 32.
30. Report dated 3 December 1929, KV 2/593. Schueller used various aliases, including Gustav Demper, Walker, Walkden and Marsden.
31. SIS summary report for MI5, 'Espionage and Communist Activities among Austrians', no CX reference, 5 February 1935, KV 2/593.
32. Report dated 3 December 1929, KV 2/593.
33. *Morning Post*, 11 April 1928.
34. A report about Schueller from an unnamed source, March 1930, KV 2/593. Schueller's wife was Helena (née Willmanovsky/Willmanovskaya).
35. CX/6561, 'Communist Agents', 4 March 1930, KV 2/593.
36. The two communist colleagues were Alois Ketzlik and Ferchlechner. CX/1387, 'Austria: Communism. Review of the Communist Movement in Austria during the first half of 1931', 25 November 1931, KV 2/593.
37. SIS report quotes *The Times* correspondent on this story, 28 April 1933.

38. CX/1387, 6 June 1933, KV 2/593.
39. See two reports in KV 2/593: 'Radical Tendencies in Austria', CX/2889, 17 December 1934 and SIS summary report for MI5, 'Espionage and Communist Activities among Austrians', 5 February 1935.
40. SIS report, no reference, dated 11 July 1935, KV 2/593.
41. Details in Schueller's personal MI5 file, KV 2/593.
42. Johann Taeubl's MI5 file, KV 2/2024. It contains reports that originate from SIS and MI6 (as SIS was later called). Taeubl was born in 1906.
43. Message intercepted on 5 December 1934, ref: 1447/A, KV 2/2024.
44. CX/1387, 1 February 1935, KV 2/2024. See also CX/12650/2009, 27 July 1935.
45. Intercepts 13 July 1934, 4 September 1934 and 13 December 1934 in KV 2/2024.
46. CX/1387, no date, KV 2/2024.
47. CX/1174, 4 November 1935, KV 2/2024.
48. Memo from SIS to MI5, 3 September 1942, KV 2/2024.
49. Details in personal file of Eva Kolmer, KV 2/2516.
50. SIS summary to MI5, CX/1387/a, 18 November 1935, KV 2/2516.
51. CX/1387, 7 February 1936.
52. Biographical summary as part of CX/1387/a, 18 November 1935, KV 2/2516.
53. CX/1387, 10 October 1936, KV 2/2516.
54. Minute from MI5 to Special Branch, 21 November 1936, KV 2/2516.
55. Special Branch report, 20 January 1937, CX/1387, KV 2/2516.
56. Minute dated 24 March 1938, KV 2/2516.
57. Personal MI5 file, KV 2/2672.
58. SIS to MI5, report dated 18 November 1937, KV 2/2672.
59. Personal MI5 file, KV 2/3068.
60. Biographical report dated 5 March 1940, KV 2/3068.
61. Information extracted for MI5 on 23 November 1940 from earlier SIS reports from Austria in KV 2/3068.
62. ibid.
63. Report dated 14 March 1941, information provided by SIS, KV 2/3068.
64. MI5 file for Paul Loew-Beer, KV 2/2186. Scholz was involved with the Austrian Centre at 126 Westbourne Terrace in London with Kolmer and another prominent communist, Dr Paul Loew-Beer.
65. SIS report to MI5, 5 May 1941, KV 2/3068.
66. Edith Suschitzky was born in Vienna in 1908.
67. Author's interview with Wolf Suschitzky, London, 19 March 2013. Wolf Suschitzky was the younger brother of Edith. He himself went on to become a renowned and highly respected cinematographer who also worked in the film industry.
68. The photographs of the poverty in Vienna were the subject of her book, *The Eye of Conscience*.
69. Alexander Ethan Tudor-Hart's personal MI5 file, KV 2/1603.
70. Edith Suschitzky's personal MI5 file, KV 2/1012.
71. Biographical report on Edith Suschitzky, 31 October 1930, KV 2/1012.
72. CX/2310, 11 December 1930, KV 2/1012.
73. Alexander Ethan Tudor-Hart's personal MI5 file, KV 2/1603.
74. MI5 to Valentine Vivian, 20 March 1931, and also CX/2310, 8 July 1931, KV 2/1012.
75. Author's interview and correspondence with Richard Deveson. Suschitzky's police reports survive in the Institut für Zeitgeschichte in Vienna and include files of the extensive questioning by police of Modern and Sonnenfeld.
76. Author's interview and correspondence with Richard Deveson.
77. Duncan Forbes, 'Politics, photography and exile in the life of Edith Tudor-Hart (1908–1973)' in Shulamith Behr and Marian Malet (eds), *Arts in Exile in Britain 1933–1945: Politics and cultural identity*, Research Centre for German and Austrian Exile Studies, 2005, pp. 45–87.
78. Summary MI5 report, 1 December 1951, KV 2/1603.

79. Biographical outline of Edith Tudor-Hart by MI5, 21 February 1934, KV 2/1012.
80. British passport number 2433. Report by Special Branch, 27 August 1937, KV 2/1012.
81. Report by Special Branch, 16 August 1935, KV 2/1012. Alexander Tudor-Hart was a qualified doctor and had obtained a new medical post at St Mary Abbot's Hospital in Kensington.
82. Paul Hardt's personal files: KV 2/1008 and KV 2/1009. According to Soviet spy and defector Walter Krivitsky, Deutsch's wife was also an agent of the OGPU and was trained as a radio operator.
83. Arnold Deutsch personal MI5 file, KV 2/4428. See also Ben Macintyre, *A Spy Among Friends: Kim Philby and the great betrayal*, Bloomsbury, 2014, pp. 38–40; and Harrison, *The Young Kim Philby*, pp. 33–34.
84. Philby's notes: 'Extract from notes handed by Philby (self-confessed Russian intelligence agent)', dated 11 January 1963, KV 2/4428.
85. Harrison, *The Young Kim Philby*, p.26.
86. MI5 minute, 12 September 1935, KV 2/1012.
87. Report dated 24 February 1947 in KV 2/1014. See also MI5 report, 1 December 1951, in KV1603.
88. Report on Arpad Haaz, 16 August 1947, KV 2/1014.
89. Summary MI5 report, 1 December 1951, KV 2/1603.
90. Hans Peter Smollett's MI5 file, KV 2/4170.
91. Patrick Seale and Maureen McConville, *Philby: The long road to Moscow*, Penguin, 1978, p. 98.
92. Biographical information, KV 2/4170.
93. Letter dated 17 November 1961, KV 2/4170.
94. Biographical information, KV 2/4170.
95. Harrison, *The Young Kim Philby*, p. 31.
96. Seale and McConville, *Philby*, p. 86. See also Cookridge, *The Third Man*, pp. 27–28.
97. Cookridge, *The Third Man*, p. 34.
98. Kim Philby, *My Silent War*, Modern Library, 2002, p. 203.
99. Arnold Deutsch personal MI5 file, KV 2/4428. See also Macintyre, *A Spy Among Friends*, pp. 38–40; and Harrison, *The Young Kim Philby*, pp. 33–34.
100. Philby, *My Silent War*, p. 7.
101. MI5 minute, 12 September 1935, KV 2/1012.
102. Brivati, *Hugh Gaitskell*, p. 38.
103. MI5 was tracking him. See his personal files KV 2/2349 to KV 2/2354.
104. During the Second World War, Gaitskell worked in the Ministry of Economic Warfare under the command of Hugh Dalton, who established SOE. In 1963, Gaitskell's early death at the age of only 56 of lupus (a rare autoimmune disease) was deemed suspicious and induced by some kind of rare poisoning. Peter Wright argued that Gaitskell had been assassinated, probably by the KGB, although this theory remains unproven. See Peter Wright, *Spycatcher*, Viking, 1987, pp. 362–63.

Chapter 4: A dangerous game

1. Jeffery, *MI6*, pp. 245–46.
2. The reports survive in KV 3/293.
3. 'Italian Intelligence Service in Yugoslavia', no date, KV 3/293.
4. 'Foreign Intelligence Services in Yugoslavia', SIS correspondence of 6 June 1936 to MI5, KV 3/293.
5. ibid.
6. 'Foreign Intelligence Services in Yugoslavia', 14 May 1936, KV 3/293.
7. Jeffery, *MI6*, pp. 424–25.
8. SIS reports on the crisis in Abyssinia and intelligence on Italian secret service agents there survive in KV 3/316.
9. Jeffery, *MI6*, p. 246.

10. Author's interview with Prudence Hopkinson.
11. An entry in Hilda's diary for Friday, 22 October 1937 reads: 'dined at the Kendricks'. See Helm, *A Life in Secrets*, p. 176.
12. Author's interview with Barbara Lloyd. Bernard Edge had a fondness for Kendrick's daughter and gave her a bound gold-trimmed copy of Rudyard Kipling's *Jungle Book* and an ebony heart necklace inscribed with her initials.
13. Smith, *Foley.*
14. Personal army record of Bertie Acton Burnell, copy given to the author by the family.
15. Read and Fisher, *Colonel Z*, p. 172.
16. ibid., p. 181.
17. Charles Drazin, *Korda: Britain's only movie mogul*, Sidgwick & Jackson, 2002, pp. 85–86.
18. ibid., p. 216.
19. Jeffery, *MI6*, p. 316.
20. Ben Macintyre, 'The real 007's cover has been blown', *The Times*, 26 September 2020; see also Conrad O'Brien-ffrench, *Delicate Mission: Autobiography of a secret agent*, Skilton & Shaw, 1979.
21. Author's interview with George Weidenfeld.
22. Fleming appears in a photograph with the naval intelligence team at Latimer House in Buckinghamshire in 1943. See Helen Fry, *The Walls Have Ears: The greatest intelligence operation of World War II*, Yale University Press, 2019, plate 19.
23. Read and Fisher, *Colonel Z*, pp. 174–80.
24. Kenneth Benton, 'The ISOS years', pp. 360–66.
25. ibid., pp. 362–63.
26. Full details of Tucek's case are in KV 3/116, which contains original Abwehr reports from 1938 and 1939.
27. 'Activities of Ast. Wien', in KV 3/116.
28. ibid.
29. Information on the SD obtained by MI14 and contained in Kaltenbrunner's files, KV 2/269.
30. SIS report in letter from SIS to counter-intelligence section of MI5, 24 December 1944, KV 2/269.
31. Author's interview with Prudence Hopkinson.
32. The list was compiled by Kendrick and the consul-general. It survives in FO 371/22320.
33. Possible Nazis or collaborators included General Dr Karl von Bardolf (president of the German Club in Vienna and former aide-de-camp of Archduke Ferdinand) and Dr Emmerich Czermak who represented the conservative wing of Christian socialism and was violently anti-Semitic.
34. Author's interview with Prudence Hopkinson.
35. Author's interview with Richard Morawetz.
36. Sandy Rosdol later became first secretary at HM Embassy Ankara and was honoured in the Queen's Birthday Honours List 1969.
37. Copy in translation in KV 3/116.
38. ibid.
39. The report refers to the Abwehr men as 'E men', KV 3/116.
40. ibid.
41. 'Information Received from H.M. Representatives regarding German Troop Movements into Austria', report to the Foreign Office, FO 371/22318.
42. ibid. Information from consul-general at Munich on 11 March 1938.
43. ibid. Information from HM ambassadors in Vienna and Budapest on 12 March 1938.

Chapter 5: *Finis Austriae*

1. Email exchange from Michael Bottenheim in 2020.
2. CX report in letter from SIS to counter-intelligence section of MI5, 24 December 1944, KV 2/269.

3. Various SIS and MI5 reports covering the same biographical information about Kaltenbrunner survive in KV 2/269.
4. Extract from conclusions of the Cabinet held on Wednesday, 16 March 1938, HO 213/1635.
5. Home Office Memorandum, 16 March 1938, HO 213/1635.
6. ibid.
7. Cypher to Mr Mack (Vienna) from the Foreign Office, 4.30 p.m., 16 March 1938, HO 213/1635.
8. Gedye, *Fallen Bastions*, pp. 307, 309.
9. *The Argus* newspaper, 20 August 1938.
10. Gedye, *Fallen Bastions*, p. 18. See also Gedye's article, 'New alarm among Vienna Jews', *Daily Telegraph*, 22 March 1938, copy in FO 395/562.
11. Summary in a telegram to the British embassy, Vienna, 30 March 1938, FO 371/21749.
12. Helen Fry, *Freuds' War*, The History Press, 2009, pp. 85–88.
13. List of public figures thought to be at risk in Vienna, no date, in FO 371/21755.
14. Jeffery, *MI6*, p. 301.
15. Smith, *Foley*, p. 125.
16. Gedye's own report, 'Three days to leave Vienna', *Daily Telegraph*, 19 March 1938. And cypher from Mr Mack (Vienna) to the Foreign Office, 19 March 1938, FO 395/562.
17. Parliamentary Questions, 4 April 1938, FO 371/21685. See also a decoded cypher from ambassador Nevile Henderson (Berlin) to the Foreign Office about Gedye's expulsion, 25 March 1938, FO 395/562.
18. Internal Foreign Office correspondence on 26 and 28 March 1938, P 1379/4/150, FO 395/562.
19. Author's interview with Robin Gedye.
20. Eric Gedye, unpublished memoirs, p. 14.
21. Gedye and Litzi officially married after the war. During the war they served in SOE.
22. Wright and Eisinger married in London in the 1930s and lived in Vienna until the Anschluss.
23. Information supplied by the family from Marjorie Eisinger's diary and notes on Kendrick.
24. *News Chronicle*, 19 August 1938.
25. Author's interviews with Acton Burnell's family.
26. 'Arrest of Captain Pollak', telegram to the Foreign Office from Michael Palairet (Vienna), 13 March 1938, FO 371/22315.
27. Pollak's account of events, FO 371/22321.
28. Report by John Taylor, 14 March 1938, FO 371/22321.
29. Pollak's account of events, FO 371/22321.
30. ibid.
31. Pollak was also the sole import agent for J.J. Coleman Ltd; George Sandeman Ltd; Peek Freans Ltd; Tanqueray; and Lipton Ltd.
32. Minutes by Creswell of meeting with Pollak, 14 March 1938, FO 371/22315.
33. Telegram from Mr Mack (Vienna) to the Foreign Office, 11 April 1938, FO 371/21755.
34. Cypher from the Foreign Office to the British embassy, Vienna, 25 March 1938, FO 371/22321.
35. Cypher to the British embassy, Vienna, 29 March 1938, FO 371/22321.
36. Author's interviews conducted in the early 2000s.
37. Telegram from Ambassador Henderson in Berlin to the Foreign Office, 12 April 1938, FO 371/21755.
38. Telegram via the diplomatic bag from Mr Mack (Vienna), 11 April 1938, FO 371/21755. Original Gestapo reports on Schuschnigg survive in GFM 33/849.
39. Report dated 25 March 1938, FO 371/22321.
40. Telegram via the diplomatic bag from Mr Mack (Vienna) to Foreign Office, 11 April 1938, FO 371/21755.

41. Cecilia Sternberg, *The Journey*, Collins, 1977, p. 135. A list of some of his property confiscated while he was in custody is contained in original Gestapo records in GFM 33/849.
42. Sternberg, *The Journey*, p. 135.
43. Seemann family business papers loaned to the author.
44. Drazin, *Korda*, pp. 42–47.
45. Author's interview with Susan Gompels.
46. In the 1950s, during the Mau Mau rebellion, the Seemann family uprooted from East Africa and travelled to Southern Rhodesia (now Zimbabwe). This new life was disrupted again at the Unilateral Declaration of Independence in 1965. William and his family moved again to make a new life in Britain.
47. Author's interview (2020) and correspondence with Susan Gompels.
48. 'Austrian Political Prisoners', 8 April 1938, FO 371/21755.
49. Author's interviews with Barbara Lloyd.
50. John Taylor's report to the Foreign Office, 15 April 1938, FO 371/21755.
51. ibid.
52. 'Anti-Semitism', report in FO 371/21663.
53. 'Note on the Situation of the Jews in Vienna', 21 March 1938, FO 371/21748.
54. *News Chronicle*, 19 August 1938.
55. Gainer's reply to A.B Hutcheon, 9 August 1938, FO 372/3284.
56. Andrew, *Secret Service*, pp. 535–36.
57. Report for Parliamentary Questions, 13 July 1938, FO 372/3284.
58. Report on staff of consulate at Vienna, 18 July 1938, FO 372/3284.
59. Gainer to A.B Hutcheon at the Foreign Office, 9 August 1938, FO 372/3284.
60. 'Staff and Office Premises of Vienna Consulate-General', 30 April 1938, FO 369/2480.
61. 'Bargain price for embassy', *Manchester Guardian*, 7 March 1939, copy in FO 741/5. The embassy and furniture had been purchased in 1873 for £39,000 and were sold to the German government in 1939 for £9,000. See also correspondence on the sale of 6 Metternichgasse in FO 741/5.
62. Letter from the legation in Vienna to the Foreign Office, 7 May 1938, FO 369/2480.
63. Letter dated 21 July 1938 in FO 369/2480.
64. Gainer's report, 21 April 1938, FO 369/2480.
65. Jeffery, *MI6*, pp. 303–04.
66. ibid., p. 303.
67. Translation of a letter from the secret police, Salzburg, to the British consulate, Vienna, 14 July 1938, FO 371/121690.
68. ibid.
69. Gainer to the Foreign Office, 18 July 1938, FO 371/21690.
70. Author's interview with Prudence Hopkinson.
71. Gainer to the Foreign Office, 18 July 1938, FO 371/21690, pp. 2, 3–4.
72. Report No. 57, British consulate to Nevile Henderson in Berlin, 25 July 1938, FO 371/21663, p. 3.
73. 'Note on the Situation of the Jews in Vienna', 21 March 1938, FO 371/21748.
74. Notes from the conference held at the Home Office on 17 March 1938, HO 213/1635.
75. Letter from the Dominions Office to the Foreign Office, 24 May 1938, FO 371/21749.
76. Parkin, Passport Control (London), 30 May 1938, FO 371/121749.
77. Letter from the Colonial Office to the Foreign Office, 21 May 1938, FO 371/21749.
78. 'Jewish Emigration to British Colonies', 30 May 1938, FO 371/21749.
79. Report for session of Parliamentary Questions to the House of Commons, 22 June 1938, FO 372/2384.
80. Letter from Mr A. Dibdin, dated 7 June 1938, India Office to the Foreign Office, FO 371/21749.
81. Around 750 visas had been granted to people in the refugee class, 150 applications were refused, 150 had been referred to London for a decision, and a further 200 visas had been issued to other people, such as businessmen.

82. Kendrick to Passport Control Department, London, 19 July 1938, FO 372/3284.
83. ibid., p. 172.
84. Kenneth Benton interview with Michael Smith in 1996. Quoted by kind permission of Michael Smith.
85. Giles MacDonogh, *1938: Hitler's Gamble*, Constable, 2009, pp. 171, 173.

Chapter 6: The spy who saved a generation

1. *The Argus* newspaper, 20 August 1938.
2. Author's interview with Roger Lloyd-Pack, 2012.
3. Author's interview with Trude Holmes, 2013.
4. Eric Sanders, *From Music to Morse*, privately published autobiography, p. 36.
5. Derrick Simon, Unpublished memoirs, pp. 147–48.
6. Creswell's additional handwritten reply dated 30 March 1938 added to the bottom of 'Permission for Jewish boy to leave Austria' (dated 24 March 1938) in FO 372/3283.
7. Author's interview with Prudence Hopkinson.
8. Correspondence from Dr Andrew Norman to the author.
9. ibid.
10. ibid.
11. Telegram from the Foreign Office to Vienna, 26 March 1938, FO 371/22321.
12. Author's interviews with George Weidenfeld, 2013.
13. Sanders, *From Music to Morse*, p. 37.
14. Author's interview with Prudence Hopkinson.
15. Author's interview and correspondence with Francis Steiner, 2013.
16. ibid. Discretion on the part of the British passport officer is confirmed in Foreign Office files, letter from J. Balfour to Edmond Howard, the Stock Exchange, London, 20 May 1938, FO 371/21751.
17. Unpublished memoirs loaned to the author.
18. Author's interview with Francis Steiner.
19. Georg Kendrick (Schwarz) enlisted in Southampton on 19 December 1944, army number 13810031.
20. Their widowed mother Fritzi Modern came out in November 1938, after Kendrick himself had left Austria.
21. Bryher, *The Heart to Artemis*, Collins, 1963, p. 278. From 1940 to 1946, Bryher moved to London and lived with her distant cousin and lover, Hilda Doolittle.
22. Correspondence with Richard Deveson during 2020.
23. Sternberg, *The Journey*, p. 205.
24. Helen Braham, voluntary part-time curator at the Courtauld Institute and keeper of the papers of Count Antoine Seilern, email to the author.
25. Sternberg, *The Journey*, p. 206.
26. Seilern's army number for the Intelligence Corps was 336967.
27. Gainer letter to A.B Hutcheon, 9 August 1938, FO 372/3284.
28. Memorandum, no date, Home Office correspondence, HO 213/1635.
29. Memorandum, no date, HO 213/1635.
30. Report dated 14 June 1938, FO 371/21751.
31. ibid.
32. Letter from Co-ordinating Committee for Refugees (London) to the Foreign Office, 13 May 1938, FO 372/3283.
33. ibid.
34. Gainer to the Foreign Office, 31 May 1938, FO 372/3284.
35. ibid.
36. Comments of Dr Weizmann reported in confidential handwritten comments 'Complaints against Miss Stamper of Passport Control Office at Vienna', 13 May 1938, FO 372/3284.

See also letter from Neville Bland at the Foreign Office to Gainer at Consulate General in Vienna, 26 May 1938, FO 372/3283.

37. Handwritten comments by Mr Bland on untitled minute, 24 August 1938, FO 372/3284.
38. ibid.
39. Giles MacDonogh, 'A most unfortunate case', *Jewish Quarterly*, 51:2 (2004), p. 60.
40. MacDonogh, *Hitler's Gamble*, pp. 208–09.
41. Gainer to the Foreign Office, 19 August 1938, FO 371/21691.
42. Author's interview with Barbara Lloyd.
43. Author's interview with Ken Walsh.
44. Author's interview with Barbara Lloyd.
45. Author's interview with Peter Barber.
46. This later enabled clothes and family correspondence of his niece's future husband to be smuggled out in three trunks via the export business in March 1939, in advance of his own exit from Nazi-occupied Europe.
47. Author's interview with Peter Barber.
48. Other members of the family did not survive. In early November 1941, Leo and Esche Fleischer and their son and daughter were deported straight to Minsk and died there.
49. 'Treatment of Mr and Mrs Cecil Rhodes-Smith at Frontier Station of Neu Bentschen', report dated 21 August 1938, FO 371/21691.
50. Rhodes-Smith was also managing director of a subsidiary company, Botany Wools Pty. Ltd. at Alexandria (Australia), and mills of James Seymour and Co. Pty. Ltd at Williamstown, Victoria. He died in 1953 and is buried at Fawkner, Victoria (Australia).
51. Abwehr report, 21 June 1938, KV 3/116.
52. Section on Ast. Wien in KV 3/116.
53. Dorril, *MI6*, p. 190.
54. Author's interview with Prudence Hopkinson.
55. Gainer to the Foreign Office, 18 August 1938, FO 371/21691.
56. ibid.
57. Gainer (Vienna) to Ambassador Henderson (Berlin), 18 August 1938, FO 371/21691.

Chapter 7: At the mercy of the Gestapo

1. *News Chronicle*, 19 August 1938. Kendrick's arrest was reported in all major international newspapers, including the *New York Times*, *Manchester Guardian*, *Irish Times* and the *Daily Mirror*.
2. Jeffery, *MI6*, p. 202.
3. MacDonogh, 'A most unfortunate case', p. 58. Sir Dudley Forwood was later equerry to Edward, Duke of Windsor.
4. Evidence provided during the first interrogation of Abwehr officer Joachim Rohleder, May 1946, KV 2/2136.
5. Gainer (Vienna) to Ambassador Henderson (Berlin), 18 August 1938, FO 371/21691. See also cypher telegram from the Foreign Office to Henderson, sent at 9 p.m. on 23 August 1938, FO 371/21691.
6. Author's interview with Prudence Hopkinson.
7. ibid.
8. Benton, 'The ISOS years', p. 364.
9. Many of the diplomatic cyphers and correspondence on Kendrick's arrest exist in FO 371/21691.
10. Cypher to Henderson from the Foreign Office, 23 August 1938, FO 371/21691.
11. Record of meeting on status of passport control officers, 2 December 1938, FO 1093/81.
12. 'Conditions in Austria', 12 August 1938, FO 371/21756. At the beginning of August, following a three-month visit to Vienna by Lady Helen Cassel, the Foreign Office discussed whether to make an appeal to Hermann Goering for Rothschild's release.

13. Code and cypher telegram sent by the Foreign Office at 9 p.m. to Henderson (Berlin), 18 August 1938, FO 371/21691.
14. The conversation between Ernst von Weizsäcker and Ambassador Henderson is reported in a cypher received by the Foreign Office at 6.40 p.m., 18 August 1938, FO 371/21691.
15. Cypher received by the Foreign Office at 6.40 p.m., 18 August 1938, FO 371/21691.
16. Vice-Consul Frank Walker was on sick leave in England and had been replaced temporarily by King. Prior to leaving Austria, he had been aiding Kendrick in saving Jews since the Anschluss and is now thought to have also been on the SIS staff.
17. Gainer to Henderson, 18 August 1938, FO 371/21691.
18. ibid.
19. Jeffery, *MI6*, p. 301.
20. Cypher from Gainer to the Foreign Office, 19 August 1938, FO 371/21691.
21. Conversation with von Ribbentrop reported in cypher from Henderson to the Foreign Office, sent 4.50 p.m. on 19 August 1938, FO 371/21691.
22. Andrew, *Secret Service*, pp. 395–96.
23. Gainer to Ambassador Henderson (Berlin), Secret Dispatch No. 71, 19 August 1938, FO 371/21691.
24. MacDonogh, 'A most unfortunate case', p. 58.
25. Benton, 'The ISOS years', p. 364. Benton returned to England briefly during the early part of the Second World War. From 1941 until 1944, he worked in Lisbon for MI6 as head of counter-espionage (Section V), identifying German spies who were passing through the region and working with MI6 officer Kim Philby.
26. Cypher sent from Henderson to the Foreign Office, 4.50 p.m. on 19 August 1938, FO 371/21691.
27. Henderson to the Foreign Office, 20 August 1938, FO 371/21691.
28. Henderson to the Foreign Office, 21 August 1938, FO 371/21691.
29. Gainer to Henderson, 22 August 1938, FO 371/21691.
30. Foreign Office memo, 20 August 1938, FO 371/21691.
31. Cypher from Gainer to the Foreign Office, 20 August 1938, FO 371/21691.
32. Cypher from Gascoigne (Budapest) to the Foreign Office, 20 August 1938, FO 371/21691.
33. Cypher from Gascoigne to the Foreign Office, 21 August 1938, FO 371/21691.
34. *Sunday Express*, 21 August 1938.
35. Copy in the Kendrick archive.
36. ibid.
37. Cypher telegram from the Foreign Office to Henderson, sent at 9 p.m. on 23 August 1938, FO 371/21691.
38. ibid. Reported also in the press: 'Captain Kendrick: No confession made', *Manchester Guardian*, 24 August 1938.
39. Cypher from Gascoigne to the Foreign Office, 21 August 1938, FO 371/21691.
40. Telegram from Henderson to the Foreign Office, 21 August 1938, FO 371/21691.
41. Consul-General O'Meara to the Foreign Office, 31 August 1938, FO 371/21691.
42. Comments in pen by Creswell on 5 September 1938 on O'Meara's (above) report, FO 371/21691.
43. 'Arrest of Walter John Howard Becker', Gainer to the Foreign Office 4 October 1938, FO 371/21691.
44. Gainer to Ogilvie-Forbes, 25 October 1938, FO 371/21691.
45. 'Arrest of Walter John Howard Becker', 8 October 1938, FO 371/21691.
46. Jebb's untitled report to the Foreign Office, no date, FO 371/21691.
47. Gainer to A.E. Hutcheon, 7 October 1938, FO 371/21691.
48. ibid.
49. 'Arrest of M. Richter Employee of the Passport Control Office, Vienna', telegram from Henderson to the Foreign Office, 24 August 1938, FO 371/21691.
50. See correspondence and discussions at the Foreign Office, FO 369/2480.
51. Letter dated 3 September 1938, whereabouts unknown.

52. Letter from the Foreign Office to Dr Hans Simon (acting as guarantor for the Richters), 16 September 1938, FO 371/21756.
53. Letter from the Foreign Office to Richard Richter, 21 September 1938, FO 371/21691.
54. Telegram from Ambassador Henderson (Berlin) to the Foreign Office, 22 September 1938, FO 371/21691.
55. Letter from Maud Richter in Foreign Office files, 23 October 1938, FO 371/21691.
56. Creswell to Selby, 15 November 1938, FO 371/21691.
57. MacDonogh, *Hitler's Gamble*, p. 308.
58. 'Germany: Captain Kendrick Expulsion', 30 November 1938, FO 371/21692.
59. IWM LBY 89/1936, No. 42, p. 105/6.
60. Letter to E.H. Rance at the Foreign Office from Maurice Jeffes at 54 Broadway Buildings, 10 October 1938, FO 366/1036. Mr Jacobsen, Miss de Fossard, Miss Lloyd, Miss St Clair and Miss Molesworth were evacuated from the passport office in Berlin; and Mr Gibson, Mr Mowbray and Miss Williams from Prague.
61. The women evacuated from the office in Vienna were Miss Steedman, Miss Wood, Mrs Howe, Miss Birkett and Miss Mapleston.
62. Jeffery, *MI6*, pp. 424–25.
63. ibid., p. 423.

Chapter 8: Secrets of the Tower

1. Rex Pearson had returned to England to plan for the dispatch of pigeons behind enemy lines for the SIS, as he had in the First World War. Instead of operating in France, he organized for pigeons to be dropped from aircraft. From locations behind enemy lines, they made the long flight back with their messages to a loft on the top floor of Broadway Buildings. SIS colleague Dick Ellis also returned to London, where he ran a high-status German agent.
2. Letter from Sinclair to Kendrick, 11 September 1938, Kendrick papers.
3. Jeffery, *MI6*, p. 317.
4. ibid., pp. 304–06.
5. Andrew, *Secret Service*, p. 399.
6. Lee Richards, *The Black Art: British clandestine psychological warfare against the Third Reich*, 2010, www.psywar.org, chapter on Section D.
7. Michael Smith, *The Secrets of Station X: How Bletchley Park helped win the war*, Biteback Publishing, 2011 edition; David Kenyon, *Bletchley Park and D-Day*, Yale University Press, 2019.
8. Major General Sir William Thwaites, 'The role of forward troops in the collection of intelligence in the field', lecture to the Royal Artillery Institution, Woolwich, 9 December 1924, Military Intelligence Museum, Chicksands. See also 'Intelligence from Prisoners of War', report by Felkin, 31 December 1945, AIR 40/2636.
9. Details of the establishment of the Prisoners of War Collecting Centre at the Tower of London are contained in WO 94/105. A map of the areas at the Tower used for Kendrick's bugging operation is in Fry, *The Walls Have Ears*, p. 7.
10. Lecture by Captain Waley from first-hand experience with GHQ in France in the First World War, no date, copy in the archives of the Military Intelligence Museum.
11. These are contained primarily in series WO 208 and AIR 40.
12. The precise area in the Tower used by Kendrick is shown in a diagram in Fry, *The Walls Have Ears*, p. 7.
13. The equipment was installed by Mr E. Barnes, Mr J. Ackroyd and Mr J. Doust, Kendrick to Rawlinson, 15 January 1940, WO 208/3458.
14. Kendrick to Rawlinson, 15 January 1940, WO 208/3458. The surveyor was Mr T.H. Rhodes, aided by Mr Jackson. The electric lighting was installed by Mr Thomas, Mr Beasley and Mr M. Read of the Office of Works. The furnishing was completed by Mr F. Rutherford and Mr W.S. Thompson.
15. Memo issued by MI1(a), 2 September 1939, WO 208/3458. The naval intelligence section was headed by Lieutenant Colonel Bernard Trench (Royal Marine Light Infantry). The unit

at this time also consisted of three captains of the Intelligence Corps, William Rose, G. Buxton and J.B. Carson, Lieutenant Commander Edward Croghan (RNVR) and army captains Charles Corner and Leslie Parkin. Lieutenant Richard Pennell (RNVR) conducted interrogations from October 1939. The daily administration of the special compound came under the jurisdiction of Captain Count Anthony de Salis, a guards officer.

16. Memo, 3 September 1939, WO 208/3458. For a more detailed background to these officers, see Fry, *The Walls Have Ears*, pp. 8–10.
17. A list of their names was compiled and this survives in WO 94/105.
18. SRA 10, 12 January 1940, WO 208/4117.
19. SR 8, 24 December 1939, WO 208/4117.
20. Clayton, *Forearmed*, p. 30.
21. Fry, *The Walls Have Ears*, pp. 27–28.
22. The family always understood that Brin had been a stool pigeon in the Tower and also spent time at Trent Park, north London. Email correspondence with Steve Mallinson in April 2015.
23. Personal army record.
24. 'Intelligence from Prisoners of War', report by Felkin, 31 December 1945, AIR 40/2636.
25. Kendrick's report, 28 October 1939, WO 208/4117. Other references to a secret weapon in Felkin's report of 31 October 1939, WO 208/5158 and conversations in WO 208/4158.
26. Felkin's report of 31 October 1939, WO 208/5158.
27. SRA 20, 29 January 1940, WO 208/4117.
28. Fry, *The Walls Have Ears*, pp. 6–23.
29. Draft Statement, no date, FO 1093/200. The principal German officers involved in this were General Wietersheim and Colonel Teichmann, although negotiations in the third week of October also involved General von Seydlitz.
30. Transcript of a telephone call from 'C' to his representative in The Hague (Payne Best), no date, FO 1093/200.
31. Summary report attached to 'C''s letter of 19 June 1941, FO 1093/201.
32. Summary report, 17 October 1939, FO 1093/201.
33. Helen Fry, *MI9: A history of the secret service for escape and evasion in World War Two*, Yale University Press, 2020, p. 171.

Chapter 9: Eavesdropping on the enemy

1. Two prisoner of war camps were located on the Trent Park estate, known as No. 1 POW Camp and No. 2 POW Camp, both directly under the auspices of British intelligence. One camp was based in the mansion house and stable block, and the other nearby at Ludgrove Hall (still on the estate). 'Minutes of Meeting held in the War Office, February 21, 1940', WO 208/3458. It is believed that the camp at Ludgrove Hall came under the command of Kendrick's colleague Colonel Alexander Scotland. This camp became known as the London Cage and in 1940 relocated to Kensington Palace Gardens; see Fry, *The London Cage*, pp. 13–15.
2. The equipment was supplied by the Radio Corporation of America. 'Inventory of Equipment Supplied and Installed at Cockfosters Camp', WO 208/3457. See also 'Installation and Use of Microphones at CSDIC (UK) P/W Camps 1939-1945', appendix G of 'The History of CSDIC', WO 208/4970.
3. Burton Scott Rivers Cope joined the naval intelligence section at Trent Park and headed it from March 1940. See the Trench diary, 12 March 1940; Derek Nudd, *Castaways of the Kriegsmarine: How shipwrecked German seamen helped the Allies win the Second World War*, Createspace, 2017, pp. 61–70; and Fry, *The Walls Have Ears*, pp. 48–51. The naval intelligence section staff were recruited by Ian Fleming of naval intelligence. The air intelligence section, ADI(K), had moved to Trent Park in mid-December 1939. The daily administration and security of the site shortly transferred from Major (Count) Anthony de Salis to the command of Major Topham. 'Minutes of Meeting held in the War Office, February 21, 1940', WO 208/3458.

4. See also 'The History of CSDIC', p. 6 and appendix F (section 9), WO 208/4970.

5. Kendrick's report, 22 July 1941, WO 3455.

6. Catherine Jestin, *A War Bride's Story*, privately published, p. 229.

7. Kendrick's report, 22 July 1941, WO 208/3455.

8. Reference to Kendrick's 'Weekly Personal Reports' in Norman Crockatt's memo, 25 July 1941, WO 208/3455.

9. For more detailed study of the intelligence given by May to Pennell about German Enigma and codes, see Fry, *The Walls Have Ears*, pp. 34–35.

10. Trench diary, 30 November 1939 and 4 December 1939.

11. Erich May's incarceration, first at the Tower and then at Trent Park, triggered the first known meeting, on 28 December 1939, between Alastair Denniston, the first head of the Government Code and Cypher School (GC&CS) at Bletchley Park, and Bernard Trench, a naval interrogator working between the Admiralty and Trent Park.

12. Interrogation reports, 8 January 1940 and 19 January 1940, WO 208/5158.

13. 'The History of Hut Eight', p. 24, HW 25/2.

14. ibid., pp. 24–25. Turing looked again at the German 'Forty Weepy Cribs' encryption. He and his colleagues noticed that two new wheels had been added to the naval Enigma machines by the Germans in December 1938 and so it had not been possible to trace the 'Forty Weepy' encryption messages, as call signs were no longer being used. They worked on them again in January 1940, using the knowledge they now had from prisoner Erich May. A further four days of cribs were broken on the same wheel order. For an explanation of the 'Forty Weepy Cribs', see Christof Teuscher, *Alan Turing: Life and legacy of a great thinker*, Springer, 2005, p. 455.

15. 'The History of Hut Eight', p. 25, HW 25/2.

16. Fry, *The Walls Have Ears*, pp. 88–89.

17. 'CSDIC Survey 3 September 1939 to 31 December 1940', WO 208/3455. Copy also in WO 208/4970.

18. ibid. See also minute NID 01789/39, 1 August 1940, ADM 1/23905.

19. Trench diary, entries for 25 May 1940 and 17 June 1940.

20. Davidson's comments in Appendix B, MI9a/683, WO 208/4970.

21. 'Intelligence from Prisoners of War', report by Felkin, section 116, AIR 40/2636.

22. SRA 37, 27 February 1940, AIR 40/3070.

23. R.V. Jones, *Most Secret War*, Coronet, 1978, pp. 234–36. The significance of this intelligence is discussed further in Fry, *The Walls Have Ears*.

24. 'Intelligence from Prisoners of War', report by Felkin, section 117, AIR 40/2636.

25. Letter from Crockatt to Kendrick, 10 April 1940, in the Kendrick archive.

26. Minute dated 25 July 1941, WO 208/3455.

27. Letter dated 11 February 1941, WO 208/3460.

28. Letter dated 21 February 1941, Stewart Menzies (head of MI6) to Crockatt, WO 208/4970.

29. Charles Deveson was born in London in 1910, studied English at the University of Oxford, then taught at an exclusive boys' boarding school in Prussia. He returned to England in 1936. At the outbreak of war in September 1939, he enlisted in the Royal Armoured Corps, and by 1941 had transferred to the Intelligence Corps.

30. Author's interview with Richard Deveson.

31. See, for example, SRA 305, 10 August 1940; SRA 441, 2 September 1940; and SRA 498, 11 September 1940, AIR 40/3070.

32. SRA 441, 2 September 1940, AIR 40/3070.

33. SRA 495, 10 September 1940, AIR 40/3070.

34. SRA 441, 2 September 1940, AIR 40/3070.

35. ibid.

36. SRX 10, 26 December 1939, WO 208/4158.

37. POWs came from the *Bismarck, Alstertor, Gonzenheim, Egerland, Lothringen* and the prize ship *Ketty Brövig*. Also from Raider 35 (Pinguin) and Raider 16, as well as the following U-boats: U-651, U-138, U-556, U-570, U-501, U-111, U-95, U-433 and U-574. For

bugged conversations from the survivors, see, for example, SRN 574, 22 July 1941, SRN 575, 20 July 1941, SRN 576, 22 July 1941, WO 208/4143.

38. Fry, *The Walls Have Ears*, p. 49.
39. 'CSDIC Half-Yearly Survey: 1 January 1941 to 30 June 1941', WO 208/3455.
40. 17 February 1941, CAB 79/9/19. See also 'Accommodation for CSDIC', p. 1, WO 208/3456. Copy also in WO 208/5621.
41. Memorandum, 7 October 1941, CAB 121/236. See also 'Interference with the work of CSDIC by the Construction of the Aerodrome at Bovingdon', WO 208/3456.
42. Army intelligence staff numbered 156; the naval intelligence section consisted of 10 officers, including five WRNS, four non-commissioned WRNS and six captured German naval officers who assisted the interrogation as collaborators; and the air intelligence section numbered just over 100. There were also warders, guards, cooks, signals specialists, couriers, a barber, medical officer and site maintenance personnel.
43. The naval intelligence team included Ralph Izzard (formerly of the *Daily Mail*), John Marriner (Reuters), John Everett, John Connell, Charles Wheeler, Colin McFadyean and Czech refugee Harry Scholar. The female naval intelligence officers included Evelyn Barron, Esme McKenzie, Jean Flowers, Celia Thomas Ruth Hales and Gwen Neal-Wall.
44. Memorandum, 7 October 1941, CAB 121/236.

Chapter 10: The Hess affair

1. For the tracking of Hess's flight by the Royal Observer Corps, see AIR 16/1266.
2. The first personnel at the scene of the crash were Mr Maclean (a ploughman), Special Constable Williamson, Captain Clark (Home Guard), Captain Flint and Signalman McBride (12th Anti-Aircraft Division, Signals) and personnel from RAF Decoy (Bonnyton Moor), 527 Searchlight Battery (Bonnyton) and 3rd Battalion Home Guard. See report on Rudolf Hess by HQ Scottish Command, no date, FO 1093/11.
3. Fry, *The London Cage*, pp. 52, 98–100.
4. 'Prologue 1: May 10, 1941', report in AIR 16/1266.
5. Copy of Roman Battaglia's interrogation of Hess in FO 1093/11.
6. ibid. See also interviews with Hess in FO 1093/1.
7. John Mair of the Intelligence Corps was later dispatched to question Battaglia about what he had extracted from Hess.
8. The units that guarded Hess or moved him to different locations while in Scotland were 3rd Battalion Home Guard and the 11th Cameronians. Hess was moved to Maryhill Barracks by L/Cpl Barty and Rifleman Browett of the 11th Cameronians and Major Barrie (Home Guard). While in a cell at the barracks, he was guarded by Pte Brearley, Sgt W. Turner, L/Cpl Hunt, Pte Skelton, 2/Lt Fulton and 2/Lt Bailey. Royal Army Medical Corps personnel who attended him were Major Greenhill, Sgt H. Moir, Pte J. Callender, Pte J. O'Brien, 2/Lt J. Loudon and 2/Lt W.J. Clark. Details in a report on Rudolf Hess by HQ Scottish Command, no date, FO 1093/11.
9. Hamilton's summary of their conversation, dated 11 May 1941, FO 1093/1. Hess told him that he had come on a humanitarian mission to stop the war, and asked if Hamilton could get together a group of leading members of his party to draw up peace proposals.
10. Hamilton's summary of their conversation, dated 11 May 1941, p. 2, FO 1093/1.
11. Report by T.A. Robertson, 13 May 1941, FO 1093/11.
12. Kirkpatrick, 'Record of Conversation with Herr Hess on May 15, 1941', FO 1093/1.
13. Hess was taken to Drymen Hospital, Glasgow. He was guarded there by 2/Lt A. McLeish, Cpl McLay, Pte H. McAreavey, Pte Durnford, Pte Reynolds, 2/Lt Ross, Capt. Greenaway, Capt. Cherry, Capt. Dunsmuir, Lt Whittle, Lt Hannigan, 2/Lt Shaw, 2/Lt McFarlane and Capt. Fraser. The officer commanding the guard was Major Sir Charles Buchanan. Details in a report on Hess by HQ Scottish Command, no date, FO 1093/11.
14. Six-page report on Hess, 13 May 1941, FO 1093/1. Lieutenant Colonel Gibson Graham, 'The case of Rudolph Hess', no date, unpublished lecture given at the Royal College of Physicians and Surgeons, Glasgow. Copy given to the author.

15. Churchill's personal minute, 13 May 1941, FO 1093/1.
16. Correspondence and directions by 'C' in FO 1093/8 and FO 1093/11.
17. Jeffery, *MI6*, p. 756.
18. Churchill's personal minute, 13 May 1941, FO 1093/1.
19. Felkin to Flight Lieutenant E.H. Baring, 23 May 1941, FO 1093/11. Baring was personal assistant to Air Vice Marshal C.E.H. Medhurst (the assistant chief of air staff (intelligence)).
20. Correspondence with the author.
21. Spenceley is listed in 'The K Album', a booklet of personnel who served with ADI(K), copy given to the author.
22. Untitled summary report, 13 May 1941, FO 1093/1. See also Report 3, 22 May 1941, FO 1093/8.
23. Kirkpatrick, 'Record of Conversation with Herr Hess on May 15, 1941', FO 1093/1; and report for Sir Orme Sargent, no date, FO 1093/11.
24. Smith, *Foley*, pp. 257–65. See also Anthony Cave Brown, *C: The secret life of Sir Stewart Graham Menzies*, Macmillan, 1987, p. 344. This theory circulated in the summer of 1941, see *Daily Express*, 8 August 1941, copy in HO 199/482.
25. Hess was escorted by Major Sheppard, Lieutenant Colonel Gibson Graham and six officers from the Glasgow region. They were Captain W. Cherry, Captain F. Dunsmuir, Lieutenant F. Harrigan, Second Lieutenant A.G. Ross, Captain W. Campbell and Second Lieutenant N.F. Cunningham.
26. Churchill's personal minute, 13 May 1941, FO 1093/1.
27. Summary entitled 'Herr Hess', including an intelligence report attached, 13 May 1941, FO 1093/1.
28. Airey Neave, *Saturday at MI9*, Pen & Sword, 2010; Fry, *MI9*.
29. Charles Fraser-Smith, *The Secret War of Charles Fraser-Smith*, Michael Joseph, 1981, pp. 135–38.
30. Four engineers were given special passes, valid for six months at a time: Mr J. Doust, Mr L. Dyer, Mr F. McGrath and Mr C. Carbury.
31. C/6720, 'C' to Henry Hopkinson (Foreign Office), 8 June 1941, FO 1093/8.
32. The orders were given to him by Colonel Coates (deputy to Alan Hunter, the director of prisoners of war), 18 May 1941, FO 1093/8.
33. Coates at the War Office to Hopkinson at the Foreign Office, 19 May 1941, FO 1093/8.
34. See FO 1093/8. Special passes to enter Camp Z were also issued to Lieutenant Colonel A. Swinton MC (officer commanding of the battalion of the guard), Lieutenant Colonel Gibson Graham (the medical officer), Captain H. Winch (guard commander) and the following officers of the guard: Second Lieutenants S.E. Smith, J. Young, P.G. Atkinson Clark, R. Hubbard and T.R. Jackson.
35. Handwritten report by Gibson Graham, 21 May 1941, FO 1093/8.
36. ibid.
37. Report No. 1, signed by 'C', copy to Hopkinson (Foreign Office), 20 May 1941, FO 1093/8.
38. Report No. 2, 22 May 1941, FO 1093/8.
39. Stephen McGinty, *Camp Z: The secret life of Rudolf Hess*, Quercus, 2011, p. 110.
40. Report from Second Lieutenant Malone to Scott, the commandant of Camp Z, 15 June 1941, FO 1093/10.
41. For the military use of drugs or 'truth drugs' on prisoners in the Second World War, see WO 193/791.
42. H. Freeman, 'In Conversation with William Sargant', *Bulletin of Royal College of Psychiatrists*, 1 (1987).
43. Remarks by H. Dale on the laboratory report on Hess's drugs, 27 May 1941, FO 1093/10.
44. Graham's report, 29 May 1941, FO 1093/8.
45. Malone's private diary, entry for 28 May 1941, quoted in McGinty, *Camp Z*, p. 74.
46. Extract from a letter from Scott to deputy director prisoners of war, 22 May 1941, FO 1093/8.

47. 'Extract from the Night Duty Officer's Report', 29 May 1941, FO 1093/8.
48. McGinty, *Camp Z*, p. 74.
49. Unsigned report on Z, 29 May 1941, FO 1093/8.
50. Graham's report, 29 May 1941, FO 1093/8.
51. Rees's report, 31 May 1941, FO 1093/10.

Chapter 11: The madness of Hess

1. David Dilks (ed.), *The Diaries of Sir Alexander Cadogan OM: 1938–1945*, Faber & Faber, 2010, entry for 13 May 1941, p. 378.
2. These are in FO 1093/7.
3. 'C' to Hopkinson at the Foreign Office, 20 June 1941, FO 1093/8.
4. Letter dated 22 May 1941, FO 1093/8.
5. C/6691, 4 June 1941, FO 1093/10.
6. Report No. 27, 6 June 1941, FO 1093/10.
7. Report No. 24, 6 June 1941, FO 1093/10.
8. Report No. 30, 7 June 1941, FO 1093/10.
9. McGinty, *Camp Z*, pp.105–06.
10. Report No. 31, 8 June 1941, FO 1093/10.
11. Frank Foley, quoted in McGinty, *Camp Z*, p. 106.
12. ibid.
13. Lord Simon was accompanied by Lieutenant Albert van Meurig-Evans (Intelligence Corps) and officers from MI5. The latter were Major R.W. Stephens, Captain Douglas Stimson and Lieutenant R. Short. See C/6720, 'C' to Henry Hopkinson (Foreign Office), 8 June 1941, FO 1093/8.
14. Complaints of headaches were reiterated by Hess; see report to Scott from Second Lieutenant Malone, on 15 June 1941, FO 1093/10.
15. Hess's interview with Lord Simon, recorded via the hidden microphones, is in 'Record of Conversations with "Dr Guthrie" (Lord Simon) on 9 June 1941', FO 1093/1. See also PREM 3/219/5; and full transcript of the meeting reproduced in McGinty, Camp Z, pp. 112–47.
16. Personal minute from Churchill to the Foreign Secretary, 14 June 1941, FO 1093/10.
17. Entry for 14 June 1941, in Lieutenant Colonel A. Malcolm Scott, 'Camp Z Diary 1941–1942', IWM, 69/66/1.
18. Report by Lieutenant Stephen Smith, adjutant of Camp Z, 15 June 1941, FO 1093/10.
19. 'Medical Report on Jonathan by Major Dicks', 9.45 a.m., 15 June 1941, FO 1093/10.
20. Report by Lieutenant Stephen Smith, adjutant of Camp Z, 15 June 1941, FO 1093/10.
21. 'Medical Report on Jonathan by Major Dicks', 9.45 a.m., 15 June 1941, FO 1093/10.
22. Report by Foley, marked urgent, 10 a.m., 15 June 1941, FO 1093/10.
23. Report No. 34, given by telephone to 'C' at 10.45 a.m., 15 June 1941, FO 1093/10.
24. Dilks, *The Diaries of Sir Alexander Cadogan*, entry for Sunday, 15 June 1941, p. 388.
25. Translation of the letters for 15 June and 16 June 1941, FO 1093/10.
26. Report No. 35, 16 June 1941, FO 1093/10. See also letter from Hunter (deputy director POW) to Hopkinson (Foreign Office), 16 June 1941, FO 1093/8.
27. 'Medical Report on Jonathan', 17 June 1941, FO 1093/10.
28. 'Camp Z Diary 1941-1942', by Lieutenant Colonel A. Malcolm Scott, IWM.
29. Letter to deputy director prisoners of war from Rees, 3 July 1941, FO 1093/10.
30. Scott to Coates [deputy director prisoners of war], 30 August 1941, FO 1093/12.
31. 'Report by Medical Officer', 19 June 1941, FO 1093/10.
32. 'Camp Z Diary 1941-1942', by Lieutenant Colonel A. Malcolm Scott, IWM.
33. Author's interviews with Barbara Lloyd.
34. Reports for July 1941 in FO 1093/10.
35. Report, 9 August 1941, FO 1093/12.
36. Kendrick's report, 30 August 1941, FO 1093/12.

37. Jeffery, *MI6*, p. 759.
38. 'Record of an Interview with Herr Rudolph Hess', 13 May 1941, p. 3, FO 1093/1. See also 'Appendix A: Comment on the Conversations', FO 1093/10.
39. Letter from Naval Intelligence to Hopkinson (Foreign Office), 18 June 1941, with accompanying Appendix A (see p. 3), FO 1093/10.
40. 'CSDIC Six-Monthly Report, 1 July 1941 to 31 December 1941', WO 208/3455.
41. C/7040, 'C' to Winston Churchill, 11 July 1941, FO 1093/12.
42. 'Deputy Führer Hess's Flight: Its Exploitation in Propaganda to Germany', and 'Hess: Observations, by German Section Ministry of Information and Political Intelligence Department of the Foreign Office', both reports undated, in FO 1093/1.
43. Summary memorandum on propaganda, Con O'Neil (Foreign Office), 22 June 1941, FO 1093/7.
44. 'The Hess Case', report dated 31 July 1941, FO 1093/8; see also SRN 583, 26 July 1941, copy in FO 1093/8; and also in FO 898/321.
45. SRA 1829, 1 June 1941, WO 208/4471.
46. Foley's report to 'C' and the Foreign Office, dated 6 March 1942, FO 1093/14.
47. Report dated 15 March 1942, FO 1093/14.

Chapter 12: A very secret place

1. Kendrick was supported at Latimer House by Lieutenant Colonel Charles Corner (assistant commandant, intelligence) and Lieutenant Colonel F. Huband (assistant commandant, administration). The daily duties at Wilton Park were overseen by Lieutenant Colonel Leo St Clare Grondona, an Australian by birth. The adjutant there was Kenneth Morgan, who had carried out interrogation duties at the London Cage in Kensington under Kendrick's colleague, Colonel Scotland.
2. Copy of a letter given to the author.
3. 'Intelligence from Prisoners of War', report by Felkin, pp. 28–29, AIR 40/2636. In August 1940, MI9 received a request for a CSDIC listening station at Cairo, in readiness for successes on the battlefields of North Africa. CSDIC sites would also open in the Mediterranean (Italy) and the Far East. See history of CSDIC-Med in WO 208/3248.
4. 'Enemy Prisoners of War: Treatment on Capture', WO 32/10720.
5. Simon, Unpublished memoirs, p. 147.
6. Matthew Barry Sullivan, *Thresholds of Peace: German prisoners and the people of Britain*, Hamish Hamilton, 1979, p. 53.
7. Nudd, *Castaways of the Kriegsmarine*, p. 70.
8. Interview with Colin McFadyean in Melanie McFadyean, 'A private war', *Guardian*, 6 July 2002.
9. Simon, Unpublished memoirs, p. 150.
10. Fry, *The Walls Have Ears*, pp. 79–82.
11. See for example, SRN 1729, 3 May 1943, WO 208/4145, SRM 444, 31 December 1943, WO 208/4137.
12. 'CSDIC Six-Monthly Report, 1 January 1942 to 30 June 1942', p. 7, WO 208/3455.
13. Simon, Unpublished memoirs, pp. 149–50.
14. Minute from Crockatt to MI14, 27 July 1941, WO 208/3455.
15. For more detailed information on Delmer's operations, see Richards, *The Black Art*. Among those figures who were turned were the anti-Nazi Max Braun, Philip Rosenthal (porcelain manufacturer), Dr Otto John (resistance leader who later defected to the Soviet Union in the Cold War) and Fritz Heine (secretary of the Social Democratic Party in Germany until 1933).
16. Author's interview with the late Elisabeth Bruegger (2011). Fry, *The Walls Have Ears*, p. 78. Few of his staff were privy to the existence of the codebreaking site, and only a small number of personnel at Bletchley knew about the CSDIC sites.
17. Letter from Marshall-Cornwall to Crockatt, 9 November 1944, Kendrick archive.

18. Letter from Rushbrooke to Kendrick, April 1943, Kendrick archive.
19. The source of this information was the late Cyril March, an RAF officer posted to Latimer House. During his time at Latimer in the war, he edited the interrogators' notes into coherent reports.
20. Information from Cyril March.
21. WO 165/39, 30 April 1941.
22. Dr Humphrey England was born in 1867 in Winchester, the son of a doctor, and studied at the University of Cambridge. He served in France in 1914 and at the end of the First World War on a hospital ship bringing back the wounded. He later married Mary Douglas Stephenson, a Scottish woman who had served as a nurse in the Imperial Yeomanry Hospital in the Boer War, stationed on the outskirts of Cape Town, South Africa. It is an open question whether she knew Kendrick during her time in Cape Town.
23. Author's interview with Patrick Filsell, 2014.
24. Reports in FO 1093/15.
25. Hess's movements to Maindiff Court in June 1942 are covered in a letter from Gepp at the War Office to Loxley (Foreign Office), 18 June 1942, FO 1093/15.
26. MF001523/07, English Heritage archives.
27. Crüwell's personal file in WO 208/3504.
28. Von Thoma's personal file in WO 208/3504.
29. Entry for August 1942 in the official MI19 war diary, WO 165/41. The files do not reveal Crüwell's location prior to his arrival at Trent Park, although it was almost certainly Latimer House where, later in the war, generals were taken before their transfer to Trent Park.
30. The meeting took place on 12 August 1942; see entry for August 1942 in WO 165/41.
31. The M Rooms were directly under the Blue Room, in the coal room and in a short tunnel next to the wine cellar – all in a secure locked area.
32. The early bugged conversations between von Thoma and Crüwell are contained in WO 208/4199.
33. By the summer of 1943, the following were being held at Trent Park: Hans-Jürgen von Arnim, Hans Cramer, Theodor von Sponeck, Gotthard Frantz, Gerhard Bassenge, Fritz Krause, Georg Neuffer, Kurt von Liebenstein, Friedrich von Broich, Ernst Schnarrenberger, Heinrich-Hermann von Hülsen; Colonel Schmidt (German air force), Colonel Buhse, Colonel Reimann, Lieutenant Colonel Köhnke (German air force), Lieutenant Colonel Wolters, Colonel Drange and Colonel Heym (German air force), Captain Paul Hermann Meixner (German navy) and other lower ranks: Dr Carius, von Glasow, Bülowius and Bock. Their names are listed in the MI19 war diary, WO 165/41.
34. Report No. 5 on ultra-long-range projectiles, 16 August 1943, WO 208/3437.
35. SRGG 659, 15 December 1943, WO 208/4167.
36. 'Enemy Prisoners of War: Treatment on Capture', WO 32/10720. See also letter from DMI to Colonel Gatesby, 29 May 1943, WO 208/3461.
37. Sullivan, *Thresholds of Peace*, pp. 51–52. After being wounded in 1940, Munro transferred to the Intelligence Corps and worked for Kendrick's colleague Major Alexander Scotland, at the Prisoner of War Home Interrogation Section (PWIS). In January 1943, he was transferred to CSDIC and to Trent Park from May 1943. For a detailed biographical background, see Fry, *The Walls Have Ears*, pp. 107–09.
38. Sullivan, *Thresholds of Peace*, p. 52.
39. GRGG 58, 22 July 1943, WO 208/4363.
40. Sullivan, *Thresholds of Peace*, p. 54.
41. Author's interview with Eric Mark. Born in Magdeburg, Germany, as Erich (Meyer) Mark, he had fled the Nazi regime in January 1935. For more about him, see Fry, *The Walls Have Ears*.
42. Author's interview with Dudley Bennett (2013).
43. The pro-Nazis consisted of Frantz, von Hülsen and Meixner.
44. Personal file in WO 208/3504.
45. GRGG 32, 10 July 1943, WO 208/5016.

46. GRGG 72, 21 August 1943, WO 208/4363.

47. Examples include SRM 424, 24 December 1943, SRM 426, 28 December 1943 and SRM 468, 2 February 1944 in WO 208/4137. See also SRGG 560, 14 November 1943, SRGG 647, 10 December 1943, SRGG 17 December 1943 and SRGG 756, 12 January 1944, WO 208/4167. A detailed study of the evidence is in Fry, *The Walls Have Ears* and Sönke Neitzel, *Soldaten: On fighting, killing and dying – The Second World War tapes of German POWs*, Simon & Schuster, 2012.

48. GRGG 189, 8–9 September 1944, WO 208/4363.

49. 'CSDIC Survey 1 July 1941 to 31 December 1941', WO 208/4970.

50. Further examples are in SRA 3468, 30 December 1942, WO 208/4128; SR 128, 5 January 1944, AIR 40/3106; SRGG 756, 12 January 1944, WO 208/4167; SRGG 1086(c), 28 December 1944, WO 208/4169; SRGG 676, 19 December 1943, WO 208/4167.

51. SIR 931, 8 September 1944 and SIR No. 938, 14 September 1944, WO 208/4296.

52. Among those US officers known to have arrived at the site were Eric Warburg, of the German banking family, Heimwarth Jestin and Joc Taylor.

53. Edgar Hoover to Kendrick, 26 September 1942, Kendrick archive.

54. This visit took place on 25 February 1943.

55. Crockatt to Kendrick, letter dated 5 January 1943, Kendrick archive.

56. Peter Hart, *Journey into Freedom*, Authors OnLine, 2003, p. 100.

57. In overall charge of the M Room was Major Frank Cassels. The squads of secret listeners were overseen by Captains Brodie, Hartje, Davis and Serin, and Lieutenants Blyth, Rowe, Read-Jahn, Reynolds, Gross, Bauers and Weber. The technical side of recording and listening in was taken care of by Captain Copping of the Royal Corps of Signals.

58. 'The History of CSDIC', appendix E, WO 208/4970.

59. Jestin, *A War Bride's Story*, p. 223.

60. Author's interview with Fritz Lustig.

61. Author's interview with Paul Douglas (2013).

62. Author's interview with Fritz Lustig. For a more detailed account of the work of the secret listeners, see Fry, *The Walls Have Ears*.

63. 'Intelligence from Prisoners of War', report by Felkin, 31 December 1945, section 303, AIR 40/2636.

64. For a history of German-speaking refugees in the Pioneer Corps, see Helen Fry, *Churchill's German Army*, The History Press, 2009.

65. Crockatt to Kendrick, 12 August 1943, Kendrick archive.

66. Correspondence with the author.

67. Author's interview with Barbara Lloyd.

Chapter 13: Special intelligence

1. 'The Present State of the SIS', report dated 9 January 1942, ADM 223/481.

2. GRGG 121, 6–12 February 1944, WO 208/4363.

3. These were U-593, U-73, U-761, U-536, U-732, U-340, U-386, U-406, U-264.

4. 'Intelligence from Prisoners of War', section 152–154, Air 40/2636. See also GRGG 344, 21 August 1945, pp. 14–15, WO 208/4178.

5. 'Intelligence from Prisoners of War', section 154, Air 40/2636.

6. CSDIC reports in KV 3/190; and 'Abwehr', report dated 18 November 1942, WO 208/3582.

7. CSDIC reports in KV 3/190; and 'Abwehr', report dated 18 November 1942, WO 208/3582.

8. Fry, *The Walls Have Ears*, pp. 150–71.

9. Chiefs of Staff memorandum, COS(43) 592 (O), entitled 'German Long Range Rockets', section 3: 'First Report of the Long range Rockets', 29 September 1943, CAB 80/75.

10. SRX 1635, 11 March 1943, WO 208/4162. Sketches of V-1 and V-2 launching equipment (ramps) contained in WO 208/4292.

11. For later comments on the German failure at Stalingrad, see GRGG 344, 21 August 1945, WO 208/4178.

12. The conversation took place on 22 March 1943 and was reproduced in a Chiefs of Staff memorandum, COS(43) 592 (O), entitled 'German Long Range Rockets', section 4: 'Von Thoma's Evidence', 29 September 1943, CAB 80/75. See also Jones, *Most Secret War*, p. 425. Information and analysis of V-weapon intelligence is also contained in CAB 120/748, including CX reports which emanated from MI6 agents behind enemy lines.

13. Jones, *Most Secret War*, p. 427.

14. Chiefs of Staff memorandum, COS(43) 592 (O), entitled 'German Long Range Rockets', section 4: 'Von Thoma's Evidence', 29 September 1943, CAB 80/75.

15. Report from Rawlinson (DDMI), 13 July 1943, WO 208/3437.

16. For more information on air intelligence acted on this information, see 'Extract from an Interpretation Report of the New Development at Peenemünde', in AIR 40/1192. Examples of the many bugged conversations on V-weapons: SRGG 319, 7 August 1943; report on secret weapon from Dutch escapists, 6 August 1943; SR 9224, 9239-9241, December 1943; SIR 395, 10 August 1944; copies of all these in WO 208/3437.

17. 'German Development of Long Range Weapons', prepared by the Ministry of Economic Warfare, 12 July 1943, WO 208/3437.

18. Minutes of a meeting held on 2 July 1943 at the Ministry of Supply, WO 208/3437.

19. Letter from Norman Crockatt (head of MI9) to Colonel Catesby ap C. Jones (MIS-X, POW branch, US intelligence) in Washington, dated 21 July 1943, WO 208/3437.

20. ibid.

21. For a more detailed argument and evidence of the trail from the bugged conversations to the bombing of Peenemünde, see Fry, *The Walls Have Ears*, pp. 150–71. The view that the bugged conversations acted as the final trigger for the bombing of Peenemünde is supported by historian Max Hastings in his *The Secret War: Spies, Ciphers and Guerrillas 1939–1945*, William Collins, 2017, p. 421. See also Most Secret Memo to Operations at Air Ministry from AI.3 (Air Ministry), 8 July 1943, AIR 40/1192.

22. The relevant conversations were SRN 1986 and SRX 1848. 'Rockets and Invasion', CSDIC to MI19, 26 July 1943, WO 208/3437.

23. Report No. 4, 27 July 1943, WO 208/3437.

24. Handwritten summary of information sent by Major Rittner (CSDIC) via scrambler to MI19 on 26 July 1943, WO 208/3437. The same message was sent by Commander Cope (NID, attached to CSDIC) to the Admiralty.

25. The bogus newspaper report is thought to have resulted in SRGG 319 in WO 208/4363. See Report No. 5 on ultra-long-range projectiles, 16 August 1943, WO 208/3437.

26. SRGG 319, 7 August 1943, WO 208/4363. See also SRGG 368, 23 August 1943, and SRGG 414, 11 September 1943, WO 208/4166; and 'The Generals: View of Senior Officer POWs', no date, WO 208/5550.

27. Jones, *Most Secret War*, p. 441.

28. Lieutenant Colonel Pryor to Rawlinson, 10 August 1944, WO 208/3437. The interrogation report of Lauterjung is reference SIR 395.

29. Le Bosquet to Rawlinson, 22 August 1944, WO 208/3437.

30. RPS/Gen/653, 6 August 1943, copy in WO 208/3437. Also report from MI19 to various departments, including CSDIC, MI6 and US intelligence in Washington, 7 August 1943, WO 208/3437.

31. Unpublished memoirs of Lt-Cdr Donald Burkewood Welbourn, RNVR, IWM, pp. 108–12.

32. Memo from MI19 to CSDIC, 8 August 1943, WO 208/3437.

33. SRX 1617 referenced in memo from CSDIC to MI19, 13 September 1943, WO 208/3437. Information on 1,600 km rocket bombs at Peenemunde was corroborated by two other POWs in SR 6473, 11 September 1943, copy in WO 208/3437.

34. Unpublished memoirs of Lt-Cdr Donald Burkewood Welbourn, RNVR, IWM, p. 110.

35. Whittle's scientific paper was sent direct to Dr Roxbee-Cox, the scientific adviser to Sir Stafford Cripps (minister for air), see unpublished memoirs of Lt-Cdr Donald Burkewood Welbourn, RNVR, IWM, p.110.
36. At the end of the war, Cleff was diagnosed with tuberculosis and severe fatigue. He was treated at the naval hospital at Greenwich and then moved to a sanatorium on the Isle of Wight. After recovery, he worked for Brigadier Blagdon, developing armoured vehicles at Chobham in Surrey. Cleff later worked for the Admiralty Engineering Department on the design of a new type of gear-grinding machine for naval gears.
37. GRGG 15, 12 June 1943, WO 208/5016.
38. GRGG 32, 10 July 1943, WO 208/5016.
39. SRGG 652, 13 December 1943, WO 208/4167.
40. SRGG 702, 25 December 1943, WO 208/4167.
41. SRGG 704, 25 December 1943, WO 208/4167.
42. Lower-rank POWs also spoke about fighting on the Russian Front. See SRM 260, 16 October 1943, SRM 282, 1 November 1943 and SRM 285, 1 November 1943, WO 208/4137.
43. GRGG 12, 7 June 1943, WO 208/5016.
44. GRGG 15, 12 June 1943, WO 208/5016.
45. GRGG 20, 16 June 1943, WO 208/5016.
46. GRGG 26, 23 June 1943, WO 208/5016.
47. SRGG 601, 30 November 1943, WO 208/4167.
48. GRGG 37, 14 July 1943, WO 208/5016.
49. Transcripts for October and November 1943 in WO 208/4167.
50. 'The Generals: Views of Senior German Officer POWs', no date, WO 208/5550.
51. GRGG 89, 4 October 1943, WO 208/5016.
52. 'The Generals: Views of Senior German Officer POWs', no date, WO 208/5550.
53. ibid.
54. GRGG 125, 12–18 March 1944, WO 208/5016. See also SRGG 558, 13 November 1943, WO 208/4167.
55. GRGG 125, 12–18 March 1944, WO 208/5016.
56. SRGG 584, 23 November 1943, WO 208/4167.

Chapter 14: D-Day and its aftermath

1. Fry, *The London Cage*, pp. 15–18.
2. New research and official documentation discovered by David O'Keefe; see his book *One Day in August: Ian Fleming, Enigma and the deadly raid on Dieppe*, Icon, 2020, pp. 244–45.
3. Appendix K, 'The Army Interrogation Section (Operational)', WO 208/4970.
4. Simon, Unpublished memoirs, p. 150.
5. SRGG 755, 11 January 1944, WO 208/4167.
6. GRGG 130, 17–23 April 1944, WO 208/5016.
7. Personal file in WO 208/3504.
8. GRGG 135, 24 May 1944, GRGG 136, 26 May 1944, GRGG 137, 29 May 1944, WO 208/5017.
9. GRGG 135, 24 May 1944, p. 5, WO 208/5017 and GRGG 138, p. 5, 1 June 1944, WO 208/5017.
10. Author's interview with Ken Walsh.
11. WO 165/39, June 1944. In June 1944, 13,742 POWs from Normandy were brought to MI19's sites in Britain, including a 'cage' at Kempton Park. In July: 18,082; August: 24,730; September: 48,444; and October: 69,493.
12. Entries for June, July and August 1944, WO 165/41.
13. Personal files in WO 208/3504.
14. GRGG 159, 15 and 16 July 1944, WO 208/5017.
15. Interview of Hennecke by Director of Naval Intelligence at Trent Park, 21 July 1944, ADM 223/475.

16. Diary entries for June, August and September 1944, WO 165/41. Other senior officers captured after D-Day, with place of capture in brackets: General Hermann Ramcke (Brest), General Erwin Vierow (Arras), General Heinrich Eberbach (Amiens); Lieutenant Generals Kurt Badinsky (Bailleul), Wilhelm Daser (Middelburg), Otto Elfeldt (Trun), Rüdiger Heyking (Mons), Erwin Menny (Maguy), Erwin Rauch (Brest), Paul Seyffardt (Marbaix), Karl Spang (Brest); Major Generals Bock von Wülfingen (Liège), Kurt Eberding (Knocke), Alfred Gutknecht (Soissons-Rheims), Hans von der Mosel (Brest), Robert Sattler (Cherbourg), Hans Schramm (Creney-Troyes), Stolberg (Antwerp), Carl Wahle (Mons); SS Oberführer Kurt Meyer (Liège); Colonels Ludwig Krug (Normandy), Rolf Müller-Römer (Paris), Hans Jay (Paris), Helmuth Rohrbach (St Gabriel), Karl von Unger (Paris), Ernst Herrmann (Cherbourg), Gerhard Wilck (Aachen), Eberhard Wildermuth (Le Havre); and Vice Admirals Schirmer (Brest), Otto Kähler (Brest), Hans von Tresckow (Le Havre) and Carl Weber (Loire).
17. Reports in WO 208/5017. See also GRGG 190 to GRGG 193, September 1944, WO 208/5018.
18. GRGG 190, 16 September 1944, WO 208/5018.
19. ibid.
20. SRGG 919, 10 June 1944, WO 208/4168.
21. Jones, *Most Secret War*, pp. 97–98, 428.
22. Personal file in WO 208/3504. By 10 July 1944 Eberbach had been appointed commander of Panzer Gruppe West.
23. SRGG 1009, 1 September 1944, WO 208/4168.
24. SRGG 1029, 4 September 1944, WO 208/4168. See also GRGG 187(c), 10 September 1944, WO 208/5017.
25. SRGG 1029, 4 September 1944, WO 208/4168.
26. SRGG 766, 15 January 1944, WO 208/4167.
27. GRGG 190, 16 September 1944, WO 208/5018. Several conversations in WO 208/5018.
28. GRGG 160, 16–17 July 1944, WO 208/4363. 'Attempted Assassination of Hitler and Subsequent Events', GRGG 161, no date, WO 208/4363.
29. GRGG 160, 16–17 July 1944, p. 6, WO 208/4363.
30. This is clear from the decision by British intelligence not to carry through Operation Foxley, the British plan to assassinate Hitler, HS 6/623. See Mark Seaman, *Operation Foxley: The British plan to kill Hitler*, Public Records Office, 1998.
31. War diary entries for September 1944 until December 1944 inclusive, WO 165/41.
32. Memorandum signed by Kendrick, 13 November 1943, WO 208/5549.
33. SIR 350, 15 June 1944, Townshend/Jestin archive.
34. From the interrogations, Kendrick's officers were able to draw a diagram of the complete structure and chain of command of the airborne troops; see appendix to SIR 462, 27 June 1944, original copy in the Jestin archive. See also SIR 232, 29 April 1944; SIR 276, 24 May 1944; SIR 350, 15 June 1944; SIR 415, 22 June 1945; SIR 514, 6 July 1944; SIR 608, 21 July 1944; SIR 1093, 21 October 1944; SIR 280, 17 November 1943; SIR 184, 31 March 1944; SIR 202, 9 April 1944; SIR 16 May 1944; SIR 251, 23 May 1944; SIR 834, 24 August 1944, Townshend/Jestin archive.
35. SIR 154, 28 February 1944; SIR 251, 23 May 1944; SIR 708, 4 August 1944; SIR 834, 24 August 1944; SIR 1055, 7 October 1944; SIR 1373, 6 January 1945 and SIR 1373, 6 January 1945, Townshend/Jestin archive. Each para training course had 480 men going through it, but the POWs admitted that – because of the urgent need for fighting forces – their training had been reduced from three months to three weeks. This gave the Allies an insight into how well trained, or not, these forces might be and the possible effect on their performance in combat.
36. Interrogation of Corporal Willi Wilhelmy, SIR 174, 24 March 1944, copy in the Townshend/Jestin archive.
37. SIR 251, 23 May 1944, Townshend/Jestin archive.
38. SIR 956, 18 September 1944, Townshend/Jestin archive.

39. Appendix to SIR 462, 27 June 1944, Townshend/Jestin archive. See also SIR 834, 24 August 1944. General Student was the overall commander and founder of the paratroops; he was captured by the Allies on 28 May 1945 near Flensburg. His bugged conversations from his time at Trent Park survive in WO 208/4178.

40. SIR 462, 27 June 1944, Townshend/Jestin archive.

41. SIR 1055, 7 October 1944, Townshend/Jestin archive.

42. SIR 611, 22 July 1944; SIR 616, 27 July 1944; SIR 906, 2 September 1944, Townshend/ Jestin archive.

43. Memo from CSDIC, 5 December 1944, WO 208/5622.

44. Hermann Ramcke, *Fallschirmjäger Damals und danach*, Lorch Verlag, 1951, p. 77.

45. Heimwarth Jestin, 'A memoir 1918–1946', unpublished memoirs, pp. 19–20. Jestin's account is borne out in official files: see GRGG 198, 24 September 1944, WO 208/5018.

46. Jestin, 'A memoir 1918–1946', p. 20. See also Ramcke, *Fallschirmjäger Damals und danach*, pp. 77–82.

47. 'The Ardennes Offensive', GRGG 330(c), 1 August 1945, WO 208/4178.

48. SIR 1423, 28 January 1945; SIR 1493, 26 February 1945, Townshend/Jestin archive.

49. SIR 1444, 1 February 1945, Townshend/Jestin archive.

50. SIR 1377, 14 January 1945, Townshend/Jestin archive.

51. SIR 1438, 31 January 1945, Townshend/Jestin archive.

52. SIR 1548, 14 March 1945, Townshend/Jestin archive.

53. In April 1945, the unit translating the documents at Latimer House was transferred to the Air Ministry building in Monck Street. 'Intelligence from Prisoners of War', section 289, AIR 40/2636.

54. They were Air Force Generals Walter Somme and Johannes Fink; Lieutenant Generals Kurt Gerlach, Karl Veith, Erwin Leister, Walter Friedensburg, Fritz Pauer, Wolgang Lange, Fritz Neidholdt, Ralph von Oriola, Richard Schimpf, Alfred Sturm, Franz Sensfuss, Hans von Boineburg, Hans von Sommerfeld, Horst von Uckermann, Karl Burdach, Max Siry, Karl Reiter, von Hernekamp (in hospital), von Kirchheim; Major Generals Alexander von Pfuhlstein, Ludwig Hellmann, Gerhard Fischer, Wilhelm Kohlbach, Walter Lindner, Richard Habermehl, Hubert Lütkenhaus, Friedrich Stemmermann, Erich Büscher, Wilhelm Viebig, Hans Erxleben, Gerhard Franz, Paul Goerbig, Maximilian Jais, Paul Steinbach, Heinrich Hoffmann, Otto Schneider, Heinrich Bruns, H. Kokott, E. König, A. Kuen, E. Stahl and Rudolf Petrauschke; Vice Admirals Wilhelm Tackenberg, Siegfried Engel and Kurt Utke; and Colonels J. Harpe, K. Hollidt and O. Hitzfeld.

55. GRGG 329, 6–20 July 1945, WO 208/4178.

56. Personal file in WO 208/3504.

57. Copy of the original letter sent to the author.

58. 'Prisoner of War Interrogation 1939–1945', p. 11, ADM 223/475.

59. Crockatt to Kendrick, 21 February 1944, Kendrick archive.

Chapter 15: Still listening

1. Simon, Unpublished memoirs, p. 151.

2. Personal minute, 16 February 1944, CAB 121/236.

3. These are contained in WO 208/5544 and primarily date to July 1945. Later reports are in WO 208/4178.

4. Contained in WO 208/5544 and WO 208/4178.

5. These reports include: 'Reflections of a German Tank Commander', with information secured from bugged conversations of General von Manteuffel (GRGG 360, 28 September 1945); 'History of the German Airborne Forces' (GRGG 359(c), 24 September 1945); and 'German Infantry Training' (GRGG 357(c), 19 September 1945), all in WO 208/4178.

6. GRGG 360, 28 September 1945, WO 208/4178.

7. GRGG 310(c) and GRGG 343(c), both dated 4 June 1945, and GRGG 318, 26 June 1945, WO 208/4178.

8. Dornberger's interrogation reports survive in WO 208/3121. See also GRGG 341, 11 August 1945, GRGG 344, 21 August 1945 and GRGG 354, 7 September 1945, WO 208/4178. His story of rocket development is in SRM 1264 and SRGG 1349.

9. GRGG 341, 11 August 1945, WO 208/4178.

10. ibid.

11. SRM 1264 and SRGG 1349.

12. GRGG 341, 11 August 1945, WO 208/4178.

13. ibid.

14. GRGG 354, p. 4–5, 7 September 1945, WO 208/4178.

15. GRGG 341, p. 10, 11 August 1945, WO 208/4178.

16. ibid., p. 11.

17. ibid.

18. GRGG 345, 20 August 1945, WO 208/4178.

19. ibid.

20. GRGG 341, p. 10, 11 August 1945, WO 208/4178.

21. GRGG 344, 21 August 1945, WO 208/4178.

22. Leo St Clare Grondona, 'Sidelights on Wilton Park', *RUSI Journal*, December 1970, p. 35.

23. Jeremy Bernstein, *Hitler's Uranium Club: The secret recordings at Farm Hall*, Copernicus Books, 2001; and Colin Brown, *Operation Big: The race to stop Hitler's A-bomb*, Amberley, 2016. See also Jim Baggott, *Atomic: The first war of physics and the secret history of the atom bomb, 1939–1945*, Icon, 2015, pp. 339-56, and CAB 126/333.

24. 'Operation Epsilon', report for 1 June 1945, WO 208/5019.

25. 'Operation Epsilon', report for 30 June 1945, WO 208/5019.

26. 'Operation Epsilon', reports for 6–7 August 1945, WO 208/5019. Although under the direction of Kendrick, Farm Hall was run on a daily basis by one of his senior intelligence officers, Major Rittner, and by Captain Brodie, both of whom had served CSDIC in the war.

27. 'Operation Epsilon', report for 17 June 1945, WO 208/5019.

28. 'Operation Epsilon', reports for 3–18 July 1945, WO 208/5019.

29. ibid.

30. Dr Stark to Kendrick, 29 August 1945, Kendrick archive.

31. Henry Dicks to Kendrick, 25 August 1945, Kendrick archive.

32. Aylmer Buesst to Kendrick, 14 September 1945, Kendrick archive.

33. Patrick Brodie, 13 July 1945, Kendrick archive.

34. Betty Cole to Kendrick, no date, Kendrick archive.

35. Albert Hollander to Kendrick, 28 October 1945, Kendrick archive.

36. Author's interview with Fritz Lustig.

37. Sternberg, *The Journey*, p. 206.

38. Author's interview with Prudence Hopkinson.

39. Letter from John Sinclair to Stewart Menzies, 19 October 1944, Kendrick archive.

40. CSDIC/CMF/SD 92 in KV 3/190.

41. No. 2 Personnel Holding Unit came under the command of Squadron Leader A. Macleod, aided by Flight Lieutenant A.A.D. Maconochie as station administration officer. See also Fry, *The Walls Have Ears*, pp. 267–68.

42. Details in a single report in AIR 29/1104.

43. Adolf Galland, *The First and the Last: The German fighter force in World War II*, Methuen, 1955, p. 125. Galland's interrogation reports survive in WO 208/4292: in particular ADI(K) report No. 311, 1945.

44. 'Intelligence from Prisoners of War', section 124, AIR 40/2636.

45. 'Intelligence from Prisoners of War', sections 253 and 254, AIR 40/2636. Subsequently, Felkin and air intelligence personnel undertook the interrogation of German air force prisoners, civilian scientists and technicians at another clandestine site known as 'Inkpot', in Wimbledon, south-west London. For the official file on Inkpot, see AIR 40/1178.

46. Copy of the letter given to the author.

47. Gil Hayward, 'Dollis Hill in the desert, 1940–44', Copy in the archives of the Military Intelligence Museum, Chicksands.
48. From autumn 1946, Trent Park was requisitioned again and became an emergency teacher training college. By 1952, it had become the subject of a compulsory purchase order for use as Barnet Teacher Training College, which also included nearby Ludgrove Hall, part of the original estate. The site then became Middlesex Polytechnic and Middlesex University, until the university vacated it in 2013. It was sold for development to Berkeley Group in 2015.
49. Personal army record, copy released to the author.
50. John Sinclair to Menzies, 19 October 1944, Kendrick archive.
51. Letter, reference C/7960, from Menzies to John Sinclair, 9 November 1944, Kendrick archive.
52. Clayton, *Forearmed*, p. 288.
53. Kendrick's personal army record says 'to MI6'.
54. Citation for Legion of Merit, WO 373/148.
55. Letter from Rawlinson to Kendrick, Kendrick archive.
56. Kendrick (aka Kaye) was played by Geoffrey Wincott and 'C' (head of MI6) by Patrick Barr.
57. Letter from Rawlinson to Kendrick, 12 June 1965, Kendrick archive.
58. *Radio Times*, 15 May 1965.
59. Inscription engraved on a silver cigar tin for his retirement from SIS.
60. Author's interview with Barbara Lloyd.

Epilogue: A life of secrets

1. Tim Milne, *Kim Philby: A story of friendship and betrayal*, Biteback Publishing, 2014, p. 37. Elliott was officially recruited to SIS in 1940.
2. ibid., pp. 39–40.
3. Author's interview with Wolf Suschitzky, London, 19 March 2013.
4. Jeffery, *MI6*, p. 379.
5. 'History of Intelligence, British Expeditionary Force, France from January 1917 to April 1919: The Secret Service', p. 9, WO 106/45.
6. Sinclair to Menzies, 19 October 1944, Kendrick archive.
7. 'Intelligence from Prisoners of War', section 122, AIR 40/2636.
8. Summary notes written by Charles Deveson in February 1941. Copy given to the author.
9. Letter from Rushbrooke (Head of Naval Intelligence) to Cope, 12 December 1944, copy given to the author.
10. Meeting of the Joint Intelligence Sub-Committee, 15 February 1945, summary of the meeting in the Kendrick archive.
11. 'Intelligence from Prisoners of War', section 125, AIR 40/2636.
12. 'History of Intelligence, British Expeditionary Force, France from January 1917 to April 1919: The Secret Service', p. 36, WO 106/45.

Afterword: Secrets to the grave

1. For example, 'Princess Michael's father was an SS officer', *Guardian*, 16 April 1985.
2. Peter Lane, *Princess Michael of Kent*, Fontana, 1986, p. 24.
3. Jackson Benson, *Haunted: The strange and profound art of Wright Morris*, Jackson Benson, 2013, pp. 39–40.
4. Wright Morris, *Solo: An American dreamer in Europe, 1933–1934*, Penguin, 1983, pp. 41–2.
5. 'Princess's mother praises "brave baron"', *The Times*, 25 April 1985.
6. Lane, *Princess Michael of Kent*, p. 36.
7. Marianne Szápáry, transcript of an interview for *The Times*, 24 April 1985.
8. Barry Everingham, *MC: The adventures of a maverick princess*, Bantam Press, 1985, p. 24; and Marianne Szápáry, transcript of an interview for *The Times*, 24 April 1985.

9. Ludgrove (Hall) was part of the original Trent Park estate; the school evacuated in 1937–38 and was used as part of Cockfosters Camp for holding Axis POWs, where, after interrogation, their conversations were bugged in their rooms by Kendrick's intelligence officers.

10. William Douglas Home, *Mr. Home Pronounced Hume*, HarperCollins, 1979, p. 48.

11. Vicar of Overbury (1948–54), rector of Richmond-on-Swale (1954–62) and of Tilehurst (1962). He died in 1984.

12. The Germans had produced a basket which could be lowered from the Zeppelin and, with various equipment, used to collect intelligence and to spy on sites below.

13. Marianne Szápáry, transcript of an interview for *The Times*, 24 April 1985.

14. ibid.

15. 'The strange marriage of Baron von Reibnitz', *Sunday Telegraph*, 28 April 1985.

16. 'Princess's mother praises "brave baron"', *The Times*, 25 April 1985.

17. ibid.

18. Everingham, *MC*, p. 22. The source given was the Israeli Archives at Yad Vashem in Jerusalem, but my correspondence with the Yad Vashem Archives in 2020 failed to find any evidence for this.

19. Lane, *Princess Michael of Kent*, p. 37. See also 'Baron nominal party member, tribunal said', *The Times*, 24 April 1985.

BIBLIOGRAPHY AND FURTHER READING

Papers and archives

Papers of Lieutenant Colonel Henry Dicks, reference: PP/HVD in the Wellcome Library, London.

Private papers of Colonel Thomas Joseph Kendrick, the Kendrick archive, Military Intelligence Museum, Chicksands.

War diaries of Bernard Trench (2017/24/27 to 2017/24/30), National Museum of the Royal Navy, Portsmouth.

The RAF Medmenham Collection.

Townshend/Jestin archive, used by kind permission of the Jestin family.

Gunther von Reibnitz file, the archives of the Vienna Wiesenthal Institute for Holocaust Studies.

Harriet Cohen papers and correspondence, British Library, ref: 1999/10.

Imperial War Museum

'Camp Z Diary 1941-1942,' by Lieutenant Colonel A. Malcolm Scott, IWM, ref: 69/66/1.

Private papers and unpublished memoirs of Eric Gedye MBE, IWM, ref: 22580.

Private papers of Squadron Officer Vera M. Atkins CBE, IWM, ref: 12636.

Unpublished memoirs of Lt-Cdr Donald Burkewood Welbourn, RNVR, IWM, ref: 99/6/1.

General Sir Walter Kirke's papers, IWM.

Interviews

This book draws on interviews with Barbara Lloyd and Ken Walsh (Kendrick's grandchildren); secret listeners Fritz Lustig, Eric Mark and Paul Douglas, and relatives of secret listeners and intelligence staff. Interviews also with former female intelligence staff: Susan Lustig (née Cohn), Elisabeth Bruegger (née Rees-Mogg), Evelyn Barron and Cynthia Turner (née Crew).

The National Archives

ADM 1/10579, ADM 1/18422, ADM 1/23905, ADM 116/4572, ADM 186/805, ADM 186/809, ADM 223/257, ADM 223/472, ADM 223/481, AIR 14/743, AIR 14/744, AIR 16/1266, AIR 29/1104, AIR 40/2394, AIR 40/2572, AIR 40/2636, AIR 40/2839, AIR 40/3070, AIR 40/3093, AIR 40/3102, AIR 40/3106, AIR 40/3108, CAB 113/41, CAB 120/748, CAB 121/236, DEFE 1/339, ED 78/418, ED 78/419, FO 366/1036, FO 369/2480, FO 371/18351, FO 371/21663, FO 371/21685, FO 371/21691, FO 371/21693, FO 371/21748, FO 371/21755, FO 371/22315, FO 371/22321, FO 372/3283, FO 372/3284, FO 395/562, FO 741/5, FO 898/320, FO 1093/1 – FO 1093/16 (Hess files), FO 1093/200, FO 1093/201, GFM 33/849, HO 213/1635, HO 405/45567, HS 6/623, HW 25/2,

HW 57/35, KV 2/34, KV 2/269, KV 2/578, KV 2/593, KV 2/1008, KV 2/1009, KV 2/1012, KV 2/1013, KV 2/1014, KV 2/2024, KV 2/2136, KV 2/2186, KV 2/2349, KV 2/2350, KV 2/2351, KV 2/2352, KV 2/2353, KV 2/2354, KV 2/2516, KV 2/2672, KV 2/3068, KV 2/3766, KV 2/3767, KV 2/4091, KV 2/4092, KV 2/403, KV 2/4170, KV 2/4428, KV 3/11, KV 3/116, KV 3/230, KV 3/293, KV 3/316, KV 4/302, PREM 3/219/5, WO 32/8112, WO 32/10720, WO 94/105, WO 106/45, WO 165/39, WO 165/41, WO 188/796, WO 193/791, WO 208/3433, WO 208/3451, WO 208/3455, WO 208/3456, WO 208/3457, WO 208/3466, WO 208/3474, WO 208/3504, WO 208/3582, WO 208/4202, WO 208/4117, WO 208/4121, WO 208/4123, WO 208/4128, WO 208/4131, WO 208/4136, WO 208/4137, WO 208/4141, WO 208/4148, WO 208/4158, WO 208/4165, WO 208/4166, WO 208/4167, WO 208/4168, WO 208/4169, WO 208/4177, WO 208/4178, WO 208/4196, WO 208/4199, WO 208/4292, WO 208/4363, WO 208/4364, WO 208/4471, WO 208/4970, WO 208/4796, WO 208/5016, WO 208/5017, WO 208/5018, WO 208/5019, WO 208/5158, WO 208/5381, WO 208/5549, WO 208/5550, WO 208/5621, WO 208/5622, WO 208/5623, WO 311/54, WO 311/632, WO 339/10993, WO 373/148

Published works

Andrew, Christopher. *Secret Service: The making of the British intelligence community*, Book Club Associates, 1985.

Andrew, Christopher. *The Defence of the Realm: The authorized history of MI5*, Allen Lane, 2009.

Baggott, Jim. *Atomic: The first war of physics and the secret history of the atom bomb, 1939–1945*, Icon, 2015.

Beach, Jim. *Haig's Intelligence: GHQ and the German army, 1916–1918*, Cambridge University Press, 2013.

Benson, Jackson. *Haunted: The strange and profound art of Wright Morris*, Jackson Benson, 2013.

Bernstein, Jeremy. *Hitler's Uranium Club: The secret recordings at Farm Hall*, Copernicus Books, 2001.

van der Bijl, Nick. *Sharing the Secret: The history of the Intelligence Corps, 1940–2010*, Pen and Sword, 2020.

Borovik, Genrikh. *The Philby Files*, Sphere, 1995.

Boyd, Andrew. *British Naval Intelligence through the Twentieth Century*, Seaforth Publishing, 2020.

Brivati, Brian. *Hugh Gaitskell*, Richard Cohen Books, 1996.

Brown, Anthony Cave. *C: The secret life of Sir Stewart Graham Menzies*, Macmillan, 1987.

Brown, Colin. *Operation Big: The race to stop Hitler's A-bomb*, Amberley, 2016.

Bryher, *The Heart to Artemis*, Collins, 1963.

de Burgh, Lucy. *My Italian Adventures: An English girl at war 1943–47*, The History Press, 2013.

Clare, George. *Last Waltz in Vienna*, Pan Books, 2007.

Clayton, Anthony. *Forearmed: A history of the Intelligence Corps*, Brassey's, 1993.

Cohen, Harriet. *A Bundle of Time*, Faber & Faber, 1969.

Cookridge, E.H. *The Third Man: The full story of Kim Philby*, Putnam, 1968.

Corera, Gordon. *Operation Columba – The Secret Pigeon Service: The untold story of World War II resistance in Europe*, William Morrow, 2018.

Dilks, David (ed.). *The Diaries of Sir Alexander Cadogan OM: 1938–1945*, Faber & Faber, 2010.

Dorril, Stephen. *MI6: Fifty years of special operations*, Fourth Estate, 2001.

Drazin, Charles. *Korda: Britain's only movie mogul*, Sidgwick & Jackson, 2002.

Everingham, Barry. *MC: The adventures of a maverick princess*, Bantam Press, 1985.

Fermor, Patrick Leigh. *Abducting a General: The Kreipe operation and SOE in Crete*, John Murray, 2015.

Ferris, John. *Behind the Enigma: The authorised history of GCHQ, Britain's secret cyber-intelligence agency*, Bloomsbury, 2020.

Foot, M.R.D. and Jimmy Langley. *MI9: Escape and evasion 1939–1945*, BCA, 1979.

Fraser-Smith, Charles. *The Secret War of Charles Fraser-Smith*, Michael Joseph, 1981.

Fry, Helen. *Music and Men: The life and loves of Harriet Cohen,* The History Press, 2008.

Fry, Helen. *Freuds' War*, The History Press, 2009.

Fry, Helen. *Churchill's German Army*, The History Press, 2009.

Fry, Helen. *The London Cage: The secret history of Britain's WWII interrogation centre*, Yale University Press, 2017.

Fry, Helen. *The Walls Have Ears: The greatest intelligence operation of World War II*, Yale University Press, 2019.

Fry, Helen. *MI9: A history of the secret service for escape and evasion in World War Two*, Yale University Press, 2020.

Galland, Adolf. *The First and the Last: The German fighter force in World War II*, Methuen, 1955.

Gedye, Eric. *Fallen Bastions*, Victor Gollancz, 1939.

Gilbert, Martin. *Auschwitz and the Allies*, Michael Joseph, 1981.

Gilbert, Martin. *The Holocaust: The Jewish tragedy*, HarperCollins, 1989.

Gilbert, Martin. *Beyond the Call of Duty: British diplomats and other Britons who helped Jews escape from Nazi tyranny*, Foreign and Commonwealth Office, 2008.

Harrison, Edward, *The Young Kim Philby*, Liverpool University Press, 2012.

Hart, Peter. *Journey into Freedom*, Authors OnLine, 2003.

Hastings, Max. *The Secret War: Spies, Ciphers and Guerrillas 1939–1945*, William Collins, 2017.

Helm, Sarah. *A Life in Secrets: The story of Vera Atkins and the lost agents of SOE*, Little Brown, 2005.

Hoare, Oliver. *Camp 020: MI5 and Nazi spies – The official history of MI5's Wartime Interrogation Centre*, Public Record Office, 2000.

Home, William Douglas. *Old Men Remember*, Collins & Brown, 1991.

Jeffery, Keith. *MI6: The history of the SIS, 1909–1949*, Bloomsbury, 2010.

Jestin, Catherine. *A War Bride's Story*, privately published.

Jones, R.V. *Most Secret War*, Coronet, 1978.

Kenyon, David. *Bletchley Park and D-Day*, Yale University Press, 2019.

Kershaw, Ian. *Hitler 1889–1936: Hubris*, Allen Lane, 1988.

Kiszely, John. *Anatomy of a Campaign: The British fiasco in Norway, 1940*, Cambridge University Press, 2017.

Knightley, Phillip. *The Second Oldest Profession*, Pan Books, 1987 edition.

Kurth, Peter. *American Cassandra: The life of Dorothy Thompson*, Little, Brown, 1990.

Landau, Henry. *The Spy Net: The greatest intelligence operations of the First World War*, Biteback, 2015 edition.

Lane, Peter. *Princess Michael of Kent*, Fontana, 1986.

Lustig, Fritz. *My Lucky Life*, privately published, 2017.

Lycett, Andrew. *Ian Fleming: The man who created James Bond 007*, Phoenix, 1996.

MacDonogh, Giles. *1938: Hitler's Gamble*, Constable, 2009.

McGinty, Stephen. *Camp Z: The secret life of Rudolf Hess*, Quercus, 2011.

Macintyre, Ben. *A Spy Among Friends: Kim Philby and the great betrayal*, Bloomsbury, 2014.

McLachlan, Donald. *Room 39: Naval intelligence in action 1939–45*, Weidenfeld & Nicolson, 1968.

Mallett, Derek. *Hitler's Generals in America: Nazi POWs and Allied military intelligence*, University Press of Kentucky, 2013.

Masterman, John. *The Double-Cross System*, Vintage, 2013.

Mayne, Richard. *In Victory, Magnanimity. In Peace Goodwill: A history of Wilton Park*, Whitehall History Publishing, 2003.

Medawar, Jean and David Pyke. *Hitler's Gift*, Richard Cohen Books, 2000.

Milne, Tim. *Kim Philby: A story of friendship and betrayal*, Biteback Publishing, 2014.

Mitchison, Naomi. *Vienna Diary 1934*, Kennedy & Boyd, 2009.

Morgan, Janet. *The Secrets of Rue St Roch*, Penguin, 2005.

Morris, Wright. *Solo: An American dreamer in Europe, 1933–1934*, Penguin, 1983.

Moss, W. Stanley. *Ill Met by Moonlight*, Weidenfeld & Nicolson, 2014.

Neave, Airey. *Saturday at MI9*, Pen & Sword, 2010.

Neitzel, Sönke (ed.). *Tapping Hitler's Generals: Transcripts of secret conversations, 1942–45*, Frontline, 2007.

Neitzel, Sönke. *Soldaten: On fighting, killing and dying – The Second World War tapes of German POWs*, Simon & Schuster, 2012.

Nudd, Derek. *Castaways of the Kriegsmarine: How shipwrecked German seamen helped the Allies win the Second World War*, Createspace, 2017.

Nudd, Derek. *Castaways in Question: A story of British naval interrogators from WW1 to denazification*, Cottage Grove editions, 2020.

O'Brien-ffrench, Conrad. *Delicate Mission: Autobiography of a secret agent*, Skilton & Shaw, 1979.

O'Keefe, David. *One Day in August: Ian Fleming, Enigma and the deadly raid on Dieppe*, Icon, 2020.

Parritt, Brian. *The Intelligencers: British military intelligence from the Middle Ages to 1929*, Pen and Sword, 2011.

Philby, Kim. *My Silent War*, Modern Library, 2002.

Prittie, Terence. *Germany Divided*, Hutchinson, 1961.

Ramcke, Hermann. *Fallschirmjäger Damals und danach*, Lorch Verlag, 1951.

Rankin, Nicholas. *Ian Fleming's Commandos: The story of 30 Assault Unit in WWII*, Faber & Faber, 2011.

Read, Anthony and David Fisher. *Colonel Z: The life and times of a master of spies*, Hodder & Stoughton, 1984.

Richards, Lee. *The Black Art: British clandestine psychological warfare against the Third Reich*, 2010, www.psywar.org

Rodgers, W.T (ed.). *Hugh Gaitskell 1906–1963*, Thames and Hudson, 1964.

Ruis, Edwin. *Spynest: British and German espionage from neutral Holland 1914–1918*, The History Press, 2012.

Sanders, Eric. *From Music to Morse*, privately published autobiography.

Sanders, Marion. *Dorothy Thompson: A legend in her time*, Houghton Mifflin, 1973.

Scotland, Alexander P. *The London Cage*, Evans Brothers Ltd, 1957.

Seale, Patrick and Maureen McConville. *Philby: The long road to Moscow*, Penguin, 1978.

Seaman, Mark. *Operation Foxley: The British plan to kill Hitler*, Public Records Office, 1998.

Smith, Michael. *Foley: The spy who saved 10,000 Jews*, Politico's Publishing, 2004.

Smith, Michael. *Six: A history of Britain's Secret Intelligence Service*, Dialogue, 2010.

Smith, Michael. *The Secrets of Station X: How Bletchley Park helped win the war*, Biteback Publishing, 2011 edition.

Sternberg, Cecilia. *The Journey*, Collins, 1977.

Sullivan, Matthew Barry. *Thresholds of Peace: German prisoners and the people of Britain*, Hamish Hamilton, 1979.

Teuscher, Christof. *Alan Turing: Life and legacy of a great thinker*, Springer, 2005.

Weidenfeld, George. *Remembering My Good Friends: An autobiography*, HarperCollins, 1994.

West, Nigel (ed.). *The Guy Liddell Diaries*, Vol. 1, *1939–1942*, Routledge, 2009.

West, Nigel (ed.). *The Guy Liddell Diaries*, Vol. 2, *1942–1945*, Routledge, 2009.

Wistrich, Robert. *Anti-Semitism: The longest hatred*, Methuen, 1991.

Wright, Peter. *Spycatcher*, Viking, 1987.

Articles, chapters in edited books and unpublished works

Bell, Falko. 'One of our most valuable sources of intelligence: British intelligence and the prisoners of war system in 1944', *Intelligence and National Security*, 31:4 (2016), pp. 556–78.

BIBLIOGRAPHY AND FURTHER READING

Benton, Kenneth. 'The ISOS years: Madrid 1941–3', *Journal of Contemporary History*, 30:3 (1995), pp. 359–410.

Forbes, Duncan. 'Politics, photography and exile in the life of Edith Tudor-Hart (1908–1973)', in Shulamith Behr and Marian Malet (eds), *Arts in Exile in Britain 1933–1945: Politics and cultural identity*, Research Centre for German and Austrian Exile Studies, 2005.

Gibson Graham, Lieutenant Colonel. 'The case of Rudolph Hess', no date, unpublished lecture given at the Royal College of Physicians and Surgeons, Glasgow. Copy given to the author.

Hayward, Gil. 'Dollis Hill in the desert, 1940–44', Copy in the archives of the Military Intelligence Museum, Chicksands.

Jestin, Heimwarth. 'A memoir 1918–1946', unpublished memoirs.

Judge, A.F. 'History of the Intelligence Corps, 1914–1929', unpublished, copy at Military Intelligence Museum, Chicksands.

MacDonogh, Giles. 'A most unfortunate case', *Jewish Quarterly*, 51:2 (2004), pp. 57–62.

McFadyean, Melanie. 'A private war', *Guardian*, 6 July 2002.

Maree, D.R. 'Bicycles in the Anglo-Boer War of 1899–1902', *Military History Journal*, 4:1 (1977) (South African Military History Society).

Oldfield, Lieutenant Colonel R.W. 'Memorandum on the work of the Section of Civic Affairs and Security, General Staff, British Army of the Rhine', Military Intelligence Museum, Chicksands.

St Clare Grondona, Leo. 'Sidelights on Wilton Park', *RUSI Journal*, December 1970, pp. 34–37.

Simon, Derrick. Unpublished memoirs.

Thwaites, Major General Sir William. 'The role of forward troops in the collection of intelligence in the field', lecture to the Royal Artillery Institution, Woolwich, 9 December 1924, Military Intelligence Museum, Chicksands.

INDEX

INDEX